Soviet-Cuban Alliance: 1959-1991

Soviet-Cuban Alliance: 1959-1991

Yuri Pavlov

North·South Center Press
UNIVERSITY OF MIAMI

To Valentina Lavrova.

The mission of the North-South Center is to promote better relations and serve as a catalyst for change among the United States, Canada, and the nations of Latin America and the Caribbean by advancing knowledge and understanding of the major political, social, economic, and cultural issues affecting the nations and peoples of the Western Hemisphere.

First edition 1994. Second printing with index and updated Epilogue 1996.

To order or to return books, contact Lynne Rienner Publishers, Inc., 1800 30th Street, Suite 314, Boulder, CO 80301-1026, 303-444-6684, fax 303-444-0824.

The cover photo, provided by *Pravda,* shows Fidel Castro and Nikita Khrushchev laying a wreath at the Lenin Mausoleum in Red Square, Moscow, April 1963. Photographs on pages 256-258 from *Viva Cuba — Visit of Fidel Castro Ruz to the Soviet Union,* published by Pravda Publishing Office in 1963; photos on pages 259 and 260 © AP/Wide World Photos; photos on pages 255 and 256 by Colonel Tanan; the rest are courtesy of the author.

Library of Congress Cataloging-in-Publication Data

Pavlov, Yuri I., 1931-
    Soviet-Cuban alliance, 1959 – 1991 / Yuri I. Pavlov.
      p   cm.
    Includes bibliographical references and index.

    ISBN-1-57454-004-1 (pbk. : alk. paper)
    1. Soviet Union — Foreign relations — Cuba. 2. Cuba — Foreign relations —
Soviet Union. 3. Soviet Union — Foreign Relations — 1945 – 1991.
4. Cuba — Foreign relations — 1959-   I. Title.
DK69.3.C9P38 1996   95-50925
327.470729 —dc20   CIP

    ISBN-1-57454-004-1 (paper)
    Printed in the United States of America
    02 01 00 99 98 97 96 7 6 5 4 3 2 1

Contents

Foreword i

Chapter 1: Origins of the Soviet-Cuban Alliance 1
Low Soviet Profile in Latin America 1
Castro Takes Power: Restrained Reaction in Moscow 3
Mikoyan Visits Havana 6
Moscow Deepens Its Commitment 13
Castro Opts for Socialism 17
Recognition in Moscow 22

Chapter 2: Soviet Missiles in Cuba 31
Khrushchev Proposes a Nuclear Gamble.............................. 31
Castro Accepts the Proposition 36
On the Brink 41
Khrushchev "Betrays" Castro 45
The Aftermath 55
Lessons of the Cuban Missile Crisis....................................... 61

Chapter 3: From Khrushchev to Gorbachev:
Gains and Losses 69
Cuba as a Showcase of Socialism in Latin America 69
Complementary Economies: Myth and Reality..................... 79
A Capricious Ally.. 83
Back to Moscow's Fold 90
Leonid Brezhnev Visits Havana 94
Political Cooperation: Living with Differences 97
The Human Rights Problem: Acting in Unison 102

Chapter 4: Movement in Opposite Directions............. 111
Gorbachev's Reforms: Reaction in Havana 111
Cuban Rectification of Errors: Assessment in Moscow 114
The Problem of Honest Reporting 117
The Rift Widens 122

Gorbachev's Visit to Cuba 126

Chapter 5: Decline in Havana's Political Influence in Moscow 141

De-Cubanization of Soviet Policy on Regional Conflicts 142

Moscow-Miami Dialogue 158

Erosion of Castro's Prestige in the USSR: Ochoa's Trial 162

Failed Attempts to Weaken Soviet Support for Castro 164

Debates in Moscow on Cuba's Future 166

Chapter 6: Cuban Lobby in Moscow 173

Castro Sounds a Bell 173

Gorbachev's Efforts to Help 176

Cuba's Achilles' Heel 185

Chapter 7: Moscow-Havana-Washington Triangle 199

Cuba in Soviet-American Contacts 200

The American Factor in Soviet-Cuban Relations 217

Chapter 8: The End of the Road 227

Defeat of the Cuban Lobby in the USSR 227

Withdrawal of the Soviet Brigade 231

Political and Economic Repercussions 239

Salvaging the Wreckage 249

Photographs 255

Epilogue 261

Index 273

About the Author 303

Soviet-Cuban Alliance: 1959-1991

Foreword

My first personal experience with Cuban affairs dates back to the days of the Cuban Missile Crisis. On October 24, 1962, I was assigned to interpret Nikita Khrushchev's conversation in the Kremlin with William Knox, vice president of Westinghouse Electric International, whom the Soviet leader had decided to use as an additional channel of communication with U.S. President John Kennedy. The tone of the conversation was somber; the content, apocalyptic. Khrushchev wanted to impress Knox with his resolve to use force if the U.S. Navy tried to intercept and inspect Soviet ships bound for Cuba. "Tell your friend in the White House that Soviet submarines are not deployed near the shores of the United States to catch tuna," Khrushchev said with dark humor. The Soviet leader gave no hint of the possibility of Moscow's concession to Washington's demands. He sounded like a man determined to have his way, whatever the cost. The nearest thing to a conciliatory gesture on Khrushchev's part, which he also asked be conveyed to Kennedy, was his personal assurance that all Soviet missiles in Cuba were and would remain under the control of Soviet Army officers.

It dawned upon me then that the hysterical threats in Soviet public statements, protesting the U.S. naval cordon around Cuba, and the furious anti-American propaganda campaign in the Soviet press were not just outbursts of Cold War rhetoric. This time it was for real! As I left the Kremlin and walked through Red Square, I was struck by the nonchalant air of the people around: none of them seemed to suspect how close we all were to a nuclear catastrophe. It was absurd to think that we were prepared to risk everything just to defend our right to deploy missiles on a faraway island! If the sole purpose of this exercise was to ward off an American invasion of Cuba, it appeared that our actions would produce the opposite effect. In any case, was it reasonable to put at stake our own survival in an attempt to save the

Cuban Revolution? Was it really so vital to our national interest? What was so special about it?

To judge by the Soviet press reports on mass meetings of workers under the slogans — "Hands off Cuba!" and "Stop American aggressors!" — all Soviet citizens were solidly behind their government in this show of solidarity with the Cuban Revolution. But the reality was different. One of the permanent features of the Soviet life-style was a chronic deficit of food and consumer goods, and Soviet workers were grumbling about Khrushchev's benevolent gestures to foreign revolutionaries at the expense of his own people. Like many other young Soviet diplomats, I was visiting Moscow factories during lunch hours to give talks and answer questions from the workers on the current international situation and various aspects of Soviet foreign policy. Questions frequently asked were the following: "Why are we giving so much assistance to Cuba? Why are we sending things there which we cannot find in our shops?" To the workers, the arguments that it was our "internationalist duty" to help the Cuban people sounded hollow. They would then ask, "And who is going to help us?"

These sentiments came into the open only a few months before the Cuban Missile Crisis during spontaneous manifestations of popular protest, triggered by a government decree on higher prices for meat and butter. In Novocherkassk, troops under the command of General Pliyev (who was soon to be sent to Cuba as commander of Soviet troops) fired into the crowd of workers, killing dozens of people. In secret reports of the Committee for State Security (KGB), which were cited recently in the Russian press, in a number of Soviet cities — Tbilisi, Gorky, Grozny, Minsk, Penza, Nizhniy, Tagil, Kemerovo, Novosibirsk, and Khabarovsk — the "instigators" of these disturbances demanded that the government cut off economic assistance to revolutionary regimes in Cuba and other developing countries.

Many years passed. Beginning in 1982, upon my appointment as Soviet ambassador to Costa Rica, I began to take a professional interest in Cuba as one of the main protagonists in Latin American regional affairs. My first visit to the "Island of Freedom" was depressing. There was an air of decay in beautiful Old Havana, a shabbiness in the hotels that struck me as oddly familiar. I had a feeling of déjà vu: the same "couldn't care less" attitude to public property and utilities, the same scarcity of consumer goods and services, the same official optimism, and the same incessant Orwellian repetition of new "achievements" of the socialist economy and of the evil designs of the enemy as I had witnessed in my own socialist motherland. But all this looked so out of place on this tropical island with its warm, cheerful, easygoing people that it seemed more like a caricature of the austere "original" socialism back in the USSR with our unfortunate Russian predisposition for autocratic rules and messianic ideas.

Soviet diplomats and economic advisers to the Cuban government, with whom I talked in Havana, were either reserved or pessimistic in their assessments of Cuba's future. Some of them doubted the very possibility of the continued existence, in a hostile regional environment, of a small socialist country not viable economically without extensive trade and economic cooperation with the United States and other industrially developed countries. From what they told me, Cuba was like a patient kept alive by machines, with an artificial respirator tube ten thousand miles long. The patient's recovery would be impossible without the restoration of normal breathing, and the longer this abnormal situation continued, the more problematic and difficult it would become.

My later experience, after I returned to Moscow in 1987 to become head of the Foreign Ministry's Latin American Department, responsible for Soviet-Cuban bilateral relations, only confirmed that impression. With or without Gorbachev's *perestroika*, Castro's policy of political-military alliance with and economic dependence on the Soviet Union was bound to give way sooner or later to a regional orientation in conformity with Cuba's natural geopolitical interests — not to regress to a position of subservience to Washington but to become an integral part of the Latin American community and one of the regional economic partners of the United States. In making his strategic decision to integrate the country economically and align it politically with the main adversary of the United States, Cuba's "maximum leader" had completely disregarded these interests.

The Soviet-Cuban alliance also had nothing in common with the normal national interests of the Soviet Union. It was born and could exist only under Cold War conditions and superpower confrontation. When this period passed into history, the USSR no longer needed and could not afford such a relationship with Cuba; it had become ruinous economically and embarrassing politically. It had also ended. The disintegration of the Soviet Union only expedited the process. But the Castro regime, which came of age and was consolidated with Soviet assistance, bears all the marks of its now-defunct Soviet totalitarian prototype and is still fighting for its survival.

The purposes of this book are to throw some additional light on salient features of Soviet-Cuban relations, which have become a function of USSR policy toward the United States, and to express judgments based in part on my experience and knowledge as a veteran officer of the Soviet Foreign Service, in the hope that these insights may contribute to a better understanding of the history of this alliance and its heritage — the present confused and contradictory Russian policy toward Cuba.

I have been able to write this book because of the excellent facilities generously offered by the North-South Center, University of Miami, and the invaluable advice and assistance given by Ambassador Ambler H. Moss Jr., dean of the Graduate School of International Studies and director of the North-South Center; Professor Jaime Suchlicki; Professor Irving Louis Horowitz; Dr. Rafael Nuñez; Dr. Richard Downes; Thelvius Winieckie, post-graduate student of the University of Miami; Jeffery Smith, president of the Institute of Geonomic Transformation; Colonel Piotr Tanan (retired); Minister-Counsellor Viktor Kropotov; and other colleagues and friends in this country and Russia, to whom I am most grateful. My special thanks go to Kathleen A. Hamman, editorial director of the North-South Center; Jayne M. Weisblatt, editor; Diane C. Duys, editorial assistant; Norma E. Laird, typist and proofreader; and Gregory Koldys and West Lockhart, graduate students; all of whom put much effort into editing the manuscript to improve its content and language. And I wish to thank Mary M. Mapes for the cover design and advice on photograph selection and Stephanie True Moss for the text design, formatting, and indexing.

Yuri Pavlov

Chapter 1

Origins of the Soviet-Cuban Alliance

Low Soviet Profile in Latin America

In the late 1950s, the new post-Stalin "collective leadership" of the Soviet Union, dominated by the enterprising Nikita Khrushchev, first secretary of the Central Committee of the Communist Party of the Soviet Union (CPSU) and chairman of the Council of Ministers of the USSR, was pursuing a dynamic foreign policy. In Europe, the aim was to consolidate the strategic positions of the Warsaw Pact by attempting to ease the three Western powers out of West Berlin through diplomatic pressure and blackmail. While maintaining its overwhelming superiority in conventional armed forces over the United States and its European allies, the Soviet Union was trying to use its successfully developed technology for ballistic missile production to catch up with the United States in nuclear strike capability. In Asia and Africa, Moscow's strategic design was to expand Soviet influence by helping to accelerate the process of decolonization and by offering economic and military aid to the newly independent states that looked as if they might opt for the noncapitalist way of development. India, Indonesia, Egypt, Guinea, Iraq, and Syria became the first recipients of Soviet large-scale economic and military assistance.

Latin America, where the process of decolonization was relevant only to a few residual British, Dutch, and French dependent territories in the Caribbean, did not figure on the list of Soviet foreign policy priorities, as it was believed to be firmly under no-nonsense U.S. control. All Latin American governments were toeing Washington's anti-communist line. This led Joseph Stalin, then in the prime of his glory and power as the despotic ruler of the USSR, to make a statement in February 1951, which became a textbook reference for all Soviet students of Latin American affairs. In an interview with *Pravda*, he spoke about "the aggressive core of the United Nations," composed of ten member countries of NATO and "twenty Latin American countries" (Stalin went to the trouble of enumerating them all), which were deciding factors in the United Nations' "problems of war and peace." He identified the position of Latin American countries with that of the United States and Canada, which were striving "to unleash a new war," and said, "It is no secret to anyone that twenty representatives of twenty Latin American countries constitute now the most solid and obedient army of the United States in the United Nations."[1] Most of the states of the region that had established diplomatic relations with the USSR before or during World War II suspended or broke them off with the advent of the Cold War.

This did not signify the Soviet leadership's abandonment of the original Comintern policy in Latin America which encouraged local communists to "...actively participate in the revolutionary mass movements directed against the landlord regime and against imperialism, even where these movements were still under the leadership of the petty bourgeoisie," specifying, at the same time, that "Communists may not under any circumstances politically subordinate themselves to their temporary ally."[2] Moreover, the policy was intensified to suit the needs of Cold War strategy. However, the political evolution of the countries of the area, and, in particular, the overthrow of the Jacobo Arbenz Guzmán government in Guatemala in 1954, engineered by the U.S. Central Intelligence Agency (CIA), demonstrated that left-wing forces in Latin America still lacked sufficient popular support to present a serious challenge to existing anti-communist regimes and U.S. domination. Neither local communist leaders nor their mentors in Moscow envisaged the possibility of a socialist revolution in the foreseeable future in any country of the region.

While Cuba did not follow the examples of Brazil, Colombia, Chile, and Venezuela, all of which broke off diplomatic relations with the Soviet Union in the late 1940s to early 1950s, Havana's official relations with Moscow were far from being friendly. In March 1949, the Cuban government sent a note of protest to the Soviet legation in Havana, accusing it of "disseminating ideologies harmful to our own regime, and even reproducing pamphlets insulting certain high personalities," and stating that it could not "permit groups subject to totalitarian ideas and to foreign political orders to find direct or indirect support in diplomatic missions."[3] The Soviet Union's relations with

Cuba were broken off by the Soviets on April 3, 1952, three weeks after Fulgencio Batista's coup d'état, on the pretext that the Cuban authorities refused entry into Cuba of two Soviet diplomatic couriers. This was followed by the publication in Moscow's *Literaturnaya Gazeta* of a sharply worded article calling Cuba "a colony of the American monopolists" and Batista "the new American viceroy."[4]

There was not a word in this article of the activities or the existence in Cuba of an internal political opposition to the Batista regime; obviously, it was not considered worth mentioning. Cuba's Popular Socialist Party (PSP) denounced Batista's military coup, but its leaders believed the country was still not ripe for a mass revolutionary movement against the regime. They branded the Moncada barracks assault and the *Granma* expedition as *putschism* (secretive plotting to overthrow the government) and even asserted that such isolated armed actions only "serve the purpose of maintaining the existing regime."[5] This view was shared in Moscow. As stated in 1966 by historian Lev Slezkin:

> Ten years ago we talked only of the inevitability of the anti-imperialist revolution in Latin America. We did not think that it would begin in Cuba. We did not know that it had already begun when, in July 1953, a group of Cuban youngsters, headed by Fidel Castro, stormed the barracks of government forces in Santiago de Cuba.[6]

Castro Takes Power:
Restrained Reaction in Moscow

The news of the seizure of power in Havana by radical left-wing revolutionaries, classified as "petty bourgeois" by Soviet experts in Latin American affairs, was received in Moscow with moderate enthusiasm. *Pravda's* first detailed report on the overthrow of Batista, published on January 3, 1959, said that it was "an evidence of the growing strength of the peoples of Latin America against the predominance of the Yankee imperialists and for freedom and national independence." According to the report, "the banner of struggle against the hated tyranny was raised by the working class of Cuba, which organized a series of powerful strikes." This struggle "was joined by peasants, a considerable part of the intelligentsia, and representatives of business circles [and] led to an insurgent movement headed by Fidel Castro, leader of the Cuban youth." *Pravda* went on to say that the resistance movement "is actively supported by the Popular Socialist

Party of Cuba, the vanguard of the Cuban working class," which viewed the insurgents "as patriots whose aim was to restore democratic freedoms in the country, transform its backward economy, carry out an agrarian reform, and do away with illiteracy."

In later commentaries by the Soviet media, Castro's anti-American rhetoric was given much publicity, but the prevailing opinion in Moscow remained that the Cuban revolutionary regime would not go beyond the limits of "bourgeois-democratic" reforms. Castro's first public statements provided no reasons for changing that assessment. In fact, in his interview with Havana television on May 21, 1959, he condemned both capitalism and socialism, saying that capitalism "resolves the economic problem but suppresses liberties" while socialism sacrificed man "as pitilessly as capitalism."[7] In other speeches, Castro vowed that his revolution would give the Cubans not only bread but also freedom.

Such public utterances, combined with Castro's sarcastic remarks about the scant participation, if any, of the Cuban communists in the armed struggle against Batista, could hardly endear Castro to the Soviet leaders. The Soviet government welcomed the overthrow of the pro-American Batista regime and informed President Manuel Urrutia, on January 10, 1959, of its "official recognition of the Provisional Government of the Republic of Cuba"[8] but, otherwise, was inclined to take a wait-and-see attitude. The USSR even abstained from expressing its willingness to re-establish diplomatic relations with Cuba, although that would have been quite in order, since they had been broken off on Moscow's initiative.

This could only be explained by the absence of any indication from Havana that the new Cuban government would reciprocate. As Khrushchev recollected later, "When Fidel Castro led his revolution to victory and entered Havana with his troops, we had no idea what political course his regime would follow.... The Communist party of Cuba had no contact with him.... The whole situation was very confused. The man Fidel appointed to be president was someone we had never heard of.... For a long time, we had no diplomatic relations with the new regime."[9]

Similar views were held at the time by such Soviet experts in Latin American affairs as Arnold Kalinin, the future Soviet ambassador to Cuba.[10] Analyzing the unstable and uncertain internal political situation in Cuba in the first months after the overthrow of the Batista regime, Kalinin concluded that it was characterized by a kind of "dyarchy," with formal attributes of power in the hands of President Manuel Urrutia Lleó and his Prime Minister José Miró Cardona and the real authority in the hands of commander-in-chief of the armed forces, Fidel Castro, who had not only an immeasurably greater political prestige and popularity than the president and the head of the government but also controlled all branches of government, the armed forces, and the security apparatus.[11] Later, some Soviet historians, looking for similarities between Castro's revolution and the Russian Revolution of 1917, even tried to compare the first months in post-Batista Cuba with the dyarchy period in Russia in 1917, when power was shared by the provisional government and the Soviets.

Meanwhile, Soviet intelligence services were charged with the task of finding out what was happening in post-Batista Cuba. The delicate mission was entrusted to, among others, Aleksandr Alekseyev, who was sent to Cuba as a journalist and appointed counselor of the Soviet embassy in Havana when diplomatic relations were renewed in May 1960. Alekseyev succeeded in establishing an excellent personal rapport with Fidel Castro and became a de facto Soviet ambassador to Cuba. With Fidel's brother, Raúl Castro, who had participated in one of the Soviet-sponsored World Youth Festivals in the early 1950s, such contacts had been established earlier, as evidenced by Khrushchev in his memoirs and confirmed by Dr. Nikolai Leonov, then a young State Security Committee (KGB) officer who met Raúl Castro in 1954 and acted as interpreter for Anastas Mikoyan in Havana in 1960 and for Fidel Castro, at his personal request, in the Soviet Union in 1963.[12]

The Soviet leadership was also getting information and advice supplied to the International Department of the CPSU Central Committee by Blas Roca, Anibal Escalante, and other leaders of the PSP, who were regular visitors to Moscow. Having committed a gross error in denigrating Castro's armed struggle, Cuban communists now faced the prospect of being left on the sidelines of his revolution. They made themselves useful to Castro and gained influence with the revolutionary regime by offering their services to help obtain the Soviet Union's economic support, which appeared to be the most effective, simple solution to Cuba's problem of finding alternative markets and sources of supply. Thus, Cuban communist leaders had a direct interest in presenting Castro's reforms to their CPSU contacts in the most favorable light — as a progressive, anti-imperialist, national democratic revolution with good socialist potential, worthy of Moscow's support and assistance. These tactics worked. Anastas Mikoyan, then a member of the ruling Presidium of the CPSU Central Committee and deputy chairman of the USSR Council of Ministers, accepted Castro's invitation to visit Cuba for the opening of the Soviet Trade Exhibition in February 1960. And he did not come to Havana empty-handed.

Mikoyan Visits Havana

By that time, Castro had sided openly with the radical wing of the 26th of July Movement and started to collaborate with the PSP, appointing communists to positions of responsibility. According to leading Soviet Cubanologists:

> By summer-autumn 1960, there were achieved a firm unity of the majority of Cuban working people around the revolutionary government and a practical blending of the PSP, 26th of July Movement, and Revolutionary Directorate into a single revolutionary stream. Thus, Lenin's thesis of the formation of the army of the socialist revolution in the course of democratic anti-imperialist revolution was confirmed in Cuba.[13]

They also believed that basic features of the "dictatorship of the proletariat" were in place in Cuba — a necessary condition for the transition to the socialist stage of the revolution.

The Cubanologists were certainly correct. Fidel Castro, having disposed of Manuel Urrutia and José Miró Cardona by forcing them to resign from their offices just months after the overthrow of Batista and taking over their powers, was acting as a full-fledged dictator, although his proletarian credentials were not very convincing. He imprisoned Huber Matos, one of the top commanders of the Rebel Army, and dealt harshly with other army officers and influential members of the 26th of July Movement who protested against his policy of alliance and close cooperation with the PSP and tried to defend the original democratic aims and principles of the revolution.

Castro's harsh treatment of his detractors hardly worried the Soviet leaders; to them, it tended to support PSP leader Blas Roca's opinion that the real power in Cuba was in the hands of the left-wing elements of the 26th of July Movement, facilitating the socialist orientation of the revolution. Matos and other opponents of Castro's political orientation and dictatorial style of government were described in Soviet media reports and scholarly works on Cuba as "rebels" who were obstructing the land reform in the interests of big landowners.[14] This was not sufficient, however, to change prevailing Soviet views on Castro's initial reforms. Reflecting these views, Sergei Gonionsky, a Soviet expert in Latin American affairs, wrote in 1960:

The main aims of the revolution, corresponding with the historic needs of the development of Cuba, are the following: independence and sovereignty of the nation, liquidation of *latifundia* [large rural estates] and the remnants of feudalism in the Cuban countryside, distribution of land among peasants, development of agricultural production and its diversification to satisfy national requirements, retrieval of natural resources, industrialization, liquidation of the monoculture system and necessary development of the economy, and liquidation of the semi-colonial dependence on foreign trade, which was practically monopolized by one country.[15]

None of that was inconsistent with the classic Marxist-Leninist notion of the "bourgeois democratic revolution," creating "objective prerequisites" for the subsequent transition to the socialist transformation of the country, provided there was a Marxist-Leninist party to give indispensable guidance and leadership to the revolutionary process. Soviet leaders were informed by Blas Roca that, with the help of Carlos Rafael Rodriguez, the only leader of the PSP who had joined Castro in the Sierra Maestra mountains, an understanding had been reached with Castro on the active participation of communists in the exercise of revolutionary power. This gave Moscow reasonable grounds to believe that Fidel Castro would not become yet another Gamal Abdel Nasser, pursuing progressive anti-imperialist policies but keeping communists behind bars. And, although the victory of Castro's guerrilla movement did not exactly fit into the classic Marxist-Leninist theory of proletarian revolutions, it did square well with Lenin's thesis of a possible progressive role for some segments of the national bourgeoisie in colonial and semi-colonial countries, fighting for their national independence. That thesis was, in fact, a theoretical basis for Khrushchev's policy of cultivating friendships with left-wing, radical, "national democratic" regimes in Third World countries regarded as valuable assets for the USSR in its global confrontation with the West and as potential converts for the noncapitalist path of development.

Anastas Mikoyan, apart from his outstanding expertise in economics and foreign trade, had a well-deserved reputation as a shrewd politician and also the advantage of being Khrushchev's trusted friend and troubleshooter. He was quick to grasp the enormous potential strategic and political value for the Soviet Union of the consolidation of a friendly revolutionary regime in an insular state within a stone's throw of the United States. The Soviet emissary, seeing the extreme vulnerability of Cuba to U.S. economic and military pressures, recommended that the Presidium of the CPSU Central Committee 1) accept Castro's offer of large quantities of Cuban sugar in exchange for Soviet oil, 2) satisfy Castro's requests for economic and technical assistance, and 3) consider seriously the possibility of meeting Cuba's needs in modern weapons and military training.

Mikoyan was empowered to sign the first Soviet-Cuban agreement on trade and payments, which provided for increased purchases of Cuban sugar on a regular long-term basis. The Soviet government committed itself to buying, at prices 50 percent higher than the world market, 425,000 tons of Cuban sugar in 1960 and 1 million tons annually for the following four years and not re-exporting the sugar to any other country. Twenty percent of the total purchases were to be paid for in hard currency. The Soviet Union accorded to Cuba a $100 million long-term, low-interest credit for importing machinery and materials and agreed to render technical assistance from 1961 through 1963.[16] Following the signing of this agreement in Havana, a Cuban governmental economic delegation, headed by Antonio Núñez Jiménez, director of the National Institute of Agrarian Reform, visited Moscow in June 1960. Jiménez met with Khrushchev and Mikoyan and signed a separate agreement on the delivery of Soviet oil and petroleum products to Cuba, a joint communiqué on trade and economic relations, and a communiqué on cultural cooperation. It was announced afterwards that Khrushchev, as head of the Soviet government, had accepted, in principle, Castro's invitation to visit Cuba.[17]

All this did not go beyond the established Soviet manner of dealing with radical anti-Western regimes in strategically situated developing countries. It was not yet part of some specific plan designed to transform Cuba into a socialist country. Rather, there were conjectures in Moscow that, with Castro's inclination to radical egalitarian reforms, communist influence in the 26th of July Movement, and Washington's implacable hostility to Castro's regime, the Cuban Revolution would be moving toward socialism and that the opportunity should not be lost. Talking privately to Arkady Shevchenko, then an expert on disarmament in the USSR Foreign Ministry, on board the *M/S Baltika* on the way to New York in September 1960, Khrushchev expressed his hope that Cuba would become "a beacon of socialism in Latin America." Khrushchev added, "Castro offers that hope, and the Americans are helping us.... Castro will have to gravitate to us like an iron filing to a magnet."[18] Khrushchev also indicated he was aware of doubts in the CPSU Central Committee about Castro's political views but would form his own opinion on the matter after meeting him.

The first Soviet-Cuban commercial agreement produced the desired political effect in Havana, encouraging Castro to go much further in his defiance of Washington and U.S. economic interests in Cuba than he would have dared in the absence of Soviet support. Commenting on the first commercial agreement with the USSR in a televised speech in Havana, on February 18, 1960, Fidel Castro said:

> In the last ten years, Cuba had a deficit in the balance of payments amounting to $1 billion. On the contrary, now, with only 20 percent provided for by the trade agreement with Russia in favor of our balance of payments, we'll have a positive balance of about $70 million in the next five years, and we'll sell 5 million tons of sugar.... If our negotiations with the United States had permitted us to receive about 20 percent in favor of our balance of payments, all our problems would have been solved.[19]

While commercial contacts were given publicity both in Havana and in Moscow, nothing was said or written about Soviet military assistance to Cuba, which was well under way soon after Raúl Castro's visit to Moscow in July 1960. To avoid raising suspicions or concern in Washington, steps were taken by the Soviets to make it appear that weapons and military advisers were sent to Cuba by Czechoslovakia and not by the Soviet Union. Soviet army officers traveled to the island with Czechoslovak passports under assumed Czechoslovak names. Thus, an element of deceit was present in Soviet-Cuban military cooperation from the beginning; however, this was regarded by the Soviet establishment as a normal part of the hide-and-seek game, which the socialist camp was playing with the West.

To an extent, this was also true of the restraint shown by Moscow's leadership in public assessments of the prospects of the Cuban Revolution and Soviet-Cuban relations. Soviet leaders had hopes that the Cuban Revolution would evolve and take a more radical course long before Castro made "the construction of socialism" his declared policy, but they did not express themselves openly, primarily for fear that such statements would strengthen anti-Castro sentiments in Washington and provoke the U.S. administration to take actions that would threaten the very existence of Castro's regime. There was also another reason behind Moscow's restraint, namely, the "bourgeois origins" of Castro and his entourage: orthodox Soviet communists, such as Boris Ponomarev, head of the International Department of the CPSU Central Committee, still had serious doubts about Castro's potential as a true socialist revolutionary. Consequently, in 1959-1960, Khrushchev avoided any definition of the social and economic reforms implemented in Cuba in his public pronouncements, limiting himself to expressions of support for the "struggle of the Cuban people for their freedom and independence, the development of their national economy"[20] and to wishes of success in "building a new life, free and independent of imperialists."[21] Khrushchev was careful not to associate Castro's reforms with socialism.

As viewed from Moscow, future prospects of the Cuban Revolution continued to be uncertain because of the ambiguous political views of its undisputed leader, who could change at will the revolution's course and orientation. Contrary to what he affirmed later, Castro was not a communist in 1953 when he started the armed struggle against Batista, nor in 1959-1960, after the triumph of the revolution. Apart from his own later assertions, intended to justify his self-appointment to first secretary of the Cuban Communist Party, there is no evidence to confirm Castro's Marxist views in the early stages of his political career. Khrushchev recollected in his memoirs that, while Raúl Castro and Ernesto "Che" Guevara were known in Moscow as communists, Fidel Castro was not believed to be one and did not behave like a communist in the first months after taking power, when he was pursuing "a very cautious policy" toward the Soviet Union. But then things started to change; "Castro was no longer sitting on the fence; he was beginning to behave like a full-fledged communist, even though he still didn't call himself one."[22]

Some Soviet officials who met Fidel Castro and observed his performance thought he was a talented opportunist who adapted his views to the demands of the moment. This view of Castro coincided with that of American political analyst Professor Howard J. Wiarda of the University of Massachusetts, who later gave a laconic but accurate description of the reasons behind Castro's transformation from a democrat to a communist. He wrote that Castro's allegiance to Marxism-Leninism "was purely pragmatic and calculating: it was a means to tweak the United States and to secure assistance from the Soviet Union" and that Castro was "a Marxist-Leninist of necessity, not of conviction."[23]

Nonetheless, the CPSU theorists were placing revolutionary Cuba into the category of countries with "progressive national-democratic regimes." These regimes placed third in order of importance for Moscow, behind the socialist and socialist-oriented countries. Soviet media ridiculed speculation in the American press regarding the existence of the "communist threat" in Cuba. In August 1959, the *New Times*, a Moscow weekly magazine, wrote that the Cuban Revolution "...was led by anti-imperialist elements among the national bourgeoisie anxious to liberate the country from foreign political domination and American monopoly exploitation. There is nothing communistic in their program or actions. The government headed by Fidel Castro does not include a single communist."[24]

The appraisal of the role of communists in the Cuban Revolution and of their ability to take over its leadership ultimately, in accordance with the tenets of Marxism-Leninism, was a crucial element in Moscow's initial evaluation of Cuba's possible eventual transition to socialism. Though the long-established Cuban Communist Party, the PSP, was regarded as one of the strongest in Latin America, its prestige and influence were seriously undermined by collaboration with Batista in the 1940s and by only lukewarm support for Castro's insurgent movement. One could hardly expect that Castro and his companions-in-arms would accept communists as equals and even less as "elder brothers." That was another reason for being cautious in estimating the chances of such a transition, even though Blas Roca was already predicting it in his speeches about the "new tasks which the Cuban Revolution will have to tackle in the course of further social development."[25]

Severo Aguirre, speaking at the end of January 1959 on behalf of the PSP at the Twenty-first Congress of the CPSU in Moscow, told the delegates of the Congress that power in Cuba "has passed into the hands of the rebel forces headed by Fidel Castro and his 26 July Organization, consisting 90 percent of peasants, rural and urban workers, and students of different revolutionary trends." He did not say who represented the remaining 10 percent who led the movement. Aguirre asserted that the PSP "played an active part in the rebel movement, insofar as it had the character of a guerrilla struggle and nothing in common with putschism or individual terrorism [and that] the Communists displayed great courage in taking part in the armed struggle and earned the love and esteem of their comrades by being in the front line of the battle." He also said, patronizingly, that twenty-five months earlier, when the insurgents began the armed struggle, "our party considered it was its first duty to help the insurgents by giving them correct orientation and securing for them support of the popular masses." He did not elaborate on Castro's political program but emphasized that "the struggle of the Cuban people is not over" and that after winning Cuba's independence, "it has embarked on a new stage, which is still harder and more dangerous."[26]

The delegates applauded this statement; Soviet communists were accustomed to believing that their fellow travelers in capitalist countries were always in the forefront of all revolutionary class struggles. The embellished image of Cuban communists and the legend of their reputed active participation in the armed struggle against the Batista regime were embraced and used extensively in accounts of the history of Castro's revolution by official Soviet propaganda and Soviet scholars. Sergei Gonionsky wrote that the PSP "was the main political force which was fighting consistently against the dictatorship...and actively participated in the liberation struggle, led by Fidel Castro." He also affirmed that a great number of the members of the PSP and its sympathizers were in the ranks of the rebels and that guerrilla detachments "were organized on the direct initiative of the party and then subordinated to Fidel Castro."[27]

This was clearly a gross overstatement; Fidel Castro and other leaders of the 26th of July Movement were telling a different story. Ernesto "Che" Guevara wrote in December 1960, in an article on the Cuban Revolution for publication in Moscow, that in Cuba "...power was taken as a result of the development of the struggle of the peasants, of arming and organizing them under the slogans of agrarian reform and of other just demands of that class.... In other words, the revolution came to the cities from the villages...."[28]

Soviet scholars and journalists began to describe the role of the PSP in the Cuban Revolution in more moderate terms only later, when the party was merged in a subordinate position with the 26th of July Movement and the Revolutionary Directorate and there was no longer any need to exaggerate its role, particularly after Blas Roca and Anibal Escalante had failed to place communist cadres in key positions in the United Revolutionary Organizations, which served as the basis for the new Castroite Communist Party of Cuba.

Apart from the public presentation in Moscow of the "heroic struggle" of Cuban communists, officials of the International Department of the CPSU Central Committee in charge of relations with Latin American communist parties were not overly optimistic from the start about the prospect of PSP leaders reaching the helm of the Cuban Revolution. However, they considered that, with the growing belligerence of Washington and the increasing internal political opposition to radical social and economic reforms, Castro would need all the support he could get from the Cuban communists and that he might be prepared to offer them, in return, a share in the new power structure, provided they gave up their aspirations for dominant positions in the revolutionary regime. Moscow curators of the PSP also surmised that its chances of gaining more influence in post-Batista Cuba would depend, to a substantial degree, on the nature and scale of Soviet support for Castro, which was bound to be reflected in his treatment of communists.

Moscow Deepens Its Commitment

With all the uncertainties, risks, and expenses involved, the temptation to consolidate a friendly regime in the backyard of the imperialist archenemy was too great to resist and led Moscow to a fateful step in reply to Washington's economic sanctions against Cuba. On July 9, 1960, the Soviet government made known its decision to increase annual purchases of Cuban sugar by seven hundred thousand tons — the exact amount of the reduction of the U.S. quota announced by the Eisenhower administration only three days earlier as a reprisal for the nationalization of American properties on the island. The Soviet leadership's rapid decision could only be explained by the importance Moscow attached to the Castro regime's survival. The USSR had no deficit of sugar; at the time, it still continued to export part of its domestic sugar production to Afghanistan, Iraq, Iran, Finland, and some other countries, altogether amounting to 242.9 thousand tons in 1960 compared to 197.2 thousand tons in 1959.[29]

This step laid the foundation of the policy which substituted Cuba's economic dependence on the United States for an even greater degree of dependence on the USSR. The pledge to become the main provider of Cuba's needs was made public in a Soviet press communiqué during Raúl Castro's visit to Moscow in July 1960, ascribing to Khrushchev the following statement:

> Forces of the countries of the socialist camp are so great at present and their economic power is so strong that they can take it completely upon themselves to supply Cuba, on the basis of normal trade relations, all the necessary goods which are denied to it now by the United States and some other capitalist states. In exchange for Cuban goods, the Soviet government is prepared to take upon itself the deliveries of oil and other products in quantities that will fully satisfy Cuba's needs.[30]

In December 1960, Castro sent to Moscow another high-level economic mission headed by Ernesto "Che" Guevara, who had talks with Anastas Mikoyan. They signed a joint communiqué that confirmed the Soviet commitment "to take all measures within its power to ensure the supply of vitally important goods for the Cuban economy when they cannot be purchased in other countries." The Soviet government expressed its willingness to increase purchases of Cuban sugar to 2.7 million tons, "if the United States of America carries out its threat not to buy Cuban sugar," and to accept the price of 4 cents per pound — double the world market price. Additionally, a government source was quoted as saying, "If the United States of America purchases some quantity of Cuban sugar, the Soviet Union will reduce its purchases of Cuban sugar correspondingly, while bearing in mind the existing agreement that the Soviet Union will purchase one million tons of Cuban sugar annually."[31] This provision was a clear indication of the political nature of the additional Soviet economic commitment.

In 1961, Cuban and Soviet representatives also signed a protocol on trade between the two countries that provided for a further substantial increase in the volume of bilateral trade. The Soviet Union undertook to export to Cuba (apart from oil and petroleum products) rolled ferrous metals, tin plate, wheat, fertilizers, chemicals, machinery and equipment, foods, and "other goods necessary to ensure the uninterrupted functioning of Cuba's industry, the successful development of its economy, and the supply of its population with necessary goods."[32] In addition to sugar, Cuba agreed to supply the USSR with nickel oxide, fresh and canned fruits, juices, tanned hides, and other products. A separate agreement provided for Soviet technical assistance in geological prospecting in Cuba for iron ore, chromites, oils, and other minerals; in building a new steel mill and enlarging the capacities of the existing ones; and in the construction of thermal power plants and a new oil refinery. Yet another bilateral document stipulated that the Soviets would 1) train Cuban students as engineers and scientists, 2) give Cuban factory workers technical training, and 3) bear all their transport, tuition, and living expenses in the USSR.

As a result, within the next twelve months, the volume of Soviet-Cuban trade more than tripled, from 160.6 million rubles in 1960 to 539 million rubles in 1961. The Soviet Union's share in Cuban exports increased from 16.7 percent to 48.2 percent and in Cuban imports from 13.8 percent to 41.1 percent. Soviet purchases of Cuban raw sugar rose from 1.5 million tons to 3.3 million tons; deliveries to Cuba of oil and petroleum products nearly doubled, from 2.164 million tons to 4.028

million tons, and machinery and equipment deliveries increased more than ninefold, from 5.8 million rubles to 54.8 million rubles.[33] The USSR had already become the principal market for Cuban sugar exports and was rapidly becoming Cuba's main source of oil, machinery, and equipment.

Even more indicative of the importance that the Soviet leadership had given to the survival of Castro's revolutionary regime in Cuba was Khrushchev's famous missile-rattling statement at the All-Russian Congress of School Teachers on July 9, 1960. After assuring the Cubans that the USSR and other socialist countries would help them withstand the U.S. economic blockade and warning that this blockade could be followed by preparation for military intervention against Cuba, he said, "It should not be forgotten that the United States is now not at such an inaccessible distance from the Soviet Union as formerly. Figuratively speaking, in case of need, Soviet artillerymen can support the Cuban people with their rocket fire should the aggressive forces in the Pentagon dare to start intervention against Cuba."[34] Khrushchev had threatened to use missiles in defense of a friendly country before, during the 1956 Suez Crisis against Britain and France, and had tried to claim credit for the withdrawal of invading foreign troops from Egypt. But this was the first time that he attempted to practice nuclear blackmail on the United States, a country by far superior to the USSR in military power and economic potential.

The Suez Crisis was, in fact, a precursor of Khrushchev's brinkmanship policy in the Caribbean. Khrushchev used the intensely anti-American revolutionary regime in Cuba and whatever opportunities it presented as the USSR's instruments to exert political and military pressure on the United States only ninety miles from U.S. territory. This was his attempt to redress the Soviet-American strategic imbalance and to improve Moscow's bargaining positions in other areas vis-à-vis Washington. By that time, relations between the two superpowers had worsened considerably compared to the second half of 1959, which was marked by the "spirit of Camp David." Soviet attempts to blackmail the three Western powers in West Berlin by threatening to sign a unilateral peace treaty with the German Democratic Republic were not producing the desired results. President Dwight Eisenhower refused to apologize for the flight of a U-2 spy plane over Soviet territory, and the Soviet leader slammed the door on the four-power summit meeting in Paris. Increasingly, the language of détente in East-West relations was replaced by familiar Cold War rhetoric.

Khrushchev's bravado raised quite a few eyebrows in Washington but was dismissed as an ill-conceived bluff, not worthy of serious consideration. In fact, Khrushchev himself seemed to realize that this time he really had gone too far. His "rocket fire" statement was not cited in Soviet press commentaries and was even omitted from subsequent reprints of his speech. At a press conference in Moscow on July 12, 1960, Khrushchev was rather vague about the exact form Soviet military assistance to Cuba might take. After expressing his belief that one day the Cubans would demand the withdrawal of U.S. forces from Guantánamo, he stated, "If the U.S. imperialists take aggressive actions against the Cuban people, defending their national independence, we shall support the Cuban people."[35] Likewise, his message to Fidel Castro on July 25, 1960, contained no mention of Soviet missiles. Khrushchev wrote that in case of "an armed intervention against Cuba," the Soviet Union would render it "the necessary assistance."[36]

However, interpreting Khrushchev's figure of speech literally was more suitable to Castro's purposes. He was quick to seize the opportunity of securing Soviet protection for his regime and apparently had no difficulty in accepting Khrushchev's rash offer to put the USSR at risk of a nuclear conflict with the United States in order to guarantee the security of the Cuban Revolution. The lengthy declaration, which Castro himself drafted and read at a mass meeting in Havana on September 2, 1960, named officially as the "General National Assembly of the People," became the foreign policy platform of the Provisional Revolutionary Government. In particular, it stated:

> The General National Assembly of the People declares that the assistance, sincerely offered by the Soviet Union to Cuba in case it is attacked by imperialist armed forces, can never be regarded as an act of intervention but only as a striking expression of solidarity.... Therefore, the General National Assembly of the People declares in front of the whole America and the whole world that it accepts the assistance in the form of the Soviet Union's missiles if the territory of Cuba is invaded by U.S. armed forces and thanks the Soviet Union for the support.[37]

In an obvious attempt to provoke Nikita Khrushchev into reaffirming his commitment as originally formulated, Carlos Franqui of Havana's *Revolución*, during an interview in Moscow on October 22, 1960, asked the Soviet leader to comment on the assertion of the "imperialists" that his statement of July 9, 1960, was "of purely symbolic importance." Khrushchev evasively replied, expressing his hope that "the imperialists' threat regarding intervention against Cuba" would not be translated into military actions and that the need to verify the validity of the Soviet commitment to "military assistance to the Cuban people" would not arise. However, Franqui pursued the matter, saying, "But if this threat is put into effect, I presume that the missiles are sufficiently prepared for this, aren't they?" Khrushchev responded, "Indisputably. You understand it correctly."[38] In December 1960, Ernesto "Che" Guevara in an article written for publication in Moscow referred to the Soviet leader's July statement as an "historic warning, which barred the military aggression being prepared in the territory of the United States and made the existence of Cuba as a sovereign state possible."[39]

The die was cast. Castro asked for a Soviet insurance policy against U.S. economic and military sanctions. Khrushchev agreed to satisfy the request. What remained to be determined was the amount and the form of the premium which Cuba was expected to pay; however, that was not something that could be negotiated and agreed upon in specific terms all at once. Rather, it was a gradually evolving process of probes and experiments, in which both sides were seeking to pursue, through their close cooperation, not only their common goal in the Third World of promoting the "struggle of peoples for their national liberation" but also their specific interests. There was little debate in Havana and Moscow about the expediency of their de facto political alliance; the great advantages seemed obvious to both sides, and the risks and costs involved appeared to be acceptable. The radicalization of the Cuban Revolution that followed and Castro's decision to convert Cuba into a totalitarian socialist state were neither required nor requested by Moscow but were prompted and made possible by its economic and military assistance.

Castro Opts for Socialism

The overriding reason for Castro's desire to seek an alliance and friendship with the Soviet Union was clearly his realistic assessment that he could not achieve his principal objectives without Moscow's material and military support. The Soviet Union was the only country with sufficient economic and military potential and the political will to withstand U.S. pressures and act against U.S. interests in the Caribbean. Castro realized that while friendship with Cuba offered unique strategic and political advantages to the USSR, it also entailed obvious risks and great economic costs that could deter Soviet leaders from making serious long-term commitments unless these disadvantages were greatly outweighed by the gains. Therefore, Castro was interested in raising Cuba's value to the USSR in order to ensure Cuba's continued inclusion on the list of Soviet foreign policy priorities.

The best way to ensure Cuba's position as a Soviet priority was to join the socialist camp. Cuban communists lost no time in educating Fidel Castro and other petty bourgeois leaders of the 26th of July Movement about the possibilities for Cuba if it were to become a member of the socialist community. Membership in this exclusive club not only ensured preferential conditions of economic and military aid from its leader, the Soviet Union, but it also promised the advantage of obtaining Moscow's "fraternal assistance" in such emergencies as internal social upheaval and/or a Guatemala-style counterrevolutionary exiles' invasion or direct U.S. intervention. By that time, the Soviet doctrine of proletarian internationalism had already passed the test in the bloody suppression of the Hungarian Revolution in 1956, although it was formulated officially years later to justify the Soviet invasion of Czechoslovakia when it became known as the doctrine of limited sovereignty or the Brezhnev doctrine.

There were, of course, other important reasons that motivated Castro's decision to declare on April 16, 1961, that his revolution was a socialist one. The Soviet model of socialism was unsurpassed in producing the most efficient system of totalitarian control wrapped in the respectable, attractive theory of Marxism-Leninism, with its appeal to the noble sentiments of social justice. Marxism-Leninism promised quick, simple solutions to the problems of underdevelopment, poverty, unemployment, and inequality. Soviet socialism gave the underprivileged classes a false, though pleasant, sense of equality and social revenge by uprooting the rich and ruining the middle class. Marxist-Leninist ideology portrayed the new ruling class, the functionaries of the party and of the state, as incorruptible servants of the people dedicated to the just cause of the revolution, and the rampant corruption in the Soviet governing elite was well hidden from the public eye. While the actual Soviet system was notoriously inefficient economically, this weakness was counterbalanced by Moscow's ability to concentrate all available resources in a few selected fields in order to guarantee substantial progress and to avoid social disturbances despite its policy of keeping popular consumption to a bare minimum.

Because of its capacity to channel resources to particular priority areas, the Soviet Union achieved spectacular results in scientific and technological fields related primarily to the defense effort and was even able to challenge the West militarily. Khrushchev bragged about his plans to catch up with the United States and to surpass it in per capita production of consumer goods. In the early 1960s, the Soviet Union presented the outside world an image of a dynamic superpower, competing successfully with the United States in military and space technology, while expanding its influence in the Third World by propping up quasi-Marxist or leftist dictatorial regimes in the newly independent countries of Africa and Asia. It was also ensuring through the use of force, if deemed necessary, the irreversibility of socialist transformations in the East European countries, as demonstrated by the suppression of anti-communist civil disturbances in East Germany in 1953 and of the Hungarian Revolution in 1956.

Against this background, Castro conveniently decided to put aside his original idea of humanistic democracy that supposedly would have avoided the evils of both capitalism and socialism, which meant, as he himself put it, that "man's dearest desire, his liberty, need not be sacrificed in order to satisfy his material needs."[40] Castro opted for Soviet-style totalitarian socialism, since it promised what he desired: 1) unlimited power without the stigma of an ordinary *caudillo* (military dictator), 2) absence of any internal political opposition and stability of the regime, 3) the semblance of an egalitarian society and resulting popular support, 4) guaranteed alliance with the Soviet Union and its economic and military assistance, 5) the luxury of reaping political benefits of an extreme anti-Americanism without fear of U.S. reprisals, and 6) the possibility of fomenting revolutionary movements in Latin America and Africa and projecting Cuba's influence far beyond the limits of the Caribbean.

In terms of the polarization and division of society, Cuba paid a very high price for the sudden turn of its revolution much further to the left than contemplated originally by Castro and his companions-in-arms. It was noted even by Khrushchev, who gave a simplistic but essentially correct summary of the process:

> Castro's policies were earning him many enemies.... Many of the men who had fought at his side during the struggle for independence were turning away from him. The reason for this was that many of them didn't want Socialist reforms. They had been fed up with Batista and eager to overthrow the corrupt old regime, but they were against Castro's nationalization of all businesses, his restrictive policies against

the landowners, and his confiscation of property belonging to wealthy Americans.[41]

Such admissions were not to be found in Soviet press reports or even scholarly works on the internal situation in Cuba; these sources invariably asserted that the majority of the populace overwhelmingly supported the socialist transformations and that only adherents of Batista's regime were against them.

Khrushchev also disclosed that he and his colleagues in Moscow were baffled by the timing of Castro's announcement of the socialist nature of the Cuban Revolution. He reasoned that, since it was bound to increase the number of political opponents of the revolutionary regime, it had to be made after the Bay of Pigs invasion was defeated and not before. For some reason, the Soviet leader failed to see the transparent logic behind Castro's timing — it was precisely because the invasion was still in the making that he hastened to take this step, intended to strengthen the Soviet Union's commitment to the defense of his regime. Apparently, he did not exclude the possibility that the invading forces would succeed, with effective American backing, in entrenching themselves on the beachhead and starting a protracted war of attrition. He could hardly foresee the eventuality that Washington would refuse to provide air and naval support to the embattled Cuban exiles and leave them to their fate.

Castro's announcement did not change President Kennedy's orders not to engage U.S. forces in combat operations supporting the invasion. It did, however, give an additional incentive to Moscow to confirm its military commitment to Cuba. On April 18, 1961, Khrushchev sent Kennedy a message voicing a strong warning, "It's not too late yet to prevent what would be impossible to control," mentioning the possibility of "a chain reaction in all parts of the world [if] the flames of war, started by the interventionists in Cuba, grow into a fire that would be impossible to put out." Making clear that this chain reaction could affect U.S. interests in Europe, the Soviet leader reasoned that it was hardly possible "to conduct matters in such a way that one will settle and put out the fire in one region while arranging a new fire in another."[42] President Kennedy reacted immediately to this threat, expressing in a message to Moscow on April 18, 1962, his hope that the Soviet government would not use the situation in Cuba as a pretext "to inflame other areas of the world."[43]

In another letter sent to Washington on April 22, 1961, in reply to this message, Khrushchev repeated his warning in more specific terms, threatening the United States with retaliatory actions against its allies in Europe:

> If you consider that you are entitled to take such measures against Cuba, to which the U.S. government resorted recently, then you should recognize that other countries also have no less grounds for acting in the same fashion with regard to the states whose territory is indeed used for preparations which pose a threat to the security of the Soviet Union.

And in reply to Kennedy's reference to the Soviet armed intervention in Hungary, Khrushchev wrote, "It's you, the United States, who crushed the independence of Guatemala by sending there your hirelings as you are trying to do with regard to Cuba as well."[44]

Cold War polemics aside, one immediate consequence of the fiasco of the Bay of Pigs invasion and Castro's declaration of the socialist course of the Cuban Revolution was the influx of massive Soviet military assistance to Cuba. According to Khrushchev, the Cuban army was given "as many arms as it could absorb."[45] Whatever doubts he and his colleagues in the Presidium of the CPSU Central Committee could have had as to the sincerity of Castro's conversion to socialism were dispelled; they were now convinced that there could be no reconciliation between Havana and Washington and that the Cuban revolutionaries had no other alternative but to throw in their lot with the Soviet Union.

Equally as important for Moscow strategists was the fact that Castro, by dealing ruthlessly and efficiently first with the internal armed opposition groups and then with the U.S.-sponsored invasion by the Cuban exiles, proved his regime's viability and capacity to hold out against heavy odds. This allayed fears in Moscow that the Cuban revolutionary regime was doomed to suffer the fate of the left-wing government of Guatemala; yet, there remained the certainty that Washington would not leave Castro in peace and was busy preparing more serious attempts to topple his regime, possibly resulting in loss of face for Moscow and loss of Soviet investments.

Not surprisingly, Castro's dramatic statement about the socialist nature of his revolution was received in Moscow with mixed feelings. On the one hand, it promised the realization of Khrushchev's most optimistic expectations and served to confirm the correctness of the Soviet leadership's decision to make an all-out effort to save Castro's regime both from economic collapse and U.S. military intervention. It also appeared to justify the enormous material expenses involved, as well as the political risks to Soviet-American relations. On the other hand, some in the Soviet government viewed Castro's precipitate public acceptance of socialist doctrine as too risky. They feared Castro's avowed socialism would further complicate Cuba's internal political situation and provoke serious repercussions in Havana's relations with Washington — making direct U.S. military intervention in Cuba much more probable and putting Khrushchev's public pledge to defend Cuba to a very dangerous test.

This explains why Castro's announcement of his belief in socialism caused a restrained public reaction in Moscow, a fact which did not pass unnoticed by Western observers. For months afterward, there was no mention in Soviet official statements and press commentaries of Castro's decision to build socialism in Cuba, except for a passage included at the insistence of Cuba in the Soviet-Cuban joint communiqué, which was signed in Moscow on September 20, 1960, by President Osvaldo Dorticós Torrado and Leonid Brezhnev, then chairman of the Presidium of the Supreme Soviet of the USSR:

> Cuba has accomplished its revolution independently and has freely opted for the road of socialist development, which will ensure in the best possible way a speedy, effective development and the highest material and spiritual level of life for its people.[46]

But neither Brezhnev nor Dorticós Torrado referred to the socialist orientation of the Cuban Revolution in the speeches they exchanged at a mass meeting in the Grand Kremlin Palace in Moscow prior to signing the communiqué.

Recognition in Moscow

The situation changed after Castro's sensational statement on December 1, 1961, asserting that he was a Marxist-Leninist and would remain one to the last day of his life. His declaration was accompanied by the accelerated nationalization of private enterprises and other socialist reforms and also by his decision to merge the 26th of July Movement, the Revolutionary Directorate, and the PSP into the United Revolutionary Organizations on a Marxist-Leninist platform. Furthermore, leaders in Moscow were increasingly confident that Cuba could become a genuinely socialist country, and they were more determined to ensure that this "beacon of socialism" in Latin America was not extinguished. At long last, the Soviet leadership acknowledged publicly the transition of the Cuban Revolution to its socialist stage. In

April 1962, Khrushchev sent a congratulatory telegram to Castro on the occasion of the first anniversary of the "crushing defeat by the Cuban people and its armed forces of the bandit gangs of foreign hirelings-counterrevolutionaries [which] demonstrated the unbreakable unity of the Cuban people, its supreme determination to defend to the end the cause of the socialist revolution."[47] It took exactly a year for the Soviet leadership to accept publicly the socialist credentials of the Cuban Revolution.

Soviet scholars were then free to write and publish their essays about the details and consequences of Cuba's transition to socialism. Sergei Mikhailov, then the director of the Moscow Institute of Latin American Studies, theorized that while previously "the national liberation movement was dealing its blows against imperialism mainly in Asia and Africa.... After the victory of the Cuban Revolution, imperialism had suffered a crushing defeat also on the continent where colonialism reigns in a disguised form — in Latin America." Mikhailov added, "The Cuban socialist revolution, which has done away with the domination of U.S. imperialism in the very center of the North American colonial domain, has put an end to the hopes of U.S. governing circles to avoid the catastrophic tremors resulting from the development of the national liberation movement in Latin America."[48]

Another aspect of the "international importance" of the Cuban Revolution, as viewed from Moscow, was emphasized by the authors of the theoretical study, *Construction of Communism and the World Revolutionary Process*, published by the Moscow Institute of World Economy and International Relations in 1966:

> Events in Cuba demonstrated graphically that, due to the growing superiority of the socialist camp over the capitalist one, there appeared greater opportunities of new countries falling off from the system of imperialism without a world war. The Cuban Revolution, the first socialist revolution to have developed in the Western Hemisphere in the third stage of the general crisis of capitalism in the absence of world war, augurs new storms on the Latin American continent.[49]

This thesis was advanced, in particular, to counter one of the especially damaging claims emanating from "bourgeois propaganda," which was based on the actual history of socialist revolutions in Russia, China, and other countries, that socialism could only triumph in wartime conditions or as a result of a major war. Cuba's case could also be used as a convincing argument to support Khrushchev's thesis — criticized in Peking as "revisionist" — that the peaceful coexistence of states with different social and economic orders did not preclude the possibility of victorious socialist revolutions in capitalist countries. A Marxist-Leninist theoretical background accompanied the leitmotif of Castro's propaganda that Cuba would serve as a model for many countries of Latin America, where the revolution, as Castro publicly affirmed, was imminent and where "the breach made by the Cuban people in the chain of imperialist oppression is of enormous importance for the peoples."[50]

Castro's proposition was echoed in the public statements of Soviet leaders and became a recurring theme in the writings of Soviet scholars on the importance of the Cuban socialist revolution. In his message to Castro on the occasion of the second anniversary of the overthrow of Batista's regime, Khrushchev wrote that the Cuban Revolution "has created new prerequisites for the further development of the national liberation movement in countries of Latin America" and that the Cuban policy of defense of national interests "has become today the banner of all progressive forces in Latin America arising to fight for liberation from the imperialist yoke."[51]

Khrushchev, in his correspondence with the Cuban leader in the aftermath of the Missile Crisis, referred repeatedly to the Cuban Revolution as a validation of Russia's revolutionary experience, as part of the common struggle against Western imperialism, and as passing through the same difficulties in building a new society as the USSR was experiencing. Welcoming Fidel Castro to Red Square in Moscow on April 28, 1963, Khrushchev said:

> Revolutionary Cuba is a beacon that shows the way to progress, freedom, and happiness to all peoples of Latin America.... A hundred years ago, the specter of communism was haunting Europe.... Since then, communism has been winning the minds and hearts of millions of working people on all continents of our planet. And now, the bright future of all mankind presents itself before the nations of the world not only in the form of ideas but also in the vivid reality of the Soviet Union and other socialist countries and in the vivid reality of Cuba. Socialism is winning one victory after another. More than a billion people are marching under its banners in Europe, Asia, and America![52]

The theme was also emphasized by the authors of the first collection of documents on Soviet-Cuban relations published in Moscow in 1963. They wrote that the Cuban Revolution "has opened the front of active struggle against imperialism in Latin America and has given a powerful stimulus to the movement of Latin American peoples for their complete national liberation."[53] In the opinion of Anatoly Bekarevich, shared by other leading Soviet experts on Latin America, it "demonstrated that, in the conditions of Latin America, the national liberation struggle of peoples for the genuine independence of their fatherland merges with the struggle for socialism [and] has become another confirmation of the invincibility and continuity of the revolutionary process started by the Great October Socialist Revolution."[54]

Historian Lev Slezkin provided a similar analysis:

Both internal and external factors were pushing revolutionary Cuba to socialism. This reflected the general trend of contemporary revolutionary national liberation movements. The completeness of this phenomenon in Cuba (despite the specific nature of local features) — the victory of the Cuban Revolution and its transition to the socialist stage — have given this revolution an international importance and have placed it among the greatest events of our time. [55]

It is difficult to determine the part played by ideological and political factors, as compared to military-strategic ones, in the Soviet leadership's decisions to make incremental, further reaching political, economic, and military commitments to Castro's regime. In the initial period of Soviet-Cuban relations, ideology and politics were certainly prevalent in Soviet leaders' thinking as they pondered the best use of their newly found ally in the interests of the USSR and of "the world revolutionary process." The weight of these factors and the depth of the USSR's commitments were increasing in direct proportion to the speed with which Cuba was being transformed into a one-party totalitarian socialist state. Yet, given Moscow's constant preoccupation with the Soviet-American confrontation and balance of power, considerations of global strategy and of Cuba's possible role in reducing U.S. superiority over the USSR in nuclear strike capability were also present in the minds of Soviet policy makers and military planners, as evidenced in 1962.

From the very beginning, Soviet policy toward Castro's Cuba was determined by the desire to project and expand Moscow's presence and influence in the Western Hemisphere, heretofore a U.S. preserve, and to sustain Cuba as a support base for revolutionary movements that were bound to follow in other countries of Latin America. Khrushchev sincerely believed, and said in his correspondence with Castro, that Soviet economic and military assistance to Cuba was motivated by "internationalist duty," not by "mercantile considerations." Since Soviet leaders, starting with Vladimir Lenin, never made a distinction between the Soviet Union's national interests and those of the world socialist revolution or, as it came to be called later, "progress of mankind," they rejected the notion that Moscow was pursuing selfish interests in trying to expand its influence in the Third World.

One thing was certain: Khrushchev and his colleagues in the Soviet leadership were not altruists. Their vision of the world scene was limited and distorted by Marxist-Leninist dogmas, but, otherwise, they were pragmatists determined to promote what they thought to be the Soviet Union's national interests and the long-term strategic goal of the socialist transformation of the world. A socialist Cuba served both purposes. This had been from the start, and remained throughout the thirty years of the Soviet-Cuban alliance, the underlying reason for the generosity of the USSR in sacrificing immense material resources to keep the Castro regime afloat. It also explained the considerable patience shown by Soviet leaders in dealing with the capricious and erratic personality of Fidel Castro, who more than matched similar traits in Nikita Khrushchev.

Notes

1. *Pravda* (Moscow), February 17, 1951.

2. Stephen Weissold, comp., 1970, *Soviet Relations with Latin America, 1918-1968. A Documentary Survey* (London and New York: Oxford University Press), 78.

3. Weissold, 1970, 213, 214.

4. *Literaturnaya Gazeta* (Moscow), April 8, 1952.

5. *Respuestas* (Havana), December 21, 1956.

6. L.I. Slezkin, 1966, *Istoria Kubinskoy Revoluitsii* (Moscow: Izdatelstvo Nauka), 5.

7. E. Gonzalez, 1974, *The Cuban Revolution and the Soviet Union: 1959-1960* (Ann Arbor, Mich.: Xerox University Microfilms), 400.

8. *Pravda*, January 11, 1959.

9. Strobe Talbott, ed. and trans., 1970, *Khrushchev Remembers* (Boston: Little, Brown), 488-89.

10. In the summer of 1991, Arnold Kalinin replaced Yuri Petrov as Soviet ambassador in Havana.

11. Collection of articles, 1961, *Natsionalno-Ocvoboditelnoye Dvizhenie v Latinskoy Amerike na Sovremennom Etape* (Moscow: Politizdat), 140.

12. Nikolay Leonov headed, in later years, the Latin American Department of KGB's Second Main Directorate.

13. V.V. Volsky and A.D. Bekarevich, eds., 1987, *Veliky Oktiabr y Kubinskaya Revoluitsia* (Moscow: Izdatelstvo Nauka), 80-81.

14. L.I. Slezkin, 1966, *Istoriya Kubinskoy Respubliki* (Moscow: Izdatelstvo Nauka), 364.

15. Sergei A. Gonionsky, 1960, *Latinskaya Amerika y SSHA: 1939-1959* (Moscow: Izdatelstvo Mezhdunazodnye Otnosheniia), 468.

16. *Pravda*, February 17, 1960.

17. *Pravda*, June 20, 1960.

18. Arkady Shevchenko, 1985, *Breaking with Moscow* (New York: Ballantine Books), 137.

19. *Pravda*, February 21, 1960.

20. *Pravda*, February 21, 1960.

21. Khrushchev's telegram to Castro on December 31, 1960. *Pravda*, January 2, 1961.

22. Strobe Talbott, ed. and trans., 1970, *Khruschev Remembers* (Boston: Little, Brown), 589.

23. Howard J. Wiarda, 1991, "Is Cuba Next? Crisis of the Castro Regime," in *Problems of Communism*, (January-April) 85.

24. *New Times* (Moscow), 1959, 33:8.

25. Blas Roca, 1961, *Kuba-Svobodnaya Territoria Ameriki* (Moscow: Politizdat), 63.

26. *Pravda*, February 1, 1959.

27. S.A. Gonionsky, 1960, *Latinskaya Amerika y SSHA: 1939-1959* (Moscow: Izdatelstvo Mezhdunazodnye Otnosheniia), 465-66.

28. A. Efimov and I. Grigulevich, eds., 1961, *Kuba. Istoriko-Ethnographicheskie Ocherki*, collection of articles, (Moscow: Izdatelstvo Akademii Nauk SSSR), 18.

29. Statistical Abstracts, *Vneshniaya Torgovlia SSSR, Statisticheskiy Sbornik, 1918-1966*, 1967, (Moscow: Izdatelstvo Mezhdunerodnye Otnosheniia), 135.

30. *Pravda*, July 21, 1960.

31. *Pravda*, December 20, 1960.

32. *Pravda*, December 20, 1960.

33. Statistical Abstracts, *Vneshniaya Torgovlia SSSR. Statistichesky Sbornik, 1918-1966*, 1967, (Moscow: Izdatelstvo Mezhdunazodnye Otrosheniia), 69, 225, 228.

34. *Pravda*, July 10, 1960.

35. *Narody SSSR y Kuby Naveki Vmeste*, collection of documents, 1963, (Moscow: Izdatelstvo Pravda), 52.

36. *Pravda*, July 26, 1960.

37. *Pravda*, September 8, 1960.

38. *Pravda*, October 30, 1960.

39. A. Efimov and L. Grigulevich, eds., 1961, *Kuba. Istoriko-Etnographicheskiye Ocherki*, collection of articles, (Moscow: Izdatelstvo Akademii Nauk SSSR), 19.

40. Irving Louis Horowitz, ed., 1989, *Cuban Communism*, seventh edition, (New Brunswick, N.J. and London: Transaction Publishers), 52.

41. Strobe Talbott, ed. and trans., 1970, *Khrushchev Remembers* (Boston: Little, Brown), 491.

42. *Pravda*, April 19, 1961.

43. *American Foreign Policy. Current Documents*, 1961, 1965, (Washington, D.C.: Department of State Publication), 296, 297.

44. *Pravda*, April 23, 1991.

45. Strobe Talbott, ed. and trans., 1970, *Khrushchev Remembers* (Boston: Little, Brown), 492.

46. *Pravda*, September 21, 1960.

47. *Pravda*, April 18, 1962.

48. *Piat Let Kubinskoy Revoliutsii*, collection of articles, 1963, (Moscow: Izdatelstvo Akademii Nauk), 23.

49. *Stroitelstvo Kommunizma y Mirovoy Revoliutsionniy Protsess*, collection of articles, 1960, (Moscow: Akademiya Nauk SSSR, IMEMO), 18.

50. Fidel Castro's telegram to Khrushchev. *Pravda*, August 16, 1960.

51. *Pravda*, July 26, 1960.

52. *Pravda*, April 29, 1960.

53. *Narody SSSR y Kuby Naveki Vmeste*, collection of documents, 1963, (Moscow: Izdatelstvo Pravda), 4.

54. V.V. Volsky, ed., 1968, *Kuba. 10 Let Revoliutsii* (Moscow: Izdatelstvo Nauka), 91.

55. L.I. Slezkin, 1966, *Istoriya Kubinskoy Respubliki* (Izdatelstvo Nauka), 441.

Chapter 2

Soviet Missiles in Cuba

Khrushchev Proposes a Nuclear Gamble

The first serious test of the tenacity of the Soviet-Cuban alliance came when the Soviet leadership decided to use the island in order to bring a substantial part of United States territory within the range of Soviet medium-range ballistic missiles armed with nuclear warheads. Khrushchev, who initiated this idea, hoped that it would help to redress the imbalance in strategic nuclear forces between the Soviet Union and the United States, which had an overwhelming superiority in numbers of nuclear warheads and the capacity to use them against the main adversary. Vital industrial and urban centers in the USSR were threatened by hundreds of intercontinental ballistic missiles (ICBMs) and SAC bombers based in U.S. territory, U.S. nuclear submarine-based missiles, and also by U.S. intermediate-range ballistic missiles (IRBMs) deployed in Italy and Turkey. Besides, Khrushchev, for all his boasts of Soviet ICBMs' strike capabilities and their supposed ability "to shoot a fly in the sky," knew that medium- and intermediate-range missiles were much more reliable and accurate, taking only five to seven minutes to reach the target and leaving the other side practically no time for effective countermeasures. As for the Soviet ICBMs, too few were operational even to make credible threats about their use in the defense of Soviet allies.

In his memoirs, Khrushchev presented this motive as secondary in importance, insisting that the principal reason for deploying Soviet nuclear missiles in Cuba was to ward off an imminent U.S. invasion of the island. That was to be expected; he had publicly spoken before, during, and after the Cuban Missile Crisis about the purported existence of the threat of such an invasion as the only justification for taking this step. Khrushchev never mentioned Soviet strategic interests publicly in the Cuban context while he was in power. He was too much of a politician — and too much of a "good communist" — to admit that Cuba's defense was more of a pretext than a real reason for this move. During his meeting with Castro in Moscow in May 1963, Khrushchev even admonished him for saying that the Soviet Union's primary interest was to use Cuba as a missile base to threaten the United States.[1]

The Cuban Missile Crisis has undergone exhaustive investigation and analysis by politicians, civil servants, and scholars, including some former members of the Kennedy administration who were involved directly in the events of October 1962. Little can be added to the factual information on the crisis as seen from Washington. However, there have been serious attempts in recent years, starting with the Hawk's Cay U.S.-Soviet Conference in Florida in March 1987, to reconstruct the events of October 1962 as they were perceived in Moscow and Havana. This conference was followed by trilateral (U.S.-Soviet-Cuban) conferences on the history of the Cuban Crisis in Cambridge, Massachusetts, in October 1987; in Moscow in 1989; in Antigua in 1991; and in Havana in 1992. They added some valuable information about the ways the crisis affected Soviet-Cuban relations. Fidel Castro, to defend himself against accusations that he was trying to push Khrushchev into initiating a nuclear war against the United States, published in *Granma* in November 1990 his correspondence with Khrushchev in October 1962. Some important clues about what actually occurred can be found in the documents from the CPSU archives, which have started to appear in the Russian press. More will certainly follow.

From the notes taken by Soviet participants in these conferences, we know that Khrushchev first introduced the concept of missiles in Cuba for consideration with other members of the Soviet government in early May 1962, when he discussed briefly with Minister of Defense Marshal Rodion Malinovsky the Soviet Union's vulnerable strategic position in the context of its global confrontation with the United States. When Malinovsky mentioned that U.S. missiles in Turkey were capable of destroying such Soviet cities as Kiev, Odessa, Kharkov, and even Moscow, Khrushchev asked if any thought had been given to installing Soviet missiles in Cuba and suggested, "Let us launch a hedgehog into the pants of those next door." The minister replied diplomatically, "We have considered this possibility, but the decision should be taken by politicians." Whereupon Khrushchev concluded the conversation, saying, "Well, we are going to do just that."[2]

From this account, it follows that in the initial discussions, Cuba was mentioned only as a vehicle for positioning Soviet nuclear weapons on the doorstep of the United States. In subsequent deliberations, Khrushchev began to emphasize Cuba's defense as the principal justification for the whole exercise — politically, this motive was much more convenient. The main purpose remained, as expressed at the time by Yuri Andropov, then secretary of the CPSU Central Committee in charge of relations with socialist countries, "to keep under our sights the soft underbelly of the United States."[3]

It was ironic that before making his decision, allegedly intended to save Cuba from U.S. invasion, Khrushchev did not even bother to consult Castro on the issue; he did not think that Castro might present a problem, although Anastas Mikoyan, according to his son Sergo, thought otherwise. But that was characteristic of the Soviet Union's treatment of its junior partners in the socialist camp at the time; more often than not Moscow just informed them, after the fact, of decisions affecting their interests. Castro, who was a newcomer to the club, had yet to learn about this particular feature of "fraternal relations" among socialist countries, which was soon to lead to the most serious crisis in Soviet-Cuban relations, nearly bringing them to the breaking point.

Early in May 1962, Aleksandr Alekseyev, then counselor of the Soviet embassy and the KGB "resident" (chief of station) in Havana, was urgently called to Moscow. He was received by Khrushchev, who, without wasting time on preliminaries, said:

> We are appointing you ambassador to Cuba. Your appointment is connected with the decision, which we have taken, to deploy missiles with nuclear warheads in Cuba. Only this can save Cuba from direct American invasion. What do you think, will Fidel Castro agree to such a step?

Khrushchev went on to say that this would be done secretly and that, after the November mid-term congressional elections in the United States, he would visit Cuba and make the operation public. "The Americans will have to swallow our bitter pill, as we had to swallow theirs," added Khrushchev, alluding to U.S. missiles in Turkey.[4] That was the linchpin of his plan, to force Washington to tolerate Cuba's conversion into a Soviet missile base, thus killing two birds with one stone: reducing U.S strategic superiority and giving a foolproof security guarantee to Cuba. Alekseyev has said he told Khrushchev that Castro "bases all his strategy of the defense of the Cuban Revolution on the solidarity of the peoples of Latin America and most probably will not accept our proposal, since the Soviet military presence will be used by the Americans to completely isolate Cuba on the Latin American continent."[5]

Similar doubts were expressed by Mikoyan, who was also consulted as an "expert on Cuba." Undeterred, the Soviet leader arranged an informal meeting of some members of the Presidium of the CPSU Central Committee, Foreign Minister Gromyko, and top military commanders, and, after informing them of Alekseyev's opinion suggested, "Perhaps we should not talk with him [Castro] about this as a decision already taken but say that, since the correlation of forces in this region of the world is not in our favor, the Soviet government could even consider, if Fidel thinks it's acceptable, the question of deploying Soviet missiles in Cuba."[6]

It took only a few days to convert the idea into a proposal, whereupon Khrushchev convened a formal meeting of the Presidium of the CPSU Central Committee, which in classic Orwellian "double-speak" and "double-think" fashion discussed and approved unanimously on May 24, 1962, his proposal for the secret deployment of Soviet troops in Cuba, code-named "Operation Anadyr," after the name of a Siberian river (presumably to confuse U.S. intelligence). Khrushchev presented the proposal's motive as the necessity to defend Cuba, and the members of the Presidium pretended to believe his argument. They then decided to send Sharaf Rashidov, a member of the Presidium and Uzbekistan's Communist party boss to Cuba, accompanied by Marshal Sergei Biryuzov, commander of the Soviet missile forces, and Aleksandr Alekseyev to obtain Castro's approval of the operation. They were instructed to emphasize to Castro that the only reason for this proposal was "the defense of Cuba against possible American aggression." No minutes were taken of the meeting. A handwritten note by an obscure general, who was asked apparently by Marshal Malinovsky to scribble some lines indicating the subject matter of the discussion, the names of the speakers, and the decision was the only trace of that history-making meeting of the Presidium.

In the months and years that followed, the legend of the "defense of Cuba" as the only reason for this decision (and the ensuing massive Soviet military buildup on the island) was promoted by Moscow's propaganda machine with such energy and consistency that most Soviet officials, scholars, and even some government and party leaders themselves came to believe it. The following propaganda cliché, repeated almost word for word in subsequent Soviet official documents, scholarly studies, and press commentaries, was first uttered by Khrushchev in his report to the Soviet parliament on the origins and the outcome of the Cuban crisis on December 12, 1962:

> In view of the intensified threat of attack from the USA, the Cuban government approached the Soviet government in the summer of this year with a request for additional assistance. Agreement was reached on a series of new measures, including the deployment in Cuba of some tens of Soviet medium-range ballistic missiles, which were to remain in the hands of Soviet military personnel.... Our objective was solely the defense of Cuba.[7]

This cliché was still being used a quarter of a century later, when General Secretary of the CPSU Mikhail Gorbachev and Foreign Minister Eduard Shevardnadze started their critical reappraisal of some aspects of past Soviet foreign policy. It was reproduced almost word for word in an article on the twenty-fifth anniversary of the Cuban crisis by Vitaly Kobysh, an *Izvestia* political observer who had a reputation for being an experienced journalist well-versed in international affairs. Like Khrushchev, Kobysh stated that the perceived main reason for the deployment of missiles was only secondary: "On our part, this decision appeared all the more justified because the United States had at that time begun to surround the entire perimeter of the Soviet Union with its missile bases."[8] The authors of *Great October and the Cuban Revolution*, published in Moscow in 1987, limited their explanation of the crisis to saying that in October 1962, "The imperialists had put the world on the brink of a thermonuclear war [and] the timely and resolute actions of the Soviet Union, support of all peace-loving forces, and the firmness and courage of the Cuban people and their government disrupted the designs of the American militarists."[9]

Similar opinions were expressed in October 1987 at the Cambridge conference on the Cuban Missile Crisis by Sergo Mikoyan, who accompanied his father Anastas Mikoyan on his mission to Havana in November 1962 to negotiate the withdrawal of Soviet missiles and bombers with Castro. He said that Khrushchev first mentioned the idea of sending missiles to Cuba to his father at the end of April 1962 and that, according to Anastas Mikoyan, the main purpose was to defend Castro's regime: "Khrushchev thought that an invasion was inevitable, that it would be massive, and that it would use all [the] American military power." Sergo Mikoyan added that Malinovsky and others talked of the strategic balance, but that was "secondary."[10] This makes one wonder: Did Anastas Mikoyan mislead his son, or had he himself been misled by Khrushchev?

In fact, as seen from Moscow and acknowledged later by Castro, the goal of improving the Soviet Union's strategic position by turning Cuba into a Soviet military base could hardly be separated from the task of defending Castro's regime. The possibility and the intention of using Cuba as a Soviet forward missile base substantially enhanced the importance that Khrushchev and his colleagues had attached to retaining Cuba as the first socialist country in the Western Hemisphere. Their fears of a U.S. invasion of the island could certainly be compared with Washington's attitude toward the prospect of "losing" South Korea or South Vietnam. They applied to Cuba the same domino theory, though in reverse, that led the United States into its massive military involvement in Vietnam a few years later.

Khrushchev believed that the Soviet Union had an obligation to do everything in its power "to protect Cuba's existence as a socialist country and as a working example to other countries of Latin America." He argued that the defeat of socialism in Cuba "would have been a terrible blow to Marxism-Leninism [and] would have gravely diminished our stature throughout the world, but especially in Latin America, [since] if Cuba fell, other Latin American countries would reject us, claiming that for all our might the Soviet Union had not been able to do anything for Cuba except to make empty protests to the United Nations."[11]

Castro Accepts the Proposition

Anastas Mikoyan and Aleksandr Alekseyev had good reasons to doubt that the Cuban leader would welcome Khrushchev's idea. Ever since Cuba joined the socialist camp, Castro vehemently refuted Washington's argument that Cuba was bound to be converted into a Soviet strategic beachhead in the Western Hemisphere, which could not be tolerated by the United States without endangering its vital security interests. Khrushchev also was doing his best to allay American fears. Speaking at a reception at the Cuban embassy in Moscow on January 2, 1961, he mentioned "alarming reports from Cuba to the effect that the most aggressive monopolists of the United States are preparing a direct attack against Cuba...[and] trying to present things in such a way as if missile bases of the Soviet Union against the United States have been or are being established in Cuba." Qualifying these reports as "dirty slander," Khrushchev asked, "Why try to get Cuba to agree to such bases on its territory? Modern technology has created for us the capability of delivering directly from one's own territory crushing second strike blows against any point on the globe."[12]

This denial was repeated in an official Soviet government statement on February 18, 1962, challenging the Americans to say "where, in what part of the island is there a Soviet military base and what kind it is: missile, air, or naval" or to find "a single platoon of Soviet soldiers." It also lectured Washington, saying that the United States "does not possess the military might that would permit it to dictate conditions to other countries [since] there are other countries possessing no less terrible weapons standing guard over peace and prepared to prevent the unleashing of a new war." In conclusion, it was stated that "the well-known warnings of the Soviet government to the enemies of the people of Cuba remain in force."[13]

That position suited Castro much better than the presence of missiles in Cuba, which could serve as a justification, if not the reason, for a U.S. attack. He issued a declaration welcoming the Soviet statement and emphasizing two points:

> [First, this statement was] a serious reminder to those who are playing with the mortal danger of an atomic war [and, second,] there are no reasonable grounds or motives for an enormous and powerful country to attack a small country which pursues an independent policy of peace and peaceful coexistence, which does not participate in military blocs, and has stated repeatedly that it has no intention to offer any part of its territory to any state for the establishment of military bases....[14]

In effect, the Cuban leader admitted, by implication, that the presence of Soviet military bases in Cuba could be regarded as "reasonable grounds" for U.S. military intervention on the island. Khrushchev's proposal for the deployment of Soviet missiles came as an unpleasant surprise to Castro. As was pointed out twenty-eight years later in the *Granma* editorial that accompanied the publication of Castro's correspondence with Khrushchev:

> Comrade Fidel and the Cuban leadership understood at once that the presence of Soviet missiles in our territory could politically affect the image of our revolution and increase the dangers of a confrontation of a different nature with the United States.[15]

However, Cuba's dependence on Soviet economic aid and military assistance and Khrushchev's public commitment to use, if necessary, Soviet ICBMs to defend Cuba — to risk a nuclear conflict with the United States for Cuba's sake — made it difficult for Castro to reject the Soviet request for a similar self-sacrificing gesture on Cuba's part in order to improve the USSR's strategic position. This was confirmed in the same *Granma* editorial, which asserted: "The true meaning of Khrushchev's proposal to improve the correlation of forces of the USSR and socialist community to imperialism did not escape comrade Fidel and the Cuban leadership either, but it would have been cowardly and an act of national egoism to reject it."

Indeed, Alekseyev confirmed that Castro was shrewd enough not to be taken in by Khrushchev's ruse about the defense of Cuba and also to see the possible ramifications for Cuba of the "bold" Soviet strategic move. According to Alekseyev's account, Castro's immediate reaction to the Soviet proposal was, "If such a decision is necessary for the socialist camp, I think we'll give our consent to the deployment of Soviet missiles on our island. Let it be — we'll become the first victims in the encounter with American imperialism."[16] When, in November 1962, Mikoyan asked Castro why he accepted Khrushchev's proposal, he again replied that he thought the Soviet leader had this (strengthening the Soviet Union's strategic position) in mind.[17]

Later, with regard to this subject, Castro enjoyed telling foreign journalists different stories, which on occasion agreed with the official Soviet version or were close to it but in most instances contradicted it. Once, he even ascribed to himself the authorship of the idea of bringing Soviet missiles to Cuba. Talking to Claude Julien, the *Le Monde* correspondent in Havana, in March 1963, Castro said, "They explained to us that in accepting them [missiles] we would be reinforcing the socialist camp the world over, and because we received important aid from the socialist camp, we estimated we could not decline. This is why we accepted them. It was not in order to assure our own defense but, first of all, to reinforce socialism on an international scale." And he added, "Such is the truth, even if other explanations are furnished elsewhere."[18]

It stands to reason that Khrushchev did not approve of Castro's revelation and told him so when they met in Moscow. As a result, Castro, speaking on May 23, 1963, at a mass meeting that concluded his visit to the USSR, eulogized the Soviet Union as "a country, which in the name of the defense of a small nation situated at a distance of thousands of miles from it, has put on the scale of a thermonuclear war its well-being, forged during 45 years of constructive labor and at the cost of enormous sacrifices."[19] Later, however, in conversations with C.L. Sulzberger of *The New York Times*, Castro returned to his original version, saying, "We had expected the Soviet Union to take a chance for us, and we had to be willing to do likewise for them."[20]

More recently, Castro repeated another version of the famous cliché at the Havana Tripartite conference in January 1992. He stated that he had not asked for nuclear missiles and accepted them only because Khrushchev thought their presence in Cuba would strengthen "the whole socialist camp." He went on to affirm that what protected Cuba "was the global power of the Soviet Union, not the missiles deployed in Cuba," and had it been a matter solely of Cuban defense, he would not have accepted them, because "the presence of Soviet missiles would have damaged our image in Latin America, turning Cuba into a Soviet military base."[21] The Soviet government, on the other hand, never admitted that Khrushchev or his emissaries spoke to Castro about strengthening the socialist camp through the deployment of Soviet missiles in Cuba. Quite likely, it was Castro's interpretation of what they said. Nonetheless, what matters is that this step was bound to increase the vulnerability of the United States to a Soviet nuclear attack, and Castro had all the reasons for interpreting the Soviet move the way he did.

At the same time, having entwined his regime's destiny with that of the USSR, Castro proceeded from the assumption that this would also enhance Cuba's security by increasing the credibility of the Soviet nuclear deterrent. Also, to Castro, the deployment of Soviet missiles and combat troops on the island, while presenting the risk of provoking Washington's military intervention, would guarantee the Soviet Union's involvement in a Cuban-American armed conflict. This, again, was mentioned by *Granma* in November 1990 as a supplementary factor in favor of accepting Khrushchev's proposition: "In addition, Cuba would have acquired strategic protection in view of the ever-present risk of a conventional war initiated by the United States against our fatherland, and, on the other hand, if for whatever reason a world war would break out, we would be affected anyway."[22]

Besides, at the Havana conference Castro admitted that in 1962 he knew nothing of the real balance of strategic nuclear forces between the USSR and the United States and, for that reason, overestimated

Moscow's capacity to force Washington to accept the presence of Soviet missiles in Cuba.

Consequently, the Cuban commander-in-chief accepted the plan without even trying to dissuade his Soviet counterpart. He objected only to the secret nature of Operation Anadyr and insisted that it should be preceded by the signing and publication of an appropriate Soviet-Cuban agreement. As he explained at the Havana conference, he thought that by accepting the missiles Cuba did not violate international law, and there was no need, therefore, to do it secretly: "I warned Nikita that the secrecy would give an advantage to the imperialists."[23] Moreover, Cuban representatives, discussing with Soviet officials Khrushchev's plan, expressed the opinion that such a large-scale operation was bound to be discovered by U.S. intelligence, in which case "...the enemy might react in an unforeseen and violent manner."[24] The Soviets rejected this argument, pointing out that the success of the operation depended on its secrecy and that it could be made public only after the deployment was completed.

Castro once again attempted to persuade Khrushchev to make public the agreement on the deployment of missiles. Through his brother Raúl, who visited Moscow in July to discuss the details of the agreement, he asked the Soviet leader what would happen if Washington discovered the plot. Khrushchev reassuringly replied, "Don't you worry. If anything happens, we'll send to the Cuban shores the entire Baltic naval fleet to demonstrate our support and solidarity."[25] Thereafter, Castro accepted Khrushchev's position, because, as he explained at the Havana conference, "the Soviets had much more military experience, and we had, therefore, an unlimited confidence in them. When we had some opinion, we expressed it, but we thought that they knew better."[26]

On June 10, 1962, the Presidium of the CPSU Central Committee heard the report on the results of Rashidov's mission to Havana and unanimously approved Marshal Malinovsky's detailed proposals on Operation Anadyr, which provided for the deployment in Cuba of a strategic missile division (24 intermediate R-14 missiles with a range of 2,200 nautical miles and 48 medium R-12 missiles with a range of 1,100 nautical miles armed with 3-megaton nuclear warheads), two anti-aircraft missile divisions, four motorized infantry regiments, two regiments of tactical nuclear rockets with a range of up to 25 miles, a helicopter regiment, a fighter aircraft regiment, a bomber aircraft regiment, a squadron of transport planes, a regiment of ground-to-sea missiles, a communications regiment, two tank battalions, one reconnaissance battalion, a battalion of field engineers, a brigade of missile speedboats, seven missile submarines, and a number of other units. A total of about forty-five thousand enlisted men and officers with munitions and other supplies for thirty days of combat were to be sent to Cuba. The plan also included sending a squadron of warships and a submarine squadron to Cuba's shores. When operational, Soviet strategic missiles in Cuba would have doubled Soviet first-strike capabilities against the United States.[27]

A Soviet-Cuban agreement on the deployment of Soviet troops in Cuba, drafted by the Soviet General Staff, was initialed in Moscow by Rodion Malinovsky and Raúl Castro. It was later revised to incorporate Castro's amendments, including a preamble on the political and legal aspects of the agreement, which was to be signed in November 1962 during the planned visit of the Soviet leader to Havana. The scope of the agreement was widened to include provisions regarding general military cooperation and mutual assistance, since it had to reflect, in the opinion of the Cuban side, "...the realistic appraisal that in case of a military confrontation between the United States and the Soviet Union, Cuba would inevitably become a strategic target."[28]

On the Brink

At the trilateral Havana conference, Russian Army General Anatoly Gribkov, who during the Cuban Missile Crisis represented the General Staff of the Soviet Armed Forces in Cuba, disclosed that there were not only strategic but also tactical Soviet nuclear weapons in Cuba.[29] Furthermore, contrary to Khrushchev's assurances to Washington that as commander-in-chief of the Soviet Armed Forces he was the only person who could authorize the use of Soviet nuclear weapons on the island, Army General Issa Pliyev (alias Pavlov, as he was known in Cuba), the commander of the Soviet troops on the island, was delegated the power to use tactical nuclear weapons in case of an American attack without first consulting Moscow.

The publicly acknowledged NATO military doctrine of "flexible response" allowed the use of nuclear weapons in Europe, in the face of overwhelming superiority in conventional forces of the Warsaw Pact countries. The Soviet leadership criticized this doctrine as "aggressive" and "inhuman," while secretly authorizing Field Commander Pliyev in Cuba to exercise his own flexible response in similar circumstances without asking for Moscow's permission. It is not clear whether

General Pliyev needed authorization from Fidel Castro to use the weapons. If he had ever requested Castro's authorization, Supreme Commander-in-Chief Castro would have granted it willingly, judging by his remarks at the Havana conference. Moreover, after listening to the expositions of Castro, Gribkov, and Alekseyev at the conference, Arthur Schlesinger, Jr. came to the conclusion that whatever was "the division of authority" between Soviet representatives in Havana and the Cuban government during the crisis, "Castro took the psychological command of all forces in Cuba — it was obvious that he had enchanted and dominated both the general and the ambassador."[30]

As for the use of Soviet strategic missiles deployed in Cuba, the following Moscow directive received by General Pliyev was signed by Defense Minister Rodion Malinovsky and Marshal Vasily Zakharov, chief of the Soviet General Staff:

> The missile forces, which constitute the basis of the defense of the Soviet Union and of the island of Cuba, should be ready on signal from Moscow to effectuate nuclear missile strikes against the most important targets in the United States of America.[31]

The directive did not specify justifying circumstances for such a signal, but linking the defense of the USSR with the defense of the "island of Cuba" (not the Republic of Cuba) as if it were part of the Soviet domain, indicated the sentiment of the Soviet military establishment. To the Soviet military, Cuba was a strategic beachhead in the Caribbean, and Soviet missiles on the island were to be used not only in Cuba's defense against the U.S. invasion but, first and foremost, in the eventuality of a general Soviet-American armed conflict possibly unrelated to Cuba.

In light of this information, it appears that the world was much closer to nuclear war than was thought previously. Arkady Shevchenko, the former adviser to the Soviet foreign minister, was correct when he wrote in his memoirs that neither Khrushchev nor anyone else in Moscow intended to use nuclear weapons against the United States during the Cuban crisis. He also correctly assumed that President John F. Kennedy did not intend to do so, either. But Shevchenko was wrong in his conclusion that "we had not been on the brink of a nuclear war."[32] U.S. forces were prepared to attack Soviet missile sites in Cuba; had Khrushchev delayed his decision to dismantle them for a few days more, or had another U.S. plane been shot down over Cuba, Kennedy may have been pressured into issuing an order to attack. Facing an overwhelming superiority of U.S. forces, Soviet commanders in Cuba would have ordered the firing of their tactical nuclear missiles. Hence, Kennedy would have had no other choice but to respond with U.S. nuclear weapons. Castro was "99 percent" convinced of that, as he said in October 1992.[33] This scenario was very close to being realized, without the U.S. administration or the Soviet government desiring or planning it.

There was also a possibility of a different scenario, though with the same catastrophic consequences, according to Piotr Tanan, a Soviet colonel in retirement, who went to Cuba in 1961 with the first group of Soviet military advisers.[34] In the midst of the October crisis, Fidel Castro appeared unannounced at a meeting of Soviet military commanders in Havana and said he wanted their advice on the proposition of shelling the *U.S.S. Enterprise* that was just outside the limits of Cuban territorial waters and could be seen on the horizon opposite Havana. Castro explained that the idea was suggested to his brother Raúl by the Chinese military attaché, who expressed surprise at the meekness of the Cuban artillerymen and said they were losing an excellent chance to deal a crushing blow to the U.S. interventionists. Upon hearing the Soviet officers' unanimous opinion that such an action from the military point of view would be sheer madness, provoking the U.S. Navy and Air Force into delivering devastating strikes against Cuba, Castro said he agreed and had already cautioned his brother Raúl against following that advice.

Castro's position and activities in October 1962, of which he is so proud, deserve closer scrutiny and analysis. He confirmed at the Havana conference that, fully realizing that the move could lead to a nuclear conflict, he, nonetheless, had allowed the installation of Soviet missiles in Cuba. Khrushchev was wrong in saying in his memoirs that Castro had failed to think through the obvious consequences of such a war for Cuba. He understood the risks involved but was playing "Russian roulette" together with Khrushchev, and he enjoyed the game. Castro revealed his predisposition to doomsday thinking when he stated publicly in a televised speech in Havana on October 23, 1962, that since the United States "threatened Cuba with a nuclear attack,... we have no choice but to run that risk together with the rest of mankind, [but] we do have the consolation of knowing that the aggressors in a nuclear war will be exterminated." He described Khrushchev's bellicose reaction to Kennedy's statement of October 22 as "an exemplary, well-argued reply, which completely exposed the aggressive policy of Mr. Kennedy." He then warned the "imperialists" that they were not "masters of the world" and that if they unleashed a war, "they should know that it will exterminate them."[35]

Castro also admitted that had Moscow consulted him regarding the composition of the Soviet missile forces to be deployed in Cuba, he would have asked for more tactical nuclear weapons because they were under the control of Soviet battlefield commanders in Cuba, who were easier to deal with than their bosses in Moscow. Castro said he was surprised that so few tactical nuclear missiles were sent to the island and regretted that they were not handed over to the Cubans.[36] Castro visited units of the Cuban armed forces, bolstering the morale of the soldiers, and maintained close contact with the commanding officers of the Group of Soviet Troops (GSF) in Cuba, who informed him that forces under their command, including three regiments of medium-range R-12 ballistic missiles, were in full combat preparedness.

Castro prodded Soviet commanders insistently to shoot down American U-2 reconnaissance planes flying over the island. He was at a loss to understand why they allowed Major Rudolf Anderson Jr. to take photos of Soviet missile sites on the island on October 14, 1962, and was delighted when Anderson's plane was shot down on October 27 by a Soviet C-75 surface-to-air missile. One can only guess why General Gennady Voronkov, who gave the order to fire a missile, and General Igor Statsenko, his commanding officer, acted apparently against instructions received from Moscow — "Open fire only if attacked." Instead, they followed the order of the Cuban commander-in-chief, given on the night of October 26 to the Cuban anti-aircraft defense forces. It is only known for certain that General Voronkov was awarded the Cuban Order of Ernesto "Che" Guevara, First Grade. In October 1991, Jorge Pollo, the author of a series of articles in *Granma* on the Missile Crisis of October 1962, wrote the following:

> On October 27, Cuban batteries opened fire against the enemy's air targets. The same day, at about 10 a.m., a U-2 plane was located by radar units. The GSF Command, respecting the order of the commander-in-chief, immediately instructed Major General G.A. Voronkov, commander of the anti-aircraft division of the Eastern region, to shoot down the spy plane.[37]

Castro was behaving like a man who had the destiny of the world in his hands. He was visibly nervous when he came to the Soviet embassy late on the evening on October 26, 1962, and he stayed there until 5 a.m. the next day. He talked to Alekseyev about the possibility of American bombing raids and invited the ambassador to join him in his command center, situated in one of the caves under Havana. While in the embassy that night, Castro dictated his infamous message to Khrushchev, in which he said, "If the imperialists invade Cuba in order to occupy it, the danger of this aggressive policy for humanity would be so great that, after this, the Soviet Union should never permit the circumstances in which the imperialists could deliver against it the first nuclear strike." Lest the full meaning of his advice not be understood by Khrushchev, Castro reformulated it in clearer terms, saying:

> Since the aggressiveness of the imperialists is becoming extremely dangerous and if they take brutal action violating generally accepted norms and morals, such as an invasion of Cuba, this would be the moment to eliminate this danger once and for all, as an act of the most legitimate defense, no matter how difficult and terrible such a solution would be, for there is no other.[38]

Khrushchev "Betrays" Castro

Castro's dramatic message, which was received in Moscow on October 27, 1962, when Khrushchev and Kennedy had reached the decisive stage in their attempts to negotiate a solution to the crisis, only strengthened the Soviet leader's resolve to accept Kennedy's conditions by ordering the dismantling of Soviet missile launching pads in Cuba in exchange for Washington's non-invasion assurances. According to Fyodor Burlatsky, Khrushchev's former speech writer, his boss commented on Castro's message, saying, "Now you see how far things can go. We have to get these missiles out of there, before the real fire starts."[39] On October 28, the Soviet leader urged his warlike Cuban ally "not to be carried away by emotions [but] to show patience, firmness, and once again firmness" and to stop firing at U.S. planes.[40] Castro complied with the request but then instructed President Dorticós to meet Ambassador Alekseyev and tell him what "many Cubans" thought of Khrushchev's "unconditional" acceptance, behind their backs, of Kennedy's demands.

Upon receiving Alekseyev's cable on his conversation with Dorticós, Khrushchev decided that Castro needed some education. On October 30, he sent him a message, in which he referred to "some Cubans" who did not agree to the withdrawal of missiles and lectured Castro on the responsibilities of national leaders:

If we, yielding to the sentiments among the people, had allowed ourselves to be carried away by certain electrified layers of the population and had refused to come to a reasonable agreement with the government of the United States, a war could have been unleashed in which millions of people would have perished, and the survivors would have blamed the leaders who had not taken necessary measures in order to prevent this war of extermination.[41]

Khrushchev rejected the Cuban complaint that Moscow had acted without consulting Havana, pointing out that the Cuban leader had already made his views known to Moscow by sending messages, "one more alarming than the other" and that since, in Castro's opinion, an American attack against Cuba was imminent within the next twenty-four to seventy-two hours, "had we continued consultations, we would have lost time, and this strike would have been delivered." Khrushchev then proceeded to speak his mind on Castro's provocative proposition:

In your cable of October 27, you proposed that we be the first to launch a nuclear strike against the enemy's territory. You realize, of course, where that would have led. Rather than a simple strike, it would have been the beginning of a thermonuclear world war. Dear comrade Fidel, I consider this proposal of yours incorrect, although I understand your motivation.

Fyodor Burlatsky confirms that Castro's message was interpreted by Khrushchev as suggesting an all-out Soviet nuclear attack against the United States.[42] When the two leaders met in Moscow in April 1963, Castro denied that he had given such advice, and Khrushchev's interpreter had to refresh Castro's memory by citing the original text of his message.[43] The exact translation superseded a later attempt by Ambassador Alekseyev to help his old Cuban friend clear his name of this accusation by attributing differences in the interpretation of Castro's message to its hasty and faulty translation into Russian in the Soviet embassy in Havana.[44] Castro repeated his denial at the Havana Tripartite Conference:

I knew Nikita well and was convinced that the situation greatly worried him. I intended to encourage him, strengthen his position from the moral point of view. I remembered that Stalin had refused to believe that the Nazis planned their attack in 1941. I did not want him to commit the same mistake. I wanted to be sure that the Soviet forces were prepared for what could happen. I was convinced that the invasion of Cuba would unleash a nuclear war against the Soviet Union. My recommendation about a preventive strike did not refer to the case of a U.S. air attack but to the case of invasion and occupation.[45]

The question is why Castro was, or appeared to be, so convinced that the U.S. invasion of Cuba would lead to a U.S. nuclear attack against the USSR. It stemmed, obviously, from his belief that the Soviet Union would use the nuclear weapons it had deployed on the island against the attacking U.S. forces. It was logical that after Kennedy's speech on October 22, 1962, Castro concluded that a U.S. air and sea bombardment or an invasion or both were imminent, since he did not envisage the possibility of Moscow's capitulation to Washington's ultimatum or the Kennedy administration's acceptance of Soviet missiles on the island. The Cuban commander-in-chief could have been misled by Khrushchev's bragging about Soviet military power. Castro was certainly in no position to know that because of the overwhelming superiority of U.S. strategic forces (a well-guarded secret in Moscow), Marshal Malinovsky had advised the Soviet leadership against running the risk of a nuclear conflict. Castro's certitude that the United States would attack Cuba and the USSR and his proposal to retaliate with a nuclear strike were based on his ignorance of the balance of power and lack of inside information from the Soviets.

It is more difficult to accept his contention that nuclear retaliation would have been "the most legitimate defense." No American invasion of Cuba, regardless of how immoral and regrettable it would have been, could justify a Soviet nuclear attack against the United States. It is true that Khrushchev himself was thinking along these lines — that if after a U.S. attack against Soviet missile sites on the island, only a couple missiles were to have survived, "We *could* still hit New York, and there wouldn't be much of New York left." But there is a difference between *could* and *would.* In practical terms, he was thinking not of a nuclear attack but of a possible retaliation in Germany, where Soviet conventional forces surpassed NATO troops, particularly in armored forces: "The Americans knew that if Russian blood were shed in Cuba, American blood would surely be shed in Germany."[46] Whatever faults could be found with Soviet strategic plans at the time, they did not envisage the initiation of a nuclear exchange.

With the world's attention focused on Cuba, Fidel Castro, noted for his pride and pretentiousness, was in for the greatest humiliation of his life, when Khrushchev, without consulting or warning him, made his public offer to Kennedy: 1) to withdraw Soviet missiles from Cuba if American missiles were withdrawn from Turkey, 2) to enter into a mutual obligation not to invade Cuba or Turkey, and 3) not to interfere in Cuban and Turkish internal affairs. This initiative produced serious, long-lasting negative effects on Soviet-Cuban relations. The Soviet proposal contained in Khrushchev's message to President Kennedy on October 27, 1962, and broadcast by Radio Moscow the same day infuriated Castro, who did not know even then that a day earlier Khrushchev had proposed a much simpler deal in a confidential message to Kennedy: withdrawal of Soviet missile forces from Cuba in return for a U.S. commitment not to invade Cuba and not to support any other invaders.

As recollected by Colonel Piotr Tanan, on the morning of October 27, high-ranking Cuban army officers, who were working with Soviet military advisers in the joint management of the emergency situation (including the formation, with Tanan's assistance, of the new people's militia battalions), expecting a U.S. invasion, were nowhere to be seen. They reappeared only in the afternoon. One of them confided to a Soviet friend that upon being informed of Khrushchev's message broadcast by Radio Moscow, Castro immediately convened a secret meeting of top government officials and Cuban army commanders and dramatically announced that "the Russians have betrayed us" and denounced Khrushchev's willingness to "exchange" Cuba for Turkey. After that meeting, Cuban army officers abruptly changed their attitude toward their Soviet counterparts and no longer treated them as trusted friends and allies but rather, with suspicion, almost as American agents.

Apart from feeling humiliated and insulted by Khrushchev's "capitulation" to Washington behind his back, Castro had to face the abrupt withdrawal of a possible foolproof guarantee of security for his regime that the Soviet missiles and support would have provided. We shall probably never know whether Castro really believed Khrushchev's earlier promises to launch Soviet missiles against American cities in order to defend Cuba. But Castro certainly could not take such pledges at face value after Khrushchev refused to risk the USSR's survival for Cuba's sake. Castro never forgot that bitter experience; he repeatedly referred to it in his correspondence with Soviet leaders. After October 1962, Castro was always fearful of Moscow "selling out" Cuba to the United States. That made him extremely sensitive to any Soviet move that could be interpreted as gaining favor with Washington at Havana's expense and forced the Soviet leadership to be very careful not to offend him or arouse his suspicions whenever they conducted business with Washington.

There was another aspect of the Kennedy-Khrushchev deal that made Castro furious: he was convinced that Khrushchev had sold out too easily, missing a golden opportunity to force the U.S. naval base out of Guantánamo. Castro believed that this would not have happened had Khrushchev insisted on Cuba's participation in negotiations on the solution of the Missile Crisis. He continued to believe that this was the case, even after he learned of the weak Soviet bargaining position. Reflecting this view, Rafael Hernández, head of the North American department of the Cuban Center of American Studies, who participated in the first tripartite conference on the Missile Crisis in Moscow in January 1989, wrote in *Granma*:

> It was a lost opportunity to guarantee our security vis-à-vis the United States because if Cuba had participated in the negotiations, that is, if they had been trilateral and not bilateral, it might have been possible to secure an agreement by virtue of which the United States may have stopped its attacks on Cuba by means of so-called 'covert action,' i.e., terrorist action and pirate raids by counterrevolutionary groups, as well as a halt to the economic blockade and the return of the Guantánamo naval base.[47]

In November 1962, Castro resorted to personal insults against Khrushchev and accused him of lacking manhood. Twenty-nine years later, *Granma* talked of the "enormous unprecedented tensions to which the Soviet leadership was subjected and the gigantic responsibilities entailed in those crucial hours, which overwhelmed Khrushchev and, despite his good faith, exceeded his capacity as a statesman." *Granma*'s editorial repeated the charge, without any attempt to substantiate it, saying that Moscow had missed a chance to get U.S. forces out of Guantánamo:

> If at least the point of the withdrawal of the Yankee naval base at Guantánamo, one of the five conditions proposed by our Party and government as a solution to the crisis, had been defended with the vigor and intelligence that the situation demanded, there would be no U.S. or Soviet troops in Cuba today.[48]

Castro's Five Conditions for Peace

One can understand the emotions of an ambitious leader of a small country, who thought he was able to dictate his conditions for peace to a superpower and then was deprived, without warning, of this cherished opportunity. Still, the question arises, what could the Soviet government have done to convince the U.S. administration to agree to close its naval base in Cuba? Khrushchev, both publicly and in confidential correspondence with Kennedy, did his best to support Castro's five conditions: 1) an end to U.S. economic sanctions against Cuba, 2) cessation of all subversive activities against Cuba, 3) cessation of pirate attacks (by Cuban exiles) from bases in the United States and Puerto Rico, 4) cessation of violations of Cuban air space and territorial waters by U.S. planes and ships, and 5) U.S. withdrawal from Guantánamo. He placed special emphasis on the Guantánamo problem, but to no avail. Obviously, Castro wanted Khrushchev to link ridding Guantánamo of the American base with Moscow's agreement to withdraw the missiles.

Fortunately, Khrushchev's "capacity as a statesman" was sufficient to enable him to see the futility of such an attempt and the immense risk involved in prolonging the crisis, which would have given Washington's hawks a good chance to get the upper hand and persuade Kennedy to attack Cuba. It is clear that if Khrushchev had consulted Castro prior to his decision to pull back the missiles, Castro would have blocked it by insisting on the linkage to Guantánamo. All doubts on this score should have been assuaged by *Granma's* article, which was written on Castro's authority by Jorge Pollo in November 1991:

> It was absolutely indispensable — and nothing prevented this — to insist on Cuba's participation in the negotiations.... Twenty-nine years later, Cuba continues to believe that there existed a real possibility to condition the dismantling and withdrawal of missile installations as part of a global settlement in which the United States would have been compelled to assume greater obligations and make greater concessions.... The solution could be reached without giving imperialism a free hand to continue its hostile policy against Cuba.[49]

Apparently, neither Khrushchev nor Castro had any pangs of conscience for bringing the world to the brink of nuclear holocaust. In retirement, Khrushchev continued to justify his decision. But he at least had a sufficiently high sense of responsibility to his countrymen to accept the inevitability of retreat unless he was prepared to go to war.

Castro, talking about his role in the Cuban crisis, publicly stated in September 1990, "The positions which I had taken then I am taking today, and what I said then I would say now, absolutely the same; I do not repent one inch of what I had done or had said."[50] He missed then and continues to miss now the utter immorality of putting at stake, by accepting Soviet nuclear missiles, the very survival of Cuba and of pushing, by his provocative behavior, the two superpowers closer to a war of mutual extermination. Recalling on October 29, 1962, the "very real dangers of war" thirty years ago, he even had the audacity to affirm that "the mistakes committed by our allies [by the USSR] increased these dangers,"[51] without mentioning his own responsibility for the events of October 1962 and pretending not to realize what might have happened had Khrushchev insisted on the Cuban "five conditions" before withdrawing the missiles.

Khrushchev, on the other hand, professed to be convinced that his gamble had paid off: the United States did not invade Cuba. In his report to the USSR Supreme Soviet in December 1962 on the origins and outcome of the Missile Crisis, he claimed that "the Soviet Union and the forces of peace and socialism" have proved to be able "to impose peace on the protagonists of war," and neither the Americans nor the Soviets lost anything during the missile crisis by making concessions in the interests of preventing thermonuclear war; "it is reason that has won." In the report he added that both Cuba and the Soviet Union "have received satisfaction: an American invasion of Cuba has been averted; the naval blockade has been lifted; the situation in the Caribbean is becoming normal; and people's Cuba exists, grows stronger, and is developing under the leadership of its revolutionary government, under its fearless leader Fidel Castro."[52]

Castro never really accepted this positive evaluation, although on occasion he had to pay lip-service to the Soviet Union's role in the survival of his regime. *Granma*, in its editorial of November 23, 1991, expressly attributed the absence of a U.S. military intervention in Cuba not to Washington's non-invasion commitment but to repeated "mistakes" of eight successive U.S. administrations that "could never find a vulnerable flank in the unity and consciousness of the Cuban people." In his interview with NBC television in October 1992, Castro stated that if he had known the consequences of the Soviet missiles' installation beforehand, he would never have accepted their presence. He blamed the "indecision of the Russians and Khrushchev's unconditional concessions" for the continuation of the U.S. "dirty war against Cuba."[53] A few days later in a speech to the Cuban National

Assembly, he again talked about "a terrible blow we received thirty years ago" and referred to "peculiar and hasty formulas, such as linking strategic missiles here with those in Turkey, and the strange proposition to withdraw the missiles, under UN control, in exchange for a promise not to invade Cuba."[54]

Some American scholars tend to support Khrushchev on this point rather than Castro, believing that Khrushchev outwitted Kennedy and deprived Washington of the possibility of using force to overthrow the Cuban socialist regime. Robert Smith Thompson, the author of *The Missiles of October: The Declassified Story of John F. Kennedy and the Cuban Missile Crisis*, agrees with Moscow's official position. Thompson says that the secret deployment of Soviet missiles was a direct result of the "American desire to overrun Cuba." He argues that considering the outcome of the crisis as a triumph for Kennedy is ambiguous — it should be judged by the fact that in the end Castro's regime has survived.[55]

That seems to be a convincing argument. However, the question is whether this would still have been the case if there had not been any attempt to install Soviet missiles on the island or assurances from Washington not to invade Cuba. Or, to put it differently, did Khrushchev's "bold move" deter an imminent U.S. invasion? Castro believes that his regime continued to exist despite, and not thanks to, Moscow's deal with Washington. For once, he was right in assuming that Moscow's main motivation was not the defense of Cuba. Threat of a U.S. invasion or no threat, Khrushchev's decision to turn Cuba into a Soviet military base could well have been taken in any case: if judged expedient, this threat could always have been invented. Besides, the presence of American missiles in Turkey alone was sufficient reason for the Soviets to justify a similar use of Cuba, as they emphasized repeatedly. As for a U.S. military intervention in Cuba, it nearly came to fruition expressly because of Khrushchev's move.

Castro may also be right to contend that his regime owed little to the Soviet missile initiative or to the Kennedy-Khrushchev understanding. The "American desire to overrun Cuba" certainly existed, but this by itself could not serve as proof that Washington had contemplated, prior to the Missile Crisis, a military intervention in Cuba. Khrushchev, guided by his proletarian "class consciousness," did not need any corroborative evidence. As he frankly put it:

> I am not saying that we had any documented proof that the
> Americans were preparing a second invasion: we did not need

documentary proof.... We knew the class affiliation, the class blindness of the United States, and that was enough to make us expect the worst.[56]

Still, the U.S. position should be given the benefit of the doubt. Former Secretary of Defense Robert McNamara categorically stated that the Kennedy administration "had absolutely no intention to invade Cuba."[57] It appears that the Pentagon had developed contingency plans for an invasion of Cuba, but prior to October 1962, the U.S. administration had not considered the plans seriously. There were CIA plans for "covert actions" against Cuba, which were implemented at least partially, including several unsuccessful attempts to assassinate or discredit Castro, but there is no hard evidence to suggest that Kennedy would have ordered an attack on Cuba if Khrushchev had not forced him to abstain from doing so.

Nor is there any documentary proof to support the thesis, which logically followed from Moscow's interpretation of the Missile Crisis, that had Kennedy failed to give non-invasion assurances, at some point his or one of the subsequent U.S. administrations would have decided to invade Cuba. Governments of sovereign states adhere to treaties or agreements concluded by them or by their predecessors only as long as they find them compatible with their interests — unless they are pressured into compliance against their interests by circumstances beyond their control. In this particular case, there was no formal agreement, no legal document, just an understanding between Khrushchev and Kennedy reached by an exchange of letters. It had no attributes of a binding formal agreement between the two states, no provisions on its duration, ratification, or other conditions of its entry into force. At most, it could be called a "gentlemen's agreement." From the U.S. side, it was just a statement of intention to apply, under certain conditions, its Law of Neutrality to Cuba, a country with which the United States officially was not at war. This did not signify a new policy toward Cuba — Washington's attempts to undermine Castro's regime were continued — but rather a more effective use of the threat of invasion to limit the Soviet military presence on the island. Any serious attempt by Moscow to violate the terms of the Kennedy-Khrushchev understanding could now be used, in an extreme case, as lawful justification for bombing or invading the island or both.

As for the Soviet side, it did not have the capacity to "punish" the United States had Washington decided to remove Fidel Castro from power by force. Since the October 1962 crisis left no doubt in the minds of the policy makers in Washington that the Soviet Union would not go to war with the United States to save the Castro regime, Moscow had no way of forcing Washington to honor its commitment not to invade Cuba. Nevertheless, successive U.S. administrations kept Kennedy's word during the next thirty years because they did not consider that an invasion would serve the best interests of the United States. Internal U.S. political pressures to invade Cuba from some factions within the Cuban exile community and some quarters in Washington were strong but not sufficiently accepted by policy makers to change their minds.

A number of factors outweighed pressures to invade Cuba: 1) large and well-trained Cuban armed forces, which Castro owed exclusively to the multi-billion-dollar Soviet grants and military assistance; 2) the size of the island and the nature of its terrain; 3) the prospect of prolonged fighting; and 4) the certainty of adverse reaction in Latin America, Europe, and in the United States to outright U.S. military intervention in Cuba. None of the different estimates of possible American casualties were politically acceptable to Washington. For all these reasons, there was no U.S. invasion of Cuba, notwithstanding Washington's continuing hostility toward the Castro regime. And the Soviet Union was clearly not prepared to shelter Cuba under its "nuclear umbrella," in spite of appearances in October 1962.

The Kennedy-Khrushchev understanding, which was scorned and denounced by Cuba's "Maximum Leader" as the Soviet "betrayal" and "sellout" of Cuba to the United States, later came to be appreciated in Havana as useful diplomatically and psychologically. It served the political interests of both Havana and Moscow to pretend that the understanding was a real deterrent to an American invasion. With Havana's blessing and, at times, at its direct prodding, Moscow sought from each new U.S. administration — and received in one form or another, with the exception of the Reagan administration — an assurance that the United States would honor Kennedy's commitment. However, these assurances, while valuable politically, did not add much to Cuba's actual security, which continued to depend more on Washington's unwillingness to pay the price of direct U.S. military intervention for the liquidation of the Castro regime than on anything else.

On the other hand, Khrushchev's commitment did add significantly to ensuring U.S. security interests in the Caribbean. It served as a deterrent against further Soviet attempts to turn the island into a base for offensive military operations. Those who reproached Kennedy for his promise not to invade Cuba in exchange for Khrushchev's undertaking to withdraw Soviet missiles and bombers from the island and commitment not to introduce offensive weapons there in the future failed to take into account the practical impossibility for the Soviets, short of starting a nuclear exchange, of "punishing" the United States for an invasion of the island. In addition, Washington had a variety of political and military options available for reacting to any Soviet move that could be interpreted as seriously violating the terms of the 1962 understanding.

Last, but not least, Castro had yet another reason to be angry with Khrushchev: if Khrushchev had followed Castro's advice and made "Operation Anadyr" public, events might have taken a different course. It would have been much more difficult for Kennedy to justify the interdiction of Soviet "offensive weapons" to Cuba or to threaten to bomb them out. After his advice was rejected, Castro was disgusted by the Soviet military's inability to take appropriate measures which would have prevented the discovery of the operation by U.S. intelligence. Castro was convinced that Anderson's spy plane should have been shot down earlier, on October 14, 1962.

On the whole, the deployment of Soviet missiles in Cuba and their subsequent withdrawal — in circumstances and on conditions legitimately regarded by the Cubans as humiliating and insulting — had these effects: 1) Washington was free to continue its policy of inflicting maximum economic and political damage to the Castro regime, 2) the Soviet-Cuban alliance came very close to the breaking point, and 3) political relations between Havana and Moscow throughout the next thirty years were affected negatively. The October 1962 Missile Crisis became a turning point in Soviet-Cuban relations; despite all the massive Soviet economic and military assistance lavished on Cuba in the ensuing years, the two governments never again reached that high degree of mutual trust and understanding that was established before the crisis. Numerous mutual protestations of everlasting friendship and loyalty notwithstanding, that mental block remained forever in Cuban leaders' minds. As the late Lev Mendelevich, former head of the USSR Foreign Ministry Latin American Directorate, said once, "After what happened in 1962, the Cubans will never be our real friends."[58]

The Aftermath

When the crisis was over, Khrushchev and Defense Minister Marshal Malinovsky had continued for some time to engage in missile rattling, warning the "aggressive circles" in the United States that an attack against Cuba would have meant "the beginning of the Third World War."[59] A more detailed formula was included in the Joint Soviet-Cuban Statement on the results of Castro's first visit to the USSR in April-May 1963:

> It was confirmed by the Soviet side that if Cuba were attacked in violation of the commitments not to invade Cuba taken by the president of the United States, the Soviet Union would fulfill its internationalist duty to the fraternal Cuban people and would render it necessary assistance for the defense of the freedom and independence of the Cuban Republic, with all the means at its disposal. The organizers of aggression must understand that an invasion of Cuba will bring mankind to the brink of a destructive thermonuclear missile war.[60]

In the Joint Soviet-Cuban Communiqué, signed in January 1964 at the conclusion of Castro's second visit to Moscow, the Soviets once again confirmed this pledge.[61]

Such statements were totally irrelevant to the actual situation in U.S.-Cuban relations and carried much less conviction than before the crisis. Furthermore, they made the hazardous and costly operation of bringing Soviet missiles into Cuba and then withdrawing them look even more ludicrous; if Moscow remained as suspicious of Washington's intentions with regard to Cuba as it was before that operation, what did it achieve? Nevertheless, Khrushchev felt compelled to issue these bellicose warnings for two reasons: first, he wanted to mollify Castro's anger, and second, it was necessary to refute the Chinese accusations that Moscow had committed a "venturesome blunder" by deploying missiles in Cuba and then "capitulated to American imperialism" by withdrawing them.[62]

Khrushchev was particularly sensitive to these accusations because he recognized the vulnerability of his position on this point in his bitter polemics with Peking. The letter, sent by the CPSU Central Committee to its Chinese counterpart in July 1963, stated:

> We also gave the obligation to the Cuban people: if the U.S. imperialists break their word and invade the territory of Cuba, we shall come to the assistance of the Cuban people. Any sensible person understands that, in case of an invasion by American imperialists, we shall come to the assistance of the Cuban people from Soviet territory, just as we would have helped from Cuban territory. It is true that, in this case, it would

take somewhat more time for the missiles to reach their targets, but this would not affect their accuracy.[63]

This sounded ominous. Yet, it was not proof that Khrushchev and his advisers had not learned their lesson; they had, but they needed time to "climb down the tree" without losing face and Soviet prestige in the Third World.

By the end of 1963, there was no more talk of using Soviet missiles for the defense of Cuba. Leonid Brezhnev, who in October 1962 became first secretary of the CPSU Central Committee, after all of Khrushchev's colleagues (except Mikoyan) had conspired to depose their leader, was even less inclined to indulge in such threats. In fact, one of the main charges that Brezhnev and other plotters brought up against Khrushchev, when he was called on the carpet at the October 1964 plenary meeting of the CPSU Central Committee, was the accusation that he had brought missiles to Cuba and then withdrawn them, damaging the Soviet Union's international prestige and its relations with Cuba. Brezhnev understood that after the Soviet retreat in October 1962, Moscow's verbal declarations could not really deter an attack against Cuba; if Moscow's words were challenged, they would only have led to another humiliating political defeat in the Cold War confrontation.

During the eighteen-year reign of Leonid Brezhnev as the secretary general of the CPSU Central Committee, Moscow hardly mentioned what the Soviet Union would do if the United States decided to ignore Kennedy's undertaking and intervene militarily in Cuba. Nobody seemed to remember Khrushchev's much-trumpeted declarations about the "internationalist duty" of the Soviet Union to defend Cuba against an invasion. Brezhnev never publicly criticized this particular aspect of his predecessor's policy, but neither did he confirm Khrushchev's pledge. On suitable occasions, there were only standard references to the Caribbean crisis based on Khrushchev's version of its origin, development, and resolution, emphasizing Kennedy's assurances against an invasion of Cuba and not even mentioning the withdrawal of Soviet missiles, Moscow's undertaking not to introduce offensive weapons to Cuba, and the Soviet Union's commitment to defend it if Washington did not keep its word.

Anatoly Gromyko Jr., once a minister-counselor of the USSR embassy in Washington, provides a typical presentation of these events in his book *President Kennedy's 1036 Days*. After dutifully repeating the official version of the events of October 1962, formulated by

Khrushchev in his December 1962 speech, Gromyko noted, "The greatest significance of Kennedy's official renunciation [of] aggressive plans against Cuba [was that it] contributed to the normalization of the situation." But then Gromyko added the following warning:

> The value of verbal promises made by bourgeois governments in foreign policy matters is, naturally, well known. It is, therefore, necessary to treat with appropriate caution the reservations accompanying the President's renunciation of an invasion of Cuba.[64]

There was no mention of the Soviets' reaffirmed pledge to defend Cuba.

Nikolai Chigir, a former TASS correspondent in Havana, offered a shorter account of the Cuban crisis with some emphasis on the role of Cuba itself:

> The imperialist circles of the United States, despite the resolute warnings of the Soviet Union that their policy of preparing an armed attack against Cuba was fraught with the gravest consequences for the world, did not heed the voice of reason and feverishly continued military preparations. Thus, the Caribbean crisis burst out. However, this time again the unshakable determination of the Cuban people to defend to the last drop of blood their freedom and independence, in conjunction with the Soviet Union's resolute support of Cuba and its active measures aimed at preventing a thermonuclear world war, forced the United States to retreat and to undertake not to attack Cuba.[65]

Again, not a word was said about the Soviet commitment to Cuba's defense renewed by Khrushchev after October 1962.

There was nothing on the subject in the Soviet-Cuban declaration signed by Castro and Brezhnev in Havana on February 2, 1974, though Castro, for all his frustration with Moscow's "betrayal" of Cuba during the crisis and skepticism about Khrushchev's renewed commitment to defend Cuba, still needed this verbal pledge in order to bolster the morale of the population of the island and to strengthen his hand in Havana's ongoing confrontation with Washington. Failing in his attempts to lure Brezhnev into reaffirming the Soviet commitment to protect Cuba in some form, Castro sought membership for Cuba in the Warsaw Treaty Organization or a degree of affiliation with its military structures. The Cuban soundings led nowhere. The most they could achieve were declaratory statements in joint Soviet-Cuban documents that the Soviet Union "resolutely demands to put an end to the economic and political blockade and other hostile actions against socialist Cuba"[66] as well as assurances of Soviet support of Cuba's demand that the U.S. military base in Guantánamo be liquidated and of continued Soviet assistance in strengthening the Cuban defense potential.

The Soviet side explained to the Cubans its unwillingness to use stronger and more binding wording because of tactical considerations. Moscow pointed out that depriving Washington of any pretext not to honor Kennedy's undertaking was much more important than stronger declarations of support that could be misinterpreted. Soviet diplomats also argued that improvement of Soviet-American relations would effectively enhance Cuba's security by neutralizing "reactionary forces" in the United States and strengthening the positions of those in Washington's establishment who were in favor of a more flexible policy toward Havana. Castro referred to the continued economic blockade and other manifestations of hostile U.S. policy designed to undermine the existing Cuban regime. He complained that improvement in Soviet-American relations, far from bringing any benefits to Cuba, would make Washington less apprehensive about the possibility that the USSR would use its power to defend Cuba.

There are grounds to believe that Brezhnev's reluctance to confirm the Soviet Union's pledge "to defend the freedom and the independence of the Republic of Cuba with all means at its disposal," as formulated in the Joint Soviet-Cuban Statement of May 23, 1963, was one of the main reasons for the absence, until 1989, of any formal political treaty or agreement between the two countries. From 1971 through 1984, the Soviet Union signed treaties or agreements of friendship and cooperation with twelve "progressive" regimes in Asia and Africa (Afghanistan, India, Iraq, North Yemen, South Yemen, Syria; and Angola, Congo, Egypt, Ethiopia, Mozambique, and Somalia) and one socialist country, Vietnam. All these documents had one common feature: they did not contain any obligation on the part of the USSR to come to the rescue of these regimes in case of "aggression." This did not suit Castro, who preferred to have no political agreement at all, rather than to sign a document that would practically cancel by omission Khrushchev's pledge. The USSR and Cuba had concluded dozens of intergovernmental agreements on economic, technical, and military (in terms of arms deliveries and training of personnel) assistance; trade and cooperation; and scientific and cultural exchanges.

They developed an extensive political cooperation and acted, for all intents and purposes, as allies in the international arena. Yet, despite all this, they did not have a political treaty which would formalize their de facto alliance.

What Castro wanted to have was a treaty of friendship and mutual assistance of the kind concluded by the Soviet Union with East European socialist countries, China, and Mongolia, which guaranteed Soviet military assistance and a "nuclear umbrella." In 1962, he nearly secured its equivalent, an agreement on "military cooperation and mutual defense," which he hoped to sign in Havana during Khrushchev's planned visit to Cuba in November 1962, but it was destined to remain in the archives of the Soviet Ministry of Defense. As years passed by, Soviet representatives, through discussions in Moscow and Havana, tried to sound out the opinion of the Cuban side on the expediency of having a political treaty. Havana's reactions were either noncommittal or negative. At least on one occasion, Cuban officials indicated that they expected equal treatment for Cuba as a socialist country and were not interested in anything less than a treaty of friendship and mutual assistance. They were told that there was no discrimination against Cuba, which was treated in exactly the same fashion as Vietnam, as a socialist country that did not have a common border with the USSR and was distant geographically. For that reason, a clause on mutual military assistance would have had little practical meaning. The subject of a treaty was dropped and not brought up again for bilateral discussions until 1988.

It was characteristic of Brezhnev that while he resisted Castro's attempts to prod him into reaffirming the Soviet defense commitment to Cuba, he could never bring himself to tell the Cubans explicitly that the USSR was not going to defend them militarily. His evasiveness made the Cubans wonder what the real Soviet position was on the issue, which was blurred further by the continued presence in Cuba of a Soviet combat motorized brigade. The unit, deployed there along with other Soviet troops in summer-autumn 1962, was left on the island after the Missile Crisis at the insistence of Castro. The enlisted men and officers of this Soviet brigade (about three thousand) were virtually Castro's hostages, whose presence ensured that the USSR would honor its pledge to come to Cuba's rescue in case of U.S. attack.

It was only after Leonid Brezhnev was replaced in November 1982 by Yuri Andropov, intellectually a much better match for Castro, that Havana was told in unequivocal terms where Moscow stood on the matter. Andropov informed Raúl Castro, who visited Moscow in March 1983, that owing to the geographical factor and the practical impossibility for the Soviet Union to maintain such extended lines of communication with Cuba in conditions of war, it would not be feasible to engage Soviet armed forces in the defense of the island. It went without saying that Soviet ICBMs and other strategic arms for Cuba's defense were also excluded. By way of compensation, the Cubans were left with the only available alternative — asking for more Soviet arms. Andropov complied with the request. This led to the greatly increased volume of Soviet weaponry shipped to Cuba in the years between 1983 and 1990 and to the Cuban leadership's development of the "people's war" doctrine as a substitute for the reliance on the assistance of the Soviet armed forces.

Lessons of the Cuban Missile Crisis

Khrushchev's secret attempt, with Castro's connivance, to deploy Soviet nuclear missiles in Cuba illustrated graphically the validity of the argument that the very existence of a totalitarian regime armed with modern weapons and able to mobilize all national resources (for achieving whatever purpose seen fit by "Big Brother") presented a potential threat to its neighbors and to international peace and stability. Saddam Hussein's attempt to annex Kuwait by force is the most recent example; this threat will be multiplied if and when totalitarian regimes are able to form alliances and conspire against other states. Suffice it to recall the Axis alliance, the Ribbentrop-Molotov pact, and the Stalin-Mao Zedong-Kim Il Sung plot against South Korea, or the Soviet-Chinese alliance, in which Mao Zedong tried to persuade Khrushchev that there would be nothing wrong with initiating a nuclear war in order to dispense with Western imperialism and then build a new socialist world civilization.

With the Khrushchev-Castro plot to deploy Soviet missiles in Cuba, two totalitarian regimes were playing with nuclear arms — and with the destiny of the world. Rationalizations that Khrushchev had not intended it to be that way, that he had just miscalculated, or that he had misjudged Kennedy and his possible reaction do not exonerate him and his associates within the Soviet leadership. Khrushchev's error of judgment, his reckless adventurism, and the meek compliance of other members of the ruling Presidium of the CPSU Central Committee (only two of them, Anastas Mikoyan and Otto Kuusinen, expressed some doubts about the fateful decision but supported it all the same) could have cost dearly — not only would the three countries directly involved and their allies have paid the price with their very existence, but so would most of the rest of the world, since nuclear fallout does not recognize borders.

On the positive side, the events of October 1962 have helped Soviet policy makers to take a realistic, sober view of Cuba's possible role in the Soviet-American strategic confrontation. The most important conclusion arrived at by the Soviet leadership that changed the nature of Soviet-Cuban relations was that saving Castro's regime was not worth risking a nuclear war. Although Cuba continued to be a factor in the minds of Soviet General Staff planners, its role was changed from being potentially the most important Soviet missile base, ready to devastate vital areas of the main adversary, to being a support and intelligence-gathering base. Soviet military presence in the Caribbean became more symbolic than real. Still, Soviet facilities in Cuba did allow Moscow to monitor American military and related activities of interest in the southeastern United States.

This is not to say that the Pentagon had no further reason to be seriously concerned with the Soviet-Cuban military connection. For once, U.S. intelligence services could only guess at the changes in Soviet military strategic thinking with regard to the Caribbean. There were indications that the Soviet Navy had an interest in establishing facilities on the island that would have enabled Soviet nuclear submarines to maintain their permanent strategic presence in the area. Cuban airfields were used by Soviet long-range reconnaissance planes. The Soviet communications military base at Lourdes, near Havana, became an important source of military intelligence information on Moscow's main enemy, and some Soviet troops remained on the island. Additionally, the Soviet Union not only equipped the Cuban armed forces with modern weapons and trained Cuban officers but also helped the Cubans set up their own defense industry. The Cubans started producing ammunition and Kalashnikovs, the principal weapon of insurgents in Latin America and other parts of the world.

All this served to cause serious tensions in Soviet-American relations, as was the case from September 1970 through January 1971 with the suspected construction of a Soviet submarine base near Cienfuegos and in 1978 with the delivery to the Cuban Air Force of modern Soviet MiG-23 fighters. Weary of adverse American reactions, the Soviets abandoned their plans for the submarine base and contented themselves with limited support and repair facilities. As for the MiG-23s, the problem was caused by their sophisticated nature, fire power, and radius of action. That led to debates and mutual recriminations when both sides resorted to equally valid arguments to justify their stands. Eventually, the United States had to accept the Soviet position that the appearance of MiG-23s on the island did not violate the Kennedy-Khrushchev agreement, but the issue was revived in 1989 and again in 1990 with delivery of MiG-29 fighters to Cuba. The complexity of this issue was illustrated by a story, told by General Rafael del Pino, the former deputy commander of the Cuban Air Force, after he defected to the United States. He disclosed that in 1983 Major Ernesto González, commander of the MiG-23 squadron, received a secret order to feed the coordinates of the Turkey Point nuclear power plant near Miami into the computers of his planes. This story was never disclaimed convincingly by Havana.[67]

An important feature of Soviet military aid to Cuba had been, almost from the start, that it was given free of charge and on a scale unprecedented for USSR relations with any other socialist country, except Vietnam and North Korea. In November 1962, Fidel Castro informed the Cuban people that the Soviet Union had written off the Cuban debt for Soviet arms and would supply them gratis in the future — a sop to his wounded pride. This enabled the Castro regime to develop a very efficient, powerful military machine at a relatively low cost to the country's economy. In terms of numbers of troops and military equipment, Cuba's armed forces were soon disproportionate to its population and limited material resources. In Latin America, they ranked second only to the Brazilian armed forces.

In defining the scale and conditions of military assistance to Cuba, Moscow used the same criteria that were applied in the 1950s to Albania. According to Khrushchev, Albania was regarded in Moscow as a "base in the Mediterranean." For that reason, it was thought "beneficial" to finance and equip, at the Soviet Union's cost, the Albanian army. The establishment of a Soviet submarine base on the Adriatic coast of Albania was the next step. Khrushchev also wanted "to turn Albania into a pearl that would be attractive to the Muslim world, especially for countries in the Middle East and Africa";[68] a similar pattern and logic were followed in Soviet military and economic cooperation with Cuba, a base in the Caribbean "right off the U.S. coast," intended to serve "as a revolutionary example to the rest of Latin America."[69]

By the same token, through the 1960s and 1970s, continued CIA undercover operations against Cuba contributed to suspicions in

Moscow that Washington was still bent on the removal of the Castro regime by force. Some Cuban exile organizations in the United States advertised their clandestine activities in Cuba; strictly speaking, such activities violated Kennedy's commitment. Yet, more often than not, they were tolerated by the U.S. authorities. These operations gave Castro an excellent reason for further militarization of Cuba and for continuing requests for Soviet arms, which were invariably complied with by Moscow.

In spite of mutual recriminations about both sides' non-observance of the letter and spirit of the Kennedy-Khrushchev understanding and their negative effects on Soviet-U.S. relations, Soviet military and political ties with the Castro regime since 1962 have not once presented the threat of an armed clash between the two superpowers. The Cuban Missile Crisis shattered the very foundation of the Soviet-Cuban alliance: Soviet commitment to defend the Castro regime militarily. The relationship has never recuperated from that blow. Subsequent "fraternal friendship and cooperation" between the Soviet Union and Cuba could be called anything but certainly not a military alliance.

There were also wider, positive implications of the Cuban Missile Crisis for relations between the two superpowers, which have been extensively analyzed and commented upon by both American and Soviet participants or witnesses to the events of October 1962. Raymond L. Garthoff summarized them in 1987, saying, "Both sides may already have learned that crises such as the one of October 1962 must be avoided. That none has occurred in the quarter-century since that time suggests that the lesson has been taken to heart."[70] Fortunately, the United States and the Soviet Union have learned to avoid policies and actions that could have turned the Cold War into a hot one.

Notes

1. Jerrold L. Schechter and Vincheslav V. Luchkov, eds. and trans., 1990, *Khrushchev Remembers: The Glasnost Tapes* (Boston: Little, Brown), 182.

2. *Ogoniok* magazine, (Moscow) November 1992, No. 44-46, an interview with General Dmitry Volkogonov, 24.

3. *Mezhdunarodnaya Zhizn* magazine (Moscow), 1992, March-April, 170.

4. *Mezhdunarodnaya Zhizn*, July 1992, 54.

5. *Mezhdunarodnaya Zhizn*, July 1992, 54.

6. *Mezhdunarodnaya Zhizn*, July 1992, 54.

7. *Pravda*, December 13, 1992.

8. *Izvestia* (Moscow), October 23, 1987.

9. A.D. Bekarevich and V.V. Volsky, eds., 1987, *Velikiy Oktiabr y Kubinskaya Revoliutsiya* (Moscow: Lzdatelstvo Nauka), 252.

10. James G. Blight and David A. Welch, 1989, *On the Brink* (New York: Hill and Wang), 238-39.

11. Strobe Talbott, ed. and trans., 1970, *Khrushchev Remembers* (Boston: Little, Brown), 493.

12. *Pravda*, January 3, 1961.

13. *Pravda*, February 19, 1962.

14. *Pravda*, February 26, 1962.

15. *Granma*, November 23, 1990.

16. *Mezhdunarodnaya Zhizn*, July 1992, 54.

17. James G. Blight and David A. Welch, 1989, *On the Brink* (New York: Hill and Wang), 251.

18. *Le Monde* (Paris), March 22, 1963.

19. *Pravda*, May 24, 1963.

20. C.L. Sulzberger, 1975, "Conversations with Fidel Castro," *Oui* magazine (Paris), January, 158.

21. *Nexos* magazine (Mexico), 1992, Vol. XV, No. 174, 66.

22. *Granma*, November 23, 1990.

23. *Nexos*, Vol. XV, No. 174, 65.

24. *Granma*, October 31, 1991.

25. *Nezavisimaya Gazeta* (Moscow), October 22, 1992.

26. *Nexos*, Vol. XV, No. 174, 65.

27. Graham T. Allison, 1971, *Essence of Decision: Explaining the Cuban Missile Crisis* (Boston: Little, Brown, 53-54).

28. *Granma*, October 31, 1991.

29. At the time of the crisis, U.S. intelligence services appeared to be unaware that some of the Soviet short-range missiles in Cuba (FROGs in NATO's terminology) were supplied with atomic warheads and could be used as tactical nuclear weapons on the battlefield against invading U.S. forces. Soviet medium-range missiles, deployed on the island by the middle of October, and intermediate-range missiles were in the category of strategic nuclear weapons, to be used against targets in U.S. territory.

30. *Nexos*, Vol. XV, No. 174, 66.

31. *Ogoniok*, No. 44-46, November 1992, 24.

32. A. Shevchenko, 1985, *Breaking with Moscow* (New York: Ballantine Books), 155.

33. *Izvestia*, October 22, 1992.

34. This story was told by P. Tanan to the author in October 1992.

35. *Hoy* (Havana), October 24, 1992.

36. *The Miami Herald*, January 29, 1992.

37. *Granma*, October 24, 1991.

38. *Granma*, November 23, 1990.

39. *El Nuevo Herald* (Miami), October 22, 1992.

40. *Granma*, November 23, 1990.

41. *Granma*, November 23, 1990.

42. *El Nuevo Herald*, October 22, 1992.

43. Jerrold L. Shlechter and Vincheslav V. Luchkov, eds. and trans., *Khrushchev Remembers. The Glasnost Tapes* (Boston: Little, Brown), 171, 183.

44. *Nexos*, Vol. XV, No. 174, 66.

45. *Nexos*, Vol. XV, No. 174, 66.

46. Strobe Talbott, ed. and trans., 1970, *Khrushchev Remembers* (Boston: Little, Brown), 494, 495, 500.

47. *Granma*, International Edition, February 26, 1989.

48. *Granma*, September 14, 1991.

49. *Granma*, November 13, 1991.

50. *Granma*, October 1, 1990.

51. *Granma*, October 31, 1992.

52. *Pravda*, December 13, 1962.

53. *Izvestia*, October 22, 1992.

54. *Granma*, October 31, 1992.

55. Robert Smith Thompson, 1992, *The Missiles of October. The Declassified Story of John F. Kennedy and the Cuban Missile Crisis* (New York: Simon & Schuster), 356-57.

56. Strobe Talbott, ed. and trans., 1974, *Khrushchev Remembers: The Last Testament* (Boston: Little, Brown), 511.

57. *Nexos*, Vol. XV, No. 174, 66.

58. Told by Lev Mendelevich to the author in 1989.

59. *Pravda*, February 23, 1963.

60. *Pravda*, May 24, 1963.

61. *Pravda*, January 22, 1964.

62. *Jenmin Jibao* (Peking), March 8, 1963.

63. *Otkrytoye Pismo Tsentralnogo Komiteta Kommunisticheskoy Partii Sovetskogo Soyuza Partiynym Organzatsiyam y Vsem Kommunistam Sovetskogo Soyuza*, 1963, (Moscow: Politizdat), 27.

64. Anatoly Gromyko, 1973, *Through Russian Eyes: President Kennedy's 1036 Days* (Washington: International Library), 181.

65. N.N. Chigir, 1973, *SSSR-Kuba: V Edinom Stroyu k Obshchei Tseli* (Moscow: Izdatelstvo Pravda), 181.

66. *Vizit Leonida Ilyicha Brezhneva v Respubliku Kuba*, 1974, (Moscow: Politizdat), 23.

67. *Moscow News*, No. 44, November 1-8, 1990.

68. Jerrold L. Shechter and Viacheslav V. Luchkov, eds. and trans., 1990, *Khrushchev Remembers. The Glasnost Tapes* (Boston: Little, Brown), 106.

69. Strobe Talbott, ed. and trans., 1974, *Khrushchev Remembers: The Last Testament* (Boston: Little, Brown), 510.

70. Raymond L. Garthoff, 1987, *Reflections on the Cuban Missile Crisis* (Washington, D.C.: The Brookings Institution), 128.

Chapter 3

From Khrushchev to Gorbachev: Gains and Losses

As Soviet-Cuban multifaceted ties and cooperation continued to develop, their relations assumed a scale and exclusiveness almost unprecedented for two countries with no common historical, ethnic, or cultural roots, so far apart geographically and so different in size and potential. Outside observers often attempted to create a balance sheet, listing what each side gained from this special relationship. Walter Raymond Duncan in his book, *The Soviet Union and Cuba: Interests and Influence,* presented an accurate general description of the Moscow-Havana axis, defining it as "one of mutual interest, costs and benefits for both sides, and with limits to the complete control by either party over the other."[1] While deciphering this formula, it is important to draw a distinction between the genuine national interests of the two countries and those superimposed by their ideologies. The Soviets' Marxist-Leninist ideology stipulated that the Soviet leaders should perceive the world as an arena of East-West class struggle. The Cubans were guided by a mixture of Marxism with Fidel Castro's extreme nationalism and *caudillismo* that constituted what has come to be known as *fidelismo.* An objective analysis of Soviet-Cuban relations also calls for a comparison of each side's expectations from the alliance, perceptions of respective gains, and the prices each one has paid.

Cuba as a Showcase of Socialism in Latin America

The failure to convert Cuba into an important military component of the Soviet-American confrontation did not depreciate its political value for the CPSU strategists as a country they hoped could be transformed into a showcase of socialism in Latin America. In Khrushchev's words, Cuba's very existence as a socialist state "right in front of the open jaws of predatory American imperialism [was] good propaganda for other Latin American countries, encouraging them to follow its example and to choose the course of socialism."[2] Soviet communist leaders needed socialism in Cuba as yet another confirmation of the credibility of the Marxist-Leninist theory regarding the inevitability of socialist revolutions in all countries and as further proof that the world revolutionary process was continuing. Khrushchev and his successors were determined to do everything they could within the limits of Soviet economic resources to ensure socialist Cuba's survival and prosperity, demonstrating to Latin America the advantages of the socialist system. No expense and effort were spared to achieve that purpose.

It seemed, for a time, that this grand design was becoming a reality. Similar to their Soviet mentors, Cuban revolutionaries were soon able to boast of the achievements of their regime, such as providing "free" education, "free" medical care, and inexpensive housing. They used the same simple, but very effective, Soviet-invented political trick of presenting all of these benefits as generous gifts from the ruling regime. The origin of the resources used to pay for such generosity was intentionally obscured. There were no statistics on indirect taxation and underpayment by the state, as the only employer, to workers and employees, who received only minimal subsistence-level wages but upon whom gratuitous social benefits rarely found in countries with private enterprise and a market economy were lavished.

Castro's egalitarian reforms — redistribution of property, dispossession of the very rich, and bringing the well-to-do people down to the level of workers and employees— also served as a source of substantial income to the state. Then came Soviet subsidies, credits, and grants, which became the largest single source of state revenue, taken by the Cuban revolutionaries as their due. Ernesto "Che" Guevara and Fidel Castro were very clear that the USSR and other "developed" socialist countries were duty-bound to sustain emerging socialist regimes in the developing countries economically and to supply them with weapons, since they were fighting the common enemy — Western imperialism. They insisted that this aid should be free, because it would be "humiliating" to pay for it. It would be "immoral" and "unjust" to apply commercial principles in trade between industrialized and developing socialist countries.[3]

All the same, Cuba could not escape the main flaws of a totalitarian socialist system. Cuba's economy was plagued by lack of incentives for efficient work and initiative, low labor productivity and waste of resources, a chronic deficit of consumer goods and services, political and economic omnipotence of the new governing elite (who became the collective owner of the national wealth), the growth of party and state bureaucracy, and generalized corruption. Combined with other features characteristic of one-party socialist regimes — arbitrariness and erratic and incompetent interventions of the political leadership (or of the leader, as was most often the case), in the formulation of economic priorities and the day-to-day running of the national economy; the militarization of society; and an excessive burden of defense expenditure and of the "internationalist" foreign policy — all this brought Cuba first to a protracted economic depression and then to an ever-deepening economic crisis years before the situation could be blamed on the disruption of economic relations with the Soviet Union and other socialist countries.

Soviet experts in Latin American affairs and Castro's court sociologists have spent a great deal of time and effort looking for common features in the October Socialist Revolution in Russia and the Cuban Revolution and comparing the experience of the CPSU and the Communist Party of Cuba (CPC) in "building a socialist society." The purpose of the exercise was to prove that the Cuban Revolution was a continuation of the cause of the Russian October Socialist Revolution of 1917 and followed its general pattern. The Institute of Latin American Studies of the USSR Academy of Sciences published a book on the subject entitled *The Great October and the Cuban Revolution* in 1987, which contained "the scientific analysis of the experience of the Cuban Revolution," confirming "the felicitous exactness of Lenin's conclusion about the historic inevitability of the repetition on a world scale of what happened with us."[4] There were also joint studies by Soviet and Cuban authors, such as *Internationalist Cooperation of the CPSU and CPC: History and Contemporaneity*, published in Moscow in 1988, in which Carlos Rafael Rodriguez, a veteran Cuban communist leader, investigated "common and specific experiences of the CPSU and the Communist Party of Cuba in the realization of the revolution."[5]

The two revolutions certainly had much in common: both were preceded by mass popular movements in favor of establishing a democratic system of government, resulted in even more severe suppression of political freedoms than under previous governments, and led to the establishment of messianic totalitarian regimes. They both gave birth to one-party rule and resorted to brutal terror against all political opposition and dissent in the form of mass persecutions and intimidation of the population, dividing societies into revolutionaries and counterrevolutionaries. They practiced forced political indoctrination of the young and promulgated a propaganda of hatred toward "the enemies of the revolution" and "Western imperialism." Both regimes developed efficient security services and pervasive networks of undercover police agents and informers.

True, there were also important features that distinguished the Cuban "path to socialism" from the Soviet experience. In Russia, it started from the establishment of the dictatorship of the Bolshevik Party, replaced later by Stalin's one-man iron rule and then transformed into a slightly less authoritarian collective rule by the CPSU Politburo's elders. In Cuba, it was from the beginning and still remains a one-man show. The Communist party structure was added afterward to solidify Castro's dictatorial regime, to give more credence to its "socialist" nature, and to make it more compatible with other socialist regimes. The Committees of the Defense of the Revolution (CDR) represented another local invention in Cuba. The nearest equivalent in Soviet Russia were the "Committees of the Poor" (*kombedy*), but they had functioned only for a brief period during the civil war of 1918-1922, and their activities were limited to the countryside. Equally original are Cuban "rapid response brigades." During Stalin's era, the CPSU and the Soviet security service organized "spontaneous" manifestations of workers and students who demanded death sentences for the "enemies of the people." Stalin's successors — Khrushchev, Brezhnev, Andropov, and Chernenko — sanctioned prison terms or psychiatric "treatment" for political dissidents, but Soviet leaders never tried to organize their harassment on a permanent basis by enlisting volunteers. The Cuban brigades are something closer to the mobs against heretics and Jews instigated, respectively, by the medieval Spanish Inquisition and the German Nazi regime.

As soon as Cuba was ordained a socialist country, it was inundated by hundreds and thousands of experts, technicians, and advisers from the Soviet Union and Eastern Europe. Scores of thousands of Cubans traveled to the USSR to learn technical, political, and administrative skills. There were intensive exchanges of high-level party and government delegations. Fidel Castro and his chieftains spent weeks touring "fraternal" socialist countries. They sat in long conferences with Soviet and East European "outstanding Marxist-Leninists" who served as the Cubans' mentors and shared their experiences in the "construction of socialism," offering free advice on how to cope with various obstacles. As a result, the Cuban socialist model presented a peculiar mixture of home-invented and imported methods of administering a highly centralized government and operating a state-owned economy under the exclusive control of Castro and his appointees.

Various components of the Cuban model were periodically changed to suit the needs of the moment or Castro's whims; yet, in essence, it began as and remained a Soviet-style model of totalitarian socialism. It had all the repulsive features of this system and was rejected by a substantial part of the population. This was illustrated by the flight from the "Island of Freedom" of hundreds of thousands of Cubans for whom individual liberties, respect for human rights, freedom of choice, and an opportunity to build their own lives without the tutelage of the party and the state were more important than free university education, guaranteed jobs, inexpensive housing, and free medical care. Many others accepted the regime, because it was able to offer these benefits, albeit to a large degree at the expense of the "Soviet brothers," which made it look attractive against the general Latin American social background.

It was ironic that as the Soviet leaders were straining themselves to implant in the minds of Cuban revolutionaries Moscow's experience in forging a totalitarian, one-party system of government in keeping with Marxist-Leninist dogmas, they were also exporting to Havana all of the Soviet system's organic defects. Both Khrushchev and Brezhnev earnestly believed that if Castro succeeded in making a carbon copy of the Soviet model with some necessary adjustments, Cuba's transformation into a prosperous socialist state, envied by its Caribbean and Latin American neighbors, would be guaranteed. In turn, they believed Cuba would provide a powerful impetus to revolutionary movements in the region, an area of great strategic and economic importance to the United States.

Limited in their vision by Marxist-Leninist blinders, Soviet leaders failed to see the basic flaws of their own system and, therefore, were unable to comprehend that its replica would not serve this purpose, that no socialist country could become prosperous. Whatever faults they found with their Cuban clone, they ascribed to the U.S. blockade, Guevara's utopian ideas, Castro's mistakes, and inconsistencies in copying the original. Consequently, they pressed for more conformity. As noted by Aleksandr Snam, a Soviet expert with personal experience of the transplantation of the Soviet model to Cuba, although the primary responsibility for Cuba's economy rested with the Cuban leadership, the USSR was by no means blameless: "Ideology, the administrative-command system, and other pathological symptoms of 'real socialism' were directly exported, [and] in specific conditions of Cuba, they have thrived and assumed even more monstrous forms."[6] Visiting Cuba in 1990, journalist Vladimir Orlov wrote about its socialist model:

> There is nothing new here. It is based on the total rejection of a market economy, prevalence of moral over material incentives, sacrifices for the idea, militarization of the state which defends itself both against the external and the internal counterrevolution, the inviolability of the party and government elite, the ban on a multiparty system and even on the discussion of the possibility of such a system.[7]

When Khrushchev was dictating his memoirs, he was still under the illusion that Castro would succeed in the realization of his plans to "revolutionize" Cuban agriculture and to dominate the international sugar market by producing ten million tons of sugar annually. The failure of this ill-fated initiative, which seriously affected production in other agricultural sectors, was followed by further efforts to double the production of sugar. In accordance with the agreement signed by Cuba in 1981 with the USSR, Bulgaria, and the German Democratic Republic, production was planned to increase to 12 million tons by 1990 and to between 13 and 14 million tons by the end of the century. Despite Soviet, East German, and Czechoslovak assistance in the mechanization of *safra* (sugarcane harvesting) and the modernization of the Cuban sugar industry, this program failed. However, Soviet mentors could not possibly reproach their Cuban disciples for failure to reach targets, since none of the Soviet much-trumpeted, numerous plans to achieve drastic increases in agricultural production by particular years had ever succeeded.

There were other notable similarities: Khrushchev tried to teach Russian peasants how to plant potatoes and cultivate corn, earning his popular nickname *koukourouznik* (corn planter). Castro initiated campaigns to mass-produce tomatoes, with the same laughable results. But there was one particular aspect in which the Cuban leader outstripped Khrushchev and his successors: he prohibited the Cuban peasants who still owned some land from selling their produce in open markets, something that even Stalin had tolerated. After the introduction of the ban, Soviet visitors to Cuba were struck by the scarcity of fruits and vegetables on sale in a tropical country; they were available only for hard foreign currency.

Massive Soviet investments into the mechanization of "socialist" agriculture in Cuba brought only limited success, such as increasing the average sugar production from 5 to 6 million tons to 7 to 8 million tons per year. Soviet expenditures did not reduce the dependence of the island on imported food products, nor did they lead to the elimination of food rationing, which soon became a permanent feature of life on the Island of Freedom, distinguishing it from the rest of the world, including the USSR and most other socialist countries. Rationing detracted, of course, from Cuba's prestige as a "beacon of hope" for Latin America. Cuban agricultural cooperatives and state farms suffered from the same ills as their Soviet counterparts: incompetent management, lack of incentives, inefficiency, waste of resources, and lack of discipline. This led to another common feature: in Cuba, private farm yields were several times higher than state farm productivity in the case of most crops, particularly vegetables.[8] Similarly, in the USSR peasants cultivating their individual gardens always outproduced collective and state farms.

The Soviet experience of running "advanced" socialist agriculture was helpful to Cuban leaders in finding plausible explanations, for the benefit of the public, for a chronic scarcity of food in a country famous for its fertile lands. Soviet leaders attempted to explain the disastrous performance of collectivized agriculture, which transformed the "bread-basket of Europe" into the biggest importer of grain, by laying the blame on the ravages of the First World War, the Russian Civil War, and foreign military intervention, and then on the devastation of the Second World War. Unfavorable weather conditions were also a frequent point of reference. Cuban leaders initially blamed U.S. economic sanctions for their agricultural setbacks; later they listed the cessation of food and fodder supplies from the USSR and Eastern European countries, droughts, and tropical hurricanes. Castro rarely held himself accountable and never impugned the Cuban socialist agricultural system.

Similarly, Soviet financial, material, and technical assistance for the development of Cuban mining and manufacturing industries was not rewarded with the expected results. The purpose of these investments was to help Cuba build a balanced economy, enabling it to make ends meet by diversifying domestic production, reducing dependence on imports, and earning, through increased exports, enough foreign currency to cover the cost of imports. Soviet investments did contribute to new industrial development and significant growth in total volume of industrial production, as they helped build more than 400 Cuban economic projects and reconstruct hundreds of enterprises (including 156 sugar plants). By 1990, Cuba's new or modernized Soviet-supported industries accounted for almost 100 percent of the domestic production of steel, cane-harvesting combines, television sets, and radio receivers; 60 percent of cotton fabrics; 55 percent of nitrates; 45 percent of electrical energy; and so on.[9] However, the growth of Cuba's industrial production did not lead to the reduction of imports, an increased capacity to pay for them, or the abolition of rationing consumer goods.

Nor did Cuba's increased industrial and agricultural production lessen the Cuban economy's dependence on Soviet assistance. Since the Soviet Union had become Cuba's principal supplier of oil, coal, pig iron, cotton, newsprint, timber, grain, and flour (90 to 100 percent); fertilizers, trucks and cars, tractors, and road-construction equipment (70 to 90 percent); and other products,[10] Cuba was no longer able to cover the total cost of these imports even by increased sugar sales to the USSR at highly subsidized prices. Castro had to ask for more Soviet trade credits to cover the deficit every year, which amounted, by a conservative estimate from the late Anatoly Bekarevich, the former vice director of the Institute of Latin America, to 8.5 billion rubles (about $13 billion at the exchange rate of 0.65 ruble to $1 that existed at the time) for the period 1960 to 1989; this figure would have been at least three times higher without concessionary prices on sugar, nickel, and oil.[11] From 1986 to 1990, Soviet trade credits amounted to 4.5 billion rubles and technical assistance to 2.5 billion rubles;[12] as a result, Cuba's official debt to the Soviet Union rose to 16 billion rubles (about $24.6 billion). Repayment was invariably postponed, albeit the Cuban government did not care to service its debt to Moscow. Soviet price subsidies were also increasing progressively.

This vicious circle of increased Soviet aid only escalated Cuba's "needs" and became a permanent headache for the officials of the Soviet State Planning Commission (GOSPLAN). Each year, Soviet planners had to stretch their imaginations to find ways and means of allocating additional funds and material resources to Cuba in compliance with the ruling CPSU Politburo's directive following yet another appeal from Fidel Castro. In classic Soviet bureaucratic fashion, top-level decisions on such requests often preceded any assessment of available resources. The standard formulation of the directive was "Find the possibility to satisfy the request of the Cuban leadership for...." In such cases, the GOSPLAN usually had two alternatives: either to re-channel resources earmarked for export to less important countries or to scale down planned deliveries of machinery, equipment, and raw materials to domestic destinations, ignoring the complaints of those affected — the "internationalist duty" had to come first.

There were different estimates of the dynamics of increases in and the total volume of Soviet economic assistance to Cuba. None could be accurate in the absence of reliable statistics and knowledge of exact amounts of "hidden" grants in the forms of non-repayable credits and overpayments for Cuban sugar and nickel, which, together with loans and price subsidies Cuba received from other socialist countries, according to Castro, in 1989 constituted 70 percent of Cuba's purchasing power.[13] In the 1980s Soviet economic assistance to Cuba averaged $5 to $6 billion per year (35 to 40 percent of the total USSR economic aid to foreign countries),[14] and technical assistance amounted to around $700 million a year.[15] Additionally, Cuba earned between $200 and $500 million a year from re-exporting Soviet-supplied oil on the world market, which in 1981-1987 constituted 30 to 40 percent of Cuba's total foreign currency income and was sufficient to service its dollar debt.[16] Soviet economists did not publicize their own overall estimate of Soviet economic, military, and technical aid to Cuba — the Soviet leadership was not interested in such calculations — but they tended to accept the rough U.S. estimates of $7 to $8 billion a year in the 1980s. Soviet economists also considered that all forms of Soviet assistance to Cuba in recent years constituted more than one-quarter of Cuba's gross national product (GNP), although U.S. sources usually gave a lesser figure of 20 percent.

Rather than admire the progress achieved in Cuba's economic growth, given the scale of Soviet aid, as well as additional substantial economic assistance from East European socialist countries, one wonders why Cuban economic growth was so insignificant in terms of balanced development and overall living standards. Soviet journalist Yuri Kornilov created a sensation by publishing a brutally candid article on Soviet-Cuban economic relations in February 1990 in *Ogoniok* magazine. He maintained that the goal of the "...creation, with our assistance and participation, of a dynamic and flourishing economy in Cuba was not achieved.... The republic's economy is in a state of stagnation, the country has introduced and is using a ration card system, prices are increasing appreciably, and Cuba, as before, is orienting its economic development primarily toward sizable material and financial 'injections' from outside." The overriding reason for this situation, said Kornilov, was that "our bureaucratic command system, with its predominance of gross figures, people's lack of interest in the results, and other organic vices inherent in it, was 'transplanted' to the island and then 'improved' to fit the Cuban way of doing things."[17]

Lenin and his followers, who invented the Soviet economic and political systems, were prisoners of the illusion propagated by Karl Marx and Friedrich Engels that the replacement of private property and private enterprise by public ownership would automatically ensure higher labor productivity and greater economic efficiency. Just the opposite was the case in all nations subjected to the most tragic social and political experiment of the twentieth century. The leaders of socialist countries proclaimed their "historic supremacy" in the East-West competition and boasted tirelessly of the "advantages" of the socialist system. Yet, none of these countries could ever approach, in terms of the living standards of their populations, the level of Western democracies, which by definition had been sentenced posthumously by Marx and Lenin to degradation and eventual disappearance, ultimately to be replaced by a higher socialist civilization. Soviet and East European communists were the first to admit the failure of this experiment and the inability of socialist economies to beat the free enterprise systems in quality and quantity of consumer goods produced and services offered. Communist leaders of China, North Korea, and Vietnam still refuse to concede this defeat. Nevertheless, Chinese and Vietnamese communists are allowing more and more free enterprise into their economic structures, and this will force them eventually either to relinquish political power or to sacrifice Marxist ideology, as was done by Boris Yeltsin.

Cuban communists will probably be the last to follow suit, but there is no reason why Cuba should be an exception to the rule. As was pointed out by Professor Jaime Suchlicki of the University of Miami, "The establishment of a Soviet-type centrally planned economy has burdened Cuba with a vast and cumbersome bureaucracy that stifles innovations, productivity, and efficiency."[18] From 1960 to 1985, the gross national product of other Latin American countries was growing at an annual rate of 6 percent, while that of Cuba at only 3.5 percent, which meant a relative deterioration in the standard of living in Cuba in comparison to the regional average.[19] Unlike other Latin American countries that were making great efforts to rid themselves of monocultural structures in their economies (some of them, like Chile, quite successfully), Cuba even increased its dependence on sugar exports.

As for labor productivity in Cuba, Carlos Rafael Rodriguez, vice president of the State Council, admitted, in his polemic with Soviet journalist Vladislav Chirkov in October 1987, that it was "indeed still low" but attempted to revise Lenin's definition of the main advantage of socialism over capitalism, asserting, "Although Lenin said that socialism will only be able to defeat capitalism after surpassing it in labor productivity, there are also other indicators of one system's superiority over the other."[20]

There were, of course, countless immediate causes for the failure of massive amounts of Soviet economic and technical assistance to bring more tangible results: poor planning, gigantomania, the low quality of Soviet machinery and lack of spare parts, defective equipment, delays in equipment deliveries to Cuba, and faulty designs of economic projects. Virtually none of the Soviet technicians sent to Cuba knew Spanish, and not all of them were skilled professionals. Eventually, the Cuban government came to the conclusion that it was better to undertake the greater expense of inviting engineers from Western Europe than employing Soviet engineers who did not speak Spanish or were incompetent or both. On the Cuban side, as reported by the Soviet press, a freeloading mentality developed because many Cubans regarded aid from the USSR as their due and ascribed Cuban economic problems to its insufficiency.[21] This attitude caused indifference, irresponsibility, and a careless attitude toward Soviet equipment. There were also errors in economic planning and definition of priorities, failures to meet contractual obligations for the supply of labor and building materials for construction projects, and delays in unloading Soviet ships.

So much for the transformation of Cuba, with Soviet assistance, into an exemplary socialist model of accelerated economic and social development to be admired and followed by other countries of Latin America. The grand design had been a nonstarter from the very beginning. Nevertheless, it took Soviet leaders thirty years and billions of dollars worth of resources to understand that the socialist experiment in the Caribbean had failed. They came to this conclusion only as they admitted the total political and economic bankruptcy of their own model of socialism.

Complementary Economies: Myth and Reality

One of the most persistent legends about Soviet-Cuban economic relations, still accepted as a valid argument in some quarters in

Moscow, is the assertion that whatever the initial motives for Khrushchev's decision were to embark upon the policy of exchanging Soviet oil for large quantities of Cuban sugar at a time when the Soviet Union was almost self-sufficient in sugar, both countries gradually came to depend on each other for these and other important products, and their economies became complementary. To prove this point, figures were cited to demonstrate that Cuba's dependence on Soviet supplies was not unilateral and that in the late 1980s, Cuban deliveries met 30 percent of the Soviet Union's needs for sugar, 40 percent for citrus fruits, and 20 percent for cobalt and nickel concentrates.[22]

The figures are probably correct but not the implied conclusion about the mutually advantageous nature of trade between the two countries, which they purported to support. Soviet-Cuban trade might have been advantageous to both parties had two conditions been met: first, if the Soviet Union's imports from Cuba had been based on a real incapacity to satisfy its own requirements through domestic production and, second, if the commodities imported from Cuba had not been available at lower prices from other external sources. Neither of these conditions existed. The Soviet dependence on imports from Cuba was created by politically motivated and economically unsound decisions. It was maintained artificially, without any serious attempt to reduce it. Those who doubted the wisdom of this policy were assured that even at subsidized prices, Cuban sugar was cheaper than domestically produced beet sugar. That might have been technically true if sugar imports had been paid in rubles, but they were exchanged for Soviet oil, which could have been sold on the world market for hard currency.

As a result of the long-term commitment to purchase large quantities of Cuban sugar annually, Soviet sugar production capacity suffered drastically because the domestic sugar industry was increasingly neglected. The acreage planted with sugar beets in the USSR was reduced, and substantial resources were channeled to increase sugar production in Cuba. The Soviets agreed to pay the Cubans ever higher sugar prices to enable them to cover, albeit partially, their costs for increased levels of imports from the USSR. Andrei Kamorin, *Izvestia* correspondent in Havana, wrote that each ton of sugar imported by the USSR from Cuba represented "an automatically satisfied request for economic aid." The USSR, by helping to build and reconstruct dozens of sugar factories on the island while freezing the development of its own sugar production, "...created a whole branch of its food industry 10,000 kilometers beyond its borders."[23]

In the early 1970s, Cuba's repeated failures to meet in full its quota of sugar deliveries caused shortages in the USSR, and Moscow attempted to decrease its dependence on Cuban sugar. In July 1972, the Soviet government issued a special decree providing for measures to ensure greater domestic sugar beet output. However, Leonid Brezhnev reconsidered; in a few months, the decree was shelved. Political considerations prevailed over common sense once again, and by the end of 1972, efforts intended to help stabilize and increase the production of sugar in Cuba were renewed and intensified. In return, the Cuban government pledged to meet its commitments in the future.

By reducing correspondingly its sugar sales in the world market, Havana did not experience serious difficulties in keeping this promise for a number of years, since the Soviet Union compensated Cuba for the resulting reduction of hard currency earnings by increasing oil deliveries, part of which Cuba then re-exported. In the late 1980s, the demands of the Soviet market reached 4 to 4.5 million tons of sugar each year, while the maximum that Cuba could deliver was 3 million tons. Consequently, the Cuban government decided to "borrow" up to 1 million tons a year from Western firms to meet these demands.

By the end of 1989, Cuba's "sugar debt" rose to 4.8 million tons, more than half of its maximum annual production. At Havana's insistent request, Moscow had to guarantee the Western firms that they would be repaid by Cuba, running the risk of paying for the borrowed sugar twice: first with oil deliveries and then with hard currency.[24] The GOSPLAN officials justified the acceptance of this economically absurd arrangement with the arguments that the Soviet Union had no reserves of hard currency for buying that much sugar in the international market and that no resources were available to increase domestic production. Political considerations excluded a much more reasonable alternative: a corresponding reduction of Soviet deliveries of oil to Cuba in order to obtain the foreign currency needed for buying sugar from other countries or to stimulate its domestic production.

Similarly, instead of investing in the domestic nickel mining industry, Soviet planners considered it more expedient to get involved in the much more costly business of building new nickel ore processing facilities in Cuba. Apart from the desire to save their own strategic mineral resources, the Soviets were looking for ways to increase their total imports from Cuba to compensate for a constant growth in the volume of raw materials, industrial products, and foodstuffs shipped to the island. Eventually, the Soviet Union became dependent on

Cuban deliveries of cobalt and nickel concentrates for the production in the Urals of high-quality steel destined almost exclusively for defense industries. Thus the Soviet military-industrial complex became a firm defender of the USSR's economic links with Cuba, even though the construction of a Soviet-designed nickel plant on the island at Punta Gorda turned into a symbol of Soviet technical inefficiency and bureaucratic muddling.

Citrus imports from Cuba were not irreplaceable either, since other citrus-producing countries were only too willing to exchange their produce — of better quality than Cuban — for Soviet oil, timber, and other raw materials. Soviet citizens who had the opportunity to taste oranges from Morocco or Israel knew the difference. As Cuban fruits were not competitive in the world market, Moscow decided to import them in large quantities to reduce, in some measure, Cuba's trade deficit with the USSR, thus diminishing the amount of its trade credits to Havana.

Another convenient half-truth was the assertion that the Soviet Union was obtaining from Cuba hard currency commodities for "wooden" rubles. Aleksandr Kachanov, then first vice minister of foreign trade, affirmed in February 1990: "...if we did not buy those Cuban products, we would have to buy them in the world market, paying for them with currency. Cuba is in a similar situation. Is it necessary to provide further evidence of the mutually beneficial nature of the Soviet-Cuban cooperation?"[25]

The full truth of the matter was that the USSR could buy the same quantity of sugar at much lower prices on the world market and sell at competitive prices part of the oil, metal, chemicals, timber, newsprint, and other convertible currency earners it was supplying to Cuba. Aleksandr Kachanov knew this, since he represented the USSR State Committee for Economic Ties with Foreign Countries in Havana, which administered Soviet economic and technical aid to Cuba.

The advocates of continuing Soviet economic "cooperation" with Havana on an inequitable basis attempted to blur the real picture by placing emphasis on the poor quality of Soviet cars, trucks, machinery, and equipment that would have been difficult to sell for hard currency. They remained silent about these goods constituting only 20 percent of the total Soviet exports to the island. The rest was taken by oil (50 percent) and other raw materials that would have sold easily on the world market. And, in any case, the same 20 percent, on average, of total Soviet exports to Cuba were given to Havana practically free, having been covered by Soviet trade credits and never repaid.

Others in the Soviet bureaucracy advanced an equally false argument that the appearance of the Soviet Union in the world market as a substantial buyer of sugar would have caused much higher world prices for this product. That could hardly have happened because Cuba would have faced the necessity of doubling its sales of sugar to the same market, thus keeping sugar prices down and neutralizing the destabilizing effect of Soviet purchases.

Finally, economic relations with Cuba cost additional hundreds of millions of dollars to the Soviet Union, since it agreed to pay all costs of transportation in both directions of the enormous volume of goods (around 24 million tons a year). The USSR Ministry of the Maritime Fleet had assigned about three hundred cargo vessels to this task on a permanent basis. On the average, there were one hundred Soviet ships docked in Cuban ports at all times (unloading and loading operations normally took up to two months). Even that was not sufficient; Soviet vessels had to be complemented by foreign chartered ships, and in 1989, they transported 30 percent of the total volume of freight to and from Cuba at a cost of $34 million to the Soviet Union.[26]

A Capricious Ally

As a developing country not aligned formally with the Soviet Union but acting for all practical purposes as a reliable friend and ally, Cuba did turn out to be quite a political asset to Moscow. Cuba was useful in winning the sympathies and support of Third World countries for Soviet "peace initiatives" in the United Nations. Up to a point, it also suited Moscow's purposes that Havana became a Mecca for Latin American revolutionaries; in some situations, it was more convenient for the Soviets to stay in the background and rely on Cubans to render them the necessary assistance. Castro's approval of Soviet foreign policy strengthened Moscow's position in its competition with Peking for influence in the Third World, and his violent anti-American rhetoric was useful in Moscow's propaganda war with Washington.

Khrushchev attached special importance to his first meeting with Castro in New York in September 1960 and was extremely pleased with its results. Castro's intense hatred of the United States and his revolutionary zeal favorably impressed Khrushchev. Castro spoke of his desire to maintain a close friendship with the USSR and asked for military aid. Referring to this meeting in his interview with Cuban radio on October 11, 1960, the Soviet leader said that he and Castro "were able to talk over many things and came to a conclusion that the views of the Soviet Union and Cuba concerning the main problems of international relations coincide."[27] Sharing his impressions of Castro with members of the Soviet delegation in New York, Khrushchev compared him to "a young horse that hasn't been broken and needs some training" and added, "but he is very spirited — so we'll have to be careful."[28]

The accuracy of that impression was soon confirmed. Notwithstanding Cuba's rapidly growing economic dependence on Soviet deliveries of oil, machinery, grain, and other necessities, Castro proved to be "difficult," more like Marshal Josip Tito of Yugoslavia, Enver Hoxha of Albania, or Nicolae Ceausescu of Romania rather than any of the other leaders of East European socialist states who were manageable or replaceable or both. The Soviets' irritation with Castro's peculiarity was aggravated by their failure to find within his entourage people whose loyalty to Moscow's interpretation of Marxism-Leninism was stronger than their fidelity to Fidel himself — a standard procedure in Soviet relations with "fraternal" socialist countries. Castro must have known about this practice, since he was careful not to allow veteran communist leaders to occupy top positions in his regime, with the exception of Carlos Rafael Rodriguez, whom he trusted. He purged them from his government twice, in 1962 and 1968, and imprisoned Anibal Escalante, one of the "old guard" Cuban communist leaders whom he accused of being too close to Moscow. Escalante and his followers, labeled a "micro-faction," were highly critical of Castro's policies and authoritarian style of governing the country and the party. One of the reasons for Castro's coolness to Soviet Ambassador Sergei Kudryavtsev was the ambassador's rumored close contact with Anibal Escalante, which led to Kudryavtsev's replacement in spring 1962.

It was surprising, under the circumstances, that there was significant give-and-take in Soviet-Cuban political cooperation. This became particularly true after the painful experience of the Missile Crisis, which made Khrushchev feel guilty for wounding Castro's pride. In the first "full-size" joint Soviet-Cuban political document, signed in Moscow on May 23, 1963, at the conclusion of Castro's visit to the USSR, the Soviets supported his "five points" or five conditions for peace, with particular emphasis on the evacuation of the U.S. naval base from Guantánamo. (See p. 50, this volume, for the five points.)

The Soviet government confirmed its commitment to defend Cuba and condemned Kennedy's Alliance for Progress as "a disguise for the continuing plundering of the peoples of Latin America." It agreed to subscribe to the formula, proposed by the Cubans, that "the Havana declarations are of historical importance for the national-liberation struggle and indicate correctly the course of events."[29] That, in effect, implied support of the main thesis of these documents, the imminence of revolutions "in many countries of Latin America" with a decisive role for the peasantry, headed by workers and "revolutionary intellectuals,"[30] in contravention of the CPSU's theoretical postulates at the time.

This was crowned by the statement that the Soviet government, "guided by the desire to contribute to the strengthening of the socialist economy of fraternal Cuba," offered, "acting on its own initiative," to raise the price on the Cuban sugar purchased in 1963. That marked a retreat from the previous Soviet practice of trading with developing countries on the basis of world market prices. Khrushchev's magnanimity in establishing this precedent cost the Soviet Union dearly. Further rises in prices of Cuban sugar followed in the years to come, becoming a routine in bilateral economic relations and a heavy burden to the Soviet economy.

In response, Castro expressed himself in favor of the policy of "the unity of the international movement of revolutionary workers and the national liberation movement" (euphemistically condemning Chinese sectarian activities). He supported Khrushchev's favorite thesis that another world war was not inevitable (again, polemics against the Chinese), supported the principle of peaceful coexistence of states with different social and economic systems, endorsed Soviet proposals for universal and total disarmament and for the ban on all nuclear tests, approved the Soviet terms of the German peace settlement and neutrality of Laos, condemned U.S. military intervention in South Vietnam, and denounced U.S. occupation of South Korea as the main obstacle to the peaceful unification of Korea.

Covering a wide range of principal items on the foreign policy agenda of Cuba and the USSR, the Joint Statement set a pattern for future close political cooperation and coordination of efforts in promoting common global and regional interests. As Soviet and Cuban policies evolved, they underwent changes in priorities and emphasis, if not substance. Such changes rarely coincided in time and direction, and this tended to widen the zone of disagreement. There were periods when their divergent views on problems they considered vital made it difficult to continue close political cooperation and produced a cooler climate in their relations. In most cases, though, both sides tried to keep disagreements "within the family" and to preserve the appearance of complete unity.

The most serious and prolonged period of estrangement in Soviet-Cuban relations occurred soon after Leonid Brezhnev replaced Nikita Khrushchev. It was not as dramatic and spectacular as the crisis of confidence between Moscow and Havana in October-November 1962 but surpassed it by far in duration and practical negative effects on their bilateral cooperation and in international affairs. The new Soviet leader showed much less disposition to tolerate Castro's adventurous exploits in Latin America and Castro's acceptance of Guevara's idealistically naive internal economic policy, which Brezhnev thought promised a quick economic collapse for Cuba. The Brezhnev government pursued a more cautious policy toward the West and proceeded to establish relations with moderate bourgeois regimes in Latin America. Accordingly, in the world communist movement, the International Department of the CPSU Central Committee was pushing a line in favor of the "peaceful road to socialism," which was attacked by the Chinese Communist Party as "revisionist." The Cuban policy, aimed at undermining feeble Latin American democracies and encouraging Sierra Maestra-style insurrectionist movements, was much closer to the Chinese interpretation of the Marxist-Leninist theory of a socialist revolution. Both Havana and Peking had little sympathy for Moscow's policy of seeking détente and some accommodation with Washington. The similarities between Guevara's economic thinking and Mao's "big leaps" theory were not entirely coincidental.

Speaking at the Tri-Continental Conference of Asian, African, and Latin American Revolutionary Solidarity in Havana on January 15, 1966, Castro affirmed that in many Latin American countries "conditions exist for an armed revolutionary struggle," referring specifically to the Dominican Republic, Venezuela, Colombia, Peru, and Guatemala, where revolutionary movements already had been going on for a considerable time. He expressed his conviction that "on this continent the struggle will assume more violent forms." Castro ridiculed those who "theorize and criticize those who theorize" about possibilities for evolutionary progressive development and stated that, due to the proximity and power of the United States, the armed struggle in Latin America "should be common and simultaneous."[31] Castro was not placated by the statement made at the conference by Sharaf Rashidov, one of Brezhnev's cronies who headed the Soviet delegation, about the Soviet Union's "fraternal solidarity with the armed struggle for liberty waged by the patriots of Venezuela, Peru, Colombia, and Guatemala against the lackeys of imperialism."[32]

In his speech on May 1, 1966, Castro implicitly criticized the Soviet Union for not reacting with sufficient firmness to the U.S. bombing of North Vietnam. He pointed out that the United States "would continue doing this — and we said so during the Crisis of October — as long as it can do it with impunity [and that] peace could be defended much better if the imperialists were given to understand what they could do and what they could not do; [whereas] letting them do what they wish, letting them continue with their piratical and Vandalic actions does not contribute to peace; it's an enormous mistake."[33]

Moreover, in the same speech, Fidel Castro questioned the CPSU program for the "construction of communism," asking rhetorically, "Can someone, some nation give itself the task of building communism in one particular country if it is not preceded by the development of productive forces and technology in underdeveloped countries of the world?" Then he boldly plunged into a quasi-Marxist theoretical exercise of explaining why a socialist nation should not strive to construct a "complete communism with abundance" if there still remained countries in need of their assistance for economic development. He also challenged another CPSU program postulate, that there were two stages in the construction of communism, the first being the "stage of socialism," and spoke in favor of "constructing socialism and communism simultaneously, in parallel," instilling in the people communist morals without waiting for the second stage.

Those were serious accusations, and they were taken seriously in Moscow. The Soviets believed it was more expedient not to enter into direct public polemics with Castro but to try to influence him through confidential correspondence. Indirectly, a public reply to some of his criticisms was given in *Pravda* on September 7, 1966, by Georgi Arbatov, a foreign policy adviser to Leonid Brezhnev. In an article, entitled "Construction of Communism: The USSR and the World Revolutionary Process," he reminded Castro that the assistance of the USSR and other socialist countries "has opened to many nations an opportunity to advance to socialism" and with this aid, "even small nations...are able to withstand the onslaught of the imperialists [as proved by] socialist Cuba, which has repulsed successfully all attacks by interventionists."[34]

Arbatov disputed the thesis of unleashing "a revolutionary war against the bourgeoisie" and pointed out, prophetically, that it was possible for short periods to maintain low living standards in a socialist country, using the "revolutionary enthusiasm of the people," but should it continue for long, it would lead to lower labor productivity and slower economic development. Noting that the world revolutionary movement needed "an effective assistance, not fine gestures," Arbatov argued that the successful construction of communism in the USSR was the greatest contribution his country could make to the world revolutionary process. He concluded with another transparent reference to Castro's theoretical exercises: "Even today doubts are expressed now and then, is it possible to build a communist society if imperialism still lasts on our planet? The question should be formulated differently: for how long will imperialism last if it were confronted by a communist society in part of the planet?"[35]

In June 1967, Soviet Prime Minister Aleksei Kosygin visited Havana after his meeting with President Lyndon B. Johnson in Glassboro, New Jersey. According to a brief TASS report, Kosygin and Castro had "a frank exchange of opinions in a comradely atmosphere on a number of questions of interest to the Soviet Union and Cuba" — a standard formula used by the Soviet media to describe difficult talks.[36] After briefing Castro on discussions with Johnson on Middle Eastern and Vietnamese problems, Kosygin raised the question of Cuban support for the revolutionary movements in Latin America. According to a report published in a Mexican Trotskyite newspaper and confirmed later by Vice President Hubert Humphrey in his memoirs, Kosygin raised the issue at Humphrey's request, only to be rebuffed in rather strong language by Castro. On July 22, 1967, Raúl Castro, speaking at a graduation ceremony at the Cuban military academy, denied the report but then made a statement, which was correctly interpreted in the West as a public confirmation of what his elder brother told Kosygin:

> Relations between Cuba and the USSR can only exist on the basis of the strictest mutual respect and absolute independence, and it is on this basis that they were born, are maintained today and will always be maintained. Our nation does not have a daddy. Should the security of a people, in this case, its very existence, depend exclusively on aid from abroad? We think not.[37]

The peak of this period of coolness and alienation was reached in February 1968, when Castro clamped down on a group of activists of the former Popular Socialist Party who criticized him, among other things, for distancing Cuba from the Soviet Union and jeopardizing Havana's friendship and cooperation with Moscow. From Raúl Castro's report at the plenary meeting of the CPC Central Committee on the activities of Anibal Escalante's "micro-faction" published by the Cuban press, it transpired that the Cuban security service was spying not only on Cuban communists but also on Soviet diplomats in Havana. Tape recordings of their conversations with Escalante and his adherents were replayed at the meeting.

The "sins" ascribed in the report to the members of the micro-faction consisted essentially of their realistic assessments of Castro's internal policy, his dictatorial behavior, and his foreign policy stance, which exacerbated differences with the USSR. The micro-faction was accused of criticizing Castro's cult of personality, his failure to practice a collective leadership, and violation of "Leninist principles of democratic centralism" in the Central Committee of the Communist Party of Cuba; of attacking Guevara's ideas and giving preference to the traditional communist parties in Latin America, rather than to revolutionary guerrilla movements; of recognizing the CPSU's leadership of the world communist movement; and even of suggesting that the Soviet Union should apply political and economic pressure to force Havana to return to Moscow's fold.[38] In effect, this amounted to the accusation that Escalante was plotting against Castro in Moscow's interests.

By that time, a firm opinion had already been formed in Moscow that confidential verbal admonishments to the whimsical Cuban leader and theoretical debates in the press were not adequate ways to influence his policy. Professing difficulties with oil supplies, the Soviet government informed Havana of its inability to continue to increase its oil deliveries in direct proportion to Cuba's growing needs. Instead, Moscow increased its sales of oil to Brazil. This coincided with the virtual suspension of Soviet arms deliveries and a freeze on technical assistance to Cuba. Castro understood the message; he realized that his critics in the micro-faction were not far off the mark.

Indeed, "Soviet comrades" were frustrated with Castro's maverick political performances and economic experiments. They were thinking either of bringing him to heel by introducing undeclared economic sanctions or, if he persisted in his stance, leaving his regime to its fate. Neither alternative was acceptable to Castro. For all his blustering,

Castro could not risk rejection by the Soviets. No other sources of such large-scale economic and military assistance were available. The People's Republic of China was no substitute for the Soviet Union as a source of such assistance, which was the basis of survival for the regime. Besides, the Chinese had already angered Castro by venturing to use Cuba for their political purposes.

Back to Moscow's Fold

Confronted with this dilemma, Castro demonstrated that he had mastered the art of political maneuvering to perfection. After removing his regime's internal critics, Castro decided to change his policy toward the USSR to reflect what Escalante had suggested. He only waited for an appropriate opportunity to avoid giving the impression that he was changing his mind under duress. Such an opportunity presented itself with the Soviet invasion of Czechoslovakia in August 1968. The leader of the Cuban Revolution, whose popularity was based on an outspoken defense of the sovereign right of a small nation to independence, faced a difficult choice. A condemnation of the Soviet Union would invoke Moscow's wrath and inflict irreparable damage on his strained relations with Brezhnev. To support the invasion of Czechoslovakia would be tantamount to the recognition of the right of a superpower to intervene militarily in pursuit of its interests in a small country.

As confirmed by those close to some members of the Cuban government at the time, none of them expected Castro to come out in support of the invasion. Moreover, he was widely believed to be preparing a strong condemnation of the Soviet military occupation of a fraternal socialist country and the detention by Soviet forces of its leaders. His televised speech on August 23, 1968, in which Castro approved Brezhnev's "doctrine of limited sovereignty," came as a shock even to some members of his entourage. Castro expressed his approval in terms that did not allow a double interpretation:

> The essential point to be accepted or not accepted is whether or not the socialist camp could allow a political situation to develop which would lead to the breaking away of a socialist country, to its falling into the arms of imperialism. And our point of view is that the socialist camp has the right to prevent this one way or another.... We acknowledge the bitter necessity that called for the sending of those forces into

Czechoslovakia; we do not condemn the socialist countries that made that decision.[39]

To soften the shock, Castro acknowledged the illegality of the Warsaw Pact countries' violation of Czechoslovakia's sovereignty and made sarcastic remarks about "fig leaves" for covering the intervention and "top personalities" in Prague who invited the Warsaw Pact forces to stop a "retrogression to counterrevolutionary positions." Therefore, the Soviet media abstained from informing the Soviet public of Castro's speech; it was conspicuously absent from *Pravda* reports on statements in support of the invasion by leaders of Latin American communist parties. Nonetheless, Leonid Brezhnev and his colleagues appreciated Castro's position very much, as their decision to invade their own East European socialist ally had come under severe criticism, not only from NATO powers but also from nonaligned countries and influential West European communist parties.

Castro's interest in patching up his quarrel with Moscow must not have been the only motive behind his support for the invasion. He hoped that setting a precedent of "defending socialism" in a socialist country by the joint military intervention of the Warsaw Pact members would help to protect his own regime against the "restoration of capitalism." In fact, he did not even bother to hide this motive. Citing the TASS statement that "the fraternal countries...will never permit to tear away even one link of the community of socialist states," Castro asked:

> Do they or do they not consider Vietnam, Korea, and Cuba links of the socialist camp to be safeguarded against imperialism? ...Will they send the divisions of the Warsaw Pact to Cuba if the Yankee imperialists attack our country or even in the case of the threat of the Yankee imperialist attack on our country, if our country requests it?[40]

Neither did Castro conceal his glee with Washington's statement that the invasion compromised any improvement in East-West relations and that it could block the ratification of the Non-Proliferation Treaty. "We ask ourselves whether the idyllic hopes of an improvement in relations with the imperialist U.S. government will continue to be maintained. We ask ourselves if, consistent with the events in Czechoslovakia, a position may be adopted that will imply a renunciation of such idyllic hopes in relation to Yankee imperialism." As for the nonratification of the treaty, that "would be the best thing that could happen." Referring to the Warsaw Pact members' decision to back a minority in Prague "in the face of a majority with rightist positions," Castro said, "I ask myself...if they will also cease to support these rightist, reformist, sold-out submissive leaderships in Latin America that are enemies of the armed revolutionary struggle, that oppose the peoples' liberation struggle."[41] He then cited with relish the statement by the Venezuelan government condemning the invasion and announcing the decision to suspend talks on the resumption of diplomatic relations with the Soviet Union and East European socialist countries.

Castro used the occasion to confirm and justify his position on all major points of his disagreement with Moscow's policy of détente with the West, limiting the nuclear arms race and developing relations with the "rightist" governments in Latin America. Castro correctly calculated that his approval of the Warsaw Pact decision to crush by force the "counterrevolution" in Czechoslovakia would make Soviet leaders more tolerant of his views and behavior. On the other hand, Castro failed to comprehend that the superpowers' common interest in finding a modus vivendi transcended their differences with regard to the ways in which the USSR controlled its sphere of influence. Castro also overestimated the negative consequences of the Warsaw Pact's invasion of Czechoslovakia on East-West relations, hoping that Moscow would be compelled to share the Cuban position of permanent hostility to Washington.

On balance, Castro managed to appease Moscow while reasserting his right to disagree with some aspects of its policy. He then took another important step toward restoring Cuba's close political cooperation with the Soviet Union: the CPC's representative at the International Conference of Communist Parties in Moscow in June 1969 joined the CPSU-led majority in denouncing Peking's "sectarian" position. Then came a "belated honeymoon" in Soviet-Cuban relations that lasted well into the 1980s. Castro's return to favor in Moscow was rewarded by the dispatch of a flotilla of Soviet warships to Cuba, followed by the exchange of visits by Marshal Andrei Grechko, the Soviet defense minister, to Havana in November 1969 and by Raúl Castro to Moscow in April and October 1970. The flow of Soviet arms to Cuba resumed and gathered momentum. The Cubans agreed to allow the construction of a deep-water base for Soviet submarines at Cienfuegos. In return, they were promised modern Soviet fighters. The reactivation of military links was the most reliable indication that relations had gone back to normal. Though all was not smooth, both sides were learning how to pursue their separate aims without treading on each other's feet.

This was confirmed, when Aleksei Kosygin, chairman of the USSR Council of Ministers, was accorded a red-carpet reception at the end of October 1971 on his second visit to Havana. The joint communiqué, published on November 1, 1971, spoke of the "complete unanimity" of the two sides:

> ...in the appraisal of the contemporary international situation and world social development, characterized by the deepening of the revolutionary process.... [They] empathized that this progressive movement of revolutionary forces is expressed in the consolidation of the world socialist system and its growing economic and military power in the accelerated development of the national liberation movement of oppressed nations, exploited by imperialism, and in the struggle of the working class in capitalist countries.[42]

This order of priorities reflected Castro's acceptance of Moscow's principal thesis regarding the paramount revolutionary role of further economic development of the Soviet Union and other socialist countries.

In return, Kosygin joined Castro in condemning "the combined attempts of imperialism and reactionary oligarchies to check the rise of revolutionary movements in Latin America." Kosygin and Castro expressed "solidarity" with the Salvador Allende government in Chile, with "structural reforms carried out by the Peruvian government," and with other Latin American countries that "asserted their political and economic independence." The Soviet side confirmed its support for Cuba "in the struggle for strengthening socialist gains and against provocations by the forces of imperialism" and denounced "the U.S. imperialist blockade against Cuba and U.S.-encouraged hostile actions."

At the end of June 1972, Fidel Castro revisited the Soviet Union for the first time since January 1964. The joint Soviet-Cuban communiqué on the results of the visit, published by *Pravda* on July 6, 1972, included an extensive section on international affairs. During the talks, Soviet leaders insistently advised Castro to think of the benefits of Cuba's economic integration with socialist countries through their Council for Mutual Economic Assistance (CMEA), whereupon he instructed Carlos Rafael Rodriguez, then secretary of the CPC Central Committee and minister of the revolutionary government, who accompanied him on this visit, to apply for an associate membership for Cuba in CMEA at its XXVI meeting, due to open a few days later in Moscow.

The Cuban delegation at the meeting, chaired by Kosygin, was headed by Rodriguez, but before he could present Cuba's case, Kosygin officially informed the heads of government of member countries present that Cuba decided to apply for full membership in the organization and that the Soviet Union supported the application. (According to a TASS report, published by *Pravda* on July 12, 1972, the head of the Cuban delegation "made a statement with the request that Cuba be admitted as member of CMEA and that it agreed to assume obligations under the CMEA Charter.")[43] The motion was carried unanimously, and it was left to Carlos Rafael Rodriguez only to thank all those present for their support.

One obvious reason why Brezhnev and Kosygin wanted Cuba to become a full member of CMEA, dominated by the USSR, was that they hoped to acquire additional means to influence its economic development and to keep Castro's economic policy under control. Another important consideration, namely, the desire to share the burden of sustaining the Cuban economy with East European socialist countries, was also present. As for Castro's motives for joining CMEA, he was thinking not only of possible economic benefits from its collective assistance programs but also of Cuba becoming "a link between the possibilities opened by socialism in Europe in the process of its integration as a cohesive and solid system and the needs of that Latin America, which was striving to free itself from conditions imposed by its dependence on the imperialist metropolis and by the defects of the world capitalist market."[44]

In December 1972, Castro traveled to Moscow again to participate in the events commemorating the fiftieth anniversary of the formation of the Union of Soviet Socialist Republics. He returned to Havana with economic agreements, referring to them as "noble and unprecedented in the history of humanity."[45] The agreements provided for new price increases on Cuban sugar (from 120 to 200 rubles per ton for the period 1973-1980), an additional Soviet credit to cover the trade deficit in 1973-1975, and the deferment of the repayment of previous credits until 1986, to be repaid then in twenty-five years without any interest.

Leonid Brezhnev Visits Havana

Castro's visits to Moscow prepared the ground for the first visit to Cuba by the Secretary General of the CPSU Central Committee

(January 28-February 3, 1974). Leonid Brezhnev and Fidel Castro signed the Soviet-Cuban Declaration, in which they proclaimed "the complete unity of their views with regard to the present world situation and the foreign policy tasks of the socialist states; the policy of defense of freedom, independence, and sovereign rights of states and peoples; and the strengthening of peace and international cooperation." The Cuban side emphasized the "great international importance" of the creation of "the material and technical base of communism" in the USSR and of the realization of the Soviet "Program of Peace." The two sides condemned "revisionism and hegemonic and chauvinist trends, contradicting the internationalist course worked out collectively by Communist and workers' parties." They welcomed "the positive turn in world affairs from the 'Cold War' to the relaxation of tension [and] peaceful coexistence of states with different social systems."

There were appropriate passages on Vietnam, the "national-liberation struggle of Arab nations against Israel's aggression," and positive developments in Europe and Africa, with references to Angola, Mozambique, Namibia, Zimbabwe, the Republic of South Africa, and Guinea-Bissau. The declaration strongly condemned the military junta in Chile and expressed solidarity with the peoples of Latin America, "waging a just struggle for national liberation, strengthening of political and economic independence and social progress" (and contained also a phrase welcoming the development by Latin American states of relations with socialist countries). Support was also expressed for "general and complete disarmament, the prohibition of the use of force in international relations, and the ban for all times on the use of nuclear weapons."[46]

The document contained no traces of Havana's "special" approach to major international and regional problems. That did not mean that Castro actually had changed his position. He had simply learned to be more flexible, accepting the necessity of presenting to the outside world the semblance of complete Soviet-Cuban unity on these problems. He never renounced his views on the questionable value of superpower agreements on peaceful coexistence and disarmament for such small socialist countries as Cuba. Castro maintained his conviction that the Cubans did not feel any safer but, on the contrary, were more insecure, since the United States could act with impunity in conditions of détente in its relations with the USSR.

Definitely not a believer in détente, Castro continued his efforts to foster revolutionary movements in Latin America. The military coup in Chile and the establishment of military rule in Argentina, Brazil, and Uruguay gave more weight to his rejection of Moscow's thesis about the possibility of a peaceful evolution of bourgeois democracies to socialism. However, he became more selective and cautious in rendering assistance to Latin American insurrectionist movements. On occasion, he even tried to maintain normal relations with the governments of the countries plagued by guerrilla groups trained and supplied by the Cubans; Colombia is one example.

As for disarmament, the Cubans were proclaiming general support for the Soviet initiatives but maintained their negative attitude to the Non-Proliferation Treaty and the Treaty of Tlatelolco on the nuclear-free zone in Latin America. Castro argued that the superpower agreements on the limitation of strategic arms were not saving millions of children who were dying of starvation and diseases in the Third World countries exploited by imperialism. Havana also continued to reject proposals for discussions on regional disarmament. The standard explanation was that Cuba was threatened by the U.S. military presence in its territory and Puerto Rico; therefore, it was entitled to acquire and to use any arms it considered necessary for its defense.

Moscow-Havana political cooperation was not limited to public declarations. Soviet and Cuban delegations and representatives in the United Nations and other international forums had standing instructions from their governments to coordinate their activities closely and share information on problems of mutual interest. At the same time, the Cubans, as a rule, avoided participation in traditional meetings of diplomatic representatives of socialist countries for informal exchanges of opinions. When pressed for an explanation of this behavior, they said they had to preserve Cuba's image of a nonaligned country. In New York, Cuban diplomats refused to take part in such gatherings in the lobby of UN headquarters — they did not want to be seen conferring with representatives of other socialist countries. This factor also influenced the Cuban position in international and regional debates on problems affecting political or economic interests of developing nations.

The congruous positions of the USSR and Cuba on most international problems, reflected in their leaders' joint statements and their voting in the United Nations, were based only in part on Cuba's interest in maintaining good political relations with its principal donor of economic and military assistance. Their complementary positions on many issues also stemmed from the community of their interests as

totalitarian socialist regimes, locked collectively in confrontation with
the West and individually with the United States. Their divergences
were more tactical than strategic. They both pursued goals of expanding
the sphere of influence of socialism, putting the United States and its
NATO allies on the defensive, and depriving them of markets and
sources of raw materials in Africa, Asia, and Latin America — to prepare
the ground for the eventual historic defeat of Western imperialism.

Political Cooperation: Living with Differences

In tactical matters, the Cubans and Soviets differed substantially.
Soviet leaders, well aware of the destructive potential of thermonuclear
weapons and the futility of Soviet efforts to outstrip the United States
in the arms race, were careful to avoid extreme provocations. Selecting
a policy of peaceful coexistence with the West had three purposes:
1) to limit the arms race that threatened to ruin the feeble Soviet
economy; 2) to erode, under conditions of détente, the cohesion of
NATO and weaken the U.S. political and military presence in Western
Europe; and 3) to create more favorable conditions in developing
countries for promoting "national-liberation" movements and the
establishment of "progressive" regimes.

The Cubans continued to be skeptical of the Soviet Union's first
two goals but were more than willing to contribute to the realization
of the third. Castro prudently avoided expressing his misgivings about
the Soviet leaders' apparent obsession with finding an accommodation
with Washington, except in his inner circle, but some of his caustic
remarks were reaching Moscow — Soviet intelligence had good
connections in Havana. Talking to his entourage, Castro did not
conceal his hope that, given the diametrically opposed policies and
global interests of the two superpowers, the periods of détente in
relations between them would only be temporary, while their enmity
would remain a permanent factor. He reasoned that the Soviet Union
valued its prestige as a champion of national liberation movements and
would not publicly criticize Havana's bellicose behavior in regional
conflict situations, even though it was hampering the improvement of
Soviet-American relations. Castro also counted on Moscow's continued
solidarity with Havana in its lingering confrontation with Washington,
and in this he was also right: Soviet leaders could be irritated by his
pugnacity in dealing with the United States, but they did not make it
a serious issue, limiting themselves to diplomatic advice on the
expediency of combining firmness with flexibility.

Through the 1970s and the early 1980s, Cuba and the Soviet Union cooperated without much difficulty and at times very closely in supporting leftist regimes in Latin America and Africa. They both welcomed the electoral victory in 1971 of Salvador Allende in Chile and did what they could to help his shaky government. Soviet and Cuban policies toward Chile were complementary, not conflicting. Moscow concentrated its efforts on developing economic, technical, and cultural cooperation with Chile; counseled the governing Popular Unity coalition toward restraint in the implementation of radical social and economic reforms; and cautioned against steps that would antagonize Washington. The Cubans had other preoccupations; while they supported in principle Moscow's line, they were busy sending security personnel (the Guardia brothers, among them) and weapons to extreme left-wing Chilean organizations and Allende's personal guard in preparation for a civil war, which they believed was inevitable, and transferred to Chile one of their centers for training guerrilla fighters. After the Allende government was violently overthrown in the 1973 military coup, leaders of the Chilean Communist Party (CCP) and socialist parties, in exile in the Soviet Union, East Germany, and Czechoslovakia, were engaged mainly in political propaganda against the Augusto Pinochet regime. The Cubans were training Chilean guerrilla fighters and sending weapons to the Manuel Rodriguez Front, which formally dissociated from the CCP and engaged in urban guerrilla activities. There were differences between Moscow and Havana on this particular point.

There was a substantial degree of Soviet-Cuban cooperation in Grenada. The Cubans were actually instrumental in persuading their Soviet friends that Maurice Bishop's New Jewel Movement (NJM), which had seized power on the exotic island, had a good chance to lead this tiny Caribbean nation to some sort of socialism and that it should be given support and encouragement. They also tried to help the Grenadian revolutionaries with advice on how to make Soviet leaders interested in rendering to Maurice Bishop's government substantial economic and military assistance and in granting the NJM the status of a "fraternal party." There were no indications of any serious differences between Moscow and Havana in Grenada. The Cubans tended to be closer to Jewel's more moderate faction, led by Maurice Bishop, whereas Soviet diplomats in Grenada and officials of the International Department of the CPSU in Moscow appeared to have more sympathy with Vincent Cord, an orthodox Marxist-Leninist, and his group, but this could hardly be linked to the tragic events that brought about Bishop's violent death and an end to the Grenadian socialist experiment.

Havana played a key role in helping the Sandinistas seize power in Nicaragua, as opposed to Moscow, which stood aloof during their armed struggle against the Anastasio Somoza regime. Castro retained his predominant political influence with the governing nine comandantes of the revolution who owed to him their unity and, to a large degree, their victory. Cuban military and security advisers helped to organize and run the Sandinista army and security services. The Soviet Union had to be content, particularly in the initial period of the Sandinista rule, mainly with the role of providing the bulk of economic assistance and military hardware. Only later, when the Nicaraguans were already weary of excessive Cuban patronage and saw advantages in taking a more balanced position between Moscow and Havana, did Moscow's influence in Managua increase considerably.

The principal political disagreement on Nicaragua between Moscow and Havana, which developed in the late 1980s, stemmed from their different approach to the Sandinista Revolution. In Havana it was regarded as a transitory revolution, destined to prepare the ground for a future socialist transformation of the country, which would not necessarily follow the Cuban precedent but would certainly possess the true qualities of socialism in good time. The Cubans counseled the Sandinista leaders to be moderate and cautious in the timing of this transformation but expressed their conviction that the very survival of the Sandinista Revolution depended on its capacity to pass to a socialist stage eventually. Therefore, the Cubans believed it was essential to educate the Sandinista cadres accordingly and to curtail the activity of the political opposition. Havana did not approve of Managua's concessions to the demands of the Contadora group (an association of Colombia, Venezuela, Mexico, and Panama formed to facilitate a peace settlement in Central America) and Central American countries on the issue of democratization, considering that they were prejudicing the survival of the Sandinista Revolution.

In regard to the Central American negotiating process, Brezhnev, Andropov, and Chernenko all emulated Foreign Minister Gromyko and paid only lip service to it. Gorbachev initially also supported this position, but Shevardnadze, who replaced Gromyko in 1986, had a different attitude: the Sandinistas would be able to preserve their power only if they practiced the principles of a mixed economy, political pluralism, and nonalignment, which they preached; Nicaragua did not have the right social, economic, and external conditions for a socialist transformation to succeed. For reasons of economic backwardness, strong internal political opposition, the U.S.-backed armed resistance to the Sandinista regime, and a hostile regional environment, the Sandinista Revolution could not evolve beyond its original goals. Some Soviets used another weighty argument to support this assessment, pointing out that the Soviet Union just did not have sufficient resources to fund yet another socialist revolution in the area. Former Vice Foreign Minister Victor Komplektov, responsible for elaborating the Soviet policy in Latin America, agreed with Shevardnadze. So did I, as head of the Latin American Directorate of the USSR Foreign Ministry. Still, some other Soviet politicians and highly placed officials continued to support the Cuban view of the nature and prospects of the Sandinista Revolution, as was the case with German Shliapnikov, the Soviet ambassador in Managua.

The differences of approach between Moscow and Havana affected Managua's negotiating position, as well as the internal policy of the Sandinista government, but they did not seriously hinder practical cooperation and joint efforts by the USSR and Cuba in support of the Sandinista Revolution. In coordination with East European socialist allies, Moscow and Havana orchestrated international propaganda campaigns of solidarity with the Sandinistas and intensive diplomatic lobbying in the United Nations and in West European, Latin American, African, and Asian capitals in favor of resolutions condemning the United States' "undeclared war" against Nicaragua. They discussed ways to satisfy Managua's needs for economic aid. This was done also within CMEA's framework, particularly with regard to the deliveries of oil. In the late 1980s, the USSR, Cuba, and East European countries were assigned quotas of oil for delivery to Nicaragua. To the East European countries and Cuba, this meant a corresponding reduction of the quantities of oil they were to receive from the USSR for their own needs.

Moscow and Havana cooperated closely in helping the Sandinistas to equip and train their armed forces. High-level Soviet, Cuban, and Nicaraguan military representatives met regularly in Havana to discuss plans for ensuring that the Sandinista Army was adequately prepared for dealing with the armed opposition. There existed a division of labor in the transportation of Soviet arms and military equipment to the Nicaraguan ports: heavy weapons (tanks, armored personnel carriers, artillery pieces, trucks, and helicopters) were shipped directly from the Black Sea ports or Leningrad to the port of Corinto on the Pacific coast of Nicaragua; whereas, portable weapons and munitions were transported first to Cuba and then, by smaller Cuban or Nicaraguan vessels, to the port of Bluefields on the Caribbean coast.

There were no tripartite meetings at a political level of representatives of Cuba, Nicaragua, and the Soviet Union to coordinate their policies in Central America. The Cubans preferred to discuss political problems with the Sandinistas in the absence of Soviet comrades. Besides, Havana was always well informed about what was going on between Moscow and Managua. Daniel Ortega kept no secrets from Castro, and Soviet representatives traveling to and from Managua via Havana were usually "debriefed" by the Cubans, as repeatedly took place whenever I came through Havana. Yet, Moscow had only rudimentary information on what was going on between Havana and Managua; the Nicaraguans and the Cubans were rarely forthcoming with information on the subject.

There were also only bilateral Soviet-Cuban political discussions of the situation in El Salvador. While accepting in principle the Soviet thesis that it was necessary for the Farabundo Martí National Liberation Front (FMLN) to combine military and political means of struggle, the Cubans placed more importance on the military. Practical cooperation between Moscow and Havana in rendering material assistance to the FMLN forces was very limited. The Cubans carried the main burden of providing, with the help of the Sandinistas, logistical support for the Salvadoran guerrilla movement.

On the whole, political cooperation between Cuba and the USSR in Latin America and the Caribbean was of a more limited nature and scope than would have been expected. Tactical and political differences aside, this could also be explained by the noticeable unwillingness of the Cubans to grant Moscow equal status in regional affairs, as they felt entitled to play the role of senior partner. They were trying, in effect, to guide Soviet policy in Latin America by sharing generously with Moscow their assessments of situations in particular countries but were much less prepared to provide detailed information on their own policy in the region.

In Africa, where the Cubans felt less at home and were dependent on Soviet logistical support for maintaining their expeditionary forces in Angola and other countries, they showed more disposition to coordinate their policy and practical steps with Moscow. Contrary to widely held opinions, they never subordinated their interests and policy in Africa to those of the Soviet Union. That was more evident in the 1960s, when the Cubans had acted in Africa independently, without any coordination with Moscow and, in some cases, at variance with its policy. Later, in the 1970s and early 1980s, it was more difficult to determine who was serving whose interests, because the Soviet and Cuban policies in that region became very close. Both Moscow and Havana were encouraging the Marxist rulers in Luanda, Addis Ababa, and Maputo to go ahead with socialist reforms. They were providing military assistance to fight the internal opposition, backed by Pretoria and Washington. And they both trained and supplied the South-West African Peoples Organization (SWAPO) and the African National Congress (ANC) forces fighting the South African regime. Notions of national reconciliation and peaceful settlement of civil conflicts through dialogue and mutual concessions were not yet popular in Moscow.

Brezhnev did not ask Castro to send Cuban troops to Angola; Castro acted without prior consultation with Moscow. Afterwards, the Cuban government began to inform Moscow about plans for sending Cuban reinforcements to Angola, since they had to be transported by Soviet ships or aircraft. An agreement was reached on Soviet logistical support for the maintenance of Cuban expeditionary forces there. On the other hand, at times Soviet military advisers and Cuban field commanders in Angola acted more like competitors "selling" the Angolan High Command their rival plans of military campaigns against the National Front for the Total Independence of Angola (UNITA) and South African forces, than as allies with a common cause; the Soviet generals and colonels often lost in that competition. Their professional training, based on Second World War experience, was no match for the Cubans' skills in guerrilla warfare, which were much closer to the types of battles fought in Africa. This did not interfere with the generally close Soviet-Cuban political cooperation in Angola, but when Moscow decided to cooperate with Washington in facilitating a political solution of the problem of Namibia and the withdrawal of Cuban troops from Angola, the situation changed.

The Human Rights Problem: Acting in Unison

Probably the best illustration of the community of interests of the Soviet Union and Cuba as members of the socialist camp was presented by their complete unanimity in categorically rejecting all criticism by the Western democracies and international organizations of their respective human rights records and any attempts to pressure them into respecting the provisions of the Universal Declaration of the

Rights of Man. These efforts were invariably described, both in Moscow and Havana, as inadmissible interference into internal affairs and slanderous concoctions of bourgeois propaganda, designed to discredit socialism. The subject matter itself was referred to in the Soviet and Cuban press only as "the so-called problem of human rights in socialist countries." The official propaganda line held that this problem did not exist. The standard explanation was simple: the socialist authentic democracy, as different from the bourgeois sham democracy, had guaranteed principal human rights — the rights to employment, housing, free education, free medical care, and so forth. Individual freedoms were regarded and treated as alien to the collectivist nature of a socialist society.

The experiences of the Russian October Revolution, years of civil war, and decades of secret police terror and Marxist-Leninist indoctrination had conditioned generations of Soviet citizens to accept constant mass violations of basic human rights as an integral part of the revolutionary process, leading to the construction of the communist society, "the ultimate dream of humanity." According to Marxist-Leninist teaching, it was mandatory for the triumphant socialist revolution to deny political rights to the former exploiting classes and apply compulsion to those who were unwilling to subordinate themselves to its interests. Khrushchev and his successors disapproved of Stalin's savage repressions against "honest communists," but they had no doubts about the expediency of Lenin's "red terror" against "hostile bourgeois elements." Neither did they hesitate to use force to quell political dissent and to imprison anyone bold enough to challenge their unlimited authority.

It was only natural, then, that Soviet leaders and official Soviet representatives in Havana did not question the necessity or morality of the terror unleashed by the Cuban revolutionary regime first against Batista's supporters and then against those who did not accept Castro's conversion to Marxism-Leninism. Nor were they concerned about the lack of individual liberties, freedom of the press, independence of judicial authorities, and other vestiges of bourgeois democracy in Cuba. Even after spending years on the Island of Freedom, Soviet journalists and scholars continued to ridicule eyewitness reports in the American press about summary executions and other abuses of power by the revolutionary government. Brushing this evidence aside, *Pravda* asserted that Cuba was "the only socialist country that has avoided mass repressions and political trials."[47]

Soviet experts in Cuba were well aware of the way the Castro revolutionary regime treated its political opponents. In fact, some senior Cuban army officers who personally executed prisoners did not even try to conceal this pastime from Soviet representatives. On one occasion in the early 1960s, Pedro Miret and other Cuban General Staff officers interrupted a conference with Soviet military advisers and left the conference hall. Reappearing an hour later and looking both contented and visibly agitated, they exchanged macabre jokes of how they hit their human targets, and then they continued to participate in the conference. The Soviet army officers present were shocked by this despicable behavior.[48] But there were other Soviet advisers, "professionals" from the USSR Committee for State Security and the Ministry of Interior, who were not disgusted by such practices. As former Cuban political prisoners testified, Soviet experts regularly inspected Cuban prisons and helped equip them.

A typical presentation for the Soviet public of this aspect of the Cuban post-revolutionary reality was given by Dr. Karen Khachaturov, former journalist and now president of the Russian Committee for Cooperation with Latin American countries. In *Ideological Expansion of the United States in Latin America,* published in 1978, Khachaturov wrote:

> The longest-playing records of anti-Castro propaganda are the slanderous inventions of the "terror" in Cuba, of the suppression of civil liberties and the rights of an individual. Organized soon after the triumph of the revolution, the open trial in Havana of the hangmen of the Batista regime, guilty of horrendous tortures and assassinations of thousands of patriots, served as a starting point for this campaign, aimed, first of all, at provoking anti-Cuban psychosis in countries of Latin America and in the United States.[49]

There was nothing original in the writings of Soviet Cubanologists on the subject. They simply toed the line of Havana's official propaganda, disregarding the growing evidence of systematic gross violations of human rights by the Castro regime and presenting to the Soviet public exultant accounts of the unity of the Cuban working people and of their achievements in the construction of socialism, despite the resistance of the enemies of the revolution — agents of American imperialism. Soviet scholars A.D. Bekarevich, B.A. Borodayev, and K.O. Leino explained the emigration of hundreds of thousands of Cubans from the island as follows:

The doors of the United States which earlier permitted the entry of only a limited number of Cubans were quickly opened for those who wanted to leave Cuba after 1959. Landowners, bourgeoisie, politicians, security agents, Batista army officers, pimps, individuals living off the vices, and even lumpen proletarians had taken this opportunity.

Evidently feeling the inadequacy of this explanation, the authors added:

One of the main purposes of this counterrevolutionary policy, apart from the cynical, disguised as humanitarian, campaign of enrolling mercenaries for future aggression, was to deprive the country of specialists and technicians. In this manner, American imperialism succeeded in taking out of the country thousands of medics and great numbers of engineers, architects, professors, research assistants, and technicians. This plunder affected even part of the skilled workers employed in industry and in important enterprises, which had earlier enjoyed the privileges characteristic of the so-called workers' aristocracy.[50]

Khachaturov, in *Confrontation of the Two Americas*, published in 1976, advanced a somewhat more original theory to explain the Cubans' exodus:

It's not only the rich or representatives of petty bourgeoisie, whose egoistic interests were affected by the people's revolution.... After the crash of the exploiters' order not only representatives of the privileged classes left the country but also those who had absorbed their ideology with their mothers' milk.[51]

Not a word was said about the real causes of this tragic situation, when one-fifth of the population had voted with their feet against the "socialist democracy" and the new way of life and many more were prepared to leave, given the opportunity.

The Soviet-Cuban Declaration of February 4, 1974, contained a section entitled "Communists of the USSR and Cuba in one fighting order in the struggle for the common cause," which set forth the agreed position of the CPSU and the CPC regarding the human rights problem in the following terms:

In present conditions of the continued ideological struggle in the international arena, of constant attempts of reactionary propaganda to encircle the countries of socialism with the smoke screen of slander to distort in the eyes of the peoples of their countries the truth about socialism in order to distract attention from the growing crisis of the capitalist system, the two fraternal parties emphasize the necessity to unmask the calumniators constantly and effectively, to rebuff resolutely all forms of the ideological diversion of anti-socialist forces, informing widely the world public of the life of the socialist countries.[52]

It was only logical that Soviet representatives in the United Nations Human Rights Commission in Geneva invariably opposed all attempts to scrutinize the situation in Cuba, to invite former political prisoners of the Castro regime to its sessions, and to condemn the systematic violations of human rights on the island. Soviet media devoted substantial space to "unmasking" Armando Valladares as "an agent of Batista's police" when he became the U.S. representative on the Human Rights Commission. In turn, the Cubans were lending their support to the Soviet Union and other socialist countries whenever they came under international criticism for similar practices.

Notes

1. W. Raymond Duncan, 1985, *The Soviet Union and Cuba: Interests and Influence* (New York: Praeger), 2.

2. Strobe Talbott, ed. and trans., 1970, *Khrushchev Remembers* (Boston: Little, Brown), 493, 505.

3. M. Gallagher, 1970, *The Public Addresses of Fidel Castro Ruz* (London), 174.

4. V. V. Volsky and A. Bekarevich, eds., 1987, *Velikiy Oktiabr y Kubinskaya revoliutsiya* (Moscow: Izdatelstvo Nauka), 3.

5. Y.L. Smirhova and F. Yrobarta, eds., 1988, *Internaatsionalnoye Sotrudnichestvo KPSS y Kubi: Istoria y Sovremennost* (Moscow: Politizdat), 37.

6. *Komsomolkaya Pravda* (Moscow), September 19, 1990.

7. *Moscow News*, No. 10, March 11-18, 1990, 12.

8. Irving Louis Horowitz, ed., 1989, *Cuban Communism* (New Brunswick, N.J. and London: Transaction Publishers), 280.

9. *Latinskaya Amerika* (Moscow), No. 4, 1990, 69.

10. *Argument y Fakty* (Moscow), April 1-7, 1989.

11. *Komsomolskaya Pravda*, October 26, 1989.

12. *Moscow News*, No. 19, May 20-27, 1990.

13. *Granma*, September 8, 1992.

14. *Nezavisimaya Gazeta*, January 9, 1992.

15. *Trud* (Moscow), April 18, 1990.

16. *Latinskaya Amerika* (Moscow), No. 5, 1990, 60.

17. Yuri Kornilov, *Ogoniok*, No. 7, February 1990, 25-6.

18. Jaime Suchlicki, 1990, *Cuba: From Columbus to Castro*, third ed. (Washington, New York, London: Brassey's, Inc.), 204.

19. Irving Louis Horowitz, ed., 1989, *Cuban Communism* (New Brunswick, N.J. and London: Transaction Publishers), 187.

20. *New Times* (Moscow), October 1987, No. 41, 17.

21. *Komsomolskaya Pravda* (Moscow), September 19, 1990.

22. *Sovetskaya Rossiya* (Moscow), September 19, 1990.

23. *Izvestia*, July 14, 1990.

24. *Moscow News*, No. 19, May 20-27, 1990.

25. Moscow Radio (program in Spanish), February 14, 1990, FBIS-SOV-91-036, February 23, 1991, 41.

26. *Pravda*, April 8, 1990.

27. *Narody SSSR y Kubi Naveki Vmeste*, 1963, collection of documents (Moscow: Izdatelstvo Pravda), 120.

28. A. Shevchenko, 1985, *Breaking with Moscow* (New York: Ballantine Books), 139.

29. *Pravda*, May 24, 1962.

30. Fidel Castro, 1968, *Revolucion Cubaine, (Textes Choisie, 1953-62)* (Paris: F. Maspero), 125.

31. *Granma*, January 16, 1966.

32. *Granma*, January 7, 1966.

33. *Granma*, May 2, 1966.

34. Georgi Arbatov, *Construction of Communism: The USSR and the World Revolutionary Process (Pravda)*, September 7, 1966.

35. Arbatov, *Pravda*, September 7, 1966.

36. *Pravda*, June 29, 1967.

37. *Granma*, July 24, 1967.

38. *Las Relaciones Cubanas-Soviéticas (1959-1968)*, 1971, (Mexico: Colegio de Mexico), 19-20.

39. M. Gallagher, 1970, *The Public Addresses of Fidel Castro Ruz* (London), 186.

40. M. Gallagher, 1970, *The Public Addresses of Fidel Castro Ruz* (London), 186.

41. M. Gallagher, 1970, *The Public Addresses of Fidel Castro Ruz* (London), 183-86.

42. *Pravda*, November 1, 1971.

43. *Pravda*, July 12, 1972.

44. N.A. Kudriashov, ed., 1984, *Kuba-Chien SEV* (Moscow: CMEA Secretariat), 2.

45. *Granma*, January 4, 1972.

46. *Vizit Leonida Iliycha Brezhneva v Respubliku Kuba*, 1974, (Moscow: Politizdat), 83-6.

47. *Pravda*, October 22, 1990.

48. Told to the author in October 1992 by a former Soviet interpreter to Soviet military advisers in Cuba.

49. K.A. Khachaturov, 1978, *Ideologicheskaya Ekspansia SShA v Latinskoy Amerike* (Moscow: Izdatelstvo Mezhdunazodnye Otnosheniia), 119.

50. A.D. Bekarevich, B.A. Borodayev, and K.O. Leino, 1988, *Kuba: Stroitelstvo Sotsializma* (Moscow: Izdatelstvo Nauka), 20.

51. K.A. Khachaturov, 1976, *Protivostoyaniye Dvukh Amerik* (Moscow: Izdatelstvo Mezhdunazodnye Otnosheniia), 264-65.

52. *Vizit Leonida Iliycha Brezhneva v Respubliku Kuba*, 1974, (Moscow: Politizdat), 87-8.

Chapter 4

Movement in Opposite Directions

Gorbachev's Reforms: Reaction in Havana

Castro was one of the few foreign leaders who saw that Mikhail Gorbachev's *perestroika* could get out of control and wreck the very system it was intended to improve. Soon after failing in his initial attempts to streamline the socialist "command administrative" economic system to make it function efficiently without changing it radically, Gorbachev decided to embark on political reforms. Castro watched this process closely, as it evolved from calls for intensive, rather than extensive, development of the economy and for accelerated introduction of modern technology (the tasks which, as he said later, were "absolutely unobjectionable") to the liquidation of the CPSU's monopoly on economic and political power and transition to a market economy. In Castro's words, "All those concepts and ideas...are shaping today's tragedy in the Soviet Union."[1] The Cuban embassy in Moscow had standing instructions to relate to Havana in detail all relevant information. Castro "interrogated" every high-level Soviet visitor to Cuba, asking questions and listening patiently to the replies. He came to an early conclusion that *perestroika* was acting like the AIDS virus, destroying the immunological defense of the socialist political system.

Still, Castro hoped that the Soviet Union, where socialism had deeper roots than in Eastern Europe, would survive *perestroika*. There was not much he could do to change or influence Gorbachev's policy. He voiced his doubts in conversations and confidential correspondence with the Soviet leader, expressing his conviction that one could not treat the ills of socialism with capitalist medicines. Gorbachev respected Castro as the leader of a victorious revolution who had reversed its bourgeois democratic course and brought his country into the socialist camp. Yet, Gorbachev could not accept him as a serious Marxist-

Leninist thinker with whom he could debate problems of contemporary communist theory and practice on an equal footing. But then Gorbachev was not swayed by the opinions of the full-fledged communist leaders of East European socialist countries, either.

Convinced of the real dangers of Gorbachev's reforms to his own brand of socialism in Cuba, Castro used his dictatorial executive power, authority, and political skills in order to limit, if not stop altogether, the spread of the Gorbachevian virus in Cuba. It was not an easy task. Scores of thousands of Cubans had received their university education or technical training in the USSR in the last thirty years, and thousands more were studying there at the time. Soviet books, translated into Spanish, and Spanish editions of Soviet magazines and newspapers were available to the Cubans. *Novedades de Moscú* and *Sputnik*, which were distributed in limited numbers until they were banned in August 1989, were hunted in Havana, sold and resold at speculative prices, and passed from one household to another. Thousands of Soviet experts and technicians were stationed in Cuba. Two generations of Cubans had been brought up in the belief that the USSR represented today what Cuba would become tomorrow.

Gorbachev's *glasnost* was of particular concern to Castro. In the USSR, uncensored news reporting gradually spread from Soviet internal politics to foreign affairs. In the Soviet press, articles appeared, critical of the situation in developing socialist nations, violating the long-established tradition of reporting only positive accounts of the events in "fraternal" countries. Public pressure mounted on the Soviet leadership to curtail expensive Soviet economic and technical assistance programs to such regimes, including Cuba. When, on October 19, 1987, the *New Times* weekly magazine published a sarcastic article by its staff writer Vladislav Chirkov, which was highly critical of the economic situation in Cuba, Castro was indignant. He ordered strong reprimands to be sent to Moscow and instructed Carlos Rafael Rodriguez, vice president of the Cuban State Council, to write a reply to Chirkov's "superficial and negative" analysis. At the express request of Cuba, the magazine duly published Rodriguez's reply.[2]

Havana was confronted with similar problems in East European socialist countries, which rapidly overtook the Soviet Union in anti-socialist political and economic reforms; as a result, their press often reported on the situation in Cuba and Castro's policy in highly critical terms, particularly on human rights issues. In October 1989, Havana hosted a meeting of journalists from socialist countries — the last one before the disintegration of the socialist community — representing Czechoslovakia, Bulgaria, East Germany, Hungary, Poland, Romania, the USSR, Mongolia, North Korea, and Vietnam, with Afghan and Nicaraguan journalists invited as observers. The Cubans made yet another unsuccessful attempt to influence their reporting. Cuban representative Julio García Luis called for basing relations between journalists' unions of the socialist countries on "mutual respect, solidarity, fraternity, loyalty, sincerity, tolerance, and support for everything positive that has been created." He spoke of the necessity of defining "a new ethic, which would consider unacceptable an exclusive or exaggerated use of Western sources when writing about events in a socialist country" and said it was "a sign of elementary respect to use, above all, the news sources of the country in question or of other socialist countries."[3]

Due to the Soviet Union's great popularity in Cuba, Castro had to do a considerable amount of explaining to his own party, government, and military cadres about why Soviet political and economic reforms were not applicable, in his opinion, in Cuba. Years before he started to criticize them publicly, he ordered the CPC Central Committee to prepare confidential analytical papers, for restricted official use only, setting forth arguments against following Moscow's example and stressing on differences between Cuba and the USSR in size, stage of economic and social development, history, culture, and traditions. The authors of one of these documents, which somehow found its way into the USSR Foreign Ministry's Latin American Directorate, pointed out, for instance, that while a decentralization of economic management could be an objective necessity in the Soviet Union with its immense territory and population, this was not the case in Cuba, where it was possible to manage the national economy efficiently in a highly centralized manner. As for *glasnost* and political pluralism, they were characterized as fraught with serious risks for political stability even in the Soviet Union and as steps that could be suicidal under Cuban conditions.

From our frequent meetings with Cuban officials in Moscow and Havana, we in the Latin American Directorate knew that Castro's arguments were not always convincing even to some members of the Cuban establishment. While the majority unflinchingly toed the official line, particularly in group discussions, some expressed sympathy with changes in the Soviet Union in private conversations and made critical remarks about the situation in Cuba. On one occasion, my Cuban interlocutor said, talking about the socialist system, that in Cuba it was called "sociolismo," not "socialismo" ("socio," in Spanish, means "business partner"). However, none of the Cubans could comprehend why the CPSU and the Soviet government allowed strikes in key industries that threatened to cripple the Soviet Union's national economy.

In addition to its political repercussions, *perestroika* was progressively undermining the Soviet Union's capacity to live up to its economic commitments to Cuba. Soviet economic reforms had limited severely the administrative powers of the government departments in charge of industry and foreign trade. A substantial part of these powers, including the choices of trading partners and export markets, was relegated to managers of state-owned enterprises who did not feel responsible for the Soviet government's foreign trade commitments and were becoming less responsive to sentiments of "class solidarity" with Cuba.

To Castro the only attractive features of Gorbachev's initiatives, judging by his speech at the Fourth Congress of the Communist Party of Cuba, were the Soviet government's draconian measures against "unearned income" and alcoholism. Homemade alcoholic beverages and intoxicating chemicals had killed thousands of people, increased private sugar consumption, increased the crime rate, and supplanted state sales of vodka, costing billions in lost revenue. The "unearned income" campaign enforced strict limits on the production and marketing of foodstuff by owners of private gardens, decreased supplies of provisions, and caused serious discontent within the population. Gorbachev's crackdown, which he later admitted was a serious mistake, corresponded with the spirit of Castro's "rectification of errors" policy and his decision to close peasant markets. *Pravda* reported at the time: "The struggle against negligence, irresponsibility, bureaucracy, and unearned income has become more acute.... Cuba's entire population approves of the strict measures taken recently with regard to embezzlers of the people's property."[4]

Cuban Rectification of Errors: Assessment in Moscow

Gorbachev's *perestroika* and Castro's "rectification of errors" campaign progressed in diametrically opposite directions. The undeclared purpose of Castro's campaign was to forestall or, if need be, eradicate any reformist ideas in Cuba prompted by the radical political and economic reforms in the USSR and Eastern Europe that could weaken

Castro's grip on power. The "errors" to be rectified were precursors of Gorbachev's reforms. Kosygin's improvements in economic management, including cost accounting, financial rewards for higher labor efficiency, and increased independence for state enterprises, were introduced in the USSR in the mid-1960s. They were transplanted partially to Cuba in the late 1970s only to become a target for public ridicule by Castro in the late 1980s.

In his speeches and interviews, Castro left no doubt that his principal reasons for initiating the rectification campaign were political and ideological. All other motives — higher economic efficiency, strengthening of discipline, and fighting against corruption — were secondary. The main fault he found with the elements of a market economy practiced in Cuba on the advice of Soviet experts was that they were breeding a "bourgeois mentality." His diatribes against private traders and "profiteers" echoed Lenin's postulate that petty private ownership constantly "gives birth" to capitalism on a mass scale. Castro argued that the introduction of market principles, starting in 1978, was a strategic mistake; whereas, earlier experiments with Guevara's ideas were "idealistic" mistakes of a tactical nature that did little damage to the "construction of socialism."

To get a clearer idea of the rectification policy "as yet another approach to the renovation of socialism," Moscow's *Latinskaya Amerika* magazine organized in Havana at the end of 1988 a round-table conference of Cuban economists to discuss the subject. Luis Suarez, director of the Center for American Studies in Havana, blamed the shift in Cuba to a system of economic management based on methods of self-accounting for the "negative trends [that] have spread to all spheres of the society, to political and ideological work." In his words, "dangerous ideological tendencies, which have begun to appear in the society, were the principal reason making the rectification necessary; [they led to] oblivion of voluntary work, an excessive attention to material stimuli, [and to] phenomena which were slipping from under the control of the party and state authorities." He also commented, "Surprisingly, already at that time Fidel foresaw a large part of the dangers, which were hidden in a thoughtless application of this system and came to the surface later." Another participant in the round-table conference, Helena Diaz of the University of Havana, argued that Guevara's ideas were "inseparable from Fidel Castro's thinking" and that Guevara had always emphasized "the necessity of struggle against the consumers' attitude to the economy, against the frame of mind which can appear in a socialist society if the formula for satisfying human needs ever more fully is followed blindly." To achieve that purpose, "we want to overcome individualism [but at the same time] to open fuller the individuality, best qualities of man, so that he would be motivated by a desire for the general well-being and not only for satisfying his own needs."[5]

Oswaldo Martinez, the department chief of the Center for American Studies, admitted at the roundtable that "a society of tramps and beggars cannot be considered socialist," but insisted that "it ill becomes us to waste ourselves, hunting the consumers' obsession of the West," and it was necessary, furthermore, "to take into account real possibilities." Martinez agreed that direct material stimulation and self-accounting could produce "quicker results" and facilitate economic development, but he thought it was necessary to take "the path that is probably longer but is more reliable." Martinez also said that Guevara "ceases to be a subject of formal worship and becomes an efficient factor of our life" and ventured the opinion that "internationalism" in Cuba's relations with the Soviet Union and other socialist countries was much more important than the "commercial aspect." To prove this point, he referred to the "road which we have traveled: from the internationalist partisan detachment in Bolivia to the internationalist army in Angola, which has been fighting successfully for the last thirteen years."[6]

To Soviet scholars, such a quasi-academic discussion reminded them of similar "debates" in the USSR before 1985, in which the participants did their best to excel in the interpretation and propagation of the "guiding ideas" of the leader, not daring to express any opinions which would contradict his. The roundtable in Havana only served to confirm the impression in Moscow that the main purpose of Castro's rectification campaign was not to reverse the increasingly negative performance of the Cuban economy during the mid-1980s but to eliminate the embryos of more reasonable and effective principles of economic management, which could eventually undermine the very basis of the command administrative economic system and totalitarian mentality, as happened in the Soviet Union. Reference to the Cuban "internationalist army in Angola" was also characteristic of Havana's set of priorities.

Indeed, it was known in Moscow that Castro was more interested in battles and skirmishes in Angola fought by Cuban troops than in the search for a solution to the economic problems of his country. When the maximum leader did occupy himself with domestic matters, he was more concerned with the ideological purity of the methods of economic management than with their performance. He was not unduly worried about a fall in industrial production — it would be compensated by a further increase in Soviet aid. To him, there was nothing wrong with one-quarter of the Cuban GNP being produced in the Soviet Union, where the population's living standards were lower than those in Cuba. It seemed that Castro did not realize the inherent dangers of this situation for the Cuban economy, to say nothing of its immorality. But then, the leader of the Cuban Revolution shared Guevara's belief that it was the "moral duty" of socialist·countries to give such economic assistance to developing nations instead of becoming "accomplices in the imperialist exploitation" by establishing normal trade relations with them.[7] Both Castro and Guevara believed that service to the common cause, which the Cubans were performing in Latin America and Africa, was much more important than "commercial aspects."

However, the worsening economic situation in Cuba did worry Soviet leaders and economic planners. They were beginning to lose hope that Cuba's economic performance would improve, making it less dependent on continued infusions of Soviet assistance. The USSR government was finding it increasingly difficult to sustain this aid economically and to defend it politically, particularly since Soviet leaders realized that the Castro regime did not show any disposition to abandon its dogmatic approach to problems of economic and social development and was not implementing the necessary reforms to solve its problems. Popular discontent in the USSR over the continued squandering of national resources for propping up this regime forced Soviet leaders to think of possible ways of reducing these expenses. The CPSU Central Committee apparatus and the USSR Foreign Ministry were directed to analyze the situation in Cuba impartially and report their findings.

The Problem of Honest Reporting

In the Soviet Union, there existed a long-standing bureaucratic tradition of presenting to the Politburo of the CPSU Central Committee only polished accounts of the political and economic situation in "fraternal" socialist countries. In fact, it was a logical extension of the unwritten rules, which guided the activities of local party bosses and government officials inside the USSR who were allowed to supply the CPSU leadership in Moscow only with "balanced" information on the state of affairs in areas of their responsibility, avoiding "extreme" negative assessments, which could be applied, by definition, only to the "decadent" Western democracies. Those who violated these rules risked being accused of "slandering the socialist reality." This tradition precluded the possibility of any Soviet diplomats supplying the Soviet leadership with accurate information on the economic situation in Cuba, including the inefficiency and waste of Soviet economic and technical assistance, the aims and consequences of the rectification campaign, and Castro's attitude toward reforms in the Soviet Union. This strict code of glossing over the truth called for presenting an "unbiased" picture of the Cuban Communist party making strenuous efforts to solve Cuba's economic and social problems, and of Castro objectively analyzing deficiencies in economic management and proposing proper steps to remedy the situation in the spirit of *perestrotka*. As for the Cubans' usage of Soviet aid, the Soviet embassy in Havana was expected, in its reports to Moscow, to emphasize the immense importance of Soviet assistance to Cuba and Soviet-Cuban friendship and cooperation and to mention only "certain defects," reassuring the Soviet leadership that everything necessary was being done to put things right.

Initially, that was exactly how the Cuban section of the CPSU Central Committee and the Latin American Department of the USSR Foreign Ministry tackled the problem of Castro's opposition to *perestrotka* and his obstinate determination to proceed in his own way. They presented a softened version of his attitudes and their implications for the rectification process, leaving room for moderately optimistic conclusions. But even that diluted picture contradicted enthusiastic reports dispatched to Moscow by the Soviet embassy in Havana. Soviet diplomats in Cuba relied exclusively on information from functionaries of the Cuban government and the CPC Central Committee and made no attempts to appraise Castro's policy or his stance on Soviet reforms critically.

Such bias was not unique to Cuba. In all socialist countries, Soviet diplomats limited their contacts to government and party officials. Making acquaintances in opposition or dissident political circles was taboo. Inevitably, their reports were overly optimistic. Furthermore, some Soviet ambassadors felt divided loyalties. They often established close personal links with the leaders of the respective regimes and received from them all sorts of perquisites and privileges, which were commonly provided in socialist countries for members of the party, government, and military elite and extended to selected ambassadors of socialist countries. As a result, they tended to associate themselves with the interests of the local leaders. They also understood that their success or failure would be judged in Moscow not on the merits of their diplomatic skills (none were professional diplomats), but on the record of the host country's leaders and the references of the latter to Moscow on their performance.

One could hardly expect anything different from Aleksandr Kapto, a professional party bureaucrat who rose to the position of second secretary of the Central Committee of the Ukrainian Communist Party in charge of ideology before he was appointed as Soviet ambassador to Cuba. He was known for his conservative, dogmatic views; he expressed misgivings about *perestroika*, believing that it contained more destructive than positive elements, as Castro did. Kapto filtered through to Moscow only positive evaluations of the situation in Cuba and admonished the embassy staff for draft reports critical of the performance of the Castro regime.

Mikhail Gorbachev, as secretary general of the CPSU Central Committee, and Eduard Shevardnadze, as foreign minister, tried to break this tradition of biased reporting. They undertook steps to ensure that Moscow had a less distorted picture of what was going on in the outside world. The CPSU Central Committee, government departments dealing with foreign affairs, and Soviet ambassadors abroad were ordered to report to Moscow nothing but the truth, no matter how unpleasant it could be. They were told that their recommendations had to be based on exact knowledge and objective analysis of the actual situation in the country concerned. However, it was easier said than done. For Soviet officials, particularly former party functionaries, changing their lifelong habits overnight was difficult; it was a slow process. What Moscow continued to get from Soviet embassies in "fraternal" countries was rarely the truth and never the whole truth.

Much depended also on the individual qualities of Soviet ambassadors. In 1988 Aleksandr Kapto was replaced by another party functionary, Yuri Petrov, who earlier had succeeded Boris Yeltsin as first secretary of the CPSU regional committee in Sverdlovsk (now Ekaterinburg), an important industrial center in the Urals. Only then could the Soviet embassy in Havana try to approximate honest reporting. Yet, these attempts were still halfhearted. Ambassador Petrov, who had a reputation as being a decent and straightforward man, was also a great admirer of Castro. He could not bring himself to debunk the myth of the wise, honest, selfless revolutionary leader who was successfully guiding his country against heavy odds to a brighter future. Petrov did his best to win Castro over to Gorbachev's side. He was genuinely disappointed when he realized the futility of his efforts. Petrov also found that, incredible as it seemed, Soviet diplomats in Havana were more isolated from the local population and less informed of the actual situation in the host country than their Western colleagues. There were few, if any, "unauthorized" personal friendships with Cuban citizens.

Moreover, the USSR embassy in Havana, like Soviet embassies in other socialist countries, was not only headed but also staffed mostly by former party or Komsomol functionaries with very few professional diplomats. The Soviet embassy in Havana resembled a regional party committee reporting on local party activities somewhere in the Ukraine or in the Urals more than a diplomatic mission. If a dispatch to Moscow admitted, for instance, that not all was well in Castro's kingdom and that substantive reforms were needed to improve the situation, it was interspersed with references to the "objective circumstances" that ostensibly made it difficult to implement such reforms, or, for that matter, to use Soviet economic assistance more effectively. Insistent prodding from Moscow was required to remind Ambassador Petrov and his staff that they were to provide information beyond that supplied by the Cuban officials and that they were also expected to evaluate the attitudes in different sectors of Cuban society toward rectification and Soviet *perestroika*, internal pressures for change, and the chances that Castro would accept necessary reforms.

With all that, Petrov's reports did arrive at some important conclusions: though Castro avoided for the time public polemics with Moscow, in his inner circle he was highly critical of *perestroika*, and he expressed strong reservations about it in contacts with Soviet representatives. It was also evident that Cuba's rectification policy was not quite compatible with Soviet reforms and that it was not likely to produce a solution to the problems of Cuba's stagnant economy. Serious changes in economic management and organization of labor were needed to generate more dynamic economic development, and something had to be done to ensure that Soviet assistance was used more efficiently by the Cubans so that they could rely more on their own resources and efforts. Ambassador Petrov recommended supplying the Cuban leadership with more detailed and authoritative information on the progress of Soviet economic restructuring and political reforms and intensifying the exchange of delegations between the two countries, particularly at the highest levels. He thought it was important to bring such information to Castro's attention and to influence his views on *perestroika*.

Gorbachev did not need Castro's approval and political support — he could well do without it — but it was thought in Moscow that to engage Castro in an in-depth discussion of Soviet reforms and, in the process, to convince him of their timeliness and expediency were the best ways to make him change his mind about what should be done with regard to Cuba's economic and social problems. The consensus in Moscow was that substantial changes on the "Island of Freedom" depended more on Castro's personal views and decisions than on any objective circumstances, such as U.S. policy toward his regime, although Castro himself disputed this point. It was also felt that any attempt to apply direct political and economic pressure on Havana to achieve the desired changes would be counterproductive. Moreover, the Soviets believed it was dangerous "to drive Fidel into a corner" because he could react unpredictably, and unwanted surprises had to be avoided, given Moscow's interests in Cuba.

Consequently, one had to persuade Castro of the necessity for such changes. The question was how? Soviet diplomats who were familiar with Havana's political scene and had watched Castro's behavior over the years thought that it would be a waste of time and effort to talk to his collaborators, since he no longer listened to their advice. On occasion, some of his closest comrades-in-arms frankly admitted, in conversations with Soviet representatives, that they were powerless to influence Fidel's thinking on a particular subject of interest to the Soviets and that it would be more productive if the Soviet leadership talked directly to him. Nor was it possible to do this through the Soviet ambassador, whom Castro increasingly ignored; for months Castro could not find time to listen to Petrov's detailed account of political and economic changes in the USSR. Gone were the good old days when the Soviet ambassador was Castro's favorite weekend companion and confidant. Therefore, Petrov's suggestion of more visits by high-level Soviet delegations headed by personalities of sufficient political weight and intellectual caliber was followed.

There were also hopes in Moscow that Castro would accept Gorbachev's standing invitation to visit the Soviet Union for some rest and recreation. Extending such invitations to the leaders of "fraternal" socialist countries and foreign Communist parties was a standard Moscow practice, which provided Soviet leaders with ideal opportunities to become better acquainted with them and to influence their thinking.[8] But Castro, who last came to Moscow for the November celebrations in 1987, refused to set even preliminary dates for another visit, despite declarations of his strong desire to familiarize himself personally with historic changes underway in the USSR. Instead, he insistently invited Gorbachev to come to Havana.

The Rift Widens

Meanwhile, high-level Soviet delegations came and went. Though there were long conversations with Castro, the results were disappointing. He was, indeed, changing his attitude toward Soviet reforms but for the worse, not for the better. As the reforms became increasingly radical and "revisionist," Castro abandoned his restraint and began castigating the Soviets publicly, ridiculing the idea of curing the ills of the socialist economy with "capitalist medicine." He launched a noisy propaganda campaign, praising Guevara's economic concepts as key to the solution of economic problems. These had been discredited and abandoned in the 1960s, after attempts to put them into practice had led to serious economic dislocation and a fall in industrial production. Guevara's economics were revived now to serve as a theoretical basis for the rectification policy — as an antidote against the *perestroika* virus. In essence, Guevara wanted to jump into "communism" when, according to Marx and Lenin, workers will be motivated entirely by moral stimuli, and Guevara emphasized industrialization — for which there were no resources.

To the Soviets, Guevara's views and Castro's diatribes against the notions of profit making as the main motivation of material production was reminiscent of Stalin's propaganda clichés that, under socialism, labor had become a matter of honor, valor, and heroism; workers should be motivated, first and foremost, by their desire to contribute to the wealth of the state; and production should be driven not by profits but be aimed at satisfying the constantly growing needs of the working people. To some veterans of the Soviet Foreign Service, who knew Guevara, this also recalled his own story of how, although a medic by profession, he had become the minister of economy in the Cuban revolutionary government. According to the story told by Guevara to his Soviet friends, when forming the government, Castro addressed a question to a meeting of his comrades-in-arms, "Is there an economist among those present?" Guevara did not hear Castro's words well and understood him to be asking if there were any communists in the room. Guevara raised his hand and was appointed minister of economy.

The close Soviet-Cuban relationship began to unravel. Apart from conceptual differences in resolving internal economic and social problems, divergences also developed regarding East-West relations; disarmament; regional conflicts, particularly in Angola and Central America; and North-South relations, including the problem of the Third World debt crisis. Growing political disagreements were exacerbated by negative trends in bilateral trade and economic cooperation. Both Moscow and Havana blamed "objective difficulties" for their failure to meet mutual trade obligations in full; each had its doubts as to whether the other side actually attempted to meet them.

It did not suit Castro's purposes to accept Gorbachev's thesis that Marxist-Leninists had no monopoly on truth and that they did not have all the answers to the pressing social and economic issues of the day. Castro still saw himself as the world's highest authority on the practical application of Marxist-Leninist theory for solving the problems of underdevelopment. He was not enthusiastic about Gorbachev's proposition that common interests of humanity had priority over class interests — Castro could find *no* community of interests with Washington. Contrary to Marx's dogma, Gorbachev theorized that world history did not, after all, boil down to a history of a class struggle that would eventually lead to the victory of socialism on a planetary scale. Castro saw this as a defeatist notion that did not help mobilize his people for the continuous struggle against U.S. imperialism. He saw no advantage to his regime in the termination of the Cold War and the end of the Soviet-American confrontation. More than ever, he was convinced that a further improvement of relations between the two superpowers would only increase Cuba's insecurity.

As for the regional conflicts, while the Cuban commander-in-chief did not object in principle to their political settlement, his insistence on applying added military pressure on UNITA and its South African allies in Angola and Namibia, on the Contras in Nicaragua, and on the Alfredo Cristiani government in El Salvador before such settlement could be achieved was obstructing progress in negotiations. Overriding Moscow's clearly expressed advice, Castro engaged in a brinkmanship policy. He sent more troops to Angola without prior notification of the Soviet government and positioned them dangerously close to the Namibian border. When Gorbachev reproached Castro for this action, Castro explained that he did not consult Moscow because he knew beforehand that the reply would be negative. He also set conditions for the withdrawal of Cuban troops from Angola, which were clearly unacceptable to the Republic of South Africa and its allies.

Similarly, from the start of the Contadora process of negotiations in Central America, Castro repeatedly cautioned Daniel Ortega against relying too much on the good offices of Latin American governments. He warned that they wanted to achieve by political means what the Nicaraguan counterrevolutionaries and Washington had failed to achieve by force. Castro's advice contributed to Managua's inconsistent and contradictory behavior, hampering progress in negotiations. The Cubans unequivocally refused to support the Esquipulas Agreement (established in 1987 as the procedure for achieving a long-standing peace in Central America), which was welcomed by Moscow without any reservations. Instead, they endorsed the position of the FMLN leaders, who declared that they did not consider themselves bound by the agreement. Havana's main objections were against its provisions on democratization and prohibiting external military assistance to irregular forces in Central America.

Castro was disappointed by Gorbachev's failure to support his pet project of persuading the developing countries to refuse payment of their debts to the industrialized countries of the North, which implied that their debts including Cuban debts to the Soviet Union and other socialist countries should not be paid either. Cuban officials in contact with Soviet representatives left hints that the Soviet Union would boost its prestige among the Third World nations if it took the initiative of canceling developing countries' debts to the USSR, thus putting effective political and moral pressure on the West to follow suit. In Moscow, even Castro's admirers shook their heads in disbelief, taken aback by the arrogant, provocative, and irresponsible nature of his proposal. The impression of Castro in the Soviet capital was that he had been carried away by his ambition to become the leader of the Third World.

To make things even worse, despite all of Moscow's assurances to Havana that political and economic reforms in the USSR would not affect its willingness and ability to continue giving the highest priority to economic cooperation with Cuba, in reality, that was exactly what was happening. Even before the falloff in the Soviet Union's industrial output, its compliance with economic commitments to Cuba was affected by the decentralization of economic management and the demonopolization of foreign trade. Soviet state-owned enterprises (except for those in energy resources and heavy and defense industries) were now free to market their products. If they had a customer in the West offering hard currency for their products, they refused to supply them to Cuba for "wooden pesos." The Cuban side lodged complaints.

In reply, Soviet officials offered explanations of the workings of *perestroika*. The Cubans were advised to negotiate directly with managers of the Soviet enterprises concerned, offering them, for instance, citrus fruits or the opportunities to spend holidays in Varadero.

There were grounds for serious Soviet grievances as well. For years, the Cubans carelessly wasted a substantial part of the Soviet-supplied material resources and made no serious efforts to increase their exports to the USSR. The trade imbalance was growing; despite increased sugar and oil subsidies, more Soviet credits were needed to cover it. According to Cuban calculations, in 1989 alone Soviet "sugar subsidies" to Cuba amounted to $2.5 billion and trade credits to $1.5 billion.[9] Castro publicly praised this abnormal practice as a model for economic relations between industrialized and developing countries, between the "rich" and the "poor." What irked Soviet officials, particularly those familiar with social conditions on the island, was that "poor" Cuba was able to offer its citizens better medical and educational facilities than could the "rich" Soviet Union. If a Soviet diplomat or technician on a mission to Cuba needed major surgery, he would use all his "connections" to have it done in a Cuban hospital with modern medical equipment imported from the West rather than go to Moscow in accordance with standard Soviet practice.

Soviet-Cuban relations became the subject of an intensive debate in Moscow among politicians, academics, and party and government functionaries. Serious doubts were expressed as to the wisdom and morality of continuing ideologically motivated, large-scale economic assistance to Havana in the midst of the deepening economic crisis in the USSR. Some Soviet parliamentarians, such as Dr. Nikolai Shmelyov, a well-known economist, were airing such views publicly. They demanded a halt to the "hidden" sugar-oil subsidies. New Cuban complaints followed. Soviet officials explained that due to the abolition of censorship of the mass media, the CPSU Central Committee and government agencies could no longer be held responsible for what was published by the press. This the Cubans found difficult to accept, since all newspaper editors and authors of critical materials were still card-carrying party members, subject to party discipline.

In the Soviet Union there was a consensus among the debate participants that steps should be taken to put Soviet-Cuban economic relations on a more equitable basis and to ensure the more effective use by the Cubans of Soviet aid. Proposals calling for the drastic reduction of this aid were rejected as "politically immature." Opinions were also divided as to how the transition to mutually advantageous trade with Cuba could be achieved: by unilateral actions or through negotiations with Cuba. Those in favor of unilateral steps believed that Castro would never agree to put Cuban trade with the USSR on a normal commercial footing unless he were forced to do so. But that would have involved the risk of affecting the political climate of relations with Havana, which Gorbachev was not prepared to take. The Soviets decided to opt for a gradual approach, talking first with Castro and then proceeding to negotiations at the expert level. Everyone agreed that if anyone could influence Castro's attitude at all, it would be Gorbachev.

Gorbachev's Visit to Cuba

Something also needed to be done to improve the political climate of Soviet-Cuban relations, which was increasingly affected by divergent internal processes in the USSR and Cuba and difficulties in bilateral trade and economic cooperation brought about by changes in the Soviet economic management system. Again, discussions on this subject revolved around the exclusive role of Castro in the formulation of the internal and foreign policy of the Cuban government. The conclusion was the same — Gorbachev's conversations with Castro were indispensable in order to dispel his forebodings about *perestroika* and persuade him to take a more positive attitude toward changes in the Soviet Union. It was even more important to urge Castro to exhibit more flexibility in his approach to the solution of Cuba's internal problems and introduce substantial changes into its policy toward the region. The confidential correspondence maintained between the two leaders was inadequate for this purpose. Gorbachev could only hope to influence Castro dramatically at a summit meeting, which would give them ample opportunities for informal, detailed discussions of the theoretical and practical problems of improving the socialist system. They particularly needed to discuss the pros and cons of socialism's economic performance, which were viewed and approached differently in Moscow and Havana.

Since Castro did not intend to travel to the USSR in the foreseeable future but repeatedly reminded the Soviet leader of his invitation to come to Havana, Gorbachev decided to visit Cuba officially. The visit was planned initially for December 1988, immediately following the Soviet-American summit in Washington. One of the arguments in favor of this timing was that President Gorbachev would be able to give

President Ronald Reagan prior information on his forthcoming visit to Havana and reassure him that it would not harm the interests of the United States in any way. On the other hand, the U.S. administration had to be informed that Gorbachev was not going to follow Washington's insistent advice — to use Cuba's dependence on Soviet economic aid as leverage to pressure Havana for democratic reforms. Nor was Gorbachev thinking of reducing, at Washington's prodding, Soviet-Cuban military cooperation.

Furthermore, care had to be taken to avoid offense to Latin American governments. The presidents of Argentina, Mexico, Uruguay, and Venezuela had traveled to Moscow in recent years and invited Gorbachev to pay return visits. Their invitations were accepted in principle, but the Soviet leader had no immediate plans to make such visits. To avoid giving the impression that the Soviet leadership's focus on implementing internal reforms and terminating East-West confrontation left it no time to think about the USSR's relations with the South American continent, it was decided to use Gorbachev's first visit to a Latin American nation for an authoritative announcement of Soviet policy in the region, to be formulated in light of new Soviet political thinking.

Soviet officials drafting policy papers for Gorbachev's visit to Cuba debated what its "political contents" should be. As already noted, there was no political treaty between the two countries. The documents signed during previous Soviet-Cuban summits were either joint communiqués and declarations on bilateral relations and international problems or agreements on trade; on Soviet economic, military, and technical assistance; and on bilateral cooperation in specific fields, such as science and technology, education, culture, sports, civil aviation, and maritime navigation. Since Cuba was the only socialist country that had not yet formalized its political relations with the Soviet Union, questions inevitably arose: Was it in our interests to have a political treaty with Cuba? If so, what should its scope and framework be? Will Fidel Castro agree to sign it?

Opponents of formalizing the Soviet-Cuban alliance doubted that a political, legal document would serve any positive purpose. They thought it would complicate Havana's relations with Washington and might weaken Cuba's position in the nonaligned movement. On the other hand, the absence of such a treaty had not proved to be an obstacle to the successful development of close friendship and cooperation over almost thirty years. In Moscow, this issue was highly debated: What is the point, then, of signing it now? Besides, there is no certainty that Castro would be interested. There have been no indications recently that it might be the case. And, if he does agree with the proposition in principle, he will most likely insist on including provisions unacceptable to the Soviets, such as a mutual military assistance clause. Wouldn't it be better not to run this risk?

Those in favor of a political treaty with Cuba argued that whatever the circumstances were that had prevented the signing of such a document in the past, something had to be done to keep Castro more in line with the new political thinking. If drafted appropriately, the treaty would help achieve that purpose. Otherwise, the widening political rift and increasing difficulties in bilateral trade and economic cooperation would complicate future Soviet-Cuban relations. As for the possibility that Castro would reject the proposition in principle or insist on provisions not acceptable to the Soviet side, this could be dealt with by arranging preliminary working-level discussions with Havana. If an acceptable document could not be agreed upon, the whole idea could be dropped without making it an issue.

The Treaty of Friendship and Cooperation with Cuba, drafted by the USSR Foreign Ministry and approved by the Politburo of the CPSU Central Committee, was modeled on treaties concluded by the USSR with socialist Vietnam and "progressive" regimes in Asia and Africa. The draft text reflected the fact that reforms in the Soviet Union at the time were still intended to democratize and restructure the socialist system in order to improve but not destroy it and were kept within the limits of the "socialist option." Accordingly, the draft preamble stated that the USSR and Cuba had decided to enter upon the treaty on the grounds of their "fraternal and indestructible" friendship and solidarity, based on their common ideology, the doctrine of Marxism-Leninism, internationalism, and identical objectives of constructing socialism and communism.

Article one of the draft spoke of the firm determination of the two countries to continue developing and improving their relations and to broaden the exchange of experience in the construction of socialism in political, social, and economic spheres, with due account of the diversity of specific conditions prevailing in each country. Article four stated that the Soviet Union and Cuba would contribute to the strengthening of relations of fraternal friendship among the socialist countries; improve and expand cooperation in all spheres, both bilaterally and multilaterally; and actively participate in promoting socialist economic integration pursuant to the resolutions of the Council for Mutual Economic Assistance.

The draft also contained standard provisions to develop and improve bilateral economic, scientific, and technical cooperation and trade and to promote contacts between state and government institutions and social organizations in the fields of science, culture, education, public health, press, radio, television, cinema, tourism, and sports. It set forth common positions of the two contracting parties on international political and economic problems. The latter were formulated intentionally in such general terms that both sides could subscribe to them even when their respective positions did not exactly coincide or even diverged. The Cubans, it was hoped, could support the formula that the two sides would continue working to reinforce peace, remove the danger of a nuclear war, ban the use of nuclear weapons and destroy their arsenals, destroy chemical weapons and other means of mass extermination, prevent the militarization of outer space, end the arms race, and attain general and complete disarmament under efficient international control.

There was nothing in the formulation of the draft treaty that could be interpreted, for instance, as relating to a nuclear-free zone or regional disarmament in Latin America, forcing Cuba to adjust its policy on these matters. Nor was there any mention of the Treaty on Non-Proliferation of Nuclear Weapons, which Cuba had refused to support. It was presumed also that Havana could endorse the obligation of the contracting parties to spare no efforts in making the principle of rejecting the use or threat of use of force a universal norm of conduct in inter-state relations, in fostering the settlement of conflicts between states solely by peaceful and political means, and in facilitating the political solution of regional conflicts through negotiations based on the recognition of the right of the peoples to self-determination and free choice of their political and social regimes without foreign interference. This language left out an important point: how were people throughout the region supposed to exercise their right to self-determination and to choose social regimes? Through democratic elections or by violent means through armed struggle?

The draft treaty had no clause on defense and security matters and no provision for bilateral cooperation or even consultations in this field, as were incorporated into similar treaties of friendship and cooperation concluded by the USSR with Afghanistan, Angola, Egypt, Ethiopia, India, Iraq, Mozambique, Somalia, and South Yemen. It just stated that the two parties: "...will continue to exchange views on important issues of mutual interest in order to enhance the interaction of the two countries in the international arena." That was the point on which, in the opinion of Soviet experts, Havana was most likely to raise objections.

Contrary to expectations, not only did the Cubans respond favorably to the proposition to sign a political treaty during Gorbachev's visit to Havana, but they also accepted the Soviet draft as a basis for discussion of the document, without submitting their own draft or suggesting any major, substantial changes in the Soviet text. Whether in spite or because of the dubious course Gorbachev's reformist movement was taking, Castro was obviously interested in formalizing Cuba's friendship and cooperation with the Soviet Union. He must have hoped that a formal political agreement would help carry this relationship through the difficult times to come.

The Cubans also agreed to the Soviet proposal to summarize the results of the Soviet-Cuban summit in a press communiqué, rather than to issue a joint political statement or declaration, as was the case in 1963 during Castro's visit to the Soviet Union and in 1974 during Brezhnev's visit to Cuba. This avoided the necessity of setting forth in detail in a political document the agreed positions on major international issues and regional problems, thus eliminating the inconvenience of publicly disclosing or confirming, by omission, the existing differences on some of them.

In the policy papers that Gorbachev took to Havana, his advisers had outlined the principal issues to be discussed with Castro: progress and difficulties in the implementation of economic and political reforms in the Soviet Union and Castro's failure to see the necessity of similar changes in Cuba, inevitable substantial revision of Soviet-Cuban trade and economic relations, more efficient use of Soviet assistance, and Havana's "special" position on a number of important international and regional problems, particularly in Central America. It was hoped that Gorbachev would find ways of telling his host some unpleasant truths, warning him of the adverse consequences of his dogmatic and inflexible posture.

However, Gorbachev had his own ideas about his mission in Havana that reflected the Soviet establishment's firm resolve to keep Cuba as a reliable political friend and a strategic asset in the game of superpower politics. Gorbachev shared with his Politburo colleagues an unwavering loyalty to the Soviet Union's ideological allies in Cuba and to Castro. In a telephone conversation with Gorbachev before the visit, Castro voiced his concern that, with its new political thinking, the Soviet Union might abandon its friends in the Third World. Gorbachev's immediate reaction was, "That will never happen. We do not forget that we have come out of the October Revolution."[10] He went to Cuba determined to strengthen Moscow's close political relations with Havana and see that the Cubans would not be harmed by disagreements on specific problems; he was anxious to avoid any steps that could confirm rumors that Castro would be "punished" for his stubborn behavior. For Gorbachev, it was particularly important to demonstrate that the reformed Soviet Union would never again attempt to bully its smaller allies.

That suited Castro's aims perfectly. He wanted Gorbachev to confirm Havana's right to continue its policy unchanged and to assure him that this would not damage Havana's privileged status in Moscow. Castro hoped to use the summit for cementing his country's political alliance with the USSR, presenting to the Cubans and the outside world tangible proof of its durability. It was also an opportunity to demonstrate his excellent personal rapport with the Soviet leader — a good defense against his critics at home and abroad — and to explain to him Cuba's economic woes and ask for the continuation of Soviet aid.

Mikhail Gorbachev, secretary general of the CPSU Central Committee, arrived in Havana on April 2, 1989; the visit was postponed due to an earthquake in Armenia. He was accompanied by Foreign Minister Eduard Shevardnadze, Secretary of the CPSU Central Committee Aleksandr Yakovlev, and Vice Chairman of the Council of Ministers of the USSR Vladimir Kamentsev. They were met at the Havana airport by Fidel and Raúl Castro — in what seemed to be a public demonstration of who was number two in the Cuban leadership and successor to the throne. Gorbachev's arrival evoked genuine enthusiasm from the Cubans. According to the Moscow Radio report from Havana, Castro said, commenting on the warm reception given to the Soviet leader by multitudes on his way from the airport, "Of course, we invited the people of Havana to this meeting. One can organize an invitation, but one cannot organize joy."[11]

In that, Castro was correct. But he omitted to mention a major reason for this spontaneous display of affection by the hundreds of thousands of Cubans who lined the route from the airport to Gorbachev's residence in the Cubanacán district of Havana. Many of them hoped that the visit of the man who had initiated revolutionary changes in the

USSR, designed to do away with some of the most odious aspects of the totalitarian socialist system, would persuade Castro to initiate a similar process in Cuba. They were to be disappointed, just as the Czechoslovaks and the East Germans were frustrated with Gorbachev's unwillingness or failure to influence the dogmatic hard-line policies of their communist leaders when he visited Prague and East Berlin.

When the talks began, Castro was visibly nervous. He apparently feared that Gorbachev would try to win him to his new creed, drawing him into discussing the polemics he wanted to avoid. He need not have worried. After the preliminaries were over, the Secretary General of the CPSU Central Committee asserted, "I am not going to impose on you my model. You can do whatever you think fit."[12] From then on, Castro relaxed. Both publicly and in confidential discussions, Gorbachev minimized the fundamental differences between Moscow and Havana over ways of improving socialism, dismissing them as just matters of tactics.

Moreover, Gorbachev echoed his host's main thesis in defense of the rectification policy, criticizing at the press conference past practices of "dogmatic copying" of Soviet methods by other socialist countries and emphasized that each country "solves the tasks of socialist transformation taking as its starting point its own conditions, the level of its development, its political experience, its traditions, [and] therefore, there is a difference in our methods, in those which are used by the Soviet Union or by the Cuban leadership." He even imparted to Castro's rectification policy the qualities of *perestrotka*, affirming, "Whatever methods we use and apply, one thing remains paramount: we are trying through these forms and methods to take people, the working people, into the arena of political and economic life as the main protagonists—through democracy, through new forms of management, through *glasnost.*"[13]

Castro's message was the same. He stated, in what was supposed to be a short introduction of Gorbachev to the Cuban National Assembly on April 5, 1989, "We do not have any disagreements with the Soviet Union, neither in international policy nor in regard to what each was doing in their own country [and] in essence, both sides and both parties proceed from the same principles, the principles of applying Marxism-Leninism in the specific conditions of each country." He went on enumerating the differences between Cuba and the USSR in territory, population, history, and problems they confronted, concluding his speech with references to the "firm defense by the new political thinking of the principle, according to which every country employs the formula suiting its conditions for the construction of socialism [and] ... absolute respect for the sovereign will of every people and every country — the golden principle of Marxism-Leninism."[14]

Castro saw fit to use the occasion to attack U.S. policies in Afghanistan, Angola, and Central America and spoke of the "task of all our peoples to struggle in the United Nations to ensure that imperialism respects the independence of Third World countries and the principles of noninterference in the affairs of other states." He also criticized the Brady Plan, which was intended to help solve the debt problem, as "yet another deception, a dreadful fraud" and confirmed his position that the only way to solve the problem of foreign debt in the Latin American countries and the Third World was its "100 percent reduction." While reasserting his "full support" for the new political thinking and the concepts set forth in Gorbachev's December 1989 speech before the UN General Assembly, Castro found it necessary to justify Cuba's defense efforts as proportionate to the "threat of U.S. aggression." In effect, he made it known that no matter what Gorbachev said in his speech, Cuba would not budge an inch from its present position on these matters.

Gorbachev began his speech to the National Assembly with effusive praise of the Cuban Revolution, which was led "by one of the most outstanding revolutionaries of the twentieth century, a man of legendary destiny [who] helped the tide of national liberation to reach unheard-of heights and came crashing down on the bastions of national oppression and humiliation." He assured the audience that the Soviet Union's solidarity with Cuba "is not subject to time-serving fluctuations" and stated that the Treaty of Friendship and Cooperation "seals what has already passed the test of time and opens up fresh vistas before Soviet-Cuban cooperation in politics, the economy, and culture."[15]

At the same time, Gorbachev's speech contained elements that could be interpreted as veiled warnings to Castro. Noting that he discussed at length with Castro "future prospects of the world and of socialism," Gorbachev said:

> Human civilization is at the crossroads. It is moving, as it were, from one phase to another. One cannot yet predict what its new image will be like. But one thing is already clear, namely, that today success will come to those who keep pace with the times and draw appropriate conclusions from the changes produced by the advent of high technologies and the decisive

role of science and intellectual effort.... We are confronted with a stark alternative. Either we continue moving down the old much-traveled track toward even greater stagnation and the economic, social, and even political dead end, with the ensuing risk of being pushed to the sidelines of progress, or we embark on an arduous but vitally important path of our society's revolutionary renewal, of imparting to socialism a new qualitative dimension that would meet the highest standards of humanism and progress.[16]

It was strong language. But Gorbachev substantially weakened the effect of his warning by saying, "We do not view our approaches and solutions as a universal remedy, [and our] problems may be similar, but each party tackles them independently, proceeding from its own ideas and distinctive features of its particular country." He also added that he fully agreed with what Castro said on this issue. When the Soviet leader reemphasized this point at the joint press conference, he was rewarded by a high compliment from Castro: "Gorbachev's wisdom lies in the fact that in coming to another country, he does not attempt to dictate what it should do. I am delighted with this."[17]

Despite these public mutual assurances, the talks between the two leaders at times resembled a dialogue of the deaf. When Gorbachev ventured the opinion that peasants should feel they are full owners of the land that they cultivate, Castro replied that small peasant farms were a form of slavery and rehashed Stalin's arguments that large collective farms were better suited to use modern, labor-saving machinery. He passed over in silence Gorbachev's statement that the CPSU intended to proceed from Lenin's understanding of the role of the party, meaning that it should provide political leadership, not take upon itself administrative functions, and implement its decisions through its members, elected into representative bodies of people's power.

Gorbachev also failed to move Castro from his entrenched positions on international and regional problems. The opposite occurred; he let himself be persuaded to support Havana's rigid stand on a peace settlement in Central America. In his speech to the Cuban National Assembly, Gorbachev announced that he and Castro had come to the conclusion that there existed a real chance to ensure peace and security in Central America and that one of the principal conditions for this was the cessation of military supplies to the region from any quarter. In effect, that made the suspension of Soviet arms deliveries to the Sandinista government dependent on the cessation of U.S.

military aid to El Salvador, similar to Castro's condition for ending Cuban assistance to the FMLN forces.

Clearly, the proposition was a nonstarter and had a purely propagandistic value. No one would expect the United States to suspend arms deliveries to the Salvadoran government before a peace settlement with the FMLN was negotiated. On the other hand, after U.S. military assistance to the Nicaraguan Contras was suspended, Washington felt it was entitled to a reciprocal step from the Soviets. The U.S. administration insisted that the USSR stop or at least reduce its arms shipments to Nicaragua and that Cuba comply with the provision of the Esquipulas Agreement, which called for an end to external military assistance to irregular forces in the area. Obviously, it was not in Castro's plans at the time to promote a peace settlement in Central America, but Gorbachev's acceptance of his position was not in correspondence with the Soviet Union's interest in such a solution and its public support for the Esquipulas Agreement.

Significantly, Castro abstained from commenting publicly on the new Soviet policy toward Latin America, as revealed in his guest's speech to the National Assembly. Gorbachev expressed support for "...enhancing the nuclear-free status of the region on the basis of the Treaty of Tlatelolco, the creation of a zone of peace and cooperation in the Southern Atlantic, and of similar zones in Central America, the Caribbean, and the waters of the Pacific off South America." Gorbachev announced that the USSR did not have and did not intend to have naval, air, or missile bases in Latin America or to deploy nuclear and other types of weapons of mass destruction there and called on other states "to take a similar approach in order to turn Latin America into a region of durable and stable peace and cooperation."[18] The Cubans obviously did not like such notions and continued to abstain from supporting the Treaty of Tlatelolco at the time, pointing to the presence of U.S. nuclear weapons in the Caribbean.

Castro's idea of completely cancelling the debts of developing countries was at odds with what Gorbachev proposed at the UN General Assembly session in December 1988. Moscow was in favor of an extended moratorium on debt repayments and was prepared to consider a total cancellation of debts only for the "least developed countries." In Latin America and the Caribbean, Haiti and, possibly, Honduras would have qualified for such benefits, certainly not Cuba. When asked at the press conference in Havana if the Soviet Union was prepared to cancel Cuba's debt, Gorbachev gave an evasive reply, saying that he had discussed these problems with Castro, and they agreed to continue their "consultations and joint analysis in order to take later concrete steps." He repeated his proposal for the establishment of a special UN body that would analyze the situation and suggest "realistic steps" to solve the debt problem.[19]

Speaking at the same press conference, Castro stated, "We are in favor of abolishing our debt to the Soviet Union. We have been wanting to abolish this debt for thirty years now." Then he affirmed that Havana never had any financial problems with Moscow: "From the very first years of this relationship, our loan repayments were either postponed or else the interest payable was simply canceled." He added that the USSR "has never refused us credits because of our debt." He also said that what Cuba was suggesting was "a general principle, and I believe the Soviet Union will likewise apply it universally."[20] A TASS report on the press conference in Havana misquoted the first part of this statement, giving the contrary impression that Castro denied he wanted to abolish the Cuban debt to the USSR. This added to some other inaccuracies in the report and led, together with *Pravda's* failure to publish in full Castro's introductory speech at the National Assembly, to complaints from the Cubans.

In his speech at the National Assembly, Gorbachev indicated that the Soviet Union intended to introduce changes in its economic relations with Cuba: "As life moves ahead, new demands are made on the quality of our interaction. This applies particularly to economic contacts; they should be more dynamic and effective and bring greater returns for both our countries, our peoples." Castro listened impassively. Later, it became apparent that this statement only strengthened his determination to delay, as long as possible, the Soviets' practical implementation of steps designed to put Soviet-Cuban trade on a normal commercial basis.

The detailed discussion of problems of bilateral trade and Soviet economic assistance was left to Carlos Rafael Rodriguez, the vice president of the State Council of Cuba, and Vladimir Kamentsev, the deputy prime minister of the USSR. There were no lofty words of "fraternal friendship and cooperation" and no pleasant talk, just a matter-of-fact, businesslike debate as the two went through a long list of claims and counterclaims. The main complaint of the Cubans was that Soviet foreign trade organizations, industrial enterprises, and agencies in charge of implementing technical assistance programs were too slow in meeting their commitments. In some cases, they refused to meet them at all. The Soviets were requested to rectify that situation.

Kamentsev cited numerous cases when Cuban state organizations failed to provide labor or building materials or both for projects constructed with Soviet assistance and failed to make sugar and nickel concentrate deliveries to the USSR on time. Referring to the Cuban complaints, he promised that the Soviet government would look into the possibility of using the system of "state orders" to industrial enterprises more extensively to ensure that they met their commitments to Cuba. Apparently, Kamentsev did not have any specific instructions to raise the problem of changing the terms of Soviet-Cuban trade, and he did not.

Overall, the much-trumpeted visit to Cuba by the CPSU secretary general left bilateral Soviet-Cuban relations much as they were prior to the summit. Castro went unpunished for his persistent efforts to put obstacles in the way of settling the Central American conflict. Gorbachev confirmed that Castro was free to continue with his anti-*perestroika* stance without fear of Soviet sanctions. There were, of course, limits to what Gorbachev could do to influence Castro's policy without openly violating the principle of nonintervention in the internal affairs of other states, but he could certainly avoid giving the impression that he accepted Castro's explanation of the rectification campaign as comparable to the changes in the USSR and aimed at achieving the same purpose of purifying and "renovating" socialism. Gorbachev smothered the difference between his aspiration to rid the socialist system in the USSR of its worst features and Castro's desire to perpetuate them in Cuba.

Gorbachev was less than sincere when he noted in his statement at the press conference that there was "a complete mutual understanding" between him and Castro. He hypocritically described Cuba as "a country with a fully developed political system, with accumulated experience in the solution of economic questions [that was] of tremendous significance for the whole world, but especially for the peoples who have embarked on the road of independent development, for the developing states." Gorbachev's conciliatory behavior during the visit and decision to sign the Treaty of Friendship and Cooperation with Cuba helped Castro convert what could have become a damaging confirmation of reports of serious disagreements between Moscow and Havana into a demonstration of their unity and his own political triumph. The summit strengthened Castro's hand both at home — in dealing with those who were trying to warn him against inviting Moscow's ire — and internationally, by dispelling the impression that the Soviet Union might be thinking of abandoning his regime.

Yet, for Castro, his triumph left a bitter taste. Discussions with Gorbachev strengthened his impression that events in the USSR were gathering their own momentum and were slipping out of the Soviet leadership's control. Gorbachev was extremely frank in describing to Castro the rapidly deteriorating economic situation and deepening social crisis in the Soviet Union. He dwelt in much detail on his political and economic reforms as the last chance to save the socialist system, to give it new life. From Gorbachev's exposition, Castro could have concluded that the Soviet leadership's freedom to maneuver was much more limited than it seemed. He must have wondered whether Gorbachev would be able to keep his promises of continued Soviet economic assistance to Cuba. Publicly, he wished Soviet *perestroika* well. Privately, he was now more critical of changes in the USSR than ever before.

The summit also had educational value for Gorbachev and his colleagues. They returned from Havana with first-hand impressions of Cuban realities, thus gaining a more sober assessment of Castro and his entourage. As a result, there were fewer expectations in Moscow that Castro would show more flexibility and would try to reform the system "from above." It became increasingly evident that unless more resolute steps were taken to reduce the economic burden of subsidizing the Cuban regime, it would continue indefinitely to sap diminishing Soviet resources. Seen in this light, the "long-term program of economic and technical cooperation with Cuba," approved by the Politburo of the CPSU Central Committee and intended to define the guidelines for Soviet economic relations with Cuba up to the year 2000, was hopelessly out of date and needed to be either revised or discarded altogether.

After reviewing the results of the summit, the Politburo instructed appropriate party and governmental departments to keep under special control and to review all matters relating to Cuba, presenting periodic reports and recommendations on the proper course of action. Economic ministries were directed to elaborate proposals that would put trade and economic cooperation with Cuba on a more equitable basis. They stipulated specifically that this should be done gradually to avoid excessive damage to the Cuban economy and to provide Havana with time for necessary adjustments. The CPSU Central Committee apparatus and the USSR Foreign Ministry were instructed to come up with recommendations on appropriate steps to be taken in order to ensure that problems in economic cooperation and political differences with Havana did not affect Soviet-Cuban friendship and cooperation.

In a survey on foreign policy and diplomatic activity of the USSR from April 1985 to October 1989, which Foreign Minister Shevardnadze presented to the Soviet parliament, Gorbachev's visit to Cuba was called "a milestone in Soviet-Cuban relations." According to Shevardnadze, "It demonstrated the commonality of the stands of the USSR and Cuba on the key problems of world development and a unified approach to changes taking place in the international arena under the impact of new political thinking."[21] In fact, the visit demonstrated just the opposite, but that was not to be mentioned in public.

Notes

1. *Granma*, December 18, 1991.

2. *New Times*, No. 41, October 19, 1987, 16-17.

3. *Granma*, International Edition, October 22, 1989.

4. *Pravda*, July 25, 1987.

5. *Latinskaya Amerika*, 1989, No.3, 41-55.

6. *Latinskaya Amerika*, 1989, No. 3, 41-55.

7. Tad Szulc, 1987, *Fidel: A Critical Portrait* (New York: William Morrow & Co.), 603.

8. At lower levels, this was done on a reciprocal basis. Each year groups of high Soviet officials spent their vacations in Cuba. Yuri Petrov, before his appointment to Havana, visited the island early in 1988 with a group of CPSU functionaries.

9. *Granma*, September 8, 1992.

10. The transcript of the telephone conversation is located in the archives of the CPSU.

11. FBIS-SOV-89-063, April 4, 1989, 34.

12. The episode was told by Mikhail Gorbachev in June 1990 to a Western leader to illustrate his point that Castro was not an easy man to deal with.

13. *Pravda*, April 5, 1989.

14. *Pravda*, April 5, 1989.

15. *Pravda*, April 5, 1989.

16. *Pravda*, April 5, 1989.

17. *Pravda*, April 5, 1989.

18. *Pravda*, April 5, 1989.

19. *Pravda*, April 5, 1989.

20. *Pravda*, April 5, 1989.

21. *Mezhdunarodnaya Zhizn*, January 1990, 74.

Chapter 5

Decline in Havana's Political Influence in Moscow

The period that followed Gorbachev's visit to Havana was characterized in the Soviet Union by rapid progress in the democratization of the Soviet political structure and further decentralization of economic management. Although the CPSU still remained, in accordance with Article six of the Constitution of the USSR, "the leading and guiding force of Soviet society, the core of its political system, state, and public organizations,"[1] other political parties were allowed, for the first time since 1918, to function legally and nominate their candidates in the elections to the Congress of People's Deputies. The Cuban embassy in Moscow was instructed to videotape the televised proceedings of the historic first session of the Congress in June 1989 for Castro's personal scrutiny. For him there was much to be worried about in what was said at the Congress. The "zone of criticism" was extended to include subjects that were still sacrosanct: a proposal was made to move Lenin's body from the mausoleum in Red Square to the Volkov Cemetery in Leningrad; the KGB was called an underground empire which had not yet yielded its secrets; the Congress formed a commission to assess legal, political, and moral aspects of the Ribbentrop-Molotov pact of 1939; and academician Andrei Sakharov characterized Soviet participation in Afghanistan's war as criminal.

In the meantime, Moscow viewed events in Cuba as developing increasing resemblance to some aspects of the Soviet past that were coming under public scrutiny and severe criticism as manifestations of Soviet totalitarian socialism. While the Congress of People's Deputies was laying the groundwork for the eventual self-destruction of this system, Division General Arnaldo Ochoa Sanchez, charged with corruption, moral degradation, and drug smuggling, was publicly confessing his "crimes" in Havana. Ochoa's trial was followed by the arrest and trial of Division General José Abrantes Fernandez, the interior minister, who was very close to Castro and was accused of "dereliction of duty, corruption and conniving with corruption, squandering state funds and their misappropriations, and the manipulation and concealment of information important to the state."[2] These unfortunate occurrences within the upper echelons of the Cuban military and government sounded all too familiar to the Soviets. In August 1989, Castro banned the distribution of Spanish editions of two Soviet publications, *Moscow News* and *Sputnik,* because they were accused of "casting doubts on certain aspects of Lenin's legacy and extolling bourgeois democracy and the American way of life."[3]

De-Cubanization of Soviet Policy on Regional Conflicts

The progressive erosion of the CPSU's previously absolute political and administrative power and authority and the growing criticism of its direct interference into affairs of state were bound to lead sooner or later to the shrinking of the communist ideology's role in the definition of priorities and formulation of Soviet foreign policy. There was a corresponding decline in the influence of the CPSU Central Committee apparatus in the foreign policy decision-making process. The USSR Foreign Ministry, which previously had largely performed the functions of a mere data bank and executor of instructions issued by the Politburo of the CPSU Central Committee, was becoming a generator of new ideas and policies. Foreign Minister Shevardnadze, while still careful not to make this new practice a subject of public discussion, encouraged his deputies and heads of departments in the foreign ministry to think and act independently, without waiting for instructions from CPSU headquarters on how to interpret and apply Gorbachev's "new political thinking."

Shevardnadze placed special emphasis on the importance of passing from general declarations about the Soviet Union's willingness to help negotiate settlements of regional conflicts to taking practical steps designed to bring this about. He stressed that in the formulation of specific policies, priority should be given to the long-term interests of the USSR and warned against yielding to the wishes of foreign ideological friends if they ran counter to these interests. He ordered a revision of Soviet positions on all regional conflicts and spoke in favor of cooperation to assist in their resolution, not only with friends but with all those who were prepared to contribute to a peace settlement.

For years this had been an area in which Castro exercised considerable influence on Soviet policy, as Cuba was involved (with Moscow's blessing) in regional conflicts in Africa and Central America and became leader of the militant group of developing countries with radical left-wing regimes. This militant group provided active political and material support to "national liberation movements" worldwide. The Cubans coordinated their strategies in the Third World with those of Moscow by way of direct contacts with the CPSU Central Committee, bypassing the USSR Foreign Ministry. It was all the more logical, since in Havana, too, all important foreign policy matters were the domain of Fidel Castro and the CPC Central Committee, not of Isidoro Malmierca Peoli and his Ministry of External Affairs. With the gradual transfer of this function in Moscow from the CPSU Central Committee departments to the USSR Foreign Ministry and with a new orientation of Soviet foreign policy toward compromise solutions of regional conflicts, Havana began to lose that influence through high party officials in Moscow.

Cuban loss of direct influence on Soviet foreign policy became apparent after Moscow, following its decision to withdraw Soviet troops from Afghanistan, embarked upon a course of businesslike cooperation with Washington in the settlement of regional conflicts, and Shevardnadze charged the relevant departments of the USSR Foreign Ministry with the task of analyzing situations and proposing specific policies on a case-to-case basis. After re-examining the situation in the Cone of Africa, as well as the respective positions and interests of the United States and the Soviet Union in the area, the Third African Department and the U.S.A. and Canada Department of the foreign ministry concluded that the interests of the two superpowers in Southern Africa were more coincident than conflicting. Hence, they surmised, it should be possible to cooperate with Washington in promoting political solutions to the internal problems of Angola, decolonization of Namibia, and dismantling the apartheid system in the Republic of South Africa. These considerations were approved by Shevardnadze and, on his recommendation, by the Politburo, making it the official Soviet policy in the region.

The Cubans were consulted following the standard procedure of discussing with them all matters affecting Havana's interests. However, this time their opinions on the "treacherous nature of U.S. imperialism" and warnings about the grave risks involved in trusting the promises of the South African government were politely ignored. They were told that Castro's linkage of the withdrawal of Cuban troops from Angola with the liquidation of South African apartheid was neither logical nor realistic and that, in any case, the Soviet Union firmly decided to join the efforts of U.S. diplomacy to bring peace to the area and saw no reason for postponing a negotiated settlement in Angola and Namibia. Havana balked and then insisted that Cuba should be invited to participate on an equal basis in the multilateral talks on the independence of Namibia. After some squabbling, Washington agreed. Faced with the prospect of continuing the Cuban military presence in Africa without Soviet political and logistical support, Castro reluctantly removed his objections against holding internationally supervised elections in Namibia and kept his promise to withdraw Cuban forces from Angola on schedule.

The Soviet Foreign Ministry used the same unbiased approach in trying to find ways of facilitating a negotiated settlement in Nicaragua. It came to the conclusion that, unlike the Reagan administration, the Bush administration, while not giving up its strategic goal of bringing about a change of government in Nicaragua, was prepared to accept a political solution. This was predicated on the conditions that the Sandinistas made true their declared policies of democratization, political pluralism, and mixed economy; agreed to hold internationally supervised presidential and parliamentary elections; reduced their armed forces; and stopped their assistance to the FMLN.

There were doubts in Moscow, however, as to whether the Sandinistas were really interested in a compromise solution, since it included the risk of losing political power through the ballot. They were still relying on force as the principal guarantee of their regime's survival. Despite the cease-fire agreement and the decision of the U.S. Congress to suspend military aid to the Contras, they showed no disposition to reconsider their long-term program of further military buildup. And, they also made it quite clear, in their contacts with Soviet representatives, that they would be prepared to continue the policy of democratization only as long as it did not interfere with the task of retaining power in their hands.

It was known that Daniel Ortega and his brother Humberto Ortega, the minister of defense, along with seven other "*comandantes* of the revolution" who composed the ruling junta of the Sandinista

National Liberation Front (FSLN), were receiving advice and counsel from Fidel Castro. Daniel Ortega regularly traveled unannounced to Havana to consult Castro on Nicaragua's political and economic problems and on strategy and tactics in peace negotiations. Humberto Ortega discussed with Raúl Castro and Cuban military advisers plans of military operations against the armed opposition and further strengthening of the Nicaraguan armed forces. "The Cuban factor" was an important part of the Central American equation that had to be taken into account and acted upon.

Evaluating this factor in one of its policy documents on the subject, the USSR Foreign Ministry noted that, while providing verbal support to the idea of a political settlement of the Central American conflict, Havana in its practical actions often contradicted the understandings reached by the presidents of five countries of the area, including Nicaragua. Such an attitude was causing a negative reaction on the part of the United States and its allies and, on a number of occasions, was putting Nicaragua and its friends, including the Soviet Union, in a delicate position. This complicated the process of normalizing the situation in the area and offered Cuba's adversaries additional arguments against the normalization of bilateral relations between the United States and Cuba.

The USSR Foreign Ministry further noted that the United States and Nicaragua's neighbors were particularly irritated by Havana's continued active support of insurrectional movements in El Salvador, Guatemala, and Honduras by supplying them with weapons and training commanding officers. Also noted was the Cuban leadership's failure to define its position publicly with respect to the documents approved by the five Central American presidents, which did not pass unnoticed in Latin America. Other governments in the Western Hemisphere interpreted the Cubans' actions as a desire to ensure they would be free to continue their policy in Central America. It was suggested that "the Cuban friends" should be persuaded to forsake their support of the armed struggle of the "progressive forces" in the countries of the region and transfer "the center of gravity" to peaceful political methods and participation in political processes, including elections.

This task turned out not to be an easy one. Moscow's attempts to convince Havana to support the negotiating process publicly, based on the Esquipulas Agreement and subsequent accords of the Central American presidents, failed. Instead, the Cubans insisted on the necessity of direct dialogue between the United States and Nicaragua and between the United States and Cuba. When consulted on new Soviet initiatives in Central America, the Cubans, more often than not, replied noncommittally, leaving it to the Nicaraguans to give a definite yes or no reply. This happened, for instance, when Moscow suggested to Havana and Managua that, in the interests of facilitating the negotiating process, the Sandinista government could declare a moratorium on arms shipments from the USSR. The Cubans said it was none of their business: "It's up to Managua to decide." Daniel Ortega gave a curt written reply — a flat "No."

Nonetheless, in October 1988, a decision was reached in Moscow, on the USSR Foreign Ministry's initiative, to suspend the delivery of heavy weapons to Nicaragua temporarily and to show restraint in the deliveries of light weapons. This decision was motivated by the suspension, since February 1988, of U.S. military aid to the Nicaraguan contras and by the consideration that in this situation Soviet arms supplies to the Sandinistas, particularly deliveries of heavy weapons, would negatively affect the formulation of the new U.S. administration's policy toward Nicaragua. The Soviets suspended heavy weapons deliveries to Nicaragua without informing Washington, Managua, or Havana to spare the Sandinista government embarrassment. As a result, no public political advantage was gained by the Soviet Union from the move, but it helped avoid considerable political damage, which would have been inevitable if Soviet arms deliveries had continued unabated despite the suspension of U.S. arms supplies to the contras.

When the Bush administration formulated its new bipartisan conciliatory approach toward Central America's problems and declared it was time for the United States and the Soviet Union to pass from confrontation in regional conflicts to cooperation in facilitating their political settlement, the USSR Foreign Ministry informed the Politburo that this presented an excellent opportunity for re-establishing peace in Nicaragua. After analyzing previous diplomatic exchanges with Washington on the issue, the situation in Nicaragua, and Havana's position, Soviet policy makers came to several important conclusions: 1) the suspension of U.S. military aid to the Contras was not Washington's propaganda exercise and made it practically impossible for them to resume major offensive operations in Nicaragua; 2) the Sandinista government already had more than sufficient Soviet arms supplies to keep the situation under control, and no additional supplies were needed; 3) continuation of Soviet weapons deliveries to Managua would only strengthen the hawks' influence in the Sandinista leadership and would be construed in Washington as proof of the insincerity of Moscow's declarations in support of a negotiated, political solution of the conflict; 4) Fidel Castro was not really interested in such a solution, and to achieve any progress in the Central American peace settlement, Moscow had to abandon the practice of making every Soviet action in the region dependent on previous approval in Havana and Managua. In May 1989, Gorbachev, without consulting Castro or Ortega, informed President Bush, "In order to promote a peaceful settlement of the conflict, bearing in mind that the attacks by the Contras' troops against Nicaragua have stopped, the USSR has not been sending weapons, since the end of 1988."[4]

Someone in Washington leaked the sensational news to the press, causing surprise and alarm in Havana and Managua. To calm these fears and explain the motives behind the Soviet move, Georgi Mamedov, as deputy head of the foreign ministry's United States and Canada Directorate,[5] and I, as head of the Latin American Directorate, traveled urgently on Foreign Minister Shevardnadze's instructions to Havana, Managua, and again back to Havana. There, we had to face the anger and suspicions of Cuban and Nicaraguan official representatives who questioned the wisdom of relying on the promises and goodwill of Washington. Jorge Risquet, Manuel Piñeiro, Sanchez Parody, and other high officials of the CPC Central Committee and of the Cuban Ministry of External Affairs insisted that Washington had always respected only force. In their opinion, the suspension of Soviet military aid to Nicaragua was putting the Sandinista Revolution at grave risk. They lectured us on the "predatory nature of American imperialists" who had never accepted and would not accept the Cuban Revolution, nor would they ever be reconciled with the existence of the Sandinista government, whatever the results of the elections, unless it capitulated under their pressure.

To increase the possibilities of influencing Havana and Managua toward supporting a negotiated settlement of conflicts in Nicaragua and El Salvador and to parry the Cubans' and Nicaraguans' reproaches about Moscow's failure to consult them before introducing substantial changes into its policy in the region, the USSR Foreign Ministry representatives were authorized to propose that tripartite consultations be held on a regular basis to coordinate the positions of the three countries on Central American problems. Managua's initial reaction to the proposal was positive, but the Cubans showed no enthusiasm for the idea, and it was dropped.

That marked the beginning of the liberation of Soviet policy in Central America from the strong influence of the Soviet Union's ideological allies in the region. The process advanced further during Shevardnadze's visits to Managua and Havana in early October 1989, which brought palpable results. Faced with the fait accompli of Moscow's moratorium on arms shipments to Nicaragua, the Sandinista government declared that it was prepared to suspend imports of arms until the February 1990 elections if the contras completely stopped their armed actions. Shevardnadze stated in Managua that the USSR was prepared "to maintain contacts with all parties in the conflict situation in Central America, with the states of the region among them, including those with which we have no diplomatic relations." He added that he was referring to both the Salvadoran government and the FMLN as well and suggested that the time was ripe for Moscow to consider the establishment of diplomatic relations with all Central American countries.[6]

Moscow did not consult Havana on these steps either. In fact, Shevardnadze was well aware that the Cubans would strongly disapprove of them: on various occasions before, the Cubans had made it known that the Soviet Union's official contacts with the governments of El Salvador, Guatemala, and Honduras, or even direct commercial transactions with these countries, would be premature, inopportune, and not in accord with the interests of the revolutionary movement in the area. The Cubans were incensed with the occasional contacts Soviet official representatives had with President Marco Vinicio Cerezo Arevalo and senior officials of the Ministry of External Relations of Guatemala from 1986 to 1989 and were not pleased with the cordial reception of Guatemalan and Honduran parliamentary delegations in Moscow. In particular, Cuban officials in Havana informed the Soviet embassy that my unofficial visit to Guatemala in February 1987, when I was still posted as Soviet ambassador to San José, my contacts with the government's representatives there, and interviews with local press and television explaining Gorbachev's *perestroika* and new Soviet foreign policy caused surprise and concern among the leadership of the Guatemalan guerrillas, as they perceived my actions were damaging to the interests of the revolutionary movement. (This information was duly passed to Moscow, and upon my return from Costa Rica in July 1987, I was asked by Vice Foreign Minister Komplektov to explain my behavior in Guatemala.)

The following day in Havana, Shevardnadze found that Castro already was well informed of his talks with Daniel Ortega in Managua.

Castro told Shevardnadze that Cuba was against suspending arms deliveries to Nicaragua and that the Soviet Union's decision could be justified only by the suspension of U.S. military aid to El Salvador, the position agreed upon during his last meeting with Gorbachev. Castro said it was not clear why the Soviet leadership had decided to change its position only a few weeks after this meeting, since the United States had not stopped supplying weapons to the Salvadoran government, to the armed opposition in Afghanistan, and to UNITA in Angola. Why then oblige Washington by suspending military assistance to Nicaragua? The Soviet foreign minister replied that the Sandinistas had enough weapons for the moment; they had reserved their right to receive more Soviet arms, if needed, and the Sandinista government would gain political prestige by announcing a moratorium on arms imports.

Castro was not convinced. Referring to the earlier Soviet-Cuban arrangement of transporting light Soviet weapons destined for Nicaragua first to Cuba for subsequent reshipment to Nicaraguan ports, he said that it would be up to the Sandinista government to decide what to do with Soviet weapons and munitions that had been promised to the Sandinistas and had already been delivered to Cuban ports. He added that the Cuban government was also fully entitled to supply Nicaragua with weapons originating from third countries. Shevardnadze, by way of commenting on these remarks, informed Castro about Secretary of State James Baker's complaint during Soviet-American talks in Wyoming that in 1989 the Sandinista government had actually received more weapons than before the Soviet Union's presumed suspension of arms deliveries to Nicaragua.

Discussing the situation in Nicaragua, the Soviet foreign minister was cautiously optimistic about the chances of the Sandinistas in the forthcoming elections but expressed concern about the deteriorating economic situation, which could affect the results of the elections. He said that Ortega's defeat would be a terrible blow to progressive forces — "worse than in Poland" — and that all possible measures should be taken to satisfy Managua's requests for additional economic assistance. He also told Castro about Baker's personal assurances that the Bush administration would accept Ortega's victory if the elections were "clean." Castro said that he shared these views and agreed that Washington would have no other alternative but to recognize the Sandinista government if Ortega defeated Chamorro. Castro thought, however, that even if Ortega lost the elections, not everything would be lost in Nicaragua because the Sandinistas would be able to maintain their control of the armed forces, since in Latin America the armies were "untouchable." In Chile when the democratically elected government came to power, it could not alter the army's high command.

Referring to El Salvador in his discussion with Castro, Shevardnadze complimented the FMLN leaders on their responsible, constructive negotiating position and noted, in particular, that Managua's statement about its willingness to suspend arms deliveries to the FMLN forces while negotiations with the Cristiani government continued to strengthen this position. But, he added, the Americans and others did not believe that the arms deliveries had been suspended. Castro replied that he was in favor of a political settlement of the conflict in El Salvador and blamed the United States for the lack of progress in negotiations between the two sides. He insisted that, since the U.S. administration continued its military aid to the Salvadoran army, Cuba had a moral right to render assistance to the FMLN forces when necessary and would not accept any unilateral obligation that would limit this right. Cuba would not turn its back on the courageous Salvadoran insurgents with whom it had been cooperating for many years. But, the FMLN no longer needed military aid from Cuba after having developed its own effective logistics.

Yuri Petrov, the Soviet ambassador in Havana, was adamant in insisting that Castro was telling the truth, but the next few weeks' events showed that Castro had intentionally misled the Soviet foreign minister. Moscow received information, not only from U.S. government sources, that Havana continued to send weapons and to train military personnel for the Salvadoran guerrillas. Moreover, there were grounds to suspect that the FMLN's November 1989 offensive in El Salvador and deliveries of surface-to-air missiles to the FMLN via Nicaragua were timed to coincide with preparations for the Gorbachev-Bush summit in Malta, scheduled for early December 1989. Consequently, a few days before the summit, Ambassador Petrov was instructed to ask for an urgent meeting with Fidel Castro to draw his attention, on behalf of the Soviet leadership, to the dangerous escalation of tensions in Central America and to the military confrontation in El Salvador, and to say that the Cuban and Nicaraguan friends should strictly observe their obligation not to transfer Soviet-supplied weapons to any other party without Moscow's consent.

Petrov also told Castro that whatever opinion he or anyone else might have of the process of negotiations in Central America, the negotiations were supported by Latin America, the United Nations, the Organization of American States, and the nonaligned movement. The

USSR regarded the Central American agreements as true opportunities to restrain the United States and establish peace in the region. The USSR was also in favor of more active participation in this process by such influential Latin American countries as Mexico, Venezuela, and, of course, Cuba. Petrov emphasized that all those who were interested in a speedy peace settlement had to define their stand clearly on this issue, for it was essential that the situation not be allowed to deteriorate to the point of endangering the negotiations. Petrov expressed Moscow's hope that Castro would accept these considerations with understanding.

Castro's reaction to the Soviet leadership's message was predictable: he professed no previous knowledge of plans for the November FMLN offensive and denied any Cuban involvement in the transport and delivery of Soviet surface-to-air SAM-7 missiles through Nicaraguan territory into El Salvador. This did not help his diminishing credibility in Moscow. It was one thing for Castro to dispute the Soviet position in confidential discussions by maintaining that the FMLN had to increase military pressure on the Salvadoran government to force it to negotiate peace or by affirming that the Bush administration was in no position to intervene in El Salvador militarily in order to save Cristiani's "crumbling puppet regime." But this time, Castro's response was an attempt to torpedo the Soviet policy in Central America. Supplying sophisticated Soviet arms to the FMLN was a clear betrayal of the Soviet policy in the area and of the widely supported negotiation process. Unable to influence this policy, Castro resorted to outright deceit, misleading Petrov and trying to dupe Gorbachev and Shevardnadze. Head of the Americas Department of the CPC Manuel Piñeiro (known by leftists throughout Latin America as "the Red Beard," in charge of coordinating guerrilla movements and communist parties' activities in the region) continued to insist in his frequent conversations with Soviet diplomats that, since the Salvadoran insurgents maintained an effective control over part of El Salvador's territory, they were entitled to a share of power even before any elections, and this could be the only basis for any peace settlement. Hence the necessity of increased pressure on the Cristiani government. As for the risk of direct U.S. interference in El Salvador, it was exaggerated in Moscow. The Cubans also implied that, in their opinion, we were giving Bernard Aronson, during Soviet-American consultations on Central America, too much information on the FMLN's position.

That was too much for the Soviets to take, even from Fidel Castro. During the November 1989 offensive in El Salvador, the USSR Foreign

Ministry proclaimed "a curse on both their houses." While denouncing the indiscriminate use of air power and artillery by the Salvadoran government forces, the Soviet Foreign Ministry also publicly criticized, for the first time ever, the FMLN offensives in densely populated urban areas. In February 1990, Shevardnadze accepted Baker's proposal, to express jointly the opposition of the United States and the Soviet Union to the use of any Central American state's territory for rendering assistance to irregular forces in the area and to support the Central American presidents' appeal that all states outside the region end military assistance to such forces. This formula, addressed clearly to Cuba, became a regular feature in passages of joint Soviet-American documents dealing with the Central American conflict.

In the meantime, the Sandinista leaders, who had succeeded in holding out militarily but were losing the battle economically, were confronted by a dilemma: either 1) hold on to power at any cost, even if they lost the elections, and resume fighting if necessary or 2) drastically change the course of their revolution and be prepared to accept a possible defeat, that is, to implement policies of political pluralism and a mixed economy. So far they had only paid lip service to these principles. The problem was debated in Managua and discussed by Daniel Ortega, Tomás Borge, other Sandinista leaders, and Castro and his lieutenants. The Cubans did their best to convince them that the actual alternatives were different: either 1) walk into Washington's electoral trap, relying on its false promises, and ruin any chances of saving the revolution or 2) continue to defend the revolution, demonstrating diplomatic flexibility but making no political concessions that would betray the revolution. Such arguments sounded convincing to Borge and his followers. Daniel Ortega, Henry Ruiz Hernández, and other "moderates" in the Sandinista leadership vacillated.

Echoes of these debates and discussions reached Moscow. In their conversations with Soviet representatives, both Cuban and Nicaraguan leaders and officials repeated the argument that the Sandinista government had already exhausted its possibilities of a political maneuver and that further concessions would lead to the loss of their "conquests of the revolution." There were even hints that Ortega might eliminate the institutions of "bourgeois democracy" altogether, by banning political opposition, nationalizing all private property, and announcing that the Sandinistas would build socialism in Nicaragua, converting the country into "an invincible fortress," parallel to Castro's actions in Cuba after the Bay of Pigs invasion failed.

The most frequent high-level Sandinista visitor to Moscow was Henry Ruiz Hernández, the minister responsible for procuring external economic assistance to Nicaragua. Vice Foreign Minister Viktor Komplektov spent hours with him, underscoring that further radicalization of the Sandinista Revolution would be suicidal and that the only viable policy included completing the electoral process, achieving national reconciliation, and normalizing relations with the United States. Komplektov did not mince words in explaining to Ruiz Hernández the real economic and political situation in the Soviet Union, which would soon force a substantial reduction in Soviet economic aid, including oil, to Nicaragua. He told him that the Sandinista government had to look for other sources of supply and make necessary policy changes in order to find them.

In a Soviet Foreign Ministry analytical document on possible future scenarios in Nicaragua, an opinion was expressed that the least desirable turn of events would be the Sandinistas' disruption of elections, at Havana's prodding, which would inevitably lead to a complete international isolation of the Sandinista regime and would entail a revision of the Soviet attitude toward the regime. That, in turn, would cause discontent among the Cubans, who viewed the prospects of national reconciliation and democratization in Nicaragua skeptically. The authors of the possible scenarios concluded that, taking into account substantial differences between Moscow and Havana both in the assessments of the internal political situation in Nicaragua and the approaches to the Central American settlement, the "Cuban factor" should be constantly kept in mind during the formulation of Soviet policy in connection with the Nicaraguan elections.

Fortunately for Nicaragua, the Sandinista leaders were not as obsessed with power and socialist dogma as their Cuban mentors and did not allow these sentiments to prevail over their common sense. They understood that for once the Soviet Union did not need, would not welcome, and would not support a socialist revolution in Nicaragua, nor, for that matter, in any other country unable to sustain itself economically, constituting an additional drain on Soviet resources. The Sandinista leaders also clearly saw that the transition of the Nicaraguan Revolution to a "socialist stage" would have led to further bloodshed, destruction, and economic ruin — a morass from which they wisely surmised their inability to escape.

In El Salvador, similar reasoning was gradually taking hold in the minds of the FMLN leaders, despite their close ties with and dependence on the Cubans. As far back as January 1989, Shafic Handal, the secretary general of the Salvadoran Communist Party, talked in Havana to Vitaly Vorotnikov, then chairman of the Presidium of the Supreme Soviet of the Russian Federation, who headed the Soviet delegation at the celebration of the Cuban Revolution's thirtieth anniversary. Handal admitted frankly that there was no chance of a socialist transformation in El Salvador. He said that no one wanted socialist revolutions that were not able to stand on their own and, although the FMLN continued to fight government forces, their purpose was not to take power but to pressure the Salvadoran establishment into substantial reforms to curb the power of the oligarchy and the military, creating conditions for a peaceful evolution toward democracy and social justice.

Another factor helped convince the Salvadoran guerrilla leaders to change their armed struggle's strategic goals and seek a negotiated settlement. Managua was increasingly reluctant to sustain further the FMLN command, communications, and logistical infrastructure in Nicaraguan territory. Ortega was under significant pressure from other Central American presidents and the U.S. administration to stop providing such assistance and support to the FMLN. Washington's strict condition for normalizing relations with the Sandinistas if they were to hold and win free elections, was for them to comply with the Esquipulas Agreement's provision banning the use of Central American countries' territory for supporting irregular forces in the area. At the same time, Havana kept reminding the Sandinistas that it was their revolutionary duty to continue to aid the FMLN. The dilemma became a subject of heated debates in the Sandinista leadership, as well as between them and the Cubans. One of the arguments that the pragmatists in Managua used to justify this concession to Washington was that it did not make sense to sacrifice the Nicaraguan Revolution, which had already become a reality, for a revolution in El Salvador that had not yet triumphed. Eventually, the FMLN leaders were informed that they would have to survive in the future without a major part of Managua's assistance.

This led to a serious rift between Managua and Havana. It widened further when President Ortega signed the Declaration of San Isidro de Coronado in December 1989, in which the five Central American presidents confirmed "their most resolute condemnation of armed and terrorist activities in the region by irregular formations" and expressed their "resolute support" of President Cristiani and his government, "demonstrating their invariable policy of supporting the governments established as a result of democratic, pluralist, and popular processes."[7] The declaration was interpreted by the Cubans and FMLN leaders as an outright betrayal. They sternly questioned Ortega, who made excuses and promised to furnish tangible proof of his continued solidarity with the Salvadoran guerrillas; after the suspension of Soviet arms deliveries, the Sandinistas depended on Cuban military supplies and had little room for maneuver.

With the end of the conflict in Nicaragua already in sight, a grave constitutional crisis erupted in Panama in May 1989. General Manuel Noriega refused to accept the electoral victory of Guillermo Endara, the opposition candidate. First, he tried to falsify the results of the elections, then canceled them altogether. Washington's sharp reaction to the establishment of an undisguised military dictatorship in Panama and an almost unanimous condemnation by Latin American governments of Noriega's blatant disregard for his country's constitution had severe repercussions in Nicaragua. Earlier, the Sandinistas had been pondering whether they should try to "correct" the results of the elections in Nicaragua if it became evident that Daniel Ortega were losing to Violeta Chamorro. Now, they had second thoughts about it.

Noriega's refusal to concede his electoral defeat led to U.S. economic sanctions against Panama and the political isolation of Noriega's government in Latin America and Western Europe. All this prompted him to seek military assistance in Havana and political support in Moscow, forsaking the traditionally cautious Panamanian policy of keeping contacts with the Soviet Union exclusively limited to commercial transactions. He informed Moscow that his government was prepared to establish diplomatic relations with the Soviet Union.

Panama, with its free trade zone, was economically important for the Cubans as the most convenient channel for bypassing the U.S. economic blockade. Foreign currency shops in Cuban tourist centers and hotels were stocked with goods brought mostly from Panama. It was also a convenient venue for Cuban intelligence operations. In 1982, Panama played host to a secret conference of representatives of Latin American insurgent movements, organized by the Cubans to coordinate their activities. Panama's conversion into a war zone was not in Cuba's interests. Yet, the prospect of dragging the United States into a protracted guerrilla war in a strategically important area was tempting to the Cubans. In addition, there were fears in Havana that a pro-American regime in Panama would cut off commercial relations with Cuba. Despite Noriega's past record of cooperating with the CIA and his scandalous involvement in the illegal drug trade, Castro decided to satisfy the general's request for arms and assistance in training the "dignity battalions." Havana advised Moscow to respond positively to Noriega's approach and establish diplomatic relations with Panama.

Opinions in the USSR Foreign Ministry were divided. There were voices in favor of giving political support to Noriega by accepting his offer and reacting strongly to U.S. pressures against his government. That would have complemented a commercial Soviet presence in Panama with a political one, a task that had eluded Moscow since General Omar Torrijos Herrera first allowed Soviet business representatives into the country. On the other hand, there were also fears that any strong political moves by the USSR toward Noriega would only serve to complicate Panama's relations with Washington further and to increase the probability of U.S. military intervention. Moscow decided not to follow the Cuban advice, rather, to limit Soviet reaction to the Panamanian crisis to expressions of disapproval of U.S. interference into the internal affairs of that country and to abstain at that stage from establishing diplomatic relations with the Noriega regime and from opening a Soviet consular office in Panama. (Moscow did not plan to open its embassy there in any case.)

The Sandinista agreement to hold free democratic elections under comprehensive international control made it easier for Soviet diplomacy to overrule Cuban objections to Soviet-American cooperation in Central America. The Bush administration proposed that the two governments agree to respect the results of free and fair elections in Nicaragua, to recognize the elected government, and to support its respect for democratic pluralism and human rights. Moscow gave Washington the benefit of the doubt and accepted the gentleman's agreement. It was incorporated into the Baker-Shevardnadze joint communiqué signed in Moscow on February 9, 1990. In fact, this was a mutual Soviet-American guarantee against the possibility of a breach in the rules of the democratic game in Nicaragua by the loser, whoever it might be.

There were still doubts in Moscow — the Cubans were doing what they could to strengthen them — as to the validity of Washington's promise to accept a Sandinista electoral victory, even if the elections were free and fair by American standards. The State Department insisted that a group of U.S. congressmen be permitted to observe the elections in Nicaragua. Yet, the Carter mission, including some members of the U.S. Congress, and UN observers were already in the country. This seemed to confirm Havana's view that the U.S. administration was looking for an excuse to declare the elections fraudulent or undemocratic and deny recognition to the Sandinistas, if they won. American press coverage of the electoral campaign in Nicaragua and Washington's strong reaction to Managua's refusal to allow official observers from the U.S. Congress into the country also contributed to these doubts.

The U.S. State Department, in turn, had serious misgivings about the willingness of Daniel Ortega to transfer power to Violeta Chamorro were she to win. It expressed concern that the Sandinistas would try to retain control of the armed forces and security service and obstruct the transfer of power or make it only partial. Assistant Secretary of State for Inter-American Affairs Bernard W. Aronson, with whom I met to prepare the Central American agenda for the Baker-Shevardnadze meeting, wanted to know how Moscow would react to such an eventuality and to a Sandinista appeal for the resumption of Soviet military assistance. Would Marshal Dmitry Yazov consider such a request from Humberto Ortega? I told Aronson that the Soviet government would deal with the elected government in Managua. Soviet arms shipments to Nicaragua could be resumed by a decision of the Soviet leadership if they were officially requested by the elected government and only if there were good reasons to justify the request. It was not Moscow's practice to defer decisions on such matters to the military. As for the possibility of Daniel Ortega clinging to power if he were to lose, there were no grounds to believe that he would do so, but if he tried he would not get any support from Moscow.

The Baker-Shevardnadze "deal" served to allay the fears of both sides and gave confidence to the Sandinistas that they would not be deprived of the fruits of an electoral victory. The Cubans were not convinced. They continued to suspect that Washington would not keep its word if Chamorro lost to Ortega and would either disqualify the elections or find some other pretext to justify U.S. refusal to normalize relations with the Sandinista government. Fortunately, Cuban consent was no longer a "must" for any important Soviet move in Central America; by that time, the USSR Foreign Ministry had definitively forsaken the traditional procedure of prior consultations with the Cubans on such matters. Policy papers on Latin American affairs submitted by the foreign ministry for the consideration of the Politburo were no longer required to have Havana's seal of approval.

When the results of the presidential elections in Nicaragua were announced and Daniel Ortega conceded his defeat, there were apprehensions in Moscow that Havana might try to use its influence in Managua to hamper the process of normal transfer of power to Violeta Chamorro. To be on the safe side, steps were taken to make it clear to both the Sandinistas and the Cubans that the Soviet Union was going to respect the results of the elections and would not condone any actions that would aggravate the situation in Nicaragua and lead to the resumption of hostilities.

Moscow-Miami Dialogue

On May 19, 1990, the Spanish news agency EFE reported, with reference to information to be published in the forthcoming issue of *U.S. News and World Report*, that a Soviet delegation was scheduled to visit Miami. It asserted that Moscow had taken note of the lessons of Eastern Europe and wanted to establish contacts with people who could be included in a new Cuban government that would replace the Castro regime if it fell. Alarmed officials in Havana instructed José Ramón Balaguer, Cuban ambassador in Moscow, to seek an urgent clarification from the USSR Foreign Ministry and to verify the information that the delegation included a foreign ministry official who was going to meet the leaders of the "anti-Cuban reactionary exile organizations." The Cuban embassy was told to ask the Latin American Directorate if there was any substance to the report and to express hope that the Soviets would avoid any steps not in correspondence with Soviet-Cuban fraternal relations.

I informed the ambassador that the report was only partially true. A Soviet nongovernmental delegation was scheduled to fly to Miami to participate in a Soviet-American conference called "Moscow-Miami Dialogue." The conference, which preceded the Bush-Gorbachev summit in Washington, would look at the settlement of regional conflicts in the context of Soviet-American cooperation. Soviet participants had no plans to meet with representatives of the Cuban exile community in Miami, but such a possibility could not be excluded if they were part of the U.S. delegation at the conference. As for my participation, I was invited to join the delegation at the request of the Americans, since the U.S. delegation would include Bernard W. Aronson, my counterpart in the State Department. It was not possible to cancel Soviet participation in the conference, because it was sponsored by nongovernmental institutions: the Soviet Peace Committee and the Institute of United States and Canada of the USSR Academy of

Sciences. The delegation included several parliamentarians who were not going to take orders from the USSR Foreign Ministry.

The next day, hours before the departure of the delegation, the Cuban ambassador sent the Latin American Directorate a letter in which he expressed regret about the conference in Miami and said he hoped that the USSR Foreign Ministry would reconsider sending its representative, since the Cuban counterrevolutionaries would use the Soviet diplomat's presence at the conference to confuse public opinion, and that would damage the interests of Soviet-Cuban friendship and cooperation. Simultaneously, a similar representation was made to the Soviet embassy in Havana. The Cuban request was discussed in Moscow at the highest political level. With Gorbachev's knowledge, it was politely declined. Gorbachev sympathized with Castro's feelings but shared the foreign ministry's opinion that this time Havana really had gone too far in attempting to dictate to the Soviets the composition of a Soviet delegation to a third country.

The Soviet delegation included well-known politicians, public figures, and journalists: Georgi Arbatov, a member of parliament and director of the Moscow Institute for U.S. and Canada Studies; Andrei Kortunov, the head of a section of the same institute; Genrikh Borovik, a member of parliament and president of the Soviet Peace Committee; Fyodor Burlatsky, a member of parliament and chief editor of *Literaturnaya Gazeta*; Nikolai Shmelyov, a member of parliament and economist; Vladislav Starkov, a member of parliament and chief editor of *Argumenty y Fakty*; Major General Kim Tsagolov, an adviser to the Soviet parliament; Sergo Mikoyan, the chief editor of *Latinskaya Amerika*; some other journalists and political analysts; and myself.

The "Moscow-Miami Dialogue" was organized by the Graduate School of International Studies of the University of Miami in conjunction with the Institute for U.S. and Canada Studies and the Soviet Peace Committee, with some support from the Florida business and Cuban communities. The U.S. delegation was led by Congressman Dante Fascell and included Wyche Fowler, the senator from Georgia; Lawrence J. Smith, a member of the U.S. House of Representatives from Florida; Jorge Mas Canosa, the leader of the Cuban American National Foundation; Spencer Oliver, chief counsel of the Foreign Affairs Committee, U.S. House of Representatives; Bernard W. Aronson, assistant secretary of state for Inter-American Affairs; Ambler H. Moss, Jr., dean of the Graduate School of International Studies, University of Miami; Sherwood Weiser, the chairman of Continental Companies;

Abel Holtz, the president of Capital Bank; Robert Ross, the president of Latin American Agribusiness Development Corporation; Robert Legvold, the director of the Harriman Institute for Advanced Study of the Soviet Union, Columbia University; Jiri Valenta, the director of the Institute for Soviet and East European Studies, University of Miami; and many other representatives of the academic and business communities of Florida and of the American press.

Inevitably, a substantial part of the debate at the conference was dedicated to Cuba and Soviet-Cuban relations. Representatives of the Cuban exile community who participated in the conference asked some sharp questions and criticized Soviet economic and military aid to Castro's regime. They protested my statement, as USSR Foreign Ministry representative, that the Soviet Union was rendering assistance to the Cuban people, not to Castro, and they did not like my assertion that since the Soviet government had abandoned its past practice of interfering in the internal affairs of other socialist countries, it could not press Castro for internal changes in Cuba. Academician Georgi Arbatov, speaking at the conference, did not mention Castro, but his allusion to him was transparent and was rewarded by the applause of the audience: "Too often the lip service to socialism paid by this or that dictatorial ruler has been considered enough of a reason for us to get involved, although the only positive sides of "socialism" for that type of ruler were a one-party system and totalitarian government."[8]

Assistant Secretary of State Bernard Aronson, while noting the Soviet Union's positive contribution to the peace settlement in Nicaragua, regretted the obvious contradiction between the basic principles of Gorbachev's "new political thinking" and the Soviet policy toward Cuba, which rejected them. He agreed with the thesis that the Nicaraguan settlement could serve as a model for the resolution of conflicts in El Salvador and elsewhere in Central America but was less hopeful about the Cuban problem, because, in his opinion, there was no will on the part of Moscow and Havana to cooperate in its solution, and there existed no rules of conduct and no institutional framework for negotiation. Unfortunately, neither *glasnost* nor *perestroika* seemed to be on the horizon in Cuba.

Jorge Mas Canosa expressed sympathy and understanding for the process of *perestroika* in the Soviet Union. He noted the convergence of interests between the reformed USSR and the Cuban exile community in the United States but rejected the argument that the new Soviet policy of nonintervention in the internal affairs of other countries had to be translated into the total lack of Soviet influence over the political situation in Cuba and called upon Moscow to withdraw its subsidies to Cuba. He noted that the USSR had not only the capacity to exercise its influence but also the responsibility, in light of massive Soviet military assistance to Havana, to ensure the peaceful nature of any transfer of power away from Castro.[9]

Apprehensions in Havana about Soviet participation in the Miami conference were justified. It did harm Moscow's friendship with Castro's regime. The episode added another dent in Soviet-Cuban political relations. After the Bush-Gorbachev summit, as the USSR Foreign Ministry representative who spoke with the leaders of the Cuban exile community in Miami and then joined Gorbachev's delegation in Washington, I was instructed to fly to Havana to inform the Cubans of the results of the Washington summit and the Miami forum. Carlos Aldana, then the secretary of the CPC Central Committee in charge of ideology, did not beat around the bush. "We know exactly what happened in Miami from our people there. Your participation in the Miami conference played into the hands of the enemies of the Cuban Revolution," he said bluntly. To substantiate this accusation, he had the videotape of the TV Martí news broadcasts on the proceedings in Miami played for my benefit. Ironically, like the Cuban exiles, Aldana had not appreciated my statement at the Miami conference that the Soviet Union was giving assistance to the Cuban people, not to Castro (it was on the videotape); he thought it was open to "double interpretation." He said that the Cuban side would consider the continuation of official Soviet contacts with leaders of Cuban exile organizations in the United States as "disloyal to Cuba and damaging to the friendship between the two countries."

I pointed out to Aldana that Havana itself should have an interest in dialogue with compatriots abroad. The Cuban exile community in the United States is very large, vocal, and plays an important role in the formulation of the U.S. administration's policy toward Cuba. Such a dialogue could help normalize Cuba's relations with Washington. Regardless of the opinion one may have of the exile groups' leaders, they claim to represent the interests of hundreds of thousands of Cubans. When a substantial part of a nation's population finds itself outside the country, its future depends to a great extent on the success or failure of the process of national reconciliation.

My arguments were brushed aside by Aldana as irrelevant. He insisted that the leaders of Cuban exile organizations in Miami had "criminal pasts" and "represented nobody." He said that there was no possibility of a dialogue with them: "The national reconciliation will be achieved but not with these people." And it will take time — in the USSR it took seventy years. "It is expected," he reiterated, in conclusion, "that the USSR Foreign Ministry will discontinue its contacts with counterrevolutionaries in Miami."[10] Not relying on the "loyalty" of the USSR Foreign Ministry, the Cubans used their influence in the CPSU Central Committee apparatus and in the Soviet academic community to torpedo the second part of the Moscow-Miami Dialogue, which was to take place in Moscow. Afterwards, the Soviet Peace Committee and the Institute for U.S. and Canada Studies said they had "financial difficulties" and could not offer hospitality to the U.S. delegation from Miami. The second part of the dialogue never took place.

Erosion of Castro's Prestige in the USSR: Ochoa's Trial

Yet, the harm to the Castro regime's image in the Soviet Union had already been done. Soviet journalists who were able to obtain for the first time first-hand information about the Cuban community in the United States wrote positive reports about the conference and the experiences and aspirations of Cuban exiles in the United States. They opened the eyes of the Soviet public to reasons for the mass exodus of Cubans from their motherland and for their hostility to the Castro regime. *Novosti* correspondent Mikhail Beliat wrote an article entitled "Dissipate My Doubts, Comrade Fidel!" in which he wondered whether two million Cubans who had fled from the island after the revolution "could all be counterrevolutionaries and criminals.... Wasn't there a much simpler explanation — that they were fleeing from injustice?" He noted that the majority of the Cuban exiles in Miami did not want Cuba to become an American protectorate again. They wanted to see it independent and democratic, with a well-developed economy.[11]

Moscow News carried an article by Aleksandr Makhov on the same subject, citing Jorge Mas Canosa as "the most influential leader of the Cuban diaspora,"[12] while *Izvestia* published an interview with Francisco J. Hernández, the president of the Cuban American National Foundation. Hernández stated that the conference in Miami was the fruit of the new political thinking displayed by both sides and that 90 percent of Cuban exiles in the United States favored the development of relations with the USSR. He added that they "were not hatching any plans of forcible action against Castro but believed that Cuba also needed reforms and political and economic *perestroika*."[13]

The "discovery" of Miami by the Soviet media helped destroy the Soviet myth of Cuban exiles as Batista's henchmen, landowners, and capitalists, serving U.S. interests. It further undermined another myth, that of the "Island of Freedom." As Aleksandr Makhov put it in his article quoted above, even a fleeting acquaintance with the "other Cuba" shattered many of the stereotypes that the Soviet people had become familiar with: "As we in the Soviet Union ripped the ideological blinders from our eyes, we realized that our friends were not better than we ourselves had been yesterday. Should we artificially prolong their period of stagnation?... We must start a large-scale reappraisal of all habitual relations with Havana, before it's too late."[14]

Even more damaging for Castro's prestige in the Soviet Union were the arrests and trials in Havana of political dissidents and human rights activists. Reported by the Soviet press without commentaries, they produced a depressing effect on Soviet readers as reminders of their own recent past. A particularly shocking impression was made by the bizarre trial of General Arnaldo Ochoa, which prompted recollections by many older-generation Moscovites of Stalin's macabre spectacles: the infamous Soviet trials of the 1930s, when Kamenev, Zinoviyev, Bukharin, and other "enemies of the people" were condemned to death after "confessing" their "horrendous crimes." The corresponding "confessions" in public court proceedings, similar accusations of "betrayal of the fatherland," and the same peculiar role of the defense were the salient features of the Ochoa trial.

Soviet Foreign Ministry officials (myself included) attempted to explain to José Ramón Balaguer and other Cuban diplomats in Moscow that the Cuban authorities, by persecuting political dissidents, were alienating public opinion in the Soviet Union from the Cuban government. I told Balaguer frankly that Ochoa's trial scenario was not convincing, and the minutes of the trial's proceedings, which had been distributed in Moscow in Russian translation by the Cuban embassy, were reminiscent of the volumes of proceedings of the Moscow trials of the 1930s. My words fell on deaf ears. It was obvious that whatever Balaguer's personal views were, he had to be careful about his reaction to the expressions of such sentiments. Rafael Mirabal, the minister-counselor of the Cuban embassy, who combined intelligence with integrity, did not return to Moscow after his sudden "vacation" in Havana. It was rumored that he was dismissed from the Cuban Foreign Service and expelled from the Communist party, presumably for being too outspoken in conversations with Soviet friends.

The officials of the Cuban embassy in Moscow were also told by Soviet diplomats that it would be politically difficult for the Soviets to go on supporting Cuba in the UN Human Rights Commission if political trials in Havana were continued. Minister-Counselor Carlos Trejo referred, by way of reply, to the high political price which Cuba had to pay for its public approval, for reasons of its "friendship and solidarity with the USSR," of the Soviet involvement in Afghanistan's war, although Castro thought it was a mistake and told Brezhnev so. (As a result, Cuba failed then to get sufficient support in the United Nations to be elected as a nonpermanent member of the UN Security Council).[15]

The implication was obvious: Havana was not going to change its behavior on the human rights issue, and Moscow was expected to continue demonstrating traditional "solidarity" with Cuba. In a different sense, Cuban diplomats in Moscow did not take such conversations lightly. On one occasion, Ambassador Balaguer even complained to Shevardnadze, asserting that a deputy head of the USSR Foreign Ministry Human Rights Department used "threatening language" when talking to the Cuban minister-counselor on matters related to the next session of the UN Human Rights Commission.

Failed Attempts to Weaken Soviet Support for Castro

By the end of 1989, the USSR Foreign Ministry analysts charged with the task of preparing recommendations on Soviet policy toward Cuba in light of Castro's obstructionist stand on the political settlement of regional conflicts and the oppressive nature of his regime came to the conclusion that Castro's Cuba was becoming more of a burden and an embarrassment than an asset to the reformed Soviet Union. They thought that, with growing social tensions on the island and Castro's obvious determination to use all means at his disposal, including force, to quell political dissent and not to allow the "restoration of capitalism," it would be unwise and irresponsible to continue feeding the voracious Cuban military establishment and maintaining the Soviet military presence on the island. As for the Soviet military presence, it was becoming increasingly irrelevant in any case due to the rapidly changing nature of Soviet-American relations. Something definitive also had to be done about Castro's disregard for human rights.

Accordingly, interdepartmental discussions on the subject were initiated, and attempts were made to formulate and submit for the consideration of the Politburo of the CPSU Central Committee proposals designed to reduce the scale of Soviet military cooperation with Cuba. It was proposed, in particular, to cancel the programmed delivery of the MiG-29 fighter bombers to Cuba and to consider the withdrawal of the Soviet combat brigade from the island. To strengthen the case, it was pointed out that the delivery of these modern combat planes, which had been planned years ago in the midst of the Cold War, was unnecessary under present conditions and could only produce a negative reaction in Washington. Their delivery would no doubt be interpreted as provocative and in conflict with Moscow's declared new policy toward the United States.

In deliberations within the USSR Foreign Ministry, arguments also were advanced that, with our changed attitude toward the human rights issue, it was illogical and immoral to continue supporting Castro's archaic treatment of this problem as Cuba's internal affair of no concern to the outside world. We felt it was necessary to criticize his policy of persecuting political dissidents and human rights activists. It was suggested that the Soviet representative on the UN Human Rights Commission in Geneva should be instructed to stop acting like a counsel for the defense in the Cuban case and, instead, Havana should be warned of the increasingly negative effects on Soviet public opinion of continuing human rights violations in Cuba, which could have dire consequences for Soviet-Cuban relations.

Such views and propositions were still regarded as heresy by more orthodox Soviet communists, particularly among the military and CPSU Central Committee personnel. For them, the notions of "proletarian internationalism" and "solidarity with the Cuban Revolution" retained their full value. To counter our proposals, the orthodox communists offered arguments that had been used repeatedly in the past to justify the "give-them-all-they-need" Soviet policy toward Cuba, such as, "Cuba is our only true friend and ally in Latin America; we have invested too much in Cuba and cannot afford to lose it; we should not succumb to U.S. pressures; the Soviet brigade should be kept in Cuba to give protection to the Soviet Communications Center at Lourdes which strategically is very important to us; and Fidel would be offended if not consulted and would complain to our boss. If consulted, he will not agree." The last argument was probably the most effective. The bitter experience in the aftermath of the Cuban Missile Crisis, when Anastas Mikoyan had to spend weeks in Havana trying to placate Castro's anger over Khrushchev's decision, made without first consulting

Fidel, to withdraw Soviet missiles from Cuba was still remembered sharply in Moscow.

As a result, the Soviet Ministry of Defense agreed to postpone only temporarily the deliveries of MiG-29s but declined the idea of canceling them altogether and rejected the proposal to consider the withdrawal of the brigade. At the UN Human Rights Commission in Geneva, the delegates of the USSR and Ukraine voted, as in previous years, against the resolution criticizing Cuba. Gorbachev's refusal to condemn political repression in Cuba was characterized by *Moscow News* as "the last manifestation of the double standard." A spokesman for the USSR Foreign Ministry tried to justify this position by references to the "confrontational nature" of the Commission's debate on the Cuban case and Cuba's "active cooperation on human rights with the United Nations."[16]

However, later in the year, Castro was not so accommodating when Gorbachev tried to sway him to support, in the UN Security Council, the use of force against Iraq. During their meeting in New York in September 1990, Eduard Shevardnadze and Isidoro Malmierca, the Cuban foreign minister, agreed in their assessment of Iraqi behavior and of the need to work for a political solution but disagreed on the specific sanctions against the aggressor. Malmierca insisted that the UN Security Council's approval of a resolution permitting the use of force in order to compel the aggressor to withdraw from Kuwait could prove "counterproductive." To persuade Castro to change the Cuban pro-Iraqi position in the Security Council, two high-ranking officials of the USSR Foreign Ministry, Georgi Mamedov and Valery Nikolayenko, were sent to Havana at the end of November 1990 as special representatives of the Soviet leadership. They carried Gorbachev's personal message to Castro with assurances that the Soviet Union would continue to be alongside Cuba and that, despite economic difficulties, Soviet-Cuban cooperation would continue. Their efforts were to no avail; Gorbachev's emissaries failed in their main mission. Castro preferred to side on this issue with Soviet "left-wing conservatives," who criticized Moscow's "unholy alliance" with Washington against the "progressive" Iraqi regime. Gorbachev's influence in Havana was definitely on the decline.

Debates in Moscow on Cuba's Future

Events in Eastern Europe and particularly in Romania inevitably posed the question: Was Cuba next on the list? The subject was debated not only in Washington and Miami but also in Moscow and among members of the Soviet leadership and officials of the CPSU Central Committee, the Soviet Foreign Ministry, and the KGB, in the academic community, and the press. The Soviet embassy in Havana was asked to assess the internal political and economic situation on the island, and the conclusions were fairly optimistic: Ambassador Petrov thought that, although the economic crisis was bound to be further aggravated, Castro's determination not to succumb to outside pressures, his continuing popularity in Cuba, and an effective Cuban state security apparatus precluded the repetition there of anything similar to what had happened in the East European socialist countries.

The longer-term prognosis of probable future developments in Cuba, elaborated in the USSR Foreign Ministry's Latin American Directorate, contained several scenarios. They all had one common ingredient: the conclusion that Castro was not likely to change his policy radically, although such a possibility could not be discounted completely, given his proven political maneuvering ability. One scenario contemplated Castro's relinquishing some of his present party and government positions, voluntarily or under pressure from his immediate entourage, in order to open the path to change. Another scenario envisaged his removal from power as a result of a military coup. Civil disturbances leading to a popular insurrection also were considered possible. It was noted that Castro's popularity was not as high as it had been and that discontent was spreading among Cuban intellectuals, party and government officials, the military, and particularly the younger generation, many of whom were influenced by the events in Eastern Europe and the Soviet Union.

In the Soviet press, academics and journalists also debated Cuba's political future. *Izvestia, New Times* magazine, *Argumenty y Fakty, Literaturnaya Gazeta, Komsomolskaya Pravda,* and *Moscow News,* all active supporters of Gorbachev's *perestroika,* ridiculed Castro's dogmatic intransigence. In March 1990, *Argumenty y Fakty* published an article entitled "Cuba: Difficult Path Toward Socialism" by V. Borodayev and G. Levykina, in which they noted:

> Far from everyone in Cuba agrees with the policy of its government.... There are supporters of reforms of the Soviet or East European type. It is no secret that many hundreds of thousands of Cubans have in the past decades "voted with their feet" for capitalism, having emigrated to the United States.... The living standards of the population are declining.

Unemployment has appeared.... An analysis of Cuba's development in recent years persuades us that the old methods of directing the country's economic and social life are exhausted.[17]

Andrei Kamorin, *Izvestia*'s correspondent in Havana, cited in his article "What is Fidelism?" the devastating words of Roberto Luque, a Cuban dissident, about Castro:

This is my truth: Fidel must go, since it is essential for the fatherland's survival. He must go, for no deal, no serious negotiations, no reconciliation are possible with him; for his consciousness comprehends only the language of violence. He must go, because he has gotten stuck in the way of the entire nation, like a fish bone in a starving man's throat, because it is necessary to reform the invented nonworking economic system which he created in his own image and likeness, and, consequently, its reform signifies self-negation for him. Because this system can only exist with Soviet subsidies, and the USSR cannot cope with its own irrational and inefficient economy while fattening ours. He must go, because his personal interests run counter to the nation's interests.[18]

The publication in the Soviet press of such harsh judgments on Castro would have been unthinkable a year earlier.

On the other hand, conservative *Pravda, Krasnaya Zvezda, Selskaya Zhizn, Sovetskaya Rossiya,* and *Trud* defended Castro's "road to socialism." Pavel Bogomolov, then vice president of the USSR-Latin America Association of Friendship and Cultural Ties, published a panegyric on Castro, "The Leader of the Nation," including:

In 1986, a new stage began in the history of Cuba — the process of rectification of mistakes and elimination of negative tendencies. Although the process is complicated, it is interesting and promising, a symbol of renewal before our very eyes.... The Soviet-Cuban summit meeting in Havana was probably remarkable in that M.S. Gorbachev and F. Castro have something in common these days.... The Soviet people believe in Cuba, the first country in the Western Hemisphere to choose the socialist path of development.[19]

Krasnaya Zvezda, expressing the opinions of the Soviet military establishment, also asserted that Soviet *perestroika* was "in the main consistent with the Cuban leadership's determination to intensify the role of the human factor in the solution of all problems, including economic ones."[20] Sergo Mikoyan, writing in *Moskovsky Komsomolets*, affirmed:

> I accept that Cuba has fallen behind us as far as the development of democracy is concerned (although not long ago it was ahead of us). Nevertheless, there is no doubt that Fidel Castro would have won in any referendum, even if in the cleanest and freest one. Of course, there is much to be desired in Cuba in the sphere of political freedoms and economic development, but things there are not so terrible as presented by the adversaries of the Castro regime.[21]

Latinskaya Amerika magazine, reflecting the views of its editor Sergo Mikoyan, Viktor Volsky, and other pro-Castro experts on Cuban affairs, also devoted a substantial amount of space to publicizing the "achievements" of the socialist regime in Cuba and justifying its rigidity by the ever-present threat of U.S. intervention. In January 1990 in Moscow, the magazine organized a round-table discussion on "totalitarianism, authoritarianism, and democracy," in which the Cuban totalitarian regime was not even mentioned as such by the participants, except for Dr. Marina Chumakova of the Institute for Latin American Studies. She referred to it as "a left-wing authoritarian regime" and stated, with regret, that as far as such regimes were concerned, "we do not, as a rule, touch upon the observance of human rights, political and civil freedoms," and if this subject were ever brought up, it was in the context of the "intrigues of imperialism, intended to destabilize progressive governments."[22]

For the majority of Soviet Cubanologists, Castro's revolution was still a "sacred cow." Not surprisingly, *Latinskaya Amerika*, while publishing serious and objective analytical articles on the situation in other Latin American countries, held the orthodox line with regard to Cuba and devoted its pages to publicizing Castro's views. In January 1990, it published without commentary excerpts from Castro's program speech of December 7, 1989, in which he stated that his government "banned without hesitation certain Soviet publications spitting venom at the USSR itself and socialism," that socialism could not be improved "by rejecting the most elementary principles of Marxism-Leninism," and that in Cuba "the revolution, socialism, and national independence are indivisible."[23]

On the whole, however, despite the efforts of Castro's propaganda machine and of his high-ranking, influential supporters in Moscow, the Soviet press coverage of Cuban realities was becoming increasingly unfavorable to Havana. The insistent popular demands to curtail economic assistance and trade subsidies to Cuba could no longer be safely ignored. More Soviet parliamentarians wanted to know if there were any good reasons to continue such massive support. Appropriate government departments were directed to give reasons for the support and presented arguments that the USSR was dependent on Cuban sugar, nickel, and citrus fruits. In public and parliamentary debates, they abandoned political or ideological rationales, though these motives — that Cuba was a socialist country and the only one in Latin America — were still the most important considerations for the CPSU and Soviet government hierarchy and were used in interdepartmental and academic discussions.

To improve his regime's image in the eyes of the Soviet public and to help its protectors in Moscow find some substitute for the depreciated arguments of "common ideology" and "solidarity with the Cuban Revolution," Castro came up with the disingenuous idea of using the advantages of Cuba's tropical climate and well-developed medical and recreational facilities for making effective humanitarian gestures, which were bound to win a great deal of sympathy for Cuba in the Soviet Union. Groups of Soviet children from areas affected by the Chernobyl nuclear catastrophe and injured Soviet veterans of the war in Afghanistan were invited to Cuba for recreation and medical treatment. Although that initiative generated some controversy in the Soviet press, it was repeatedly used by Castro's sympathizers in Moscow as one of the main reasons for continuing friendship with Cuba.

Notes

1. *Konstitutsiya (Osnovnoy Zakon) Soyza Sovetskykh Sotsialisticheskykh Respublik,* 1978, Moscow: Politizdat, 7.

2. *Pravda,* August 2, 1989.

3. *Pravda,* September 8, 1989.

4. *Time,* June 4, 1990, 39.

5. Russian vice foreign minister.

6. *Pravda,* October 6, 1989.

7. *The Miami Herald,* June 12, 1990.

8. *U.S. News and World Report,* May 28, 1990, 23.

9. Institute for Soviet and East European Studies, 1990, Occasional Papers Series, Volume III, No. 4 (Coral Gables: University of Miami Graduate School of International Studies), 22.

10. Aldana's conversation with the author in Havana in June 1990.

11. Mikhail Beliat, 1990, "Dissipate My Doubts, Comrade Fidel!" *Sputnik* (Moscow), No. 11, 9-11.

12. Aleksandr Makhov, *Moscow News,* September 21-26, 1990.

13. *Izvestia,* December 15, 1990.

14. Aleksandr Makhov, *Moscow News,* September 21-26, 1990.

15. Trejo's conversations with the author in Moscow in February-March 1990.

16. *Moscow News,* March 19-25, 1990.

17. *Argumenty y Fakty,* No. 11, March 17-23, 1990.

18. *Izvestia,* June 29, 1990.

19. *Selskaya Zhizn,* July 26, 1989.

20. *Krasnaya Zvezda* (Moscow), May 8, 1990.

21. *Sputnik,* No. 11. 1990, 16.

22. *Latinskaya Amerika,* No. 2, 1990, 57-61.

23. *Latinskaya Amerika,* No. 2, 1990, 42-44.

Chapter 6

Cuban Lobby in Moscow

Castro Sounds a Bell

When I accompanied Shevardnadze on his visit to Havana in October in October 1989, I had the rare opportunity to hear Castro's views on the situation in the Soviet Union and Eastern Europe. He did not conceal his alarm about the electoral defeat suffered by the Polish communists, and the political developments in other East European countries that were undermining the foundations of their socialist regimes. Castro wondered why, whenever there was a change of government in socialist countries, the new leaders did their best to discredit their predecessors. He also wanted to know more about steps taken by the Soviet leaders to resist similar "destructive" political trends in the USSR and talked forcefully about the ever-present threat of U.S. intervention. Castro asked, "What will be Cuba's place in this world? We have no doubts about your policy and applaud your successes, but why does the United States think of peace only with the Soviet Union and does not guarantee peace to such countries as Cuba?" To make his point clear, he added, "How would you feel in Moscow if you had, immediately to the north of the Soviet Union, a hostile superpower with a population twenty-four times greater than that of the USSR?[1] Shevardnadze did his best to calm his fears, but Castro was not reassured.

Events that followed soon after Shevardnadze's visit to Havana confirmed Castro's misgivings. Marshal Sergei Akhromeyev, who visited Cuba in January 1990 as Gorbachev's unofficial emissary, found Castro and his entourage in a dejected mood. In his report to Gorbachev on the results of his visit, Akhromeyev wrote that Castro and other Cuban leaders understood the objective necessity of *perestroika* in the USSR, but they were worried by the profound nature of social changes and the speed of the restructuring. They were also concerned by the failure of Soviet authorities to take measures provided by law in a number of cases when anti-socialist forces openly defied the social and state order, in particular in Transcaucasia and the Soviet Baltic republics. The Cuban leadership hoped, nonetheless, that "given the revolutionary vigor and the consciousness of the Soviet people, the proficiency and staunchness of the CPSU, and the secure guarantees against the external threat, the Soviet Union will cope with *perestroika*."[2] The reference to the "secure guarantees against the external threat" had a special meaning. Gorbachev's emissary went on to relate Castro's oral message which continued as follows:

> The Communist Party of Cuba is using, depending on circumstances, the experience of *perestroika* in the Soviet Union, but it is not possible today to implement profound reforms in Cuba — the military situation around the country is becoming more complicated, and we should be constantly prepared for armed provocations on the part of the United States and should not exclude the possibility of a direct American armed invasion of Cuba.

That was, in effect, a confirmation of Castro's refusal under a seemingly convincing pretext to embark on a program of democratic reforms in Cuba. It also contained unsolicited friendly advice to Gorbachev to get tough with the "anti-socialist forces" — counsel Gorbachev apparently immediately tried to follow (or else coincidentally had already decided to do) in Lithuania where Soviet troops took the Vilnius television center by assault. They carried out similar military operations in the Latvian capital, Riga — another unfortunate coincidence, and also in Georgia's capital, Tbilisi, where the use of Soviet troops had tragic consequences, just days after Gorbachev's visit to Havana in April 1989.

Be that as it may, Castro was not sitting idle, waiting passively for his worst premonitions to come true. He was actively trying to set Gorbachev on the course of saving what still could be saved of the "foundations of socialism" in the USSR, and he kept his fingers crossed. Addressing the Congress of the Federation of Cuban Women in March 1990, Castro blasted Cuba's East European friends (Bulgaria, Czechoslovakia, Hungary, and Poland) for their vote in the UN Human Rights Commission in favor of the resolution condemning Cuba. He said that they were "behaving in a way similar to the Yankee empire, the enemy of mankind," but he drew a clear distinction between them and the USSR:

> The Soviet Union has not fallen into the hands of counter-revolutionaries, and let us hope that it doesn't. The Soviet Union has not disintegrated, and let us hope it does not. No civil war has started in the USSR, and let us hope none does, although the real threat exists, a real threat.[3]

This particular passage of Castro's speech caused surprise in Moscow at a time when even the die-hard Soviet conservatives were not thinking in terms of unleashing a civil war in defense of "socialist values." Obviously, Castro extrapolated his own stand on the issue, "socialism or death," thus giving yet another piece of advice to the defenders of the socialist cause in Moscow.

For Havana, the most important task was to ensure that Moscow kept Gorbachev's pledge to Castro, given before the 1989 summit: "Whatever the changes in the Soviet Union, Soviet-Cuban relations will remain unchanged. There will be no difficulties."[4] Castro's principal preoccupation was that Gorbachev would succumb to internal political pressures combined with those of Washington and would follow the example of East European countries by terminating special treatment of the Cuban regime—they had ended trade subsidies and condemned violations of human rights on the island. Hungary and Poland had already proposed to the Council for Mutual Economic Assistance that all trade among CMEA countries, including Cuba, be put on a normal commercial footing and based on world market prices. Cuban representatives in CMEA protested vehemently against the proposal.

Since the Cuban economy depended largely on Soviet subsidies to function, preserving Cuba's "fair" economic relationship with the Soviet Union became an obsession with Castro. Talking to Shevardnadze in October 1989, Castro expressed his indignation with the Polish-Hungarian proposition that CMEA countries should introduce world market prices into trade among themselves and said that for Cuba "it would be a catastrophe." He asked Shevardnadze to something about it. Castro repeatedly aired this subject publicly, starting with his speech on December 7, 1989, when he expressed outrage at some Soviet publications' demands to end

> ...equal and fair trade relations that have taken shape between the USSR and Cuba in the course of the Cuban revolutionary process [and to] change over to unequal trade with Cuba, i.e.,

charge ever-higher prices for its wares and beat down the prices of our farm products and raw materials — exactly what the United States is doing to the Third World countries — and that the USSR should eventually join the American blockade of Cuba.[5]

Castro reiterated this thesis in his speech in Havana at the Sixteenth Congress of the Trade Union Center of the Workers of Cuba in January 1990. Calling the USSR policy toward Cuba "magnanimous," he argued that if Cuban sugar was sold at higher prices than in the "world garbage pit," the prices were nonetheless fair, "because in this way an end has been put to inequitable trade relations." In his opinion, Soviet policy toward Cuba was also "mutually advantageous." He saw two dangers for Cuba, stemming from changes in the USSR: one from the economic difficulties there and another from trends within the Soviet Union "which are undoubtedly connected with reaction to imperialism and which campaign openly for relations of this kind to end." Elaborating further on the subject, he added that people (in the USSR) who represented these trends were "not in the government and not in the party, but in the mass media and in parliament."[6]

Gorbachev's Efforts to Help

This was not just wishful thinking. President Gorbachev and the head of the USSR government, Nikolai Ryzhkov, were still determined to continue economic assistance and price subsidies to Havana, despite the political pressures at home and Washington's linkage of U.S. economic and technological aid to the USSR with the termination of Soviet material support of the Castro regime. After his meeting with President George Bush in Malta in December 1989, Gorbachev reported to the USSR Supreme Soviet that "the winds of the Cold War" still prevailed in the U.S. position on relations with Cuba. He assured Soviet parliamentarians that the Soviet Union continued to maintain "fraternal relations of cooperation with Cuba."[7]

Disregarding internal economic problems and popular sentiments against squandering material resources on politically motivated aid to ideological friends, Soviet leaders continued to drag their feet on the practical implementation of the USSR's declared intention to change the nature of economic relations with Cuba. They kept postponing the introduction of world market prices into Soviet-Cuban trade, although Cuba's East European trade partners had already done so in accordance with the decision of the CMEA session in Sofia in February 1990.

The influential "Cuban lobby" in the Soviet Union was not limited to former Soviet ambassadors in Havana who came to occupy high positions in the CPSU Central Committee and the government, such as Vitaly Vorotnikov, member of the Politburo of the CPSU Central Committee; Konstantin Katushev, the minister of external economic relations; and Aleksandr Kapto, the head of the Ideological Department of the CPSU Central Committee. The Cuban lobby also included innumerable Soviet government officials, party functionaries, journalists, army generals and officers, factory managers, and experts, who at one time or another had spent months or even years in Cuba. Among them were Marshal Dmitry Yazov, the defense minister; Karen Khachaturov, the chairman of the Soviet Committee of Solidarity with the Peoples of Latin America; Sergo Mikoyan, the editor of *Latinskaya Amerika* magazine; Oleg Darusenkov, the head of the Cuban section of the CPSU Central Committee; Aleksandr Kachanov, the first vice minister of external economic relations; Dmitry Venedictov, the head of the Cuban section of the State Commission on External Economic Relations; Viktor Volsky, the director of the Institute for Latin American Studies; and Pavel Bogomolov, a *Pravda* columnist. They were able to influence decisions on many matters related to Cuba and news coverage of Cuban affairs by the Soviet media.

The conservative majority of the Politburo and Secretaries of the CPSU Central Committee, Oleg Baklanov, Vladimir Kryuchkov, Yegor Ligachev, Ivan Polozkov, Nikolai Ryzhkov, Oleg Shenin, and others, shared Castro's ill feelings about the radical course *perestroika* was taking. In their opinion, "excessive" *glasnost* and democracy were endangering socialism in the Soviet Union and needed to be checked. Ligachev sounded exactly like Castro, when he stated in an interview with *Argumenty y Fakty* in October 1989: "We have no need for private property.... Socialism has a colossal potential. It cannot be improved by methods of capitalist economy.... Socialist democracy can develop quite well within the framework of a one-party system."[8] Ivan Polozkov, the first secretary of the newly formed Russian Communist Party, the main stronghold of the defenders of socialism, expressed similar sentiments.

Soviet conservatives were in favor of retaining the Communist party's monopoly on political and economic power and propagating the re-establishment of "order and discipline" in the Soviet Union. They rejected the notions of political pluralism and mixed economy. In their opinion, re-establishing order and discipline was much more important than guarantees of individual liberties, "unbridled" freedom of expression, and other paraphernalia of "bourgeois democracy." Their political program coincided on a number of major points with Castro's rectification policy. The Soviet conservatives wished Castro well in his firm stand in defense of the socialist system of government and communist monopoly on political and economic power and could not have cared less about the violations of human rights in Cuba. In that sense, they all belonged to the "Cuban lobby."

When Julio Camacho Aguilera, the Cuban ambassador to Moscow and member of the Politburo of the CPC, complained to Yuri Solovyev, then the first secretary of the Leningrad CPSU Regional Committee, that the U.S. ideological services attempted "to use their country's proximity [to Cuba] for their subversive aims," the latter replied that similar attempts to "preach bourgeois values and Western morality" were also being made against the Soviet Union.[9] This community of ideological interests continued to exist until August 1991. It found its expression in the USSR Foreign Ministry's statement on April 6, 1990, that the Soviet Union condemned the beginning of TV Martí broadcasts to Cuba and regarded them as a violation of international law and "interference in Cuba's internal affairs through subversive actions and the use of international radio frequencies in violation of existing international convention."[10]

Added to this, the powerful Soviet military establishment still highly valued Cuba as the only strategic Soviet outpost in the Western Hemisphere. During decades of the most extensive military cooperation, close ties had developed between Soviet officers and the Cuban military. Some generals and colonels of the Soviet General Staff exploded when foreign ministry officials tried to talk them into supporting the idea of the withdrawal of the motorized brigade from Cuba.

I made this very suggestion, to withdraw the motorized brigade from Cuba, to Lieutenant-General Nikolai Derbentsky in a telephone conversation. He fumed, "What do you think you are suggesting? Our forces are being driven out of Eastern Europe, abused in the Baltic republics, Tbilisi, and Baku, and now you want to withdraw them from Cuba? Isn't that too much?" After this emotional outburst, the general gave me a lecture on the U.S. military bases still surrounding the Soviet Union, on the absence of reciprocity on the part of the United States, and the inadmissibility of unilateral disarmament.

It was a poorly kept secret in Moscow that the Cubans had files on all Soviet party and government leaders, parliamentarians, officials, and public figures whose opinions could affect Havana's interests. They divided them into three categories: 1) true friends of the Cuban Revolution who always could be counted on to do what they could to help Cuba, 2) those whose loyalty to Havana was weakened by *perestroika* and the new political thinking but could still be useful, and 3) people who had never been Cuba's real friends and had become staunch opponents of the Cuban Revolution. The Cuban embassy in Moscow was charged with recommending what could be done to win over the waverers and neutralize the opponents. The usual practice was to invite "promising" Soviet politicians, public figures, and officials to Varadero "for rest and recreation," combined with some official business in Havana; the cold shoulder was given to those who were "hopeless cases."

Mikhail Gorbachev, Aleksandr Yakovlev, Eduard Shevardnadze, Vadim Bakatin, Yevgeny Primakov, and other reform-minded members of the Soviet leadership fell into the second category; none of them were unfriendly or hostile to Castro, although they could not be pleased with the more odious aspects of his policy and the difficulties they created for the USSR's relations with the United States. They all shared the notion that, while the Soviets should persist in their efforts to correct Castro's internal policy and his regional behavior and to introduce changes in Soviet-Cuban economic cooperation, the USSR should also continue to provide the Cuban regime political support and economic and military assistance. As for the transition to more equitable economic relations, it was necessary but should be gradual to avoid excessive damage to the Cuban economy.

These were the instructions given to Vice Chairman of the USSR Council of Ministers Leonid Abalkin when he went to Havana in April 1990 as head of the Soviet delegation at the Twentieth Session of the Soviet-Cuban Intergovernmental Commission for Economic, Scientific, and Technical Cooperation. He was also directed to explain to Castro the necessity of elaborating a practical program of putting bilateral trade on a normal commercial basis. The session was preceded by difficult negotiations on the problem of increasing the efficiency of Soviet-Cuban cooperation; the Soviet side won some important positions. During the session itself, the Cubans were pleasantly surprised when Abalkin gave away these positions without receiving anything in return. He signed a protocol on Soviet-Cuban trade and payments for 1990, which provided, unrealistically, for an increase in the volume of bilateral trade of over 8 percent compared to 1989. Speaking at a press conference in Havana, Abalkin expressed his confidence that "with the correct organization of matters," this growth could continue right up to doubling the scale of Soviet-Cuban economic cooperation.[11] As for elaboration of the program, of making it advantageous not only for Cuba but also for the Soviet Union, the two sides decided to set up a special working group for the purpose.

We in the Latin American Directorate were surprised when Leonid Abalkin, the reputedly gifted Soviet economist, was charmed by Castro. Abalkin sent a very optimistic report from Havana to Moscow on the results of the work of the Commission and about his long conversations with Castro, who succeeded in convincing him of the virtues of his economic and social policy. He was impressed with "construction contingents" and moved by Castro's offer to receive up to ten thousand Soviet children annually who suffered from the Chernobyl nuclear plant catastrophe[12] and five hundred Soviet veterans of the war in Afghanistan for recreation and medical treatment. According to Gennady Sizov, the press officer of the Soviet embassy in Havana, on the eve of Abalkin's arrival, Fidel Castro decided to meet him at the airport and attend all meetings of the Commission, making it necessary to revise the original schedules of the Soviet delegation.[13] The Cuban leader lavished his attention on Abalkin, personally accompanying him on his tour of the Cuban capital.

It was worth the expense of Castro's time. Abalkin became an active proponent of the Cuban regime and of Soviet economic assistance to Havana. In a series of interviews with the Soviet press, he argued that it was necessary to continue it both on humanitarian grounds — "This small country has always been among the first to extend to us a helping hand in hard times." — and for pragmatic reasons, for without Cuban sugar, nickel, and citrus, Abalkin said, "We would have to pay capitalist countries from $1.5 to $2 billion for the same produce."[14] There was no mention of the billions of dollars the USSR could get from additional annual sales in the world market of the 13 million tons of Soviet oil and oil products annually delivered to Cuba or of the fact that a substantial part of Soviet raw materials and manufactured products sent to Cuba were supplied on a credit basis, with no prospect of repayment in the foreseeable future.

The next Soviet dignitary to visit Cuba, as a continuation of attempts to counterbalance negative trends in Soviet-Cuban relations, was Oleg Baklanov, the secretary of the CPSU Central Committee responsible for the Soviet defense industry. He headed a Soviet parliamentary delegation to Cuba in May 1990. According to a TASS report, Castro listened "with great attention and interest" to Baklanov's account of the "progress of the restructuring processes in the USSR and the preparations for the Twenty-eighth CPSU Congress." In his response, Castro "gave his evaluation of the rectification process under way in the country, which consists of a complex of measures directed at perfecting the running of the economy and ensuring sovereignty of the people." Castro also "touched on the efforts being undertaken in the sphere of national defense."[15]

In an interview with *Pravda*, the chief overseer of the Soviet military-industrial complex, who later was destined to play a key role in the August 1991 coup in Moscow, discounted "idle talk about a decline in Soviet-Cuban economic ties" as devoid of any foundation. Noting that the delegation's visit coincided with the thirtieth anniversary of the restoration of diplomatic relations between the USSR and Cuba, he said, "We may be proud of the path we have traveled together and are convinced that there are fruitful joint projects, mutually beneficial cooperation, and the strengthening of sincere friendship ahead of us."[16]

Addressing the ceremonial meeting in Havana, which commemorated this anniversary, Baklanov emphasized that "a key element" of the relations between the two countries was "the fraternal collaboration between the CPSU and the Cuban Communist Party." He noted, "In transforming the image of Soviet society, we are trying to impart to socialism the features of a truly humane democratic system" but then added, "We are not seeking to impose our model on anyone." Moscow's emissary thought it was appropriate to defend Castro's regime against criticism on the democracy issue, saying, "Certain countries' attempts to teach others their style of democracy evoke our condemnation. We believe that the United States should demonstrate a genuinely democratic approach to other countries and Cuba in particular."[17]

Baklanov assured both Fidel and Raúl Castro that the Soviet Union's rapprochement with the United States would not interfere with the continuation of traditional close ties between the armed forces of the two countries and Soviet military assistance to Cuba, and that the arms deliveries would continue as planned, including MiG-29s. (General U. Rosales del Toro, chief of the Cuban General Staff, asked Marshal S. Akhromeyev in January 1990, if the Soviet side would change the nature of Soviet-Cuban military cooperation in 1990-1995, and if it would honor the agreement on the delivery of MiG-29s.)[18]

Soviet military links with Cuba were the least affected by *perestroika* and economic difficulties. The flow of Soviet arms to Cuba continued unabated in accordance with plans, and the Ministry of Defense maintained its regular contacts and exchanges with the Cuban military. General Rosales del Toro visited Moscow in April 1990 at the invitation of General Moiseyev, chief of the General Staff of the Soviet Armed Forces. A convoy of Soviet warships arrived in the port of Havana for an official visit in June 1990. General Moiseyev came to Havana in October 1990 after completing his visit to the United States. He was received by Fidel Castro and had talks with Raúl Castro. Moiseyev assured them that the Soviet side remained faithful "to the roots of our friendship, and especially to the obligations under contract agreements concluded after President Gorbachev's visit, pertaining to economic, political, and military relations."[19] The only concession the USSR Ministry of Defense made to the political demands of avoiding excessive activity in Soviet-Cuban military cooperation, prone to be interpreted as provocative in Washington, was to postpone, at the insistence of the Soviet Foreign Ministry, a visit to Cuba of Defense Minister, Marshal Dmitry Yazov.

The Soviet military's interest in Cuba was one of the few subjects that still remained taboo for the Soviet press, despite *glasnost*. But in July 1990, *Izvestia* carried an article by Yelena Arefyeva, questioning the truthfulness of the official arguments in favor of the continuation of Soviet economic assistance to Cuba. She noted that the advocates of this policy based their reasoning on moral and humanitarian grounds and also on the "advantages" of being able to get Cuban sugar, nickel, and citrus without spending hard currency. They never mentioned "the real gain which had been programmed in the past years — ideological and military-strategic." Arefyeva affirmed that the maintenance of close political ties with Cuba was subordinated to strategic tasks inherited from the past and originally intended to serve the purpose of confrontation with the United States. In her opinion, the Soviet policy toward Cuba was judged in Washington "not by the correlation of sugar and oil prices but by the information about our military bases and the colossal station for monitoring the United States, located on the Island of Freedom."[20]

Ten days later, *Izvestia* published a reply by Marshal Sergei Akhromeyev, former chief of the Soviet General Staff, who stated categorically that there were no Soviet naval or air bases, nor military bases for ground forces in Cuba, only "a single ground forces training center comprising a few hundred people who help to retrain junior commanders and officers in Cuba's revolutionary Armed Forces." Admitting that there was "a grain of truth" in what Arefyeva wrote about the electronic communications center at Lourdes, Marshal Akhromeyev referred to the U.S. intelligence-gathering facilities around the borders of the USSR: "Northern Norway is literally crammed with U.S. intelligence-gathering facilities.... Every day three to five U.S. spy planes gather intelligence along Soviet borders." He asserted that U.S. policy toward the USSR "is still contradictory and still includes, alongside the line of cooperation, strong-arm pressure toward our country."[21]

This was a rare public admission of Cuba's continued important role in the Soviet military strategy by Akhromeyev, a man who was an expert on the subject. He failed to mention the Soviet submarine support facility near Cienfuegos and the use of Cuban airfields by Soviet long-range reconnaissance planes, but this was done a few weeks later by José Raúl Viera, then first vice foreign minister of Cuba, in an interview published by *Moscow News*. When asked what motivated the Soviet Union in continuing its subsidies to Cuba in spite of its own economic difficulties, Viera said, "Gorbachev realizes that the United States presents a threat to Cuba, and he, therefore, feels a moral responsibility toward it. In addition, the USSR, like any other country, needs allies. After all, the United States has not removed its military bases from either Turkey or Europe." Viera admitted that Cienfuegos had perfectly suitable conditions for the entry of submarines but insisted, "If the Soviet submarines did indeed come here regularly, the world would long have known it from American photographs."[22]

At the end of October 1990, Cuba was visited by another high-level Soviet delegation headed by Oleg Shenin, a Politburo member and CPSU Central Committee secretary in charge of organizational affairs, who later would also be involved in the August 1991 putsch. During his stay in Havana, Shenin took the unusual step of publicly denouncing criticism in the Soviet press of Cuban realities and Soviet-Cuban relations as "wholesale vilification..., an insult to the Cuban people." Shenin insisted that the Soviet government "should make an official statement about it." He added, "Those who are attempting to nullify with the stroke of a pen decades of our friendship and cooperation forget the old saw: A friend in need is a friend indeed." Shenin also argued that since the going was extremely tough for Cuba at the moment, "We should not aggravate the situation but, rather, quietly analyze the multitude of complex issues, seek solutions, and restructure outmoded cooperation mechanisms in our peoples' interests." Defending his hosts against accusations of dogmatism and inflexibility, he affirmed that the Cubans "are beginning to change many things in the Party."[23]

Shenin's angry diatribe against "certain Soviet publications" was prompted by an article in *Komsomolskaya Pravda* of October 18, 1990, by Aleksandr Novikov, the newspaper's former Havana correspondent. It contained sensational (for the Soviet public) information about the personal lives of Fidel Castro and Raúl Castro. José Ramón Balaguer, the Cuban ambassador in Moscow, took the unusual step of publishing his protest against the article in another Moscow newspaper, *Pravda*, in order to bring it to the attention "of readers of the serious Soviet press." Balaguer expressed his regret that the Soviet media "has been publishing articles distorting the essence of Cuban-Soviet relations and cooperation and deforming the picture of reality" and complained that "their authors even interfere in our internal affairs, and this coincides with attacks on Cuba and Cuban-Soviet relations from the most reactionary Western press." He accused Novikov of defaming Fidel and slandering Raúl Castro, drawing his information from Western "yellow" magazines. Ambassador Balaguer wrote in conclusion that "disdain for the truth," shown by Novikov, reflected "the hatred felt by the defiler of the Cuban Revolution for a steadfast defender of socialism."[24]

What was also disquieting to Havana and to Castro's friends in Moscow were the continued public attacks by Soviet parliamentarians against the Soviet policy of "friendship and cooperation" with Cuba. In October 1990, this was done by Oldzas Suleimenov, a member of the USSR Supreme Soviet from Kazakhstan, during the debate on Soviet foreign policy. Anatoly Lukyanov, the chairman of the Supreme Soviet, denounced Suleimenov's critical remarks on Cuba and Soviet-Cuban relations as "an insult to our Cuban friends" and stated that Soviet parliamentarians "condemn and disavow" his insinuations.[25]

The Cuban leadership's serious concern with "slanderous" publications in the Soviet press and statements in the Soviet parliament prompted Carlos Lage, an alternate member of the Politburo of the CPC Central Committee, to refer to this problem in his speech on the occasion of the seventy-third anniversary of the Russian October Revolution. He stated that among different ideological currents in the Soviet Union "appear perceptions critical of our revolutionary process and interpretations which reflect a profound ignorance of our history, of the circumstances in which the construction of socialism in Cuba is developing, and of our reality." Lage accused "voices" in the USSR which, "showing an absolute absence of ethics, attempt to distort the sense and the substance of our relations, falsifying our reality" and said it was important "to understand that those who reveal themselves as enemies of the Cuban people and its revolution are also enemies of socialism and of the Soviet people." He then expressed confidence that, as in the past, "there will be no lack of honest and revolutionary minded people in the USSR who will put the truth in its place."[26]

Speaking in Havana on the same occasion, Ambassador Yuri Petrov joined Lage in criticizing articles on Cuba in the Soviet press "...which can be regarded as an attempt to interfere in the internal affairs of sovereign states" and said, "In this connection, I must state with all responsibility that the authors of such publications do not express in any way the sentiments of the Soviet people nor the position of the president or the government of the Soviet Union."[27]

Cuba's Achilles' Heel

The main difficulty with the Cuban lobby in Moscow, as well as for Castro in Havana, was that despite all the political will of the Soviet leadership to minimize the negative effects of economic reforms in the USSR on Moscow's trade and economic cooperation with Havana, Soviet-Cuban economic relations were proceeding from bad to worse. The joint working group set up to draft proposals for changing the mechanism of economic cooperation in accordance with the decision of the February 1990 CMEA session had its first meeting in Havana in June 1990, which failed to work out agreed upon recommendations for approval by the governments. Nevertheless, the Soviets informed the Cubans officially that as of 1991 the USSR would assess the value of commodities in trade with Cuba at current world prices and settle accounts in hard currency.

Further exacerbating the Soviet-Cuban problems, the Soviets were having trouble keeping their now autonomous producers interested in complying with commitments to Cuba, and they began to experience difficulties in delivering to Cuba some essential products still completely controlled by the Soviet government in quantities provided for by Soviet-Cuban trade contracts. The progressive decline in oil production in the USSR cut Cuba's annual quota from thirteen to ten million tons. The total volume of Soviet-Cuban trade in 1990, compared to its planned growth, suffered a 10 percent reduction compared to 1989.[28] According to Castro's report to the Fourth Congress of the CPC, the shortfall in deliveries of goods by the Soviets constituted 1 billion rubles (out of the total of 5.13 billion rubles planned), including 559 million for 3.3 million tons of oil, which it failed to supply.[29]

That was the beginning of the end of the thirty-year period of Cuba's bonanza, when Castro could justifiably define his domain as "a small country with the resources of a great power."[30] Soviet aid was a determining factor that enabled him "to put Cuba on the political map of the world" and to make himself an important player in the arena of international and regional politics. How long Castro's regime would have survived in its original form — without the Soviet helping hand — is anyone's guess. Castro himself admitted on several occasions that the chances of Cuba's survival would have been questionable. Indisputably, Cuba's intensive activities in the nonaligned movement, which turned Havana into one of the major capitals of the Third World; its extensive support for insurrectionist movements in Latin America; and its costly exploits in Africa were made possible only by constant infusions of massive Soviet economic and military assistance. There is no question that its preponderant economic dependence on the Soviet Union became Cuba's Achilles' heel.

True to his reputation as a resourceful and unscrupulous politician able to extract benefits from any situation, Castro exploited to his political advantage temporary delays in the delivery of Soviet grain and oil. By blaming the disintegration of the socialist camp and the reduction of Soviet supplies for the economic crisis and the fall of industrial production in Cuba and by manipulating statistics of Soviet-Cuban trade and distorting facts, Castro directed the popular discontent against Moscow. Many Cubans believed that the Russians, not Castro and his regime, were responsible for their increased economic hardships. Castro's petty maneuvering caused irritation in Moscow, where government officials were doing what they could under the circumstances to ensure uninterrupted supplies to Cuba and were offended by the Cubans' lack of appreciation of their efforts.

In January 1990, the Cuban government reduced bread rations, publicly putting the responsibility for this unpopular measure on the delay in the delivery of Soviet grain. Even though Soviet ships loaded with grain arrived a few days later, reduced rations remained in force. That episode was widely, and negatively for Havana, commented upon in the Soviet press. In August 1990, the Cuban authorities introduced emergency measures to save aviation fuel, gasoline, and electricity, blaming the country's fuel shortage on a shortfall of two million tons of promised but undelivered Soviet oil. According to Soviet sources, the shortfall did not exceed 580,000 tons.[31] The Cubans even refused to refuel Aeroflot planes en route to Latin America. In September 1990, they decided to save newsprint, publishing only one daily paper, *Granma*, and again blamed the USSR for this measure. The Cuban government was exaggerating shortfalls in Soviet deliveries to conceal the accumulation of "strategic reserves" of raw materials, which it decided to build up in anticipation of the "special period," as the crisis came to be known.

In reality, Cuba began to experience serious economic difficulties long before there was any reduction in supplies from the USSR and Eastern Europe. The Cuban GNP was declining between 1986 and 1989 at an annual rate of 0.8 percent, labor productivity fell by 2.5 percent, and the budget deficit increased 4.5 times.[32] All the same, Castro blamed the Soviet economic model, which the Cubans had copied, not his own economic policy or the waste of resources on fighting a war in Angola and on preparations for a suicidal "people's war" in Cuba. In essence, that was a continuation of his traditional well-tried tactics: somebody else, not the maximum leader, had always been to blame for Cuba's economic difficulties. But even when Cuba's economy did begin to suffer directly from the increasing fall in Soviet deliveries, the crucial questions went unanswered: Who is responsible for this dependence on one single source of supplies? And, why didn't Cuba diversify its trade earlier?

Castro and his apologists in Moscow put all the responsibility on Washington. Their standard argument was that in the face of the U.S. economic blockade, turning to the USSR and other socialist countries was the only alternative the Cuban revolutionaries had. That might have been the case initially, although there is no evidence that they had really tried and failed to find other alternatives. But, even if other alternatives were available in the early 1960s, that does not account for the continued growth of Cuban dependency on the Soviet market in the 1970s and 1980s. By that time, the U.S. government had already given up its ineffective attempts to pressure American friends and allies into joining the economic blockade of Cuba. The Cuban government received billions of dollars in loans and trade credits from Western countries, and it was Cuba's own fault that it did not use them wisely, lost its financial solvency, and eventually had to reduce its imports from Western Europe, Canada, and Japan. The share of these countries in Cuba's foreign trade fell from 27.7 percent in the period from 1976 to 1980 to 10.8 percent from 1981 to 1985. In the same period, the Soviet

Union's share in Cuba's trade increased from 62.3 percent to almost 70 percent.[33]

The U.S. economic blockade does not explain why Castro reneged on his regime's original intention to diversify Cuba's economy and to end its predominant dependence on sugar exports. Sugar's average share in the value of Cuba's total exports throughout the post-revolutionary period stayed near the same 80 percent (vacillating slightly) as before 1959, and the area under sugar cane cultivation, which had been reduced during the 1959-1963 period by 25 percent, then increased again and by 1984 exceeded the 1958 level by 11 percent, making it practically impossible to increase the production of other agricultural crops, meat, and milk substantially and, thus, impossible to reduce the dependence of the country on food imports.[34]

Castro himself gave this explanation for Cuba's economic strategy: had Cuba exported all its sugar at world market prices, it could have paid for only 20 percent of the oil it needed, with nothing left to pay for timber, cotton, grain, other foodstuff, machinery, and equipment — all of which it obtained from the USSR.[35] According to some estimates, Soviet sugar-petroleum subsidies in the 1970s-1980s amounted, on the average, to $2 billion a year.[36] Soviet "trade credits" added up to another $1 billion per year. Obviously, the Cubans did not have pressing economic reasons to look for alternative markets or to go to the trouble and expense of developing untraditional exports while they had a guaranteed and lucrative market for sugar in the Soviet Union and other CMEA countries. Who else, and for what reasons, would have been prepared to offer them such generous terms of trade? With the United States out of the game, only the Soviet Union could have geopolitical and ideological motives for buying Cuba's friendship and loyalty at a price of several billion dollars a year.

That was, however, only part of the whole picture. When, in the late 1960s, Castro's hopes of imminent Cuban-model socialist revolutions in Latin America dwindled away, and he made a strategic decision to bind Cuba politically and economically even more tightly with the Soviet Union and other countries of the "socialist camp," he sacrificed the last vestiges of Cuban economic independence. Speaking at a meeting with Cuban students in Moscow on July 2, 1972, Castro stated:

> In the modern world of large economic and human communities, no small country like Cuba can rely only on its own forces in striving for a high level of material and scientific development.... We consider ourselves to be part of Latin

America and will wait patiently for the time of the revolution in Latin America, for the integration of Latin America, which is possible under socialism. We shall not integrate with landlords and bourgeoisie; we shall not integrate with the United States. Farther away from them! We have an allergic incompatibility with their traditions, their culture.... Our integration with Latin America would be natural. But, for the time being, we shall integrate with the socialist camp.[37]

The continuation of monocrop dependence was a logical consequence of that decision. Cuba's membership in CMEA meant that economically it was no longer a free agent. Members of that organization were supposed to coordinate their plans of economic development following the principle of the "socialist division of labor." In CMEA, there existed the consensus that the only viable way to integrate Cuba's economy with that of the East European socialist community was to perpetuate the island's role as a sugar supplier. Soviet experts asserted that it was cheaper to import Cuban sugar, even at high subsidized prices, than to increase its domestic production.

Accordingly, it was decided to promote sugar production on the island and ignore the Marxist dictum that a monocultural economy was one of the principal symptoms of colonial dependence. With CMEA's help, Cuba was expected to reach and surpass the ten million tons per year target that had eluded Castro in 1970. At the July 1981 CMEA session, Cuba signed, with the Soviet Union, Bulgaria, and East Germany, a "General Agreement on the Integral Development of Sugar Production," which set for Cuba a target of producing twelve million tons of sugar in 1990 and provided for assistance in the modernization of its sugar industry.[38]

So much for the "distribution of guilt" for Cuba's economic dependence on the USSR and the East European countries. The main responsibility lay with Havana, although Washington and Moscow were also at fault. At the same time, the U.S. economic blockade had nothing to do with Cuba's continued reliance on sugar exports; only Havana and Moscow were to blame for that. Many Soviet intellectuals, including people who did not have much sympathy for Castro's regime, had feelings of guilt and moral responsibility for the economic hardships that the transition to world market prices was bound to bring to Cuba. These sentiments strengthened the hand of Castro's admirers who used them as additional arguments against a drastic revision of Moscow's relations with Havana. This view was expressed by Viktor

Komplektov, vice minister of foreign affairs, in an interview with Radio Moscow (in Spanish) on January 2, 1991:

> ...the Cuban economy was regrettably built on our model, [and] in order to adapt to the recent changes in Eastern Europe and the Soviet Union, which affect the nature of our links and mutual economic agreements, there must be a transitional period — changes cannot be introduced in a rushed or drastic manner.[39]

In Moscow on December 29, 1990, after prolonged and difficult negotiations, the USSR and Cuba signed their trade agreement for 1991, and on January 20, 1991, signed "transitional protocols on the new mechanism of mutual economic and trade relations." The Cuban side applied strong political pressure on Moscow to acquire what Castro later called "reasonable" terms; during 1990, he sent several letters to President Gorbachev and Prime Minister Ryzhkov, arguing Cuba's case.[40] The documents were to cover only one year, not a five-year period, as was the practice before. There were other important changes. Prices of commodities were calculated in U.S. dollars to make them comparable to world market prices; sugar prices were reduced from about $800 to $500 per ton, although they still remained 2.5 times higher than the world market price. As a result, the Cuban buying capacity in the Soviet market was diminished by $1 billion; planned Soviet exports to Cuba were $6 billion compared to the $7.9 billion planned for the previous year, approximately at the actual level of 1990.[41]

The USSR agreed to supply Cuba with oil (up to 10 million tons, circumstances permitting), ferrous alloys, tin, sulfur, caustic soda, fertilizers, timber, machinery, equipment, foodstuffs, and other products in quantities which, according to Cuban sources, were in line with the requirements of the "special period" in Cuba,[42] but the Soviets stopped deliveries of durable consumer goods, such as television sets and refrigerators, to Cuba. The supply of sugar to the Soviet Union was to remain at the average level of the last five-year period, and the supply of citrus was to increase by 50 percent. To reduce their deficit in bilateral trade, the Cubans agreed to supply the USSR substantial quantities of high-technology medical equipment and pharmaceutical products, which they previously had exported almost exclusively to hard currency countries. Cuba's practice of meeting its commitments with sugar borrowed from third countries against Soviet loan guarantees was discontinued. For the first time, Cuba had to pay part of the shipping costs; previously, the Soviets had paid 100 percent.

In an interview with *Granma,* Cuban Foreign Trade Minister Cabrisas praised "a very constructive climate" and "a spirit of mutual understanding" during the talks and noted an important role, which was played by the visits to Cuba "by several Soviet leaders" during 1990, when they were able "to note the development of such branches of the economy as the pharmaceutical and biological industries, tourism, and the outlook for further economic cooperation between the two countries."[43] He emphasized that there would be no change in the structure of Soviet exports and that, despite the decentralization of economic management in the USSR, the Soviet government agreed to guarantee centrally the deliveries of fuel, foodstuffs, chemicals, and some other products. However, Cabrisas noted that this was not a 100 percent guarantee, as before.

Minister Cabrisas was particularly pleased with the willingness of the Soviet side to continue in 1991 the practice of granting credits to cover the Cuban trade deficit and to proceed with participation in joint construction projects on the island; for that purpose, the Soviet government approved a credit covering all energy projects, including the first and second reactors at the Juraguá nuclear plant; prospecting, extracting, and refining oil; the Antillana iron and steel works; and projects in such fields as chemicals and petrochemicals, electronics, machinery, light industry, transportation, communications, the sugar industry, agriculture, the food industry, geology, and the pharmaceutical industry. He said in this interview that all this reflected "the will and political determination of Soviet authorities and government officials to uphold relations with Cuba, [even though] many inside and outside the Soviet Union predicted the contrary."[44]

Even after signing the document, which provided for the introduction of the new mechanism into their economic relations with the USSR, the Cubans continued to refer to the old system as if it were going to remain in force. On January 25, 1991, Vice Foreign Minister Raúl Roa stated in an interview with Radio Moscow, "In the field of economic cooperation, Cuba and the Soviet Union maintain relations which have been described as exemplary by President Fidel Castro." He added that, ever since Cuba joined CMEA, it advocated the eradication of "unequal exchange" from relations among developed and underdeveloped socialist countries and that "in our relations with the USSR we have eliminated that unequal exchange."[45] These comments gave the impression that Havana still hoped to leave things essentially as they were and to limit changes to the formal side of commercial transactions without seriously affecting the real terms of trade with the Soviet Union, at least as far as sugar was concerned.

Cuban hopes were strengthened by the willingness of the Soviet side to continue its program of technical assistance in the construction or refurbishing of dozens of projects in Cuba. In 1990, the Soviet Union helped complete the construction of twenty projects: the Santa Clara automobile repair and mechanical plant, a repair shop in Moa, a soap factory in Havana, and others. In the course of negotiations on bilateral economic cooperation in 1991, the Soviet side proposed not to initiate any new joint construction projects in Cuba but to concentrate all efforts on completing the current ones. This reflected Moscow's intention to start the process of reducing its long-term economic commitments to Cuba. The proposal was accepted.

To demonstrate that changes in the economic field did not affect the political climate of Soviet-Cuban relations or cooperation in foreign policy matters, Moscow and Havana intensified their political contacts and exchanges. In January 1991, Raúl Roa and Soviet Vice Foreign Minister Vladimir Petrovsky held political consultations in Moscow. TASS reported that they "focused on ways to strengthen global and regional security, particularly in light of the Gulf war, [and had] a constructive dialogue on bilateral cooperation at the United Nations and other international organizations, including the agenda of the forthcoming session of the UN Human Rights Commission." They also discussed "Latin American problems and ways to strengthen Soviet-Cuban relations."[46] There was no criticism of the Cuban position on the human rights problem and no indication that the Soviets would deprive Cuba of its traditional support in the UN Human Rights Commission in Geneva.

Later, Russian Foreign Minister Andrei Kozyrev, characterizing Soviet foreign policy in the last years of the existence of the Soviet Union, referred to Moscow's continued friendship with dictatorial regimes in Cuba, Iraq, Libya, and North Korea to illustrate his thesis that Gorbachev's new political thinking was largely "an indeterminable philosophical concept; in fact, it was simply a new front." In his opinion, the Soviet Union's relations with these countries "had undergone only cosmetic changes," Moscow "simply toned down the wording of congratulatory telegrams," and, in practice, "the old machine was working full steam and opposed all the feeble steps made by Shevardnadze."[47]

One can dispute the harshness of Kozyrev's judgment, but, in essence, he was right. The substance of Soviet relations with ideological friends and allies did not change. This was confirmed by Nikolai Paltyshev, deputy of the USSR Supreme Soviet, who headed a group of Soviet parliamentarians on a visit to Cuba in February 1991. He stated in Havana, "It will be politically illiterate, wrong in human terms, and, in future, economically unprofitable to sever links between the Soviet Union and Cuba."[48] Two weeks later, Soviet Vice President Gennady Yanayev, Secretary of the CPSU Central Committee Valentin Falin, Chairman of the USSR Supreme Soviet Anatoly Lukyanov, and Chairman of the Supreme Soviet's Committee on International Affairs Aleksandr Dzasokhov reaffirmed the Soviet leadership's determination to maintain friendship and cooperation with Cuba when they received in Moscow General Juan Escalona as head of the National Assembly's delegation. Dzasokhov emphasized, "We always think of Cuba as a reliable and permanent ally [and] at the current transitional period of our relations — which affects the form but not the political substance of such relations — we appreciate Cuba's understanding of our problems."[49]

That was the intention of the Soviet leadership, to change the form but not the substance of relations with Havana, to preserve the Soviet-Cuban alliance, and to help maintain the socialist system in Cuba. Escalona's Soviet hosts were thinking of possible ways to curb and then stop the process of erosion of socialism in the USSR, before it was too late. These men were grateful to Castro and his comrades-in-arms for their "understanding" of the CPSU's problems. They admired his steadfastness in resisting similar changes in Cuba, defending one of the few remaining outposts of socialism and preserving its "purity." General Escalona, a man who agreed to play a shameful role in the judicial assassination of General Ochoa, had no difficulties in finding a common language with Soviet leaders.

At the end of May 1991, Castro had "a fraternal meeting" in Havana with Ivan Melnikov, a secretary of the CPSU Central Committee, who stated, referring to "the difficult times" for both Moscow and Havana, "It is precisely when there are difficulties that comrades-in-arms should stick together, help each other, and solve problems together."[50] The last important Cuban visitor to Moscow before the August 1991 coup was Carlos Aldana, secretary of the CPC Central Committee, then a rising star on Havana's political horizon, who headed a delegation of the Communist Party of Cuba. On June 28, 1991, he was received by Gorbachev in his capacity as the secretary general of the CPSU. TASS reported that they had "a frank and comradely conversation." They

"...confirmed their desire for consistent strengthening of the traditional friendly ties between the peoples of the Soviet Union and Cuba and stressed the urgency of consolidating the positive changes that are taking place in world politics on the path toward equal and mutually beneficial cooperation among all states."[51]

Aldana also had meetings with Yanayev; secretaries of the CPSU Central Committee Falin, Kuptsov, and Shenin; and *Pravda*'s editor-in-chief Andrei Frolov. Moscow Central Television informed the Soviet viewers that Yanayev and Aldana expressed "mutual interest in the further strengthening and development of traditional relations of friendship between the Soviet and Cuban peoples and between the USSR and the Cuban Republic."[52] *Pravda* reported that Aldana, during his meeting with Frolov, noted "the economic difficulties [in Cuba] that are adversely affecting the domestic political situation [and] the determination of the Cuban people to continue their chosen path of socialist transformations and friendship with the Soviet Union." Frolov spoke about "the complex processes and changes" in the USSR and the situation in the CPSU, confirming "the desire of the Soviet political leadership to develop and improve friendly relations with Cuba."[53]

The form of words had changed. There was no more talk of "fraternal friendship and solidarity" and no mention of Soviet economic or military assistance to Cuba. The emphasis was on "traditional relations of friendship" and "mutually beneficial cooperation." Moscow and Havana found a new modus vivendi, which allowed them to reform their economic relations gradually and to maximize the remaining positive elements of their political relationship. That was confirmed by Aldana in a lengthy interview published by *Pravda* on July 15, 1991, entitled "Cuba: Changes Are Needed, But What Changes?" He stated that the problem of the reduction of Soviet deliveries, which brought about "a marked deterioration" of Cuba's economic situation, "has now been largely resolved thanks to the mutual understanding that has been reached between the two countries' specialists and economic organizations and thanks to the political will of the Soviet and Cuban leadership."[54]

Cuba's chief ideologist also commented on the internal political scene in the USSR. "We respect the decisions adopted on various matters by the Soviet leadership and the majority of the population, and we have faith in the ideological, ethical, and moral potential of the Soviet society and of the communists." He admitted, watching the developments in the Soviet Union, "Frankly, we sometimes do not understand their underlying causes, trends, or the motives for the decisions adopted"; and added, "for Cuba, the situation in the USSR is a sphere of vital interest, because thirty years ago we linked our fate to yours."[55]

Talking then about the disintegration of the socialist community, Aldana resorted to the same primitive argument that was often used by Soviet conservative critics of Gorbachev's policy: "If these processes did not suit the geopolitical interests of the West, and first and foremost of the United States, the latter would hardly have supported the new political thinking." He excluded any possibility of Cuba following the Soviet example when he said:

People are constantly giving us all kinds of advice. If we were to follow that advice precisely, the Cuban Revolution would already be over. The self-preservation instinct tells us what not to do if we want to survive. Some people are proposing a course of political suicide to us. We Cubans are convinced that capitalism is not in the interests of the Third World countries.[56]

Notes

1. Notes taken by the author during Shevardnadze's conversation with Castro in Havana on October 5, 1989.

2. The document, dated January 15, 1990, is located in the archives of the former USSR Ministry of Defense.

3. *Izvestia*, March 11, 1990.

4. *Latinskaya Amerika*, No.1, 1990, 10.

5. *New Times*, No.5, January 30-February 1, 1990, 20.

6. *Pravda*, January 30, 1990.

7. Moscow Radio (program for Cuba), June 26, 1990, FBIS-SOV-90-128, July 3, 1990, 23.

8. *Argumenty y Fakty*, No.42, October 21-27, 1989.

9. *Leningradskaya Pravda*, February 3, 1988.

10. TASS report from Moscow, April 6, 1989, FBIS-SOV-90-068, April 9, 1990, 24.

11. *Izvestia*, April 20, 1990.

12. In July 1990 Castro raised the offer to receive for treatment thirty thousand children a year who had health problems related to the Chernobyl disaster.

13. *Sankey Shinbun* (Tokyo), April 13, 1990.

14. *Sovetskaya Rossiya*, May 5, 1990.

15. FBIS-SOV, May 7, 1990, 42.

16. *Pravda*, May 23, 1990.

17. *Krasnaya Zvezda*, May 10, 1990.

18. Akhromeyev's report to Gorbachev of January 15, 1990.

19. *Granma*, October 10, 1990.

20. *Izvestia*, July 25, 1990.

21. *Izvestia*, August 4, 1990.

22. *Moscow News*, September 2-9, 1990.

23. *Pravda*, November 6, 1990.

24. *Pravda*, October 26, 1990.

25. *Granma*, October 16, 1990.

26. *Granma*, October 16, 1990.

27. *Granma*, November 8, 1990.

28. *Granma*, October 18, 1991.

29. *Granma*, October 18, 1991.

30. As told to the author by Costa Rican communists in San José in May 1987, a high-level Cuban representative in Managua quoted Castro's definition of Cuba during a conversation with Sandinista security officers.

31. *Komsomolskaya Pravda*, September 1, 1990.

32. *Cuba in the Nineties*, 1991, (New York and Washington: Freedom House), 72.

33. M. A. Manasov, 1988, *Kuba: Dorogami Sversheniy* (Moscow: Izdatelstvo Nauka), 90.

34. Irving Louis Horowitz, ed., 1989, *Cuban Communism* (New Brunswick, NJ and London: Transaction Publishers), 278, 285.

35. Rhoda P. Rabkin, 1991, *Cuban Politics: The Revolutionary Experiment* (New York: Praeger), 134.

36. Rhoda P. Rabkin, 1991, *Cuban Politics: The Revolutionary Experiment* (New York: Praeger), 133.

37. Fidel Castro, 1973, Collection of Speeches (in Russian), Budushcheye Prinadlezhit Sotsialismu (Moscow: Gospolitizdat), 355.

38. N.A. Kudriashov, ed., 1984, *Kuba-Chlen SEV* (Moscow: CMEA Sekretariat), 29.

39. FBIS-SOV-91-003, January 4, 1991, 11.

40. *Granma*, October 18, 1991.

41. *Granma*, October 18, 1991.

42. *Granma*, International Edition, January 20, 1991.

43. *Granma*, International Edition, February 3, 1991.

44. *Granma*, International Edition, February 3, 1991.

45. FBIS-SOV, January 29, 1991, 26.

46. FBIS-SOV, January 29, 1991, 26.

47. *Moscow News*, No. 23, June 7-14, 1992.

48. TASS report from Havana, February 4, 1991, in FBIS-SOV-91-024, February 5, 1991, 21.

49. Moscow Radio (in Spanish), February 20, 1991, in FBIS-SOV, February 22, 1991, 20.

50. *Granma*, International Edition, May 26, 1991.

51. FBIS-SOV, July 1, 1991, 25-26.

52. FBIS-SOV, July 1, 1991, 25-26.

53. *Pravda*, June 26, 1991.

54. *Pravda*, "Cuba: Changes are Needed, But What Changes?" July 15, 1991.

55. *Pravda*, July 15, 1991.

56. *Pravda*, July 15, 1991.

Chapter 7

Moscow-Havana-Washington Triangle

During the Cold War, apart from Moscow's messianic expansionism, Washington's reactions to the "communist threat," the nuclear arms race, and the East-West confrontation in Europe, particularly in Berlin, no other single aspect of the Soviet Union's foreign policy affected so negatively and for so long the superpowers' relationship as the Soviet-Cuban alliance. It first caused the most dangerous crisis, which brought the USSR and the United States to the brink of a nuclear war, and then remained, almost to the very end of the Soviet Union's existence, a constant, major factor hampering the progress of mutual efforts by Moscow and Washington to narrow their differences in periods of détente and exacerbating their contradictions in times of heightened tension. The negative influence of the Moscow-Havana connection on Soviet-American relations has become more pronounced with the sweeping internal changes in the Soviet Union, and the radical reorientation of its foreign policy has effectively brought to an end the historic rivalry between the two superpowers. During this period of change, Fidel Castro has remained the odd man out, refusing to face reality while maintaining Cuba as one of the last bastions of totalitarianism.

Castro found nothing wrong with the arms race and tensions between Moscow and Washington, as long as this precarious "balance of terror" guaranteed the survival of his regime; moreover, Castro actively contributed to Soviet-U.S. tensions. Whenever possible, he attempted to obstruct the improvement of Soviet-American relations on the correct assumption that continued animosities would help maintain Moscow's interest in Cuba. He could see no place for Cuba in a world without Soviet-American enmity. Castro failed to understand that the growing expenses of Soviet global confrontation with the West and Marxist revolutionary experiments in developing countries were expediting the eventual bankruptcy of Soviet socialism. Taking on these excessive economic burdens had irreparably damaged the USSR's already inefficient economy and was threatening not only the Cuban but also its own life-support system. Blaming Gorbachev and other Soviet leaders for the "errors" that destroyed the socialist system in the USSR instead of improving it, Castro conveniently failed to mention his own contribution to its demise by making the Soviet Union foot the bill for the "construction of socialism" in Cuba. The Soviet Union also paid for Castro's exploits in Latin America and Africa, bankrolling him as a big player in deadly "national liberation" games but also helping bury the Soviet-American détente of the 1970s, which brought about a new spiral in the superpowers' arms race — the last straw that broke the back of the socialist camel.

Cuba in Soviet-American Contacts

In April 1961, Khrushchev put Cuba on the official Soviet-American agenda, when he addressed two messages to President Kennedy protesting the Bay of Pigs invasion and warning Washington that if exiles, who were not content with political regimes in countries they had left, were allowed to attack these countries with arms, this "would inevitably lead to conflicts and wars — [it was] a slippery road which [could have led] the world to a new world war." He also stated that the USSR "cannot recognize any U.S. rights to decide the fate of other countries, including Latin American countries."[1] The subject was initiated by Khrushchev in his conversation with Kennedy in Vienna in June 1961. President Kennedy was on the defensive; he said that his giving a green light to the Cuban exiles' invasion of the island was a mistake on his part, with the implication that it would not be repeated. But Kennedy also added that he continued to sympathize with opponents of Castro's regime.

During and after the Missile Crisis of October 1962, an exchange of messages between Khrushchev and Kennedy led to a Soviet-American understanding on the security aspects of the Cuban problem, which set certain limits both to Soviet-Cuban military cooperation and to Washington's ability to use force against the Castro regime. These aspects remained the order of the day in Soviet-American diplomatic exchanges and summit meetings throughout the ensuing twenty-nine years, with both sides tending to give different interpretations to the 1962 understanding and acting, on a number of occasions, in ways that could be construed by the other side as violating the letter or spirit of the understanding. Mutual recriminations around this issue continued well into the post-confrontation period.

Moreover, while the Soviet side never attempted to call into doubt the validity of this understanding, Washington was intentionally vague at times about its willingness to keep Kennedy's non-invasion assurance and even questioned whether it was valid at all, since it was conditioned upon Castro's consent to on-site inspections in Cuba, which he never gave. Apparently, some U.S. policy makers thought it was better to keep Moscow and Havana guessing about Washington's intentions with regard to Cuba. This made Havana nervous and prompted Moscow's diplomatic efforts to procure Washington's confirmation of the non-invasion commitment to calm Castro's fears. Yet, on occasion, these efforts were motivated by considerations which had more to do with Soviet strategic plans in the Caribbean than with Havana's worries about American intentions.

Such was the case in August 1970, when Yuli Vorontsov, the Soviet chargé d'affaires in Washington, was instructed by Moscow to call on Henry Kissinger, secretary of state, and inform him that "in the Cuban question" the Soviet side proceeded, as before, from the "understanding on this question reached in the past" and expected that the American side would also "strictly adhere to this understanding."[2] In a few days, the Soviet embassy was given a reply ("Kissinger's memorandum") that noted with satisfaction the assurance of the Soviet government that the understandings of 1962 were still in force and reaffirmed, in return, that the United States would not use military force to bring about a change in the governmental structure of Cuba.

Henry Kissinger was puzzled when his memorandum was followed almost immediately by a Soviet attempt to establish a submarine base in Cienfuegos; in fact, there was nothing illogical in Moscow's tactics: first, to reassure the Nixon administration that the Soviet Union was not thinking of violating the Kennedy-Khrushchev understandings and then to proceed with actions that it hoped would be tolerated by Washington, particularly in view of Richard Nixon's planned meeting with Leonid Brezhnev in Moscow in the coming year. As in the case of the Soviet missiles deployment in Cuba in 1962, the Soviet embassy in Washington was not informed of these plans. There was also another similarity; Moscow again miscalculated. At the end of

September 1970, Henry Kissinger summoned Soviet Ambassador Anatoly Dobrynin and told him that the continued construction in Cienfuegos of what unmistakably would be a submarine base would be viewed with the "utmost gravity" by the U.S. administration, which would not shrink from appropriate measures, including public steps, if forced to do so.

The Soviet side thought it expedient not to aggravate the situation further, and on October 5, Ambassador Dobrynin handed over to Kissinger a message from Moscow with reference to recent exchanges about the Kennedy-Khrushchev understanding and an assurance that the Soviet side "has not done and was not doing in Cuba now — that includes the area of Cienfuegos — anything of the kind that would contradict that mentioned understanding." The ambassador affirmed orally, on behalf of the Soviet government, that Soviet ballistic missile submarines would never call on any Cuban port in an operational capacity.[3] This new round of Soviet-American diplomatic exchanges on Cienfuegos led to a formal incorporation of submarines and sea-based ballistic nuclear missiles into the 1962 understanding, although it took several further protests from Washington to Moscow to ensure that the Soviets kept their word.

Yet another series of Soviet-American confidential and public exchanges on the interpretation of the 1962 understanding was triggered in November 1978, by reports of the Soviet delivery to Cuba of advanced MiG-23 fighters, which, in the opinion of American military experts, could have the capacity for carrying nuclear weapons. Washington hinted that this might impede the ratification of the Soviet-American Strategic Arms Limitation Treaty (SALT II) by the U.S. Senate. This time Moscow stood its ground. Aleksei Kosygin, the chairman of the USSR Council of Ministers, told a group of U.S. senators visiting Moscow that the MiG-23s given to Cuba could be used only for defense, and they had nothing to do with SALT. After these exchanges, President Carter stated on November 20, 1978, that the Soviet government had assured him both publicly and privately that the MiG-23 jet fighters recently delivered to Cuba were for defensive purposes only.[4]

The controversy around Soviet military links with Cuba flared up again in September 1979 in connection with a "discovery" by the United States of the presence on the island of a Soviet combat motorized brigade. Moscow and Havana both believed that the U.S. announcement was timed to coincide with the summit conference of nonaligned nations, which began in Havana on September 3, 1979, and that it was an attempt to discredit Cuba as a leader of the nonaligned movement. Some strong statements were made regarding the Soviet motorized brigade. In the U.S. Congress, Senator Frank Church, the chairman of the Senate Foreign Relations Committee, expressed his opinion that the SALT II treaty would not get the necessary two-thirds majority in the Senate unless Soviet troops were removed from Cuba. Senator Henry Jackson accused the USSR of turning Cuba "into a fortress capable of threatening the United States, our allies, and friends in this hemisphere." They were supported by presidential candidate Ronald Reagan, who said the Soviet Union should also withdraw the MiG-23 fighters from Cuba.[5]

President Carter took a middle position; he stated, on September 7, 1979, that the presence of Soviet combat troops in Cuba was "a very serious matter" and called on the Soviets "to respect our interests and our concerns" so that relations between the two countries would not be "adversely affected." At the same time Carter said that the Senate had to approve SALT II "on its own merits."[6] *Pravda* published, on September 10, 1979, an editorial asserting that there were no Soviet combat troops in Cuba, only a limited number of Soviet military personnel, who "have helped Cuban servicemen master Soviet military equipment" and that "neither the number nor the functions of the Soviet personnel have changed." It also accused the "U.S propaganda apparatus" of spreading misinformation "to undermine the prestige of Cuba as one of the most active and authoritative member states of the nonaligned movement." It took intensive diplomatic exchanges to find a compromise acceptable to both sides. The compromise was not to Castro's liking, but Brezhnev ignored his objections: again, as in 1962, more important Soviet interests — in this instance, the ratification of the SALT II treaty — prevailed over loyalties to the Caribbean ally. On October 10, 1979, President Carter made a nationwide television appearance, informing the American people of the assurances he had received "from the highest levels of the Soviet government" to the effect that the Soviet military unit in Cuba was a training center, that its function and status as a training center would not be changed, that it would not be a threat to the United States, and that the Soviets reaffirmed "the 1962 understanding and the mutually agreed-upon confirmation in 1970" and would abide by it in the future. Carter stated that the United States, for its part, reaffirmed this understanding and called upon the Senate to ratify the SALT II treaty.[7]

With a dramatic increase in the Cuban military presence in Africa and Cuba's established destabilizing role as a major source of outside military assistance for insurgent movements in Latin America, particularly in El Salvador, Washington began to press Moscow for the reduction of its arms supplies to Havana, even though Soviet shipments rarely included weapons that could be regarded, with some justification, as offensive; therefore, the Kennedy-Khrushchev understanding could not be invoked. The agenda of Soviet-American bilateral exchanges on Cuba was further expanded to include, at the insistence of the United States, the problem of Soviet economic assistance to Castro's regime, which made it possible for the Cubans, according to Washington, to indulge in fostering revolutions in Latin American countries and supporting Marxist-Leninist or "progressive" leftist regimes in Africa. There were also representations sent to Moscow about the Cuban intransigent position on conflicts in Central America and Angola, obstructing their negotiated settlement. Moscow, in turn, urged Washington to change its policy of implacable hostility to the Castro regime and to bring the U.S. economic blockade of Cuba to an end.

Predictably, the USSR government reacted to American pressures for reducing Soviet economic and military assistance to Cuba with indignant remonstrations about the inadmissibility of outside interference into relations between two sovereign states. The opening strong language was then followed by suggestions that Washington would do better if it relaxed its economic sanctions against Cuba. This was not demagoguery on Moscow's part. From the start, Soviet leaders had not been happy with the U.S. economic blockade of Cuba, despite the undeniably important part it played in helping to bring Castro into alliance with the USSR. It was never easy for the USSR to play the role of principal provider for Cuba's needs. The percentage of the Soviet Union's GNP spent on economic assistance to its Caribbean ally might appear insignificant, but the Soviet economy was not export-oriented and was never able to satisfy its own domestic needs properly in most of the commodities supplied to Cuba. Because of the USSR's chronic deficit of raw materials and manufactured products for domestic consumption, shipping them elsewhere at giveaway prices or for nothing in return was always politically costly and economically painful.

For that reason, Soviet appeals to Washington for the normalization of U.S.-Cuban relations have always had a sincere ring to them. Moscow was doing its best to play the role of an honest broker, trying to persuade Washington that it had to learn to live in peace with Castro, just as the Soviet Union had learned to live with some of its neighbors, including members of NATO. Khrushchev, in his message to Kennedy on November 11, 1962, even lectured the U.S. president on this subject, asking him to understand the feelings of the leader of a small country who felt threatened by a large and powerful neighbor, saying that a different appraisal of the Cuban Revolution "should not prevent us from finding agreed solutions in the interests of peace.... One should treat both sides with understanding and take into account the actual...situation in Cuba which has chosen the way for its development in accordance with the will of the people."[8] Yet, nobody in the USSR Foreign Ministry seriously believed that the United States would respond positively to such appeals. Moscow had very little political capital at this time in Washington — all the Soviets could do was to express such sentiments for the sake of polemics, as well as to demonstrate to Havana that the USSR was trying to use its improved relations with Washington in Cuba's best interests.

Similarly, few people in the U.S. Department of State could be expected to think that the Soviet Union might abandon its trusted friend and ally in the Caribbean, unless for some unavoidable, crucial reasons. But, with the various U.S. administrations' hostility toward the Castro regime and apparent desire to see it fall, they could not provide such reasons. The deliverance from Castro and the Soviet-Cuban alliance was important for the United States but not important enough to justify the application of severe political or economic sanctions or both against the USSR for continuing to support it, to say nothing of losing thousands of American servicemen in an invasion of Cuba. Nor was there any guarantee that such sanctions would accomplish that purpose. Sanctions certainly did not help remove Soviet troops from Afghanistan. Thus, both the Soviets and the Americans engaged in more polemics and plain demagoguery in their public positions and official contacts with Cuba than they spent time on issues of substance, but this should not be surprising as they both also followed the same pattern on the issues of disarmament and other outstanding international and regional problems.

In November 1985, Gorbachev and Reagan decided during their meeting in Geneva to initiate regular bilateral meetings of the U.S. State Department and USSR Foreign Ministry representatives to discuss regional conflicts, seeking to find ways of promoting their negotiated settlements. On the Central American conflict, such meetings were held in 1986 and 1987 between Assistant Secretary of State for Inter-American Affairs Elliot Abrams and the head of the first Latin American Directorate, Vladimir Kazimirov. After Kazimirov was appointed Soviet ambassador to Angola and I replaced him in the Latin American

Directorate, we had two more sessions with Elliot Abrams in 1988, in London and Rome, before he was replaced in 1989 in the Bush administration by Bernard Aronson. During the meeting in London, Abrams suggested that although, strictly speaking, Cuba was not on the agenda of Soviet-American talks on the Central American conflict, it would be difficult to discuss the situation in the region without touching on Cuba's involvement in this conflict as one of the principal supporters of the Sandinista government and the FMLN. Abrams also proposed that we exchange opinions on Soviet-Cuban relations, since Soviet aid to Cuba had direct bearing on its policy and actions in Central America. I agreed with these propositions on the condition that the U.S. policy toward Cuba would be discussed as well.

Debating with Elliot Abrams the subject of Soviet economic assistance to Cuba, I admitted frankly that it was a heavy burden that the Soviet Union would like to lessen. I told Abrams that Moscow would be prepared, in principle, to consider the reduction of this assistance only if Washington agreed to relax its economic sanctions against Cuba. His reply was negative: the United States could not possibly take such a step without substantial changes in Castro's internal policy and in light of his revolutionary activities in the Third World. From this, it followed that Washington wanted to induce changes in the Castro regime or strangle it economically, not lighten Moscow's burden of keeping it afloat.

In accordance with this logic, U.S. congressmen and political analysts came up with various "incentives" for the Soviet Union to cut economic assistance to Cuba. Thomas E. Cox, of the Heritage Foundation, proposed that in order "to accelerate Castro's departure," the U.S. administration should link "economic concessions" to the USSR with "significant and fully verifiable reductions in Moscow's military and economic aid to Cuba." Cox's recommendation was that until this linkage was undertaken the United States should oppose granting credits to the USSR through the U.S. Export-Import Bank; oppose Soviet membership in the American Overseas Private Investment Corporation; prevent Moscow from raising money by issuing bonds in U.S security markets; and require, as a condition of USSR membership in the European Bank for Reconstruction and Development, a substantial cut in Soviet aid to Cuba.[9] There were other suggestions of a similar nature; some were advanced in the U.S. Congress in order to pressure Moscow.

Nevertheless, the Soviet government categorically rejected such linkage, and I emphasized to Abrams that there should be no illusions in Washington as to the possibility of Moscow succumbing to these pressures. Our debate then took a different turn. Conceding the point that the Soviet Union was "doomed" under the circumstances to continue its economic assistance to Cuba, the assistant secretary of state argued that the USSR government should use Cuba's economic dependence to pressure Castro into more responsible international behavior in keeping with Gorbachev's new political thinking. I replied that it was not Moscow's practice to attach political strings to its economic aid. My reply was not quite sincere — I should have said that the Soviet government resorted to such practices only in extreme cases and that Cuba was not yet considered to be such a case. In fact, the possibility of exerting economic pressure on Fidel in order to bring his policy in line with *perestroika* was never discussed as a serious proposition in Moscow. Havana's policy was thought to be regrettable, but not deserving of such sanctions. On the contrary, everything possible within the limits of dwindling Soviet export resources was being done to keep Fidel Castro happy.

Later, when the Gorbachev government desperately sought economic assistance from Washington, the Bush administration was quick to link consideration of the request with the issue of Soviet aid to Cuba. At one point, Secretary of State James Baker even handed over to Soviet parliamentarians a rough U.S. estimate of the total volume of Soviet aid to Cuba, accompanied by friendly suggestions for better use of these resources, such as solving some acute social and economic problems in the USSR. This pressure, combined with an internal political controversy in the Soviet parliament and media around the issue, contributed to Moscow's subsequent decision to discontinue both economic and military aid to Havana, but this became possible only when the CPSU was removed from power and the Soviet economic crisis reached a critical stage.

After the two superpowers decided to pass from confrontation in regional conflicts to cooperation in their political settlement, Cuba became a permanent item on the agenda of Gorbachev-Bush summits and numerous Shevardnadze-Baker meetings, and it continued to be discussed at the bilateral working level. The Bipartisan Accord on Central America, signed by President Bush and the congressional leadership on March 24, 1989, which served as a basis for Washington's new approach to a solution of Central American problems, made reference to the "continued aid and support of violence and subversion" in that area by the Soviet Union and Cuba in violation of the Esquipulas Agreement, which they both publicly endorsed. The Accord also expressed the expectation that President Gorbachev's impending visit to Cuba represented "an important opportunity for both the Soviet Union and Cuba to end all aid that supports subversion and destabilization in Central America, as President Arias has requested and as the Central American peace process demands."[10]

In fact, Havana's policy of stirring up trouble for the West in Latin America and Africa still remained a bone of contention between Moscow and Washington, since in most cases it was believed to be encouraged, supported, and financed directly or indirectly by the USSR. However, when Gorbachev and Shevardnadze accepted Baker's proposal to cooperate in finding ways to contribute to negotiated settlements of regional conflicts, traditional mutual recriminations regarding the Cuban role in South-West Africa (Namibia) and Central America gave way to a discreet coordination of efforts intended to interest Havana in bringing an end to these conflicts. Most of the talking with Havana was being done by Moscow, since Washington was not prepared for bilateral dialogue with Castro. Havana was kept informed of Soviet-American contacts on regional conflicts and of what Washington had to say about the Cuban policy — and that was also a way to influence it. In its turn, Havana tried to use Moscow to influence Washington's position.

This intricate diplomacy has proved to be extremely helpful in finding solutions to the problems in Angola and Namibia. Soviet-American joint efforts were less productive in attempts to secure Cuba's cooperation in reestablishing peace in Nicaragua. Havana refused to admit its active behind-the-scenes involvement there and took the position that Cuba was not a party to the conflict and that it was up to Washington to stop its undeclared war against the Sandinista government and normalize relations with Managua. When peace was restored in Nicaragua, Bernard Aronson in our meetings switched his main emphasis to the Cuban role in El Salvador. His particular worry was that the continuing Soviet military cooperation with Cuba enabled Havana to supply the FMLN forces with modern weapons and ammunition in quantities sufficient for large-scale offensive operations and that the FMLN leaders, therefore, lacked incentives for negotiating a peace settlement with the Salvadoran government.

I pointed out to Aronson that the same argument could be applied just as well to U.S. military assistance to the Salvadoran government and army. Confident of the continuation of this assistance, they could not be so willing to talk peace. Moreover, if they knew that their opponent would be deprived of outside military aid, they would have even fewer incentives for making political concessions, which were indispensable for a negotiated settlement. As for the USSR military assistance to Cuba, the possibility of its reduction should be linked with some reciprocal moves on the U.S. side. I told Aronson that intensive U.S. military activities around Cuba made it difficult to justify any reduction in Soviet-Cuban military cooperation. We agreed that this particular problem deserved separate consideration.

The idea of bilateral negotiations on this issue was first suggested by the authors of the Santa Fe II document in August 1988. They proposed initiating high-level talks with the Soviet government, "...with the objective to bring about the Soviet military withdrawal from Cuba [and,] when these talks reach a conclusion or at least a promising stage, the United States should open talks with Castro or his successor in order to prepare for a post-Castro Cuba."[11] The proposal was not taken up by the Reagan administration; it was a nonstarter in any case, if only because Moscow would not have agreed to negotiate such a withdrawal just on the vague promise of Washington's future talks with Havana, while the linkage to talks with Castro was hardly acceptable to President Reagan. Moreover, it was far from certain that Castro would be willing to negotiate matters pertaining to a transition to a "post-Castro Cuba."

Gorbachev, on the eve of his departure for Cuba in the beginning of April 1989, received a message from Bush, informing the Soviet leader of the Bipartisan Accord on Central America and warning him that if the Soviet side continued its previous policy in Cuba and Central America, this would inevitably affect relations between the United States and the USSR. President Bush expressed hope that Gorbachev, during his visit to the Caribbean, would seriously consider new possibilities for securing a peaceful settlement in Central America. He suggested that cutting off the Soviet and Cuban flow of arms to this region would be most beneficial, demonstrating the willingness to contribute to a political settlement — not only with words but also with deeds. Gorbachev, on his return to Moscow from a trip to Havana and London, sent a message to Bush assuring him that the Cuban leadership, as confirmed by his conversations in Havana, was prepared to contribute to the establishment of a just peace in the region based on a reasonable balance of interests. He then tried to convince Bush of the benefits of the Soviet proposal for a complete embargo on arms deliveries to Central America from all sources, which was supported by Castro.

Throughout 1989, the Bush administration continued to press the Gorbachev government to do something about Cuba, while Moscow defended Castro's record and argued for the expediency of the normalization of U.S.-Cuban relations. In June, during bilateral talks on Central America in Moscow, Assistant Secretary of State Bernard Aronson criticized Cuban policy in the region and warned Soviet Vice Foreign Minister Viktor Komplektov that Cuban and Nicaraguan military assistance to General Noriega could have grave consequences. Komplektov emphasized the necessity of direct dialogue between Washington and Havana on regional problems and referred to Cuba's constructive role in the negotiated settlement of the situation in Namibia. At Havana's request, we also told Aronson that the TV Martí transmissions to Cuba could lead to serious repercussions.

Secretary of State James Baker, talking to Foreign Minister Eduard Shevardnadze, when they discussed regional conflicts with participation of the State Department and Soviet Foreign Ministry experts on these problems during their meeting in Wyoming in September 1989, again accused Cuba of hampering a peace settlement in Central America. He asked the Soviet foreign minister to explain the twofold increase in shipments of military supplies and weapons from Cuba to Nicaragua, compared to the previous year, although Moscow informed Washington that Soviet arms deliveries to Nicaragua had been suspended since the end of 1988. He implied that the Soviet Union continued to ship weapons to Nicaragua via Cuba.

Shevardnadze reaffirmed that there were no arms deliveries to the Sandinistas from the Soviet Union in 1989 and added that, although he could not speak for the Cubans, there were great changes in their policy after the Soviet Union and the United States started to cooperate toward resolving regional problems. On the other hand, he thought that the normalization of U.S.-Cuban relations would have contributed to the improvement of the situation in Central America and the Caribbean. Referring to Cuba's military assistance to Nicaragua, Shevardnadze questioned the reliability of Baker's information but then promised to look into the matter, noting at the same time that the Soviet government was not under any obligation to stop arms deliveries to Cuba. That was true, and Baker did not dispute the right of the USSR to supply weapons to Cuba, but he objected to their transfer to Nicaragua.

What Baker did not know was that, after stopping direct arms deliveries to the Sandinista government at the end of 1988, the Soviet

Union continued in the first six months of 1989 — in violation of its declared policy — to transport lethal weapons and munitions to Cuba that were destined for further shipment to Nicaragua by the Cubans, in accordance with the existing Soviet-Cuban arrangement. In this particular case, Castro was a willing tool of the double-track Soviet policy toward Nicaragua, but only a tool. Not until the end of June 1989 did the Politburo of the CPSU Central Committee decide to suspend, until February 1990, the delivery of weapons and munitions to Nicaragua via Cuba. As a member of the Politburo, Shevardnadze was aware of the real situation, but even senior officials of the Soviet Foreign Ministry were misled into believing that all arms deliveries to Nicaragua from the Soviet Union had been stopped at the end of 1988, and they, in turn, were unintentionally misleading their American counterparts.

In October 1989, Shevardnadze informed Baker that, as promised, he had talked to Castro about the problem of ending Cuban arms deliveries to Nicaragua and the FMLN, but Castro had confirmed his previous position, linking it directly with U.S. policy in Central America: Havana could assume such an obligation only within the context of a multilateral agreement that ended military supplies to the region from all sources. Shevardnadze indicated that Castro was interested in the normalization of relations with the United States and thought that the USSR could play a useful role in bringing this about. Accordingly, Moscow was prepared to offer its good offices by helping to start a Washington-Havana dialogue.

Baker was not impressed. In November 1989, he responded in a letter to Shevardnadze that as far as the prospects of the termination of Cuban support for subversion in the region were concerned, he saw no basis for optimism. He did not conceal his belief that Castro's inflexible position was made possible by Soviet support and said that Soviet policy in the region ultimately would be judged by the Soviet arms supplied to Cuba. In this context, Baker expressed strong disappointment with indications that Moscow was providing Cuba with advanced MiG-29 aircraft capable of delivering nuclear weapons, thus raising serious concern about Soviet compliance with the 1962 understanding.

By the time Baker's letter was received in Moscow, the spokesman of the USSR Foreign Ministry at a press briefing in Moscow had already denied, with reference to the reports in the American press, that the delivery to Cuba of MiG-29 interceptor fighters with anti-aircraft defense functions (in accordance with an agreement concluded several years before) would violate the 1962 Soviet-American understanding. He stated that the United States was attempting to give it an expanded interpretation and added that nothing the Soviet Union was doing in Cuba was inconsistent with its obligations under this mutual understanding and that the USSR would continue to observe it, provided that the United States also observed its obligations.

The November 1989 offensive of the FMLN forces in El Salvador threatened to cause a crisis of confidence between Moscow and Washington because there was evidence that the Sandinistas not only continued to supply the FMLN with Soviet-made small arms and ammunition (despite their repeated assurances to the contrary) but also had delivered surface-to-air missiles to the Salvadoran guerrilla fighters for the first time. Yuri Dubinin, the Soviet ambassador to the United States, was urgently instructed to inform Secretary of State Baker that the Soviet government was also concerned with the developments in El Salvador and was not aware of the origin of the surface-to-air missiles in question. However, the Soviets were bringing this concern to the notice of the Cubans and the Nicaraguans, to remind them of their obligation to use Soviet-supplied weapons only for their own defense, and to confirm the Soviet position in favor of settling Central American problems by political means, on the basis of the Esquipulas Agreement and other agreements of the region's countries. After talking to Baker, Dubinin cabled to Moscow that the secretary of state seemed to be satisfied with the message but asserted once again that in 1989 (that very year), Cuba had doubled its arms deliveries to Nicaragua, proof of the colossal amount of current Soviet military assistance to Havana.

The next round of Soviet-American exchanges regarding Cuba took place during the Gorbachev-Bush summit in Malta in the beginning of December 1989. The same arguments were repeated by both sides without any substantial alterations. At a press conference in Valletta on December 3, 1989, both leaders refused to be provoked by journalists into publicly stating their differences on the subject, with Bush saying that he had absolutely no influence on Castro and with Gorbachev relating what he had told the U.S. president, that in Central America conditions were ripening for positive changes and that "different parties" (including Cuba) wanted to normalize relations, not only in the region but also with the United States. The Malta summit gave fresh impetus to U.S. State Department and USSR Foreign Ministry officials to search for ways and means of promoting a peace settlement in Nicaragua and El Salvador and neutralizing Cuba's negative influence on some of the principal protagonists of this regional conflict.

A few days after the summit, Washington presented Moscow with some new ideas, suggesting particularly that the Soviet Union could reduce its military and economic assistance to Cuba in order to ensure that the Cubans did not increase further arms deliveries to Nicaragua to compensate for the suspension of Soviet supplies and to rearm the FMLN forces. It was further suggested that the United States would not take advantage of this step by threatening Cuba's security, provided that Cuba did not threaten the security interests of the United States. Although this proposal was not acceptable to the Soviets, it contained an element that could serve as a basis for further discussions on the issue: a recognition by the United States of the principle of reciprocity, essential for any progress in finding ways for Moscow to reduce its military assistance to Havana.

In May 1990, this problem was publicly debated at the Soviet-American conference on regional problems in Miami, the Moscow-Miami Dialogue, which preceded the Bush-Gorbachev summit in Washington. Professor Jaime Suchlicki of the University of Miami proposed that the Soviet Union should remove its MiG-29 fighters and other sophisticated weapons from Cuba in return for a U.S. promise to close its naval base in Guantánamo and never to invade Cuba, but this idea found no support in Washington. During the working-level Soviet-American diplomatic contacts on the subject, the closure of the Guantánamo base was not discussed, since Bernard Aronson categorically excluded any possibility of making it one of the elements of an understanding on mutual confidence-building measures around Cuba. He indicated that the United States was interested in the cancellation of Soviet plans for the delivery of MiG-29s and in the withdrawal of the Soviet brigade from the island. I replied that these propositions could be discussed but only on the basis of reciprocity; Washington had to take substantial steps aimed at the reduction of U.S. military activities in the area.

Several rounds of talks between representatives of the USSR Foreign Ministry and the State Department followed on possible confidence-building measures of a military-political nature with regard to Cuba. Moscow expressed its willingness to reduce considerably the volume of its military cooperation with Havana, if Washington were prepared to take appropriate steps to lessen the military tension in the region, including confirmation by the U.S. government of nonaggression assurances. The United States agreed, in principle, with this approach and took note of Moscow's statement that it would have to coordinate its position with Havana and keep it informed of progress in the talks.

In conversations with Gorbachev in Washington and Camp David in June 1990, Bush noted that Castro was swimming against the current — there were no positive developments in Cuba — and suggested that changes in the nature of Soviet-Cuban economic relations could push the Cuban leader toward greater openness. Gorbachev said that attempts to isolate Cuba would lead nowhere and tried once more to persuade Bush of the merits of direct contacts between Washington and Havana. Speaking about Soviet economic ties with Cuba, he asserted that they were already changing, but things were not so simple; the Soviet Union needed Cuban sugar, and although the price was high, the supply was guaranteed. Bush did not exclude the possibility of some improvement in U.S.-Cuban relations if Havana were to terminate its support for the FMLN, but he emphasized that relations could be normalized completely only after radical changes took place in Cuba. He concluded by saying that Soviet military and economic assistance to Cuba remained a serious irritant in American-Soviet relations. At a working level, I tried to convince Bernard Aronson that Washington should define its priorities; it was unrealistic to expect that Castro would be prepared to change simultaneously both his foreign and domestic policies. A few days later in Havana, Cuban Vice Foreign Minister Sanchez Parody and other officials listened with particular interest to my verbal account of Gorbachev's exchanges with Bush — and mine with Aronson — relating to Cuba; their comment was that my information only confirmed their opinion regarding the absence of any positive changes in the U.S. policy toward Cuba.

The Soviet-American dialogue on Cuba continued without any tangible results well into 1991. Given the positions of the two sides, the dialogue could not be fruitful. Shortly before the August 1991 coup in Moscow, the USSR Foreign Ministry issued a directive to Soviet embassies around the world to the effect that the removal of the Cuban problem as an "irritant" in Soviet-American relations was one of the tasks of Soviet diplomacy, but it had to be accomplished without threatening the "legitimate interests" of Cuba and the Soviet Union. Washington needed to comprehend the futility of its high-pressure policy toward Havana, as well as the expediency of lowering the level of confrontation in U.S.-Cuban relations. Washington had to see that gradually normalizing relations with Cuba and eventually initiating a direct dialogue with Havana would be in the best interests of the United States.

Moscow's intention was to achieve a change in the official U.S. attitude toward the Castro regime and the Soviet-Cuban alliance, without making any substantial corrections in its own policy toward Cuba. The 1991 foreign ministry directive stated that the USSR invariably pursued a policy of maintaining traditionally friendly close relations with Cuba and intended to continue them, despite "irresponsible" efforts of "certain forces" in the United States to drive a wedge into these relations. Therefore, all attempts to link the development of Soviet-American relations with demands to terminate Soviet-Cuban cooperation had to be resisted as "inadmissible and absolutely unacceptable."

Similarly, the Bush administration was not disposed to make substantial concessions in order to weaken Soviet links with Cuba. In the post-Cold War world, the Cuban problem was losing its urgency for Washington. In the United States, the conviction was growing that the Castro regime was doomed anyway and that Cuba was losing its importance as a political ally and a military base for the Soviet Union. After all, the USSR had ceased to be the principal adversary of the United States and was now more vulnerable to American political and economic pressures to reduce its cooperation with Cuba than ever before. Besides, the way things were going in the USSR, it was clearly only a matter of months, not years, before Moscow lost the practical ability to continue its economic assistance to Havana, whatever its political will. Consequently, the United States could afford to wait a little longer without making any concessions to Moscow or Havana and even to make its conditions more stringent for the normalization of U.S.-Cuban relations.

Additionally, Washington had come to the conclusion that the chances of influencing Castro's regional behavior and domestic policy through Moscow were limited, partly because of the Gorbachev government's reluctance to put stronger pressure on Castro but primarily due to Castro's defiant attitude to any outside influences, which made it unlikely that such pressures would succeed. That was clearly demonstrated by the failure of persistent Soviet diplomatic efforts to persuade Havana to support the Esquipulas negotiating process in Central America and contribute to a peace settlement in El Salvador. Gorbachev was not able to change Castro's mind on the use of force against the Saddam Hussein regime in Iraq, either.

Still, Soviet-American exploratory talks continued on possible confidence-building political and military measures around Cuba. Moscow was trying to get Washington to consider making a public statement addressed to Cuba that contained the following: 1) confirming the 1962 non-invasion assurance, 2) reducing U.S. military personnel and armaments at the Guantánamo base, 3) notifying Cuba in advance of military maneuvers and other important U.S. military activities in the region, 4) reducing or canceling U.S. military maneuvers around Cuba, and 5) ending the flights of U.S. reconnaissance aircraft over Cuba.

In return, subject to Havana's approval, the Soviets were prepared to 1) suspend deliveries to Cuba of MiG-29s, 2) reduce gradually the total volume of Soviet military supplies and the number of Soviet military advisers on the island, and 3) consider other steps aimed at changing the nature and reducing the scale of Soviet-Cuban military cooperation, depending on the progress toward normalizing U.S.-Cuban relations. These ideas that arose from the Soviet-American talks went nowhere — Castro would not hear of anything less than the withdrawal of U.S. forces from Guantánamo, and Gorbachev was not prepared to ignore his objections. The U.S. administration, in turn, had to take into account the strength of anti-Castro sentiments on Capitol Hill and the Pentagon's unwillingness to consider closing down the U.S. naval base in Cuba. The situation was deadlocked. Nevertheless, the talks did prepare the groundwork for the subsequent sensational Soviet decision after the failed coup attempt in Moscow to withdraw the brigade from Cuba without linking this to Guantánamo; the United States took some steps to reduce its military activities around Cuba.

In 1991, Moscow was still pursuing the aim of preserving the Soviet-Cuban alliance, albeit at a lesser economic and political cost. Moscow's interest in Cuban internal changes did not extend beyond the hope that Castro would allow some reforms to ensure an increased efficiency of the Cuban economy, lower social tensions, an embellished public image for the regime, and improved Cuban-American relations. That was very different from the principal aims of U.S. policy toward Cuba, but it coincided partly with Washington's immediate interests, insofar as democratic reforms were concerned. Thus, apart from Moscow's and Washington's common interest in obtaining Havana's cooperation in the settlement of regional conflicts, there appeared another common element in their policy toward Cuba: they both wanted the Castro regime to change.

As the Soviet Union progressed to a semblance of political pluralism and Gorbachev, while still defending the "socialist option," began to talk about a transition to a market economy, Moscow moved somewhat closer to Washington's understanding of political democracy, the value of individual freedoms, and the advantages of private enterprise. Yet, there remained major differences in their approaches to promoting internal political and economic changes in Cuba, differences that also existed, if not within the U.S. administration itself, certainly in the Congress and among the American people. Gorbachev and his colleagues believed that the general improvement of the political climate around Cuba would help to dissipate the "besieged fortress" mentality in Havana and positively influence the internal policy of the Cuban government. More specifically, they thought that the best way to aid the liberalization of the Cuban regime was to free it from U.S. pressures and develop more trade and other contacts with Havana. Washington's policy of increasing outside political pressures on Castro's regime and strangling it economically by depriving Cuba of energy supplies and other vital resources was viewed in Moscow as inhuman and dangerous. The Soviets believed that this could lead to a social explosion with tragic consequences for the Cubans and to destabilizing the situation in the area.

That kind of reasoning was rejected in Washington and by influential Cuban exile organizations in the United States, although it found considerable support in other sectors of U.S. public opinion. Judging by opinion polls, Americans strongly supported the Bush administration's advocacy of democratic changes in Cuba, but at the same time many favored increased travel, social, and business ties with the island. Notwithstanding, the U.S. opponents of the "gradualist" approach were convinced that, since Castro was a dictator who still embraced communism, it would be naive to expect Cuba to evolve toward democracy, individual freedoms, and a market economy as long as he remained in power. They admitted that a further deterioration of Cuba's economic situation could lead to civil disturbances and violence but considered it to be an unavoidable risk. Furthermore, most Americans blamed the Soviet Union for prolonging the suffering of the Cuban people by continuing to supply Castro's regime with most of its basic needs.

The American Factor in Soviet-Cuban Relations

Moscow's obsession with the task of lessening tension between Havana and Washington reflected the underlying truth, which first came to the surface in October 1962: for the USSR, relations with Cuba and the preservation of socialism on the island could never become more important than "peaceful coexistence" with the United States. Having learned this lesson during the Cuban Missile Crisis, Khrushchev and his successors were determined to avoid such untenable future situations, as they were unwilling to risk a serious conflict with the United States for Castro's sake. The Soviets counseled restraint on Castro's part, urging him to avoid actions that might provoke U.S. retribution. After the Missile Crisis, the Soviets were also more conscious of the limits of their actions in Cuba that would be tolerated by the United States and the limits within which the Soviet Union could safely continue using the Cuban territory for strategic purposes. With the dramatic change of priorities in Soviet foreign policy during the late 1980s, these motives were considerably reinforced by Moscow's desire not to allow the Cuban factor to interfere with the radical improvement in relations with Washington and with Soviet-American cooperation in assisting negotiated settlements of regional conflicts.

Strange as it may seem, Castro and his entourage were doing very little, if anything, to strengthen the validity of the arguments advanced by the "optimists" in Moscow and the "liberals" in the United States, Western Europe, and Latin America who still hoped for orderly democratic evolution in Cuba. On the contrary, their behavior tended to confirm the opposite point of view, that Castro had no intention of liberalizing his regime under any circumstances and would try to use the normalization of Cuban-American relations to consolidate it. Moscow attributed Castro's stubborn persistence in refusing to take steps that would ease U.S. and international pressures to his apprehension that any real move toward democratization would cause a snowball effect, as in Eastern Europe and the USSR, and would rapidly lead to his loss of control of the country. In this sense, *perestroika's* denouement in the Soviet Union has diminished, if not altogether eliminated, the possibility of moves toward democratization by the present Cuban regime, unless such changes were to be imposed by circumstances beyond its control. It was also thought in Moscow that, to a large degree, Castro's stubbornness was reinforced by Washington's implacably hostile policy, giving him a good excuse to persevere in maintaining his brand of totalitarian socialism. At times, I wondered whether he really wanted the United States to change its policy.

Indeed, an undisguised U.S. enmity to the Cuban revolutionary regime had been from the start and remained an important factor in consolidating Castro's personal grip on power. As Soviet economic assistance guaranteed the survival of his regime, Castro could well live with this enmity for as long as Washington did not decide to invade Cuba. For him the advantages of the normalization of Cuban-American relations could be outweighed by the removal of the ever-present external threat, which helped to justify his one-party system, thought control, and the absence of individual freedoms. He was often irritated by Moscow's insistent prodding that was intended to push him into initiating a new policy of improving Havana's relations with Washington. He may have suspected, not entirely without reason, that this prodding reflected the Soviet Union's self-interest and desire to promote such changes in Cuba's regional policy and its internal regime, which would make it more acceptable to its northern neighbor. Keeping these suspicions to himself, Castro said to the Soviet leaders, with justification, that the United States would be prepared to normalize relations with Cuba only if Cuba distanced itself from the USSR, and this, he swore, could only happen over his dead body.

The situation changed with the collapse of socialism in Eastern Europe and unmistakable signs of a similar transformation building in the Soviet Union, along with the radical change in Soviet-American relations. Castro was clever enough to foresee the inevitable effects these events portended for Cuba. For him, accustomed as he was to thriving on the rivalry and confrontation between the two superpowers, the termination of the Cold War and the disappearance of the "socialist camp" signified the end of Cuba's role as a Soviet beachhead in the Western Hemisphere. As such, it had reaped great political and material benefits, befitting a strategic outpost in wartime. The basis of Castro's grand design for the duration of the Soviet-Cuban alliance was ensuring generous Soviet economic and military support while excluding practically any possibility of a substantial improvement of Cuba's relations with the United States. Now this particular obstacle to such an improvement was being eliminated, whether Castro wanted it or not, but Washington's other conditions for the acceptance of his regime — cessation of Cuba's "subversive" activities in the Third World and democratic elections on the island — remained, and he was running the risk of being left in limbo, with Soviet support dwindling and the United States hardening its position in order to expedite the demise of his regime. In such a situation, his anti-American bravado was becoming a luxury he could ill afford.

This new Soviet-U.S. atmosphere made Castro more receptive to Gorbachev's repeated offers of Soviet good offices in persuading Washington to agree to a direct political dialogue with Havana and explained Gorbachev's and Shevardnadze's persistence in raising this problem with Bush and Baker. Replying in October 1989 to Shevardnadze's optimistic remarks about Cuba's "growing international prestige," particularly in Latin America, and some indirect indications of possible positive future changes in U.S. policy toward Cuba, Castro said that it was necessary to work to that goal and that the Soviet Union could play an important role in the normalization of Cuba's relations with the United States. He talked about the colossal damage to Cuba from the U.S. economic blockade, which was obstructing Cuba's efforts to increase and diversify its exports, and said he was tired of Cuban-American confrontation.

After the withdrawal of Cuban troops from Africa, Castro bitterly complained to Shevardnadze that before the Cubans left Angola, Washington had hinted at a possible improvement in its relations with Havana. Yet, when this condition was met, U.S. representatives started putting emphasis on Cuban assistance to the FMLN forces. There was no doubt in Castro's mind that when there was a peace settlement in El Salvador, the Americans would come up with other new conditions: a multiparty system, democratic elections, and guarantees of human rights. Why, then, try to please the Americans, who thought that socialist countries would not be able to cope with their difficulties. Why should the Americans talk to Cubans? Only when the Americans were convinced that the socialist camp would not disappear, would favorable conditions for the normalization of Cuban relations with the United States be created.

In the months that followed, similar sentiments were expressed by Foreign Minister Isidoro Malmierca Peoli; his first deputy, José Raúl Viera; Vice Foreign Minister Ramón Sanchez Parody; and other Cubans in conversations on the subject with Komplektov and myself; one Cuban official told me bluntly that the Americans would never normalize relations with Cuba while Fidel Castro was in power. Much later, in June 1991, Sanchez Parody said, in his interview with *Latinskaya Amerika*, that as far as this problem was concerned, there was "no light at the end of the tunnel," and he rejected the arguments of the Soviet press that Cuba had lost its chance of improving relations with the United States when Malmierca declined Baker's proposal to join the anti-Hussein coalition in the UN Security Council. Analyzing the position and role of the Cuban exile community in the United States, the Cuban vice foreign minister asserted that it had no influence in Washington: the Cuban exile community "...has been and remains a tool of the most aggressive circles of the American establishment...and has always been used only for political purposes." He was particularly sarcastic when talking about the Cuban American National Foundation and claimed that it exaggerated its importance in the United States and its contacts with the Soviet side, but he then admitted that "there are individuals and even groups in the USSR interested in establishing such contacts and undermining cooperation between Cuba and the Soviet Union."[12]

Still, in spite of this deliberate pessimism, the Cubans showed great interest in what U.S. leaders and State Department officials had to say to Soviet representatives about the U.S. policy toward Cuba and the Cuban position on international and regional problems. Castro did not hesitate to give his advice to the Soviet leadership on Cuba-related issues that could be raised by the U.S. administration in its contacts with Moscow. The Cubans also asked the Soviet Foreign Ministry to raise, in conversations with the Americans, questions on Cuba's behalf related to Radio Martí, TV Martí, Central American problems, and anti-Castro resolutions in the UN Human Rights Commission. They usually made such requests prior to Soviet-American summits and meetings of experts on regional problems. Since the foreign ministry had abandoned obtaining Havana's approval in advance of planned Soviet diplomatic moves intended to help solve these problems, the ministry simply informed the Cubans of these events ahead of time, enabling them to make comments, if they so desired. They usually did.

On the eve of Soviet-American consultations on Central America in Moscow in June 1989, the Cubans thought it was important for the Soviets to insist that the United States should initiate a direct dialogue with Nicaragua and Cuba on questions of bilateral relations and regional problems. The Cubans wanted the USSR Foreign Ministry to bring to the attention of Assistant Secretary of State Bernard Aronson the increased infiltration of Contras from Honduras into the territory of Nicaragua and their attacks against the civilian population. According to the Cubans, these attacks were aimed at 1) establishing grounds for discrediting the Nicaraguan electoral process, 2) creating in Nicaragua a situation similar to the one in Panama, and 3) pressing the Sandinistas for more concessions.

In a sense, apart from reflecting Cuba's interest in the normalization of relations with the United States, Havana's emphasis on "direct dialogue" with Washington was a form of making it clear to Moscow that it was none of its business to discuss specific problems of Cuban-American relations with State Department representatives, except when specifically asked by Havana to do so. The Cubans were concerned with the increased confidentiality of Soviet-American contacts and were particularly sensitive to any indication that Soviet officials were using them to exchange opinions, among other things, on the internal situation in Cuba. On one occasion, they learned of my conversation with U.S. Senator Bob Graham (D-Florida) in the Latin American Directorate in Moscow and complained, through unofficial channels, of my "disloyalty" to them during that conversation. (I did not see any reason for withholding from the senator my assessment of some aspects of Castro's foreign and domestic policies.) Ostensibly to avoid "interference in the internal affairs" of Nicaragua, the Cubans declined to discuss with us in the Soviet Foreign Ministry the internal policy of the Sandinista government and asked us specifically to abstain from doing so in Soviet-American contacts.

At the end of 1989, Havana was alarmed by the delay in the planned deliveries of Soviet MiG-29 fighters. The Cubans suspected, or probably even knew for certain from their friends in the USSR Ministry of Defense, that the reasons for the delay were not technical in nature, and they took what turned out to be effective countermeasures. Raúl Castro spoke about the matter to the chief Soviet military adviser in Cuba and asked him pointedly whether the Soviet Union was going to succumb to American pressure again, as it had in 1962. This caustic remark produced the desired effects in Moscow. When this question was raised again by General Rosales del Toro in a conversation with Marshal Sergei Akhromeyev in Havana in January 1990, Gorbachev's military adviser gave him a reassuring reply, and Chief of the Soviet General Staff General Moiseyev, during his visit to Cuba in October 1990, officially confirmed that MiG-29s would be delivered.

This incident put the Cubans on guard, and when Moscow informed Havana of its plans to exchange opinions with Washington on confidence-building measures in the political-military field with regard to Cuba, they expressed dismay at this intention. We explained to them that for economic reasons, the Soviet Union would soon have to start reducing its military assistance to Cuba anyway, and it was only reasonable to try to get some concessions in return from the United States, which would diminish the American threat to Cuba's security. In particular, the Soviets intended to propose that the U.S. government confirm in some form its undertaking not to engage in aggressive actions against Cuba and not to interfere in its internal affairs. This would allow Havana to reduce its military expenditure, concentrating resources on solving its social and economic problems. The main criteria for the Soviets in conversations with U.S. representatives would be actual effective guarantees of Cuba's security; they would coordinate their position with Havana and would keep the Cubans informed of progress in the talks.

It was difficult for the Cubans to reject these arguments, but Sanchez Parody did not conceal his strong doubts with regard to the possibility of obtaining such concessions from Washington. The Cubans eventually agreed to the proposition, correctly concluding that if they didn't, Moscow would have a free hand in negotiating with Washington. Soviet-American contacts on the problem dragged on for months, with the USSR Foreign Ministry having problems in elaborating negotiating positions; it had to conciliate differences of approach not only with the Cubans but first with the USSR Ministry of Defense. Soviet General Staff officers insisted that the Soviet concessions had to be limited, in essence, to the planned reduction of military supplies to Cuba, leaving intact the Soviet motorized brigade, the Lourdes communications base, and the Cienfuegos submarine support facility. It appeared that the State Department had similar problems with the Pentagon, which seemed to insist on the liquidation of the Soviet military presence in Cuba without giving much in return. Eventually, Havana blocked any possibility of a Soviet-American understanding on the issue by insisting on the withdrawal of U.S. forces from the Guantánamo base as a condition for any substantial reduction in Soviet-Cuban military cooperation.

There was another incident early in 1990 that illustrated Havana's particularly strong influence in Moscow on military matters; on occasion, this superseded Gorbachev's interest in avoiding steps bound to cause adverse reaction in Washington. The Cuban military asked the USSR Ministry of Defense to send to the island an old, deactivated, Soviet meduim-range missile "R-12," of the type deployed there in 1962, to be installed as an exhibit at the Museum of the Cuban Armed Forces. The obvious purpose of the exercise was to have a permanent visual reminder to the Cuban public and Soviet visitors of Cuba's "hour of glory," a symbol of its defiance of the "Evil Empire" and of the Soviet commitment to defend the island.

When consulted on this request, the USSR Foreign Ministry proposed declining it on grounds that the installation of such an exhibit in Cuba would not be politically expedient; it would give the wrong signal to Washington, and, in particular, it could be used by American opponents of the Soviet-American Strategic Arms Limitation Treaty, negotiated in Geneva, as an argument against its ratification by the U.S.

Congress. However, Minister of Defense Marshal Yazov and Chief of the General Staff General Moiseyev overruled the objections of Foreign Minister Shevardnadze and secured Gorbachev's approval of the scheme. They argued that the Cubans had already gone to the expense of constructing a stand for the exhibit after receiving a preliminary positive reply from the USSR Ministry of Defense and would be offended if Moscow reneged on its promise. The missile's exterior framework was duly shipped to Cuba and installed on a pedestal.

As mentioned above, in 1979 the Soviet government, in order to appease Washington, officially renamed the Soviet combat brigade in Cuba as "No. 12 Training Center" after the "mini-crisis" caused by Washington's "discovery" of its existence. The Cubans did not conceal their disgust, qualifying this step as a deplorable, needless concession to Washington, although at the time Castro contained his anger and even publicly supported Moscow's explanation of the functions and status of the brigade. Nonetheless, for all practical purposes, Fidel and Raúl Castro continued to regard Soviet servicemen in Cuba as hostages, proceeding from the original understanding reached with Anastas Mikoyan in Havana in November 1962 that the Soviet brigade was committed to combat in case of a U.S. invasion. When Yuri Andropov, then secretary general of the CPSU Central Committee and commander-in-chief of the Soviet armed forces, informed Raúl Castro in 1983 that the Soviet Union could not defend Cuba militarily, the brigade was not mentioned specifically because the implication seemed obvious from the Soviet viewpoint — Soviet troops in Cuba would not have any combat role.

However, the Cubans preferred to interpret this differently. In January 1990, General Ulises Rosales del Toro, talking in Havana to Marshal Sergei Akhromeyev, referred to the "worsening situation around Cuba" and to the possibility of a "direct invasion by U.S. armed forces." He then asked what the actions of the Soviet motorized brigade would be in case of U.S. aggression against Cuba, as if he were unaware of Andropov's verbal statement to Raúl Castro. Marshal Akhromeyev avoided a direct reply, saying that he was no longer with the USSR Ministry of Defense and was not dealing with "specific problems of the utilization of troops."[13] That was a strange response, as Akhromeyev could not possibly have been ignorant of Andropov's conversation with Raúl Castro.

Even more peculiar — when we in the Latin American Directorate, acting on Shevardnadze's instructions, began to discuss with the Soviet

General Staff officers a draft reply to General Rosales del Toro's inquiry, they professed total ignorance of the Soviet leadership's position as related by CPSU Secretary General Andropov to Raúl Castro. Only after they were shown a transcript of Andropov's verbal message did they agree with our suggestion that the Cubans should once again be informed of the USSR's inability to defend them militarily. However, the USSR Foreign Ministry was never informed whether this had been carried out.

The problem of U.S. policy toward Cuba was one of the subjects often discussed both during high-level meetings and working-level political consultations between Moscow and Havana. When Carlos Aldana met Foreign Minister Aleksandr Bessmertnykh in Moscow in July 1991, they stressed "the importance of intensifying joint efforts and international actions to eliminate tensions around Cuba on the basis of Cuba's security, sovereignty, and self-determination [stating that] one of the premises for improving the situation in the region is avoiding conflicts and achieving a normalization of relations between the United States and Cuba, on the basis of equality, mutual respect, and noninterference in the internal affairs of others."[14]

In an interview with *Prensa Latina*, Aldana discarded the possibility that the Soviet Union would succumb to Washington's pressures for ending cooperation with Cuba and referred to "the Soviet government's firm and upright position, its determination not to submit to any kind of blackmail nor accept any such pressures." He also said that all attempts by the United States "to confuse things and cast a shadow over Cuban-Soviet relations were useless, because there existed a stable and clear communication between Cuban and Soviet leaders."[15]

Notes

1. *Pravda*, April 23, 1962.

2. Henry Kissinger, 1979, *White House Years* (Boston: Little, Brown), 632, 634.

3. Henry Kissinger, 1979, *White House Years* (Boston: Little, Brown), 647.

4. *Facts-on-File Yearbook*, 1978, (New York: Facts-on-File, Inc.), 905, 1016.

5. *Facts-on-File Yearbook*, 1979, (New York: Facts-on-File, Inc.), 674.

6. *Facts-on-File Yearbook*, 1979, (New York: Facts-on-File, Inc.), 673.

7. *Facts-on-File Yearbook*, 1979, (New York: Facts-on-File, Inc.), 638.

8. *Problems of Communism*, special edition, Spring 1992, 108.

9. *The Backgrounder*, 1990, (Washington: The Heritage Foundation), 13 (May 14).

10. *American Foreign Policy*, 1989, current documents, (Washington, D.C.: Department of State), 691.

11. Committee of Santa Fe, 1988, *Santa Fe II: A Strategy for Latin America in the Nineties*, 31.

12. *Latinskaya Amerika*, 1991, No. 10.

13. Marshal Akhromeyev's report to President Gorbachev of January 15, 1990.

14. *Granma*, International edition, July 14, 1991.

15. *Granma*, July 3, 1991.

Chapter 8

The End of The Road

Defeat of the Cuban Lobby in the USSR

The desperate attempt of the conservative forces in the Soviet Union to prevent the disintegration of the Soviet empire and to save what they thought still could be saved of the socialist totalitarian system was expected and hoped for in Havana. After the resignation of Eduard Shevardnadze in December 1991 and his public warning that the country was sliding toward dictatorship, it became fashionable in the political and diplomatic circles of the Soviet capital to discuss the modalities of a possible coup. There were even opinion polls to establish the degree of public support for a coup. Since the Cubans had extensive contacts at all levels of the CPSU, the Soviet government, and the USSR Supreme Soviet hierarchy, they were in a good position to know that their fellow travelers in Moscow were resolved not to allow the "foundations of socialism" in the Soviet Union to be undermined any further.

As was pointed out in a *Komsomolskaya Pravda* commentary, the junta formed by the putschists included "the most influential pro-Havana lobbyists of the recent Soviet leadership,"[1] some of whom had recent personal contacts with Fidel Castro. Therefore, the assertion of General Rafael del Pino, the former deputy commander of the Cuban Air Force who defected to the United States, that Castro knew of the preparations for the coup was not as farfetched as it might seem.[2] There was no reason why Yanayev, Lukyanov, and Shenin could not be frank with General Escalona and Carlos Aldana when they met in Moscow in February and June 1991, or Kryuchkov with Castro in May 1991 in Havana — not necessarily in terms of informing them of their specific intentions, but in sharing their concern with the activities of the "enemies of socialism" and expressing their determination to do something about it.

During the coup, Castro cautiously abstained from welcoming it publicly, but a closer analysis of the way the Cuban mass media were covering the events in Moscow reveals that he wished the putschists well and was prepared to grant recognition to their figurehead Gennady Yanayev as the new Soviet president, had they succeeded in keeping power. On August 19, 1991, *Granma* published, without any commentary, an official Soviet TASS agency report under the heading: "Yanayev Assumes Presidential Functions in the USSR." The next day it published a detailed TASS report entitled "Yanayev Affirms that Most Energetic Measures Will Be Taken to Get the USSR out of the Crisis" and the complete text of the "Appeal to the Soviet People," issued by the "State Committee for the State of Emergency" (GKChP). Again, there was no commentary and nothing about the resistance to the coup headed by Boris Yeltsin. On the strength of that information, Cuban readers could only conclude that the coup was met by Soviet citizens "with understanding" and that the situation in the USSR was being "normalized."

On August 21, 1991, when it became clear that the coup had failed, *Granma* mentioned for the first time Yeltsin's call for civil disobedience and resistance to the coup and published the "Statement of the Government of Cuba on the Events in the Soviet Union," which spoke of its "profound preoccupation" with these events and gave a summary of the address of "Provisional President of the USSR" Gennady Yanayev to heads of state and government and the UN Secretary General. It hypocritically asserted that while the Western media "promoted various speculations," producing a "contradictory, tense, and confused" view of the situation, and the Soviet media insisted that the "tendency to normalization is prevalent," the Cuban press "limited itself strictly to news reports proceeding from different sources, taking into account particularly, as we have always done, Soviet information agencies."

The Cuban statement continued that it was not appropriate for the Cuban government to pass judgments on the events in the USSR; however, "in the present circumstances, it is our most fervent wish that the Soviet people can peacefully overcome their difficulties and that great nation can remain united, exercising its international influence, which is its due, as an indispensable counterweight to those who want to impose absolute hegemony on the world." It said in conclusion: "The Yankee imperialism, international gendarme, aspiring to become a master of the world, has no right to take advantage of this painful situation." That was actually what motivated the statement — the fear that Cuba would be left alone face-to-face with the United States, without its ever-present Soviet political, economic, and military support.

On August 29, 1991, *Granma* printed a lengthy editorial entitled "Our Most Sacred Duty is to Save the Nation, the Revolution, and Socialism," which dwelt in more detail on the "tragedy" in the Soviet Union and stated, "No matter what happens in the USSR, we will not depart from the path we have chosen." The same fears were reiterated as follows:

> As a poor and underdeveloped country, situated right next to the United States, we are fully aware of the mortal danger which U.S. hegemony represented for all peoples and understand, therefore, a historic need for the Soviet Union to preserve its unity and integrity, no matter what legal structure it adopts to do this, as a factor of real power on the planet, on whose existence will depend, in great measure, that the third millennium does not reserve a Third Reich to us.

There were no congratulatory messages or telephone calls from Fidel Castro to Mikhail Gorbachev and Boris Yeltsin. The above editorial summarized the real Cuban perspective in this sentence: "We cannot, as many Western leaders have done, rejoice in this tragedy." There was, however, a letter dated August 21, 1991, to Boris Yeltsin from Jorge Mas Canosa, the leader of the Cuban American National Foundation, congratulating the Russian president on the victory of the democratic forces and asking him "...to use his enormous moral authority to ensure that the Soviet Union withdraws its troops from Cuba and puts an end to all subsidies that the militarist regime of Fidel Castro receives by the decision of the same political elements who wanted to deprive your people of freedoms and hopes."[3]

The failure of the August coup was followed by the accelerated process of removing ideology from the USSR's relations with the outside world and a reassessment of friendships and priorities. No exception was made for Cuba. With the CPSU deprived of political power, its activities banned, and the principal protectors of Castro's regime in prison or out of jobs, Havana tasted the first bitter fruits of that process when Jorge Mas Canosa and Francisco J. Hernández of the Cuban American National Foundation, together with Lawrence Smith, a member of the U.S. House of Representatives, and Armando Valladares, then the U.S. representative on the UN Human Rights Commission, arrived in Moscow in early September 1991. They carried a letter from Dante B. Fascell (D-Florida), then chairman of the U.S.

House of Representatives Foreign Affairs Committee, asking for the cessation of Soviet aid to Havana, and they had meetings with Russian President Boris Yeltsin and the USSR Foreign Minister Boris Pankin, which were reported by Moscow television on September 6, 1991, as sensational news. Yeltsin told them that the Soviet subsidies to Cuba would end when the current trade agreement expired. Pankin admitted that some aspects of Soviet assistance to Castro's regime were "immoral."

With all that, Gorbachev was still trying to remain loyal to Castro, though Castro was not exactly loyal to him during the coup. Explaining Moscow's policy toward Havana to the American audience on ABC television on September 6, 1991, the Soviet leader added little to what already had been said by the USSR government on Soviet economic relations with Cuba. He avoided the issue of Soviet economic and military assistance to the Castro regime and spoke only of trade relations, saying that they were being put on a mutually beneficial basis and that the USSR would continue to supply Cuba with oil and other raw materials in exchange for sugar and minerals. His words were reported by *Granma* under the heading: "The USSR Will Maintain and Expand Cooperation with Cuba, Declares President Gorbachev to North-American Television."[4]

Cole Blasier of the U.S. Library of Congress, in his analysis of changes in Soviet policy toward Cuba in the aftermath of the August coup, correctly pointed out that "the widespread repudiation of the old authoritarian system that followed the coup's collapse gutted the pro-Castro forces among the old guard [and that] in the post-coup setting, elimination of aid to Cuba ceased to be a potential foreign policy embarrassment and came to be viewed as progressive by reformists."[5] It was certainly true about Yeltsin and Russian Foreign Minister Kozyrev, but for Gorbachev, with his fidelity to the "socialist option," it was more difficult to come to the realization that it was immoral for a democratic country to sustain a totalitarian regime at great economic and political cost. Had the Soviet Union continued to exist with Gorbachev as its president, he probably would have attempted to use what was left of his power to preserve a few more vestiges of the Soviet-Cuban alliance. In any event, major structural and quantitative changes in economic relations with Cuba could come only with the expiration of bilateral agreements for the year 1991.

Withdrawal of the Soviet Brigade

S hortly before the events of August 1991 in Moscow, President Bush used his stay in the Soviet capital during his last summit meeting with the president of the USSR to name publicly, in a speech at the Moscow Institute of International Relations on July 30, 1991, three obstacles for further development of U.S. relations with the Soviet Union: 1) the lack of progress toward a solution of the Soviet territorial problem with Japan, 2) Moscow's resistance to the independence of the Baltic states, and 3) the continuing Soviet military assistance to Cuba. In conversations with President Gorbachev and Foreign Minister Bessmertnykh, President Bush and Secretary of State Baker reiterated that close Soviet-Cuban ties were impeding the expansion of cooperation between Washington and Moscow and referred specifically to Moscow's military links with Havana. On August 1, 1991, speaking to the press on the results of the summit, Vitaly Churkin, foreign ministry spokesman, noted that much more was said on this problem in public than in confidential talks and affirmed that the Soviet Union would continue its close relations with Cuba, despite objections by the Americans at the Moscow summit, and would observe all agreements concluded with Cuba.[6]

In other words, there was no progress at the summit on Moscow's military links with Cuba. The main reason for this deadlock was that Havana blocked Soviet-American talks on confidence-building measures for Cuba. Moscow was not yet prepared to reach a mutually acceptable accommodation with Washington on this issue, against Castro's objections. Havana continued to use every opportunity to dramatize the threat to Cuba from U.S. military activities in the vicinity of the island, trying to persuade Moscow that undiminished Soviet military assistance was needed more than ever before, that Washington's non-invasion assurances were not to be trusted, and that the Soviet brigade could not be withdrawn from Cuba if U.S. forces were to remain in Guantánamo. *Granma* wrote on September 6, 1991, that the U.S. forces "are practicing sea landings, while Bush demands the suspension of military aid to Cuba."

It took the transfer of real political power in Moscow from Gorbachev to Russian President Yeltsin and the removal from office of most active and influential supporters of Castro's regime before the way could be cleared for withdrawing the Soviet brigade from Cuba. It was Yeltsin who stated, in reply to a question from a Cuban exile in Miami, when interviewed by the ABC television network on September

6, 1991, that the withdrawal of Soviet troops stationed abroad should continue, including a gradual withdrawal from Cuba.[7] During the same interview, Gorbachev abstained from any comments on the subject, and *Granma* chose to omit Yeltsin's statement in its report on the interview. There were, obviously, still some hopes in Havana that the Russian president would not be able to push Gorbachev to such an extreme. Otherwise, Castro would have immediately raised an outcry on the issue to try to avoid his second startling public humiliation at the hands of Soviet leaders.

Gorbachev's announcement at a joint press conference with Secretary of State Baker in Moscow on September 11, 1991, that the Soviet government had decided to negotiate the withdrawal of the Soviet motorized brigade from the island produced a sensation in the world press, exultation in Washington and Miami, and deep shock and indignation in Havana. The next day Soviet Foreign Minister Boris Pankin, speaking at a press conference in Moscow, poured more oil on the flames. He stated that the decision to withdraw the Soviet military contingent was intended to lessen tensions around Cuba and improve Soviet-American relations. Pankin added that the USSR took the line of gradually reducing military aid to Cuba, based on Cuba's plentiful military supplies and adequate defense capabilities. Pankin also said that the Soviet brigade in Cuba was "a symbol of a past epoch in international and Soviet-U.S. relations of which we must rid ourselves" and expressed hope that this withdrawal would enhance productive discussions with Washington on working out additional security measures regarding Cuba, which initially could involve a reduction in the strength of U.S. forces at Guantánamo, a reduction in the number of calls of U.S. warships to that base, and advance announcement of military maneuvers in the area.[8]

Immediately after Gorbachev's announcement, the Cuban Foreign Ministry issued a statement, qualifying it as "an intolerable practice from the viewpoint of international norms and existing agreements between the two states," since it was not preceded by either consultations with or prior notification of the Cuban side. The statement also pointed out that Secretary of State Baker, who "expressed appreciation and satisfaction for this decision, even though he considered it a small step, made no reference to U.S. troops stationed in Guantánamo, a territory illegally occupied by the government of his country against the will of the people and the government of Cuba."[9] On the whole, it was moderate in tone and touched only indirectly on the substance of the matter, concentrating more on Moscow's failure to consult Havana.

Castro's righteous anger over Moscow's second major "betrayal" of the Cuban Revolution, which he compared to Khrushchev's conduct during the Missile Crisis, found its full expression in *Granma*'s editorial on September 14, 1991, authored most probably by the maximum leader himself and entitled "Cuba Will Never Let Itself Be Turned Over or Sold Out to the United States." Written in verbose, emotional language characteristic of his style, the article affirmed that the unilateral and unconditional decision to withdraw the Soviet brigade, taken without prior consultation with Havana, "has grave political connotations, which compromise our security" and was equivalent to giving the United States "a green light to carry out its plans of aggression against Cuba."

The editorial brushed aside Pankin's references to the "so-called measures of confidence with regard to Cuba [as] secondary and undeserving of any comment" and characterized as "extremely modest" Moscow's "expectations" of the reduction of U.S. military personnel in Guantánamo and "other equally insignificant measures, [which] would always be subject to the arbitrariness of the United States and could be cancelled at any moment, as is traditional in United States' conduct, especially now that it considers itself the master of the world, while the steps the USSR declared itself ready to take would be irreversible and unconditional." The analysis was concluded by an allegation that "concessions in respect to Cuba were negotiated and finalized with the United States, acceding to its demand without even a single word spoken to our country" and were all the more surprising "after seeing a few days earlier how Mikhail Gorbachev, president of the Soviet Union, had dealt capably with the subject of Soviet relations with Cuba while speaking on U.S. television."

With these preliminaries, the editorial formulated the Cuban position on the subject: "We would be willing to accept the simultaneous withdrawal from our country of Soviet military personnel and U.S. military personnel. This would be the only equitable, just, and honorable method in present circumstances." It added that there were "issues that must be discussed with us as one of the interested parties" and that Cuba was prepared "to sign an international agreement to that end, backed by the United Nations." That was, in fact, a public confirmation of Havana's inflexible position in its earlier confidential discussions with Moscow on possible solutions to the problem of reducing military tension around the island and also an indication of its interest in making the problem of foreign military presence on the island a subject of trilateral negotiations with Cuban participation.

Full of ire, the Cuban commander-in-chief's article expressed his long-suppressed feelings of humiliation and extreme resentment with Moscow's behavior toward Havana, accumulated during the thirty-odd years of the Soviet-Cuban alliance. The *Granma* editorial sarcastically noted that there was nothing new in the practice of great powers "to make public their intentions and thus turn them into faits accomplis; ...nor should it surprise those of us who experienced the outcome of the Missile Crisis, one of whose results, following numerous conversations between our leadership and Anastas Mikoyan in Havana from November 3 to 22, 1962, and the corresponding agreement signed in Moscow on May 29, 1962, was precisely the permanence of the military contingent."

The second point was illustrated by an emotional description of the "painful and unforgettable experience, which the Soviet-U.S. agreement on the withdrawal of nuclear missiles without consulting Cuba signified for our young revolution," after Cuba "had risked nuclear extermination for the sake of strengthening the defensive capacity of the socialist community — above all of the USSR." In the logic of Castro's thinking, "enormous dangers," which Cuba faced "for the sake of everyone's security," and "the agreements, which were violated in those days," gave the Cuban leadership "the right to demand at least that minimal Soviet military presence, which was accepted."

On both points, Castro certainly had a case. He did learn of Gorbachev's decision on the withdrawal of the brigade from news agency reports. And, as confirmed by Sergo Mikoyan, Castro, in conversations with Anastas Mikoyan, did make it as a condition of his acceptance of the Soviet pullback from Cuba that a Soviet combat unit should remain on the island as a guarantee against an invasion or rather as a guarantee of the Soviet involvement in a Cuban-American armed conflict, and this condition was accepted.[10] Later Soviet General Staff officers insisted in conversations with us in the Foreign Ministry's Latin American Directorate that there was no written agreement on the brigade; it was verbal. However, to put the historical record completely straight, the permanent Cuban commander-in-chief should have added that not only did he willingly agree to participate in Khrushchev's nuclear gamble but he also tried, in desperation, to push the Soviet Union and the United States even closer to the brink of a nuclear catastrophe in the belief that it was the only way of saving his regime or, if worst came to worst, of giving him the consolation to think that the "evil empire" (borrowing Reagan's term for the USSR and applying it to the United States) would also be destroyed.

Castro also took his revenge on Moscow for Leonid Brezhnev's conduct in the 1979 "mini-crisis" in Soviet-American relations upon the "discovery" by Washington of the presence of the Soviet combat brigade in Cuba, when, according to *Granma,* "the then-Soviet leadership, without taking into account our opinion, which was opposed to denying the presence of that brigade, and with consultations still unfinished, yielded to public pressure from the United States and, through official statements and with sibylline lenience of the United States' rulers, transformed overnight in theory this combat unit, which was committed to act in the event of a U.S. invasion, into a supposedly inoffensive training center." Here, again, he had a case — Brezhnev's government did succumb to persuasive arguments by President Carter, who was then under pressure from the internal Republican opposition for a firmer stand on the Soviet military presence in Cuba.

The analysis of the *Granma* editorial would be incomplete without mentioning the most striking twist of Castro's mind on the Soviet Union's "historic, political, and moral responsibility" to Cuba. To give an idea of this responsibility, Castro referred to Havana's "own experience, [when] out of loyalty to certain principles which cannot be renounced without failing to be what one was when those principles were adopted, we withstood all pressures and even the offers of various U.S. administrations in exchange for recanting and breaking our close ties with the Soviet Union." He lectured Gorbachev sternly, "We always firmly and loyally met our commitments. No state, great or small, and much less a great power, no matter who leads it, can turn its back on the legitimate and historical agreements and commitments it has made."

That was a classic example of trying to make a virtue out of necessity. It was certainly true that U.S administrations were putting out feelers time and again in Havana, promising a substantial reward to the Castro regime if it distanced itself from Moscow. In fact from 1961-1962 on, this had been Washington's first condition for any serious improvement of its relations with Havana, and Fidel Castro mentioned it in some of his speeches — only to reassure his listeners that Cuba would never abandon its friendship with the Soviet Union. To the best of Moscow's knowledge, Castro never flirted seriously with Washington. The question is why? Given the earlier evolution of Castro's political views and convictions, rather than accept his explanation of fidelity to the USSR, there are more grounds to believe that he saw no alternative to his alliance with the Soviet Union that could be chosen without endangering his regime; he knew that Washington would not be content with only the "de-Sovietization" of Cuba's foreign policy and would press for internal political changes.

Shortly before Gorbachev's announcement, Havana was incensed, among other things, by Yeltsin's reception of the Cuban American National Foundation's leaders, to whom *Granma* referred as "Batista followers, redeemed by the State Department, knocking impatiently on the doors of the Russian Federation's leaders, trying at all costs to persuade them to join the U.S. blockade," and whom it evidently suspected of playing a role in the decision on the brigade: "There they were, in the front row, enjoying the news." Their presence in Moscow during the joint Gorbachev-Baker press conference added insult to injury.

Finally, *Granma* spitefully noted that it was difficult to understand "...what is happening under the present circumstances, when the East-West conflict is considered to be over with the disappearance of one of the blocs, and when in the name of new thinking in international relations, regrettable practices, which were manifested in some very difficult moments in bilateral relations between Cuba and the USSR, seem to reappear." And its editorial betrayed once again Castro's doomsday thinking, prophetizing:

> We are startled and indignant when we think that we could be moving toward a world order, in which small Third World countries like Cuba, whose social system is not to the liking of the United States, have no alternative except to risk disappearing; and in which there is no room for ideological loyalties or even the most elementary ethical principles, without which our civilization will be threatened with the possible emergence of a new barbarism, based on the United States' technological power and hegemonic delirium.[11]

To sum up, the Gorbachev-Yeltsin decision to withdraw Soviet troops from Cuba and the manner of its announcement was Moscow's coup de grace to the agonizing Soviet-Cuban alliance, deprived in August 1991 of its ideological foundation. Since the United States was no longer regarded by the Soviet leadership as the USSR's potential enemy, Cuba lost much of its former strategic value for Moscow as a support base for Soviet military activities in the Western Hemisphere. However, appearances of close Soviet-Cuban military cooperation were still preserved, symbolized by the presence of Soviet troops on the island; it was important for Castro to keep up these appearances. As pointed out by Cole Blasier in his article, "Moscow's Retreat from Cuba," the announcement of the coming withdrawal of the Soviet military contingent was "a staggering blow to the Castro regime not so much because of its immediate practical importance, but because of its symbolic and political implications."[12] This conclusion was borne out by Havana's hysterical reaction expressed in the *Granma* editorial, which spoke also of the symbolic importance of the presence of Soviet forces on the island: they were not significant for Cuba's defense in numbers but, at the same time, "had great significance as an expression of friendship and solidarity in the face of threats from the United States."

The Cuban leaders were aware that since 1983 the Soviet motorized brigade on the island had no longer been committed to combat action, apart from the improbable eventuality of generalized military conflict between the two superpowers, but they took care to keep that knowledge to themselves. The Cuban public and outside observers could only guess at what Moscow's standing orders to the brigade were for the eventuality of U.S.-Cuban armed conflict. The matter was complicated further by the absence of any written bilateral agreement specifying the purpose and conditions of Soviet troop deployment on Cuban territory. This certainly helped Havana maintain the impression that the Soviet Union continued to be committed in some way to Cuba's defense.

The delicate task of explaining to the Cubans the reasons behind the Soviet decision and of pursuing the matter further was given to Vice Foreign Minister Valery Nikolayenko, who had talks with Cuban First Deputy Foreign Minister Alcibiades Hidalgo on September 21-22, 1991. At a press conference in Havana, he described them as "very difficult" but stated optimistically that "the results are positive: we have achieved understanding by the Cubans of the motives that served as a basis for the Soviet initiative on the stage-by-stage withdrawal of the brigade." Asked about the guarantees of Cuba's safety, Nikolayenko mentioned "Washington's assurances that any Soviet step to reduce its military presence in Cuba will not be used to harm the security of the Republic" and stated that any reduction of the Soviet military presence in Cuba "will not be detrimental to Cuban security" and that U.S. military activities in the area have already been partially reduced. Referring to Cuba's insistence on the simultaneous pullout of U.S. forces from Guantánamo, he said that this "just demand of the Cuban people" was not directly linked with the withdrawal of Soviet troops.[13]

This optimism seemed excessive in light of Hidalgo's remarks at the same press conference:

Cuba reiterated to the Soviet Union its opinions of the [Soviet] initiative, which were published on September 14, and fully explained the reasons for this position. Cuba's position is that the only acceptable formula under the circumstances is that the Soviet proposal be accompanied by negotiations for the end of the U.S. military presence at the Guantánamo Naval Base, maintained against the Cuban people's will.

Hidalgo insisted that the problem of the withdrawal of Soviet troops was "crucial to Cuba's national security."[14]

The Cuban side confirmed this stand during the first round of talks on the implementation of the Soviet decision, held in Havana in November 1991. Soviet special envoy Viacheslav Ustinov, who was supposed to negotiate a time schedule and other modalities of the withdrawal of Soviet troops, returned to Moscow empty-handed. In an interview with *Izvestia*, he admitted that the discussion "has been mainly about politics [and said that] we have now reached a stage where the two countries' high leaders in Moscow and Havana have to reflect and adopt an appropriate decision."[15] In another interview, the special envoy rejected the Cuban arguments, noting that the problem of Guantánamo went back to the beginning of the century and was regulated by agreements between Cuba and the United States. To make his point quite clear, he referred to precedents in Greece and the Philippines, where similar problems were tackled on the basis of bilateral agreements.[16]

A few days later, Castro, in an interview with the Mexican *Sol de Mexico*, blasted the Soviet president, accusing him of doing "a great damage" to Cuba and increasing the risk of U.S. armed aggression against Cuba. He attributed Gorbachev's decision to U.S. pressures and said it provoked "contradictions and even irritation and tension" in relations between Cuba and the USSR. Castro added that he proposed "to discuss and analyze" this issue, confirming that he would agree only with the simultaneous withdrawal of Soviet troops and U.S. forces from the island.[17]

Castro's defiant and arrogant public stand on the issue could have been disregarded as a characteristic expression of his wounded self-esteem and grave concern with political consequences of the Soviet decision, had it not also reflected his awareness of the vested interest of the Soviet military in preserving its presence on the island and the knowledge that he could depend on its support. In fact, the USSR government itself hastened to dispel the impression that the withdrawal of the brigade would mark the beginning of the culmination of Soviet-Cuban military cooperation. Nikolayenko made it quite clear in his statements in Havana that this was not the intention of the Soviet side. Furthermore, Moscow decided to send Admiral V. Chernavin, commander-in-chief of the Soviet Navy, on an official visit to Havana. It was timed to precede the talks on the pullback of "training center No. 12" and was intended to "soften" Cuban resistance to that step. The admiral failed in this mission, but he succeeded in reassuring Raúl Castro of Moscow's desire to continue its military links with Cuba and in voicing this message to the public.

As it transpired afterwards during the first round of talks, Havana actually tried to blackmail Moscow by linking the presence of Soviet ground forces in Cuba with the further Soviet use of a submarine support base at Cienfuegos and electronic surveillance facilities at Lourdes. That was confirmed by Sergei Yushenkov, a deputy of the Russian Supreme Soviet, who said, talking to the press in December 1991, that the issue of the "training brigade [proved] much more serious than it might seem at first." He explained that, in the opinion of the Soviet military, the Soviet Union continued to have strategic interests in Cuba, relating primarily to the facilities at Cienfuegos and Lourdes, and it would be premature to withdraw from that country completely.[18] It stands to reason that the Cuban ambassador in Moscow denied this linkage in an interview with *Nezavisimaya Gazeta* in January 1992.[19]

Political and Economic Repercussions

In the meantime, there were other developments in relations between the two countries that did not augur well for Havana. In October 1991, the Russian Television Network reported on the meeting of Gennady Burbulis, the Russian secretary of state, with a delegation of the Liberal Union of Cuba, headed by its president, Alberto Montaner. According to the report, they reached an understanding on establishing direct contacts between this Cuban exile organization and the Russian leadership. Coming after meetings of Russian President Yeltsin and Soviet Foreign Minister Pankin with Jorge Mas Canosa, this was yet another snub to Castro. The Liberal Union of Cuba delegation came to the USSR at the invitation of the Russian Social Democratic party, and its visit coincided with the establishment in Moscow of the Committee for the Defense of Human Rights in Cuba, the first Soviet organization concerned with human rights in a socialist country. The committee was headed by Yuri Karyakin, a prominent Soviet writer, and included such well-known figures as historian Yuri Afanasyev, playwright Aleksandr

Gelman, philosopher Igor Klyamkin, film producer Elem Klimov, writer Ales Adamovich, and leader of the Democratic Party of Russia, Nikolai Travkin.

Before the August coup, Soviet economic relations with Cuba were already being transformed, under bilateral arrangements reached in December 1990, along the lines of the reduction of price subsidies, credits, and technical assistance with the aim of eventually putting them on a commercial basis. At the Fourth Congress of the CPC, Castro presented detailed information on how the USSR was fulfilling its obligations under the 1991 trade agreement. In January-May 1991, Soviet supplies to Cuba were limited almost exclusively to oil and petroleum products (4,160,000 tons as planned). There were no deliveries of rice, beans, vegetable oil, powdered milk, condensed milk, butter, canned meat, sulfur, caustic soda and other chemicals, rolled steel, non-ferrous metals, tires, cotton, spare parts for domestic appliances, and other products previously exported to Cuba. Cuba received only 5 percent of the planned deliveries of fertilizers and almost no newsprint, animal fats, and spare parts for machinery and equipment. Of the total value of $710 million for products supplied, oil and its products accounted for $650 million.[20]

However, some programs of economic assistance to Havana continued, despite the catastrophic financial situation and declining industrial production in the USSR. In the first five months of 1991, when the USSR state budget deficit skyrocketed to almost 40 billion rubles (actual income was 45.6 billion, while expenditures were 84.8 billion), 4.7 percent of the expenditures went to finance what was officially called "external economic activities" — Soviet economic and military aid to Afghanistan, Cuba, and other friendly regimes still considered indispensable.[21] The Soviet Union participated in 1991 in the construction of eighty-four economic projects in Cuba, such as a nickel plant at Camarioca, thermal power plants, a nuclear power plant at Juraguá, and an oil refinery.

The Fourth Congress of the Cuban Communist Party in October 1991 was the first forum of Cuban communists that did not receive a congratulatory message from the CPSU Central Committee — it no longer existed. However, that event did not pass unnoticed in the Soviet Union. For months before the Congress, Soviet analysts were making bets: Will Castro introduce meaningful changes into his policy, or will he continue the orthodox line? There were even rumors that he might vacate one of his posts, that of prime minister, and embark on a program of economic liberalization, while maintaining tight political and administrative control, similar to the recent Chinese model of development. The Congress all but stopped this debate. As the *Moscow News* stated, "The division of Cuban affairs analysts into optimists, who hoped that the Fourth Congress of the Communist Party would pave the way for reforms, and pessimists, who entertained no such hopes, lost all relevance as soon as the Congress opened."[22] It became abundantly clear both to Moscow's sympathizers and critics of Castro that he was now more than ever convinced of the wisdom of his decision to resist any changes that would risk weakening the "foundations of socialism" in Cuba.

Nonetheless, commentaries on the Congress by Soviet correspondents in Havana — A. Moiseyev for *Pravda* and A. Kamorin for *Izvestia* — and other reports in the Soviet media were different in tone and content, reflecting Soviet conservatives' and democrats' divergent attitudes toward Castro and his brand of socialism. In Moiseyev's judgment, the main result of the Congress was that the Cuban Communist Party would continue to lead the country "forward with optimism, without changing course." He noted that the delegates "resolved to show combat spirit, oppose pessimistic sentiments and distrust of socialism, and put a stop to criminal antisocial activities." And, Moiseyev emphasized that they "unanimously advocated retaining the anti-imperialist and internationalist thrust of their country's foreign policy and spoke in favor of the principles of respect, sovereignty, and each nation's right to self-determination." The only somber note in his report was a reference to a "local observer's opinion" that Castro's slogan 'Socialism or Death!' "may perhaps acquire more dramatic meaning on the island."[23]

Izvestia's Kamorin, on the other hand, took a critical and somewhat sarcastic position, commenting that although the intention to hold the Congress behind closed doors was known in advance, "not many people supposed that the doors would be closed so firmly." He thought that Castro's interventions did not contain any important points not made already by him in previous speeches and noted that the Cuban leader openly expressed his negative attitude to recent changes in the USSR, particularly with regard to the situation with the CPSU. In conclusion, Kamorin cited one of his Western colleagues in Havana who said, "The communists have decided at the Congress what to do with the country. Now the country will have to decide what to do with the communists."[24]

The report on the Congress in *Moscow News* was entitled "Ovations Without Reforms" and contained ironic references to "a bill for a billion dollars" presented to Moscow for its "base behavior in 1991" and to the "powdered milk that the Cuban children living on a lush and fertile land will now be deprived of because of the Soviet Union."[25] A scathing commentary was made by L. Levchenko on a Moscow Radio program in Spanish on October 16, 1991. Summing up what one could expect in light of the results of the Congress, he said, "The Cubans will have to tighten their belts even further because of food shortages. They will have to prepare to repel aggression from their eternal enemy: U.S. imperialism. Cubans will have to die to defend the revolution and socialism."[26]

With all his references to the right of the Soviet people to choose their own path of development, which "should be respected," Castro commented at length in his report at the Congress on events in the USSR. He said that he had accomplished his "historic duty" in warning the leaders of the USSR and East European socialist countries against "the tendency to copy capitalism" as far back as 1987. And he also reminded the delegates of the Congress that in July 1989 he had spoken about the possibility of civil conflict in the USSR and the disintegration of the country. The obvious implication of this "I told them so!" exercise was that if the proponents of the "perfection of socialism" in the USSR had listened to and acted upon his warnings, conditions would have been different.

Having meticulously cited statistics of the shortfalls of Soviet deliveries to Cuba in the first five months of 1991, Castro gave the following figures for the nine-month period ending on September 30, 1991: the USSR supplied commodities worth $1.3 billion. Oil and petroleum products amounted to $985 million, about 95 percent of the planned amount. The following list shows percentages of planned amounts of goods actually delivered to Cuba: grain, 45 percent; beans, 50 percent; vegetable oil, 16 percent; condensed milk, 11 percent; milk powder, 22 percent; butter, 47 percent; canned meat, 18 percent; fish products, 11 percent; fertilizers, 16 percent; timber, 47 percent; rolled steel, 1.9 percent; non-ferrous metals, 54 percent; tires, 1.6 percent; soap, 5 percent; animal fats, 13.5 percent; ammonium, 54 percent; construction and transport equipment, 38 percent; spare parts for this equipment, 10 percent; and spare parts for television sets, refrigerators, and other appliances, 1.1 percent. There were no deliveries of rice, sulfur, caustic soda, detergents, or cotton and other textiles. Castro added that these shortages of Soviet supplies negatively affected the construction, with Soviet participation, of eighty-four "projects of economic cooperation."[27]

Judging by these figures, by the end of September 1991, oil deliveries continued to be stable, and the situation with other Soviet exports to Cuba improved considerably compared to the period January-May 1991. Castro stated at the Congress that he could testify to the efforts taken by the Soviet government to meet its commitments to Cuba, but "with chaos and disorganization in that country, it's very difficult." He complained about the uncertainty of Soviet oil deliveries in future:

> Nobody knows if oil will be available next year, what price our sugar will have, or whether the USSR will be in a position to export oil at all. We know that it needs our sugar, but will it be able to export? Who will export: the USSR or the Republics? What price will they pay for sugar? Will they want the garbage sugar price? With what enterprises will we have to negotiate? All these are problems and difficult uncertainties. Therefore, I am saying that fuel is our weakest point (Fourth Congress of Cuban Communist Party, 1991).

In effect, one of the keynotes of Castro's speech was his message that the USSR, the pillar of the Cuban economy for thirty years, was no longer able to play that role and that no other country could replace it as a provider of 13 million tons of oil per year as a market for millions of tons of Cuban sugar. New sources for financing Cuba's economic development projects had to be found. In this context, Castro elaborated on the advantages of foreign investments, citing Lenin to prove that one could use them without detriment to the "dictatorship of the proletariat." He said, "We always thought Latin American integration was necessary" and offered preferential treatment for Latin American investments, asserting that he always regarded Cuba's integration with the CMEA countries as "transitory and conjunctural" and that "the natural stage of our economic integration had to be Latin America."

That statement was only partly true. Castro had expressed this idea seventeen years ago but in a somewhat different form, as cited earlier: that Cuba would integrate with Latin American countries only if they underwent socialist transformations. He had stated then that Latin American integration would become possible only after capitalism gave way to socialism. It was in that sense that he spoke in the early 1970s about the "transitory" nature of Cuba's membership in CMEA.

Now that CMEA, as a "temporary substitute," had disappeared and no revolutionary changes were in sight in Latin America, this condition was conveniently forgotten. Latin American "capitalists" and "landlords" were suddenly no longer an obstacle to Latin American integration or to Cuba's participation in this process. The leader of the Cuban communists remained true to Lenin's motto that Marxism was not a dogma but a guide, proving once again that he was a man of action.

The obvious primary purpose of Castro's complaints about the shortfalls of Soviet deliveries and events in the USSR was widely commented on. However, taken in the context of his eulogies about the glorious past of the Soviet Union, his complaints also served to tell the delegates of the CPC Congress and the Cuban nation that the leader of the Cuban Revolution had made the only right decision thirty years ago, opting for friendship with the USSR, and he could not be blamed for what was happening in Cuban-Soviet relations, particularly since he had made every effort to prevent that from occurring.

The Fourth Congress of the Cuban Communist Party was like a funeral service for the deceased benefactor of a household, with the bereaved heir lauding the virtues of the late provider and explaining to the family members — loudly enough for the neighbors to hear — what they had lost. His eulogy stressed that now they were on their own and needed help, but charity would be accepted only on the condition that he as the heir would be allowed to practice, as before, the religion of the deceased and to run family affairs in accordance with his own interpretation of that religion.

In the last months of 1991, Castro repeatedly raised the alarm about the progressive reduction of Soviet oil supplies. He spoke of the impossibility for Cuba to import sufficient quantities of oil in exchange for its sugar *if Cuba were to pay world market prices*. Castro called this metamorphosis of the exchange rate (from 7 to 1 in 1959-1960 to 1.4 to 1 in 1991) "the Achilles' heel of the Cuban economy," pointing out that to get 13 or 14 million tons of oil, Cuba would have to sell 10 million tons of sugar, which it could not produce.[28]

On November 28, 1991 Castro presided over the meeting of the Politburo of the CPC Central Committee, which examined "growing difficulties and the tense situation caused by the state of deliveries of fuel and other raw materials from the USSR." It was noted that the shortfall in Soviet oil supplies increased from 400,000 tons at the end of September to 540,000 tons by the end of October and that the situation with fuel deliveries from the USSR was becoming "more and more uncertain."[29] On December 6, Castro publicly complained that the USSR had not yet shipped "a single ton of oil promised for December."[30]

On December 20, 1991, *Granma* published "information for the population on additional measures for reasons of scarcity of fuel and other imports," issued by the Cuban Council of Ministers' Executive Committee, which gave details of shortfalls or total absence of Soviet supplies of oil, foodstuffs, chemicals, and other products in 1991 and complained that, due to the changes in terms of maritime transportation between Cuba and the USSR, the Cuban side had to transport at its own cost by Cuban or chartered ships "more than one million tons of products, which previously were transported by the USSR, with the corresponding expense of convertible currency." The document set forth further measures for reducing the consumption of fuel and other material resources, effective immediately.

According to Castro's speeches, he was increasingly worried by indications that Moscow would no longer be prepared to buy Cuban sugar at prices that had allowed the Cuban side until 1991 to import seven or eight tons of Soviet oil in exchange for one ton of sugar, and in 1991, only four tons of oil.[31] On December 6, he referred to "influential persons" in the Soviet Union who thought that the terms of trade should be based on world prices, with the result that "for our sugar we would be paid in USSR rubbish-heap prices, and we would pay for oil in USSR, or in what is left of the USSR, monopoly prices of petroleum." According to his calculations, in this case, Cuba could get only 1.3 to 1.4 million tons of Soviet oil for 1 million tons of sugar, while in the 1980s, it could satisfy its needs completely, importing 13 million tons of oil a year in exchange for only 2 million tons of sugar. He thought that it was necessary to discuss with the Soviets "some reasonable formula, if one wants to maintain some exchange of sugar for oil with the USSR or with what is left of the USSR."[32]

On December 16, 1991, Castro stated that whereas Cuba was "in no way responsible" for the disintegration of the USSR, it had to "suffer terribly the consequences of this disaster," and while that was also true of "the whole revolutionary movement, the whole world progressive movement, and socialism, our country has to suffer more than any other country, because during the thirty years we have been implementing our program of economic and social development, based on the solid foundations of our economic relations with the socialist camp and the Soviet Union, and all this has collapsed practically in twenty-four months!" He went on to talk of the "new economic blockade" of Cuba, with the U.S. blockade still continuing, when "the greatest part of all equipment is of the Soviet or of the old socialist camp's origin; the greatest part of buses, locomotives, tractors, equipment, machine tools — and not a single spare part is received." And he reiterated that, with present oil and sugar prices, "all of the sugar we are producing will not be sufficient to satisfy the country's needs in fuel..., and we have to buy many other things, not only oil."[33]

Continuing to analyze the adverse consequences for Cuba's economy of the disintegration of the USSR and the catastrophic fall in its industrial and agricultural production, Castro also mentioned possible rises in world prices on foodstuffs imported by Cuba, as a result of their increased purchases by the Soviet Union. He used milk powder as an example, which already had almost doubled it previous cost, and expressed his apprehension that if Soviet oil production were not restored to its normal level, this could lead to a rise in the world "monopoly" price of oil, making it even more difficult for Cuba to import oil in quantities sufficient to satisfy its basic needs.[34]

Castro was obviously worried by reports from Moscow that the representatives of the Cuban exile community in the United States were offering sugar to Soviet foreign trade organizations and spoke on December 27, 1991, about "the enemy moving in all places, moving most actively in Moscow, ...making offers and other things, attempting to harm our economic ties with what is left of the USSR; attempting to impede, by all means possible, our efforts to obtain even one-third of the fuel, with which we shall probably have to be content."[35] His worry was not groundless: offers of the Cuban American National Foundation seemed to be one of the factors which forced Havana to stop insisting on retaining "sugar subsidies" in trade with Moscow.

In his speech on December 16, 1991, Castro mentioned yet another negative effect of the events in the Soviet Union on his regime, resulting from "our mistake of the deification of the USSR." He admitted that when "worse horrors about socialism and Soviet history than those published in the United States" started to emanate from Moscow, many Cubans, "including honest people," yielded to the influence of the "ideological venom," because they were "accustomed to believe literally everything that was written or pronounced in Moscow," and this had "inflicted considerable damage." Yet, he apparently was not among the deluded majority: "It was already evident to us, when all this was being written, that it was a matter not of improving socialism but of destroying it. We saw this clearly then, and we see it now."[36]

Indeed, there were indications that the provident Cuban leader had suspected from the moment the USSR started its transition to a more radical stage of *perestroika*, that the time was coming when Havana, to preserve the present regime, would have to distance itself from increasingly contagious Moscow. As far back as 1989, instructions were given by the Cuban leadership to stop teaching Russian as a foreign language in Cuban schools and to switch to English. Later, explaining the reasons for this decision, Castro said that the introduction of the study of Russian in all Cuban schools was a mistake:

> You will not find in Russian any new literary work — you had to wait ten or fifteen years before they published it in the USSR — or a scientific work; and what is most important, almost all scientific works, written in Japan, in Europe, or in any other country, are immediately translated into English. It became an international language, and we, idiots, abandoned English.[37]

Furthermore, in most branches of the Cuban government the number of Soviet advisers was reduced substantially. Young Cubans who had received their university degrees in the Soviet Union now had fewer chances to be appointed to responsible positions in state enterprises and organizations, and, in turn, fewer Cubans were sent to the USSR for their university studies.

There was also another factor that led to the deterioration of Cuban-Soviet cooperation, which had nothing to do with ideology: the Cubans, from their long experience of economic and technical cooperation with the Soviet Union, learned that the USSR was falling further behind the West in its industrial and technological development. The Cubans used the USSR as a source of cheap energy resources, raw materials, basic industrial machinery and equipment, means of transportation, foodstuffs, consumer goods, and free arms and other military supplies, but for more sophisticated and modern equipment and technology, they always shopped in the West. Castro's pet projects — the Biotechnological Center, pharmaceutical factories, and new hospitals — were provided with Japanese and Western equipment purchased with hard currency. Part of that currency came from re-exports of Soviet oil, but until 1990, pharmaceutical and biotechnological products were exported exclusively to the West and Latin America in order to earn more hard currency. When the Soviets tried to extend to Cuba the practice of establishing joint ventures as one way of making the bilateral economic cooperation beneficial also for the USSR, the Cuban side balked — it had more interest in establishing such links with Western firms.

Castro was quite familiar with the many deficiencies of Soviet-produced planes, trucks, and other machinery, as shown by references to some of them in his speeches at the end of 1991, but he was willing to continue importing this equipment as long as the Soviet Union was prepared to subsidize it. It was harder to comprehend how he could fail to see the unfairness to the Soviet side of this arrangement, which he chose to describe as fair and even advantageous for Moscow:

> It was convenient for the Soviets to buy our sugar, paying for it with their industrial products, paying for it with fuel. It was much more expensive for them to produce sugar. Thus, when they delivered to us several tons of oil for one ton of sugar, they were buying sugar at a lower expense than the cost of production.[38]

Even if that had been the case, given the inefficiency of Soviet agriculture and the generally higher cost of production of beet sugar (in the USSR, it was cheaper to produce eight tons of oil than one ton of beet sugar), this particular example did not justify the lopsided trade situation, when the Soviet Union could have exchanged on the world market several times fewer tons of oil for the same quantity of sugar but continued instead its uniquely inequitable arrangement with Cuba. There was only one explanation — Soviet leaders were consciously subsidizing the Castro regime to maintain it economically and politically to preserve Cuba in its role as one of Moscow's staunchest allies, a sort of Soviet "Trojan horse" in the Western Hemisphere. There were no good reasons, however, to continue this wasteful practice once there was no need for such an expensive "friend."

The self-appointed leader of Cuban communists was well aware of the inadequacies not only of the Soviet economic system, which he criticized quite severely, but also of state-run socialist economies in general, as illustrated by his joking reply several years ago to a question from visiting Japanese journalists on whether he thought that the whole world would become socialist. Castro said, "No, there must be at least one capitalist country left to buy goods from." The joke was not new — it had been circulating in Moscow in Khrushchev's time — but Castro was probably the last man who could be expected to repeat it, given his public polemical outbursts against market economy systems in defense of socialism. Castro and his comrades-in-arms were trapped in a quagmire: they could not make the Cuban economy function without giving up "socialist principles" and could not sacrifice them without losing power.

Finally, the end of the Soviet-Cuban political alliance also affected cultural ties between the two countries. Culturally, Russians, Ukrainians, Byelorussians, and other nations of the USSR were too different and too far from the Cubans to develop a strong affinity and kinship during the long period of their political friendship. Common ideology was a poor substitute for a natural mutual interest and served more as a barrier than a stimulus to its growth. Both governments had made strenuous efforts over the years to promote cultural exchanges, but, more often than not, they were politicized and stifled by formalism. Soviet participants at the round-table discussion on this subject, organized by *Latinskaya Amerika* in Moscow in June 1989, noted that real cultural contacts were replaced by empty protocol visits from incompetent functionaries; sincere words, by formal speeches. Between 1959 and 1989, only one Cuban dramatic performance traveled to the USSR, and only three Soviet theatrical companies performed in Cuba. Works of many Russian and Soviet authors were translated into Spanish and published in Cuba, and the books of a number of Cuban writers were translated into Russian in the Soviet Union, but few were outstanding or creative pieces of literature, as the criteria for translation were political.[39]

For all of these reasons, Soviet-Cuban cultural ties were superficial. As soon as the political friendship was over, most of the trappings of the artificially created image of the cultural affinity between the two countries fell apart. By that time, the Soviet government had placed all cultural exchanges with foreign countries, capitalist and socialist alike, on a commercial basis. As for the Cuban government, in recent years it could hardly have been expected to finance cultural exchanges with renegades to the socialist cause; therefore, such contacts dwindled to a trickle. There remained, however, thousands of mixed marriages and true personal friendships not subject to political factors, and this presented a serious problem for the Cuban authorities charged with the task of protecting the population of the island from pernicious Soviet ideological influences.

Salvaging the Wreckage

With the community of ideological and political interests effectively ended and cultural ties largely curtailed, all that was left of the "multifaceted" Soviet-Cuban cooperation after the victory of democratic forces in Moscow were weakened military links; remnants of economic and technical assistance programs (which were to be discontinued, as announced, or put on a commercial basis as of 1992); and dwindling bilateral trade, which was almost completely paralyzed by the cessation of Soviet subsidies, falling oil production, and general economic dislocation in the Soviet Union. Politically, relations between the two governments were in the most serious crisis since 1962. The breakdown stemmed from Gorbachev's September 1991 public snub of Castro, but this time from the Soviet viewpoint there was very little reason to seek reconciliation with Cuba.

However, Havana still had some grounds to hope that not everything was lost. The Cuban lobby within the Soviet establishment had been dealt a crushing blow but did not disappear altogether. It made itself felt through the tolerance and patience shown by Vice Foreign Minister Nikolayenko and Special Envoy Ustinov in their Havana talks on the withdrawal of the Soviet brigade and through Soviet government officials' efforts to achieve the impossible, as they attempted to arrange the uninterrupted flow of Soviet supplies to Cuba. Apart from the references to contract obligations, these officials argued that Cuba was "a special case" and that even if one disliked Castro and his associates, the Cuban people should not be "punished" for that. On November 19, 1991, a Soviet Ministry of External Economic Relations spokesman confirmed, in a Moscow Radio program for listeners in Cuba, that current Soviet oil shipments to Cuba were being carried out on a regular basis; 95 percent of the oil came from Venezuela and other Latin American countries, and in return, Soviet oil was being exported to Europe to meet Latin American commitments there. He added that some delays in Soviet shipments to Cuba were caused by a fall in oil production and difficulties with the Soviet merchant fleet, but everything possible was being done to resolve these problems.[40]

Pravda reacted angrily to the statement by Assistant Secretary of State Aronson that the United States did not want to provide "oxygen" to Havana. Admitting that "the real conditions of life for ordinary Cubans and observation of their civil rights are far from ideal, like much else in Cuba," columnist Bogomolov wrote, "All this in no way justifies Washington's fervent effort, hardly compatible with the status of a great power, to 'squeeze' its opponent at all costs, condemning it to hunger, suffering, and social upheavals. Some people evidently want to obtain certain changes in Cuba, not rationally and gradually, but at any price, even if it is the price of complete paralysis of the Cuban economy." He concluded his commentary, saying, "The consequences that pathological hatred toward the island could have are too dangerous: this island, overcrowded with huge stocks of modern weapons, is capable of changing for the better only gradually, not in convulsions of oxygen starvation."[41]

Pravda's columnist omitted mentioning who was responsible for oversaturating Cuba with modern weapons. Soviet military representatives in Havana were doubtful at times of the wisdom of complying with all Cuban requests for more and more weapons. At one point, after the Cubans requested that more Soviet tanks be transported to Cuba to allow for the formation of additional armored battalions, a Soviet adviser told the minister of the Revolutionary Armed Forces, "Raúl, you shouldn't ask for that much! The island won't keep afloat — it'll sink into the sea under the load!"[42] That does not exonerate, of course, Soviet leaders and military strategists in Moscow of their responsibility for stimulating Castro's appetite for arms by offering them gratuitously, thus making it possible for his regime to build up a large, sophisticated military machine, whose continued maintenance was bound to constitute, particularly in the absence of free military supplies, an unbearable burden for Cuba.

In another commentary, *Pravda* asked, "Is it not too early to place the final kibosh on the Cuban regime?"[43] Interviewed by Radio Moscow on October 5, 1991, Yuri Petrov, who shortly before the August coup left the post of Soviet ambassador in Havana to become head of Boris Yeltsin's office, spoke of the necessity to keep the Cuban economy "operational" and to avoid haste in moving to balanced Soviet-Cuban trade. Talking about military cooperation, he said, "The USSR supplied Cuba with a considerable amount of war material, [and] as everyone knows, some of this material must be replaced and repaired."[44]

On their part, the Cubans were doing their best to salvage whatever possible from the wreckage of their economic and military ties with Moscow and to establish direct contacts with the former Union Republics. After the actual disintegration of the USSR became a fact and only days remained before it was formally dissolved, Castro formulated "new important tasks" and a "new policy" for Cuba in the new situation:

> We intend, as logical [steps]...to recognize all independent states and to develop, as far as possible, our commercial, diplomatic, and political relations, as we do with any independent state. In these circumstances, we proceed from historical ties, developed with each republic which constituted the Soviet Union. During thirty years there were many

contacts, ties, and friendships, which developed with all these
republics, apart from relations with the Soviet Union. Thousands
and thousands of Cubans studied in that country, practically
in all of the republics.... There are also established economic
ties; just as many of them consumed our products and need
them, we consumed their products and need them.[45]

He noted that trade with the former Soviet Union had turned into "a
most difficult task," because now Cuba had to conduct trade and solve
problems of transportation with each republic separately and also with
the "innumerable enterprises of these independent republics."[46]

Castro did not single out Russia as the most important Cuban trade
partner among the members of the Commonwealth of Independent
States; that was done by the Cuban ambassador in Moscow. Ambassador
Balaguer stated in an interview with *Nezavisimaya Gazeta* that 80
percent of Cuba's trade and economic interests in the territory of the
former USSR "involve Russia." He said that the Cuban government had
no reason to change relations with Russia and believed that trade and
economic and political ties should be preserved and "should not be
influenced by the fact that we have different attitudes toward the so-
called Cuban opposition, which is not really an opposition but an
expression of the interests of U.S. policy." Talking about the chances
of Russia's participation, at Washington's insistence, in the economic
blockade of Cuba, the ambassador said that he could not make such
predictions: "Yeltsin has never made statements directed against Cuba
[and] has always been cautious in his assessments."[47]

On December 26, 1991, the Cuban Ministry of External Relations
issued a statement to the effect that the Cuban government "took note
of the declaration in Alma Ata by the highest authorities of the
Republics of Armenia, Azerbaijan, Belarus, Kazakhstan, Moldova, the
Russian Federation, Tajikistan, Turkmenistan, Uzbekistan, and Ukraine,
that with the formation of the Commonwealth of Independent States,
the Union of Soviet Socialist Republics has ceased to exist" and has
decided to recognize them as independent states. It expressed the
desire of the Cuban government "to continue to develop ties of
friendship and cooperation, established in the last three decades, both
with each of the new states individually and with joint entities and
institutions set up for coordinating their common actions in internal
and foreign policy."[48] The independence of Estonia, Latvia, and
Lithuania had already been recognized by Cuba in September 1991.

Notes

1. General Rafael del Pino's letter on the subject was published in *Izvestia* on September 14, 1991.

2. *Komsomolskaya Pravda*, September 3, 1991.

3. *Fundación*, (Cuban American National Foundation), No. 3, 1992, 1-2.

4 . *Granma*, September 7, 1991.

5. Cole Blasier, "Moscow's Retreat from Cuba," *Problems of Communism*, November-December 1991, No. 6, 98.

6. *Granma*, August 2, 1991.

7. INTERFAX report, September 6, 1991; in FBIS-SOV, September 10, 1991, 13.

8. FBIS-SOV, September 16, 1991, 19; and *Granma*, September 13, 1991.

9. *Granma*, September 12, 1991.

10. James G. Blight and David A. Welch, 1989, *On the Brink*, 267.

11. *Granma*, September 14, 1991.

12. Cole Blasier, "Moscow's Retreat from Cuba," *Problems of Communism*, November-December 1991, No. 6, 98.

13. TASS report from Havana, September 23, 1991 in FBIS-SOV, September 24, 1991, 23.

14. *Granma*, International Edition, October 6, 1991.

15. *Izvestia*, December 3, 1991.

16. INTERFAX report, December 2, 1991 in FBIS-SOV, December 4, 1991, 29.

17. TASS report from Mexico, December 4, 1991 in FBIS-SOV, December 4, 1991, 19.

18. INTERFAX report, December 25, 1991 in FBIS-SOV, December 27, 1991, 49.

19. *Nezavisimaya Gazeta*, January 9, 1992, 2.

20. *Granma*, October 18, 1991.

21. Soviet government background information on the economic situation of the country.

22. *Moscow News*, October 21-28, 1991.

23. *Pravda*, October 17, 1991.

24. *Izvestia,* October 21-28, 1991.

25. *Moscow News,* October 21-22, 1991

26. L. Levchenko, FBIS-SOV, October 18, 1991.

27. *Granma,* October 18, 1991.

28. Fidel Castro, Speech at the Fifth Congress of the Trade Union of Agricultural Workers in *Granma,* November 26, 1991.

29. *Granma,* November 30, 1991.

30. *Granma,* December 10, 1991.

31. The last year of subsidized Soviet trade with Cuba was 1991: the USSR was still providing Cuba with cheap oil and paying high prices for Cuban sugar. Moscow introduced world market prices only in 1992.

32. *Granma,* December 10, 1991.

33. *Granma,* December 18, 1991.

34. *Granma,* December 24, 1991.

35. *Granma,* December 31, 1991.

36. *Granma,* December 18, 1991.

37. *Granma,* December 24, 1991.

38. *Granma,* December 10, 1991.

39. *Latinskaya Amerika,* 1990, No. 1, 73-83.

40. FBIS-SOV, November 21, 1991, 16.

41. *Pravda,* November 16, 1991.

42. This story was told to the author by a former Soviet interpreter for Soviet military advisers in Cuba.

43. *Pravda,* October 24, 1991.

44. FBIS-SOV, October 8, 1991, 20.

45. *Granma,* December 24, 1991.

46. *Granma,* December 18, 1991.

47. *Nezavisimaya Gazeta,* January 22, 1992.

48. *Granma,* December 26, 1991.

Raúl Castro with Lieutenant General Aleksey Dementyev, chief Soviet military adviser to the Cuban government, at the Havana airport, November 1962.

Soviet Ambassador Aleksandr Alekseyev with Fidel Castro, Ernesto (Ché) Guevara, and Oswaldo Dorticós at the Havana airport, November 1962.

(Photos by Colonel Tanan)

(Photo by Colonel Tanan)

Anastas Mikoyan, Ernesto (Ché) Guevara, and Oswaldo Dorticós at the Havana airport, November 1962.

Anastas Mikoyan and Fidel Castro at the welcoming ceremony for Castro, Murmansk airport, April 1963.

(Photo courtesy of Pravda)

From left: Marshal Klim Voroshilov, Defense Minister Marshal Rodion Malinovsky, Fidel Castro, Nikita Khrushchev, Leonid Brezhnev, Anastas Mikoyan, Mikhail Suslov, and Aleksey Kosygin at the Lenin Mausoleum during the May Day military parade in Red Square, Moscow, May 1, 1963.

Leonid Brezhnev (then chairman of the Presidium of the Supreme Soviet of the USSR), Nikita Khrushchev, and Fidel Castro after Castro was awarded the title "Hero of the Soviet Union" in the Kremlin, May 1963.

(Photos courtesy of Pravda)

Nikita Khrushchev, Yuri Andropov (then secretary of the CPSU Central Committee in charge of the Soviet Union's relations with socialist countries), Foreign Minister Andrei Gromyko, Aleksandr Alekseyev, and Fidel Castro at the opening of official talks with Castro in Moscow, April 1963.

Fidel Castro and Mikhail Gorbachev raise their arms in accord after Gorbachev addressed the National Assembly in Havana on April 4, 1989.

*Ambassador Yuri Pavlov inspecting the honor guard in front of the
presidential palace (La Moneda) in Santiago, Chile, December 1990.*

*Ambassador Yuri Pavlov with President Patricio Aylwin after presenting
his credentials, Santiago, December 1990.*

(Photo © AP/Wide World)

Castro surrounded by cheering Cubans, May Day 1992. Now support is waning.

Epilogue

There were both gains and losses for the USSR and Cuba in the thirty-year period of their close political, military, and economic relations. All of the Soviet leaders, including Mikhail Gorbachev, maintained that the political and strategic benefits from close cooperation with Cuba had justified the enormous economic expenditure involved in preserving this de facto alliance. That was disputed, however, by democratic political forces in Moscow, as they began to voice publicly their opinion on Soviet foreign policy problems and demanded an end to this immoral and impractical relationship.

The alliance with Cuba had been an enormous, constant drain on the Soviet Union's national resources and was one of the factors that accelerated its economic and political demise. The relationship with Cuba was the biggest single expenditure of the USSR on a friendly political regime, amounting to hundreds of millions of tons of oil and other raw materials, machinery, equipment, and foodstuff worth scores of billions of dollars, which could have found a better use domestically or brought greater returns if exported at normal prices elsewhere. Cuba indisputably occupied the first place among recipients of Soviet economic and military aid and headed the list of Moscow's debtors. The economic "benefits" from friendship with Cuba — guaranteed supplies of sugar, nickel, and citrus fruits — were not in any way commensurate with the Soviet Union's expenditure, compensating for only 20 to 30 percent of the real cost of Soviet supplies to Cuba.

As for the Castro regime, it has survived for so many years, notwithstanding U.S. economic sanctions and hostility and despite its own economic inefficiency, owing largely to Soviet assistance and support. But the historic failure of the totalitarian socialist system in the Soviet Union and Eastern Europe has turned a similar social experiment in Cuba into a zero sum game and has doomed Fidel Castro to the unenviable role as one of the last defenders of this bankrupt system.

The maximum leader proved to be either incapable or unwilling to face the task of rectifying his monumental blunder — forsaking the original democratic goals of the 26th of July Movement and jumping on the bandwagon of communism — which produced disastrous economic and social consequences for Cuba.

The task of rebuilding Cuba will have to be tackled by a nation without Fidel Castro. Thirty years after the overthrow of the Batista regime, which relied on U.S. political and economic support, Cuba found itself in a situation of even greater dependence on another superpower, but this time its benefactor was plagued by political turmoil, economic chaos, and disintegration. The Soviet Union, by 1991, had reduced the flow of supplies to Cuba to a trickle, leaving its erstwhile ally to its own fate. Cuba's economy was put on starvation rations, as the country faced the prospect of economic collapse. After enjoying lush economic premiums and bonuses as a privileged member of the socialist community for decades, Cuba had to do without them, learning to survive the hard way.

Among the multitude of questions that have arisen following the disintegration of the Union of Soviet Socialist Republics and the emergence of the Russian Federation as its successor, one that stands out is Russia's future policy toward Cuba. There were certain grounds for hope in Havana that President Boris Yeltsin would show some consideration for the Island of Freedom. In the past, like other Soviet leaders, he had established good personal relations with Fidel Castro. In March 1987, he visited Havana twice and was given a red-carpet reception on the way to and from Managua, when he headed a Soviet parliamentary delegation to Nicaragua. They met again in Moscow in November 1987. By that time, Yeltsin had resigned from the Politburo, was ousted from the position of the leader of Moscow's Communist Party organization, and had become a political outcast. That did not prevent Castro from saluting him warmly at the reception in the Kremlin. Yeltsin was impressed by this gesture. It was not surprising that during his visit to Miami in September 1989, Yeltsin was careful not to be provoked into any offensive remarks about Castro. Later, President Yeltsin's decision to appoint his old friend Yuri Petrov, then the Soviet ambassador in Havana, as the president's chief-of-staff seemed to open a reliable channel of communication between Havana and the first elected president of Russia. In the summer of 1991, Castro told Latin American visitors in Havana that despite Yeltsin's dramatic break with communist ideology, he would be able to maintain good relations with Russia's new leader.

All this was a poor substitute for the past close political ties and extensive economic cooperation based on the common Marxist-Leninist ideology, identical political objectives, and mutual interest in waging the Cold War against the West. None of that was left. The 1989 Soviet-Cuban Treaty of Friendship and Cooperation became a dead letter. The Russian parliament held unprecedented public hearings on systematic violations of human rights in Cuba. In February 1992, Sergei Kovalev, a former Soviet dissident, who was appointed the first Russian representative to the UN Human Rights Commission in Geneva, issued a public apology for Moscow's past support of Castro's oppressive regime and voted for the resolution condemning the persecution of political dissidents on the island. Despite Havana's protests, the Russian government and parliament established and continued to maintain contacts with representatives of Cuban exile organizations in the United States and Spain. With the expiration of the Soviet-Cuban commercial agreement and protocols on trade and economic cooperation for 1991, there was no legal basis for doing business between Russia and Cuba, and the Yeltsin government showed no interest in establishing it. Castro's emissaries in Moscow, who tried to negotiate new barter deals (sugar and oil) on the old preferential basis, got nowhere, and the Cubans had to content themselves with a contract for a limited amount of Russian oil (1.8 million tons) in exchange for 1 million tons of sugar at prices close to world market level. Deliveries to Cuba of other raw materials, foodstuff, and manufactured goods were stopped completely. In January 1992, addressing a workers' meeting in Leningrad (later renamed Saint Petersburg), Yeltsin confirmed this policy, saying that fifty thousand tons of food supplies, which had been destined for Cuba, would be used in Leningrad. Castro's attempts to persuade Moscow to reconsider the decision on the withdrawal of Russian troops from Cuba also failed. On June 17, 1992, American congressmen were pleased to hear President Boris Yeltsin state, in his speech to a joint session of the U.S. Congress, that Russia "has corrected the well-known imbalances in its relations with Cuba, and Cuba has become just one of Russia's Latin American partners" (*Miami Herald,* June 18, 1992).

However, Yeltsin's policy toward Cuba caused sharp controversy and heated debates in the Russian parliament, the press, and academic community, with communist and ultra-nationalist parliamentarians accusing the government of damaging Russia's national interests by yielding to Washington's pressure and cutting trade and economic cooperation with Cuba severely; this policy also encountered stiff opposition on the part of former Soviet politicians, senior officials, and the military, who still exercised influence in the Russian establishment and preserved personal links with their former Cuban counterparts or perhaps simply sympathized with Castro and his regime on ideological grounds. The government itself appeared to be divided on the issue. Sergei Stankevich (Yeltsin's political adviser), Yuri Petrov, and some other members of Yeltsin's entourage argued that Russia, in its disastrous economic situation, could not afford the luxury of trading only with democratic countries and advocated a pragmatic course of developing normal political relations and substantial economic ties with Cuba while preserving the existing military links. Their reasoning was supported by senior officials of the Russian Ministry of Foreign Affairs, the Ministry of External Economic Relations, and the Ministry of Defense.

President Yeltsin was responsive to these pressures. Castro's more flexible tactics, when he stopped criticizing Moscow for its "anti-Cuban" stand in the UN Human Rights Commission and withdrew in September 1992 his objections against the Russian motorized brigade's departure, also helped improve the political climate of Russian-Cuban relations. By the end of 1992, Russia's almost hostile attitude toward the Castro regime became more lenient, evolving to the exchange of personal messages between Yeltsin and Castro and the resumption of regular political consultations between senior representatives of the Russian Foreign Ministry and the Cuban Ministry of External Affairs. In a July 1992 speech in Ekaterinburg, Boris Yeltsin referred to Castro as his "friend" who promised to comply with his personal request for additional deliveries of Cuban sugar to Russia. In November 1992, the two governments concluded a Russian-Cuban trade agreement establishing a legal base for bilateral trade and maritime communication. The trade protocol for 1993 provided for an increase of Cuban sugar exports to Russia to 1.5 million tons in exchange for 2.3 million tons of oil. In May 1993, Russian Vice Premier Vladimir Shumeiko visited Havana and was received by Fidel Castro. New documents on bilateral economic cooperation were signed, designed to ease the difficulties experienced by Cuba's sugar and oil-refining industries and to ensure increased sugar exports to Russia. For the first time, Havana accepted Moscow's proposals on establishing joint Russian-Cuban ventures in Cuba. The Russian government officially confirmed its interest in the continued use of the Soviet-built communications center at Lourdes, and to avoid hard currency expenses, offered to pay the rent for this base with deliveries of spare parts for Soviet-made weapons supplied in the past to Cuba. In July 1993, the Russian government, in a reversal of its earlier decision to discontinue technical assistance credits to Moscow's former clients in the Third World, provided Cuba with a $350 million credit for completion of twelve Soviet-sponsored projects and a $30 million credit for conserving the Juraguá nuclear power plant.

There were at least three major reasons for this evolution of the Russian policy toward Cuba in 1992-1993 that also explain why the Russian government, contrary to what Yeltsin said in Washington, was not actually prepared to treat Cuba on the same basis as other countries in the region. First, in the short term, the disintegration of the USSR and its deep economic crisis increased Russia's dependence on imported sugar. In the Soviet Union, the Ukraine produced half of all the beet sugar. Moscow's initial plans to reduce the dependence on imported sugar (by augmenting the acreage under beet sugar crops and modernizing the Russian sugar industry with the help of West European investments and technology) had to be shelved for the foreseeable future due to crisis conditions and the lack of resources. In 1992, the deficiency of sugar supplies, blamed by the opposition on the drastic reduction of sugar imports from Cuba, added to the population's discontent with Yeltsin's free market economic reforms. That made the Russian government particularly vulnerable to the criticism of its policy toward Cuba and to charges that it was, once again, ideologically motivated, this time in reverse. With no foreign currency reserves available for purchasing large quantities of sugar in the world market, the Russian government opted for going back to barter trade with Cuba and to Moscow's old practice of helping boost the falling sugar production on the island, despite Washington's displeasure.

The second reason for special treatment of Cuba — seldom mentioned but very much present in the minds of Russian politicians, economists, and government officials — was that Castro's regime proved to be more resilient than expected and capable of withstanding the initial shock of the overnight disappearance of Soviet and East European sources of essential supplies and massive economic assistance. In Moscow, the possibility was not excluded that the socialist regime in Cuba would not collapse suddenly, as happened in Eastern Europe, but, rather, would undergo a gradual transformation, with Castro retaining his grip on power at least for several more years. On the other hand, the Cubans needed Russian supplies more desperately than ever before and were prepared to meet Moscow's new conditions for doing business. Consequently, it was considered unwise to mistreat Castro and miss the opportunities for regaining positions of influence in Cuba's economy. Resumed participation in selected joint construction projects and new joint ventures on the island might ensure some returns from past enormous investments in the Cuban economic infrastructure and possible future repayment, albeit partial, of Havana's debt to Moscow. Furthermore, in influential political quarters it was believed that it would not be to Russia's advantage to accelerate the demise of Castro's socialist regime by joining the U.S. economic blockade of Cuba. In fact, the Russian government was under internal pressure to renew the old Soviet policy of trying to persuade the U.S. government to lift its blockade and to offer its good services to Washington and Havana in helping bring about the normalization of relations between them. Not only the communist *Pravda* and *Sovetskaya Rossiya*, but also pro-government newspapers came out in support of this position.

The third factor that prevented a more comprehensive break of close relations with Cuba was related to the continued interest of Russian military strategists and foreign policy planners in preserving some Russian military presence in the Caribbean — including particularly the electronic communications base near Havana, which they treasured for its high intelligence-gathering capacity and its possible bargaining value in Russian-American talks on further measures of mutual disarmament. In the opinion of the Russian General Staff and intelligence services, these facilities were not to be given up without corresponding concessions on the part of the United States.

Tumultuous political developments in Russia in 1993 reflected the ongoing economic crisis and the growing popular discontent with Yeltsin's "shock therapy" methods of the transition to a market economy, which brought the majority of the population below the poverty line. They culminated in Yeltsin's decision to dissolve the parliament, the use of army tanks to quell the armed resistance of the parliament's supporters, and the December 1993 parliamentary elections, which led to a substantial change in the balance of political forces in favor of Vladimir Zhirinovsky's ultra-nationalists, communists, and their allies. Together, these conservative forces were able to slow down radical economic reforms and force President Yeltsin and the ruling coalition of pro-Western democratic parties to compete with them in promoting nationalist ideas of Great Russia and its special role in world affairs, as opposed to the Russian democrats' original notion of the Russian Federation joining the Western countries and becoming an integral part of the world democratic community.

In Havana, these developments tended to reinforce Castro's position. In some ways, they could be interpreted as confirming the wisdom of Castro's repeated public warnings and protestations about the catastrophic consequences of treating the ills of the socialist society with "capitalist medicines" and as justifying his refusal to follow Gorbachev's reforms, which Castro said would destroy the socialist system in Cuba. In more practical terms, Zhirinovsky's and the Russian communists' demands for increased trade, including arms sales, with the former Soviet Union's friends in the Third World sounded promising for the Cubans, who still remembered Zhirinovsky's statement during the presidential election campaign in Russia in 1991, in favor of continuing trade with Cuba and using the island as a recreational facility for Russian army officers.

Since the end of 1993, Russian-Cuban relations have been a mixed bag of favorable developments and adverse trends, particularly in the economic field. The Russian government, business community, and the public at large reacted positively to the introduction of elements of market economy in Cuba and Havana's steps intended to improve its relations with Washington. There were renewed hopes in Moscow that the Castro regime would be able to evolve gradually to the market economy and political democracy, avoiding violent transition scenarios.

In 1994, Russia supported the U.N. General Assembly resolution calling for the United States to lift its economic blockade of Cuba, while in previous years Moscow had abstained during votes on such resolutions. In October 1994, the Russian State Duma called on the U.S. Congress to repeal the Torricelli bill. In December 1994, in preparation for hearings in the State Duma's International Affairs Committee on the state and prospects for Russian-Cuban relations, a group of Russian parliamentarians visited Cuba. The hearings, held in January 1995, were dominated by those who supported re-establishing extensive trade and economic relations with Cuba. They criticized the government for failing to honor its financial commitments to Cuba and failing to recognize the damage inflicted on the Cuban economy from 1991 to 1992 by Russia's rupture of trade ties and economic cooperation with the island. In May 1995, the State Duma condemned the Helms-Burton bill and appealed to the U.S. Congress not to pass it.

There was some further progress in the military field. For the first time since the disintegration of the Soviet Union, in November 1993 an official Cuban military delegation visited Moscow. The delegation was received by Defense Minister General Pavel Grachev. The discussions centered on financial conditions of maintaining the Russian radio-electronic base at Lourdes. (The Russian-Cuban agreement on the base, signed in November 1992, provided for its continued operation for the next twenty years on a commercial basis, with rent to be paid in U.S. dollars or in deliveries of spare parts for Russian-made weapons and military equipment, ammunition, and building materials.) The Cuban side insisted that Moscow pay $1 billion each year for the use of the base. The Russian Ministry of Defense declined this demand as unreasonable and excessive. This problem eventually was solved in November 1994, during the visit to Havana of General Mikhail Kolesnikov, Chief of the Russian General Staff. It was agreed that the rent would amount to $200 million per year.

On the other hand, improved political relations between the two countries were not accompanied by any substantial growth of trade and economic cooperation. Both sides have difficulties in meeting their contract obligations. Under the Protocol on Trade and Payments for 1994, the Russian and Cuban governments pledged to exchange 2.5 million tons of crude oil for 1 million tons of sugar. Annex II to the Protocol enumerated commodities, apart from oil and sugar, which were merely "recommended" by the two governments to respective trade organizations and companies participating in bilateral trade (from Russia, rolled iron and non-ferrous metals, ammonia, fertilizers, herbicides, synthetic rubber, lumber, pulp, cardboard, fish, agricultural machinery and spare parts, tires, spare parts for motor transport, and nickel plant equipment; from Cuba, nickel and cobalt concentrates, medicines and medical equipment, citrus fruit and other tropical agricultural products).

However, Havana's hopes for effective Russian assistance in modernizing and developing Cuban export industries, hopes raised by Moscow's promises of credits and supplies of goods essential for preventing a further fall in Cuba's sugar production, turned out to be unrealistic. The $350 million Russian credit, announced in July 1993, has remained on paper. Moscow kept only its commitment with regard to the $30 million credit for the preservation and maintenance of the unfinished Juraguá nuclear power plant. The "Rus-Cuba" project (promoting new Russian investments in Cuba through the consortium of Russian and Cuban companies, established in 1993) has suffered a similar fate: The Trade Protocol for 1994, signed in December 1993, went into force only in March 1994. As a result, in 1994 the first tankers carrying Russian oil, scheduled to reach Cuban ports in January, arrived in May, too late to save the 1994 sugar harvest. Neither side was able to follow through on its intentions to complement oil and sugar with other commodities. The following year, Russian and foreign business interests, working through their lobbyists in the Boris Yeltsin government to re-direct Russian sugar purchases to the open world market, delayed the signing of the protocol of trade with Cuba in 1995 for months, defying President Yeltsin's instructions to expedite the matter.

Russian-Cuban economic relations are complicated further by the refusal of the Cuban government to recognize Cuba's debt to Russia (16.7 billion "old" rubles, in 1991 equivalent to $28 billion), inherited from the Soviet Union. Cuba heads the list of foreign debtors to Russia, followed by Mongolia, Vietnam, Ethiopia, Angola, and other former Soviet clients in the Third World. In 1991, the payments of the Cuban ruble debt had been deferred by the Soviet government until the year 2000, but Havana has not made a commitment to repaying it after that date. The Cubans point out that the Soviet Union, the country with which the debt had been incurred, no longer exists, and that, in any case, it cannot be repaid in U.S. dollars at the artificially low 1991 official rate of exchange for the Soviet ruble. (Officially, in 1991 a ruble equaled 58 cents.) There were also statements in Havana to the effect that if it were possible to assess in material terms the assistance given by Cuba to the Soviet Union in pursuit of its strategic interests in the Western Hemisphere, Cuba would be Russia's creditor, not a debtor. In January 1995, when asked in the State Duma to explain reasons for freezing this credit, the Russian government representative referred in particular to Havana's unwillingness to recognize its debt.

Havana had fewer difficulties in establishing normal political relations and developing barter trade with the other fourteen former Soviet Union republics than it had with Russia. They all valued Cuba as a market for their low-quality manufactured products, which would not sell in other, more competitive and demanding markets, and they needed Cuban sugar. Most of the newly independent states were still ruled by communists, who were prudent enough to board the train of nationalism in time, while preserving old command administrative economic systems and communist party structures essentially intact, though under new names. All of them professed their allegiance to the causes of democracy and market economy, but none, except three Baltic states, practiced what they preached and kept pace with Russia's political and economic reforms. There was also a similarity with Castro's methods of ensuring popular support in the way the leaders of the Baltic states, the Ukraine, and some other former Soviet republics instigated the nationalistic fervor of their populations and castigated

"Russian imperialism" for all the ills that had befallen them since independence.

Such is the story of the Soviet-Cuban alliance, as I see it. On a personal note, like many of my compatriots, in 1959 I was thrilled with the victory of the Cuban Revolution. In 1962, my doubts about the wisdom of Khrushchev's decision to convert Cuba into the Soviet forward missile base in the Caribbean did not detract from the admiration that my colleagues in the Soviet Foreign Ministry and I felt for the courageous Cuban nation and its fearless leader challenging the heretofore undisputed supremacy of the United States in the Western Hemisphere. On April 28, 1963, several buses took us from the foreign ministry to Red Square for participation in a mass meeting arranged by the government to give a hero's welcome to Fidel Castro upon his arrival in Moscow on his first visit to the Soviet Union. In his appearance, as he stood side by side with short, fat, and bald-headed Nikita Khrushchev, he contrasted favorably with the aging Soviet leader. Castro's words seemed to come from his heart; the ideas he expressed sounded fresh and original. The Moscovites applauded him enthusiastically, while reacting with skeptical smiles and derisory remarks to Khrushchev's blabbering speech that was filled with worn-out propaganda clichés. To us, Castro was an embodiment of an honest revolutionary, an authentic folk hero, dedicated to the noble cause of liberating the Cubans from foreign domination, social injustice, and misery. At the time, we did not know anything about the shady aspects of the Cuban Revolution, about thousands upon thousands of Cubans being imprisoned, tortured, and murdered for their political beliefs. Or, to be more exact, we did not want to hear anything about all this, sincerely believing that Western press reports on the situation in Cuba were malicious slander and pure fabrications of imperialist propaganda.

Over the years, my own communist views had evolved to an understanding of the duplicity and corruption of the Soviet governing elite, the misery of day-to-day life for most Soviet people, the inherent economic inefficiency of our system, and the falsity of our claims of its superiority over the West — in short, of the glaring gap between the promised socialist paradise, which my father had fought for during the Russian Civil War, and the bleak socialist reality. Whatever hopes I had for the gradual transformation of the Soviet system into "socialism with a human face" died when Soviet tanks entered Prague and crushed Alexandr Dubchek's experiment. By the time I began to deal with Cuban affairs in the line of my official duties in the USSR Foreign Ministry, I no longer believed in the Marxist-Leninist utopia and saw the futility of Gorbachev's efforts to improve Soviet socialism and make it work. Nor did I have many illusions about its Cuban replica. Yet, it was still difficult for me to equate Castro with Soviet or East European communist leaders. I still thought he was different. However, the more I learned about what was happening in Cuba, the more doubts I had about him. The intensified persecution of Cuban dissidents and, in particular, the infamous "Ochoa trial" severely shattered my ideas about Castro's personal integrity and the nature of his regime. My last illusions finally disappeared after I came to Miami and talked to many Cubans who had passed through Castro's prisons and torture chambers. It became clear to me that Castro and his comrades-in-arms were not and could not be different from Russian Bolsheviks or Chinese communists. Radical revolutionaries, irrespective of their original intentions and motives, are doomed to become dictators and subjugators of the very people they want or pretend to want to liberate, since their ideology denies the value of individual freedoms and justifies the use of indiscriminate violence, mass terror, and the establishment of totalitarian control over the society for achieving their aims. That was the case in Russia and Eastern Europe. This is still the case in China and North Korea, Iraq, and Libya. And also in Cuba.

To conclude, a few words about the prospects of Russian-Cuban relations. There exist objective economic factors, which will continue to stimulate the mutual interests of the present and future Russian and Cuban leaders, irrespective of their political and ideological orientations, in maintaining and developing trade and economic cooperation between the two countries. In all probability, Russia will remain for years to come the biggest single buyer of Cuban sugar. The lifting of the U.S. economic embargo will not lead to the restoration of the Cuban sugar quota in the U.S. market, and Russia is further away from self-sufficiency in sugar than ever before. Cuba can get oil from countries other than Russia, but important sectors of the Cuban economy will depend on Russian deliveries of industrial and transport equipment and spare parts for the foreseeable future. The same is true of the Cuban military establishment.

Furthermore, the recent trend of Moscow's more nationalistic and self-assertive foreign policy stance is not likely to fade away. On the contrary, it may well become stronger and acquire a distinctly anti-Western coloring, as the Russian economy recuperates and Moscow restores its capacity to project Great Russia's image and influence abroad. This being the case, there may arise a situation when some jingoistic-minded Russian leaders will find compelling political and/or strategic reasons for a rapprochement with Cuba, provided that Fidel Castro or his nominees still govern the island and that in the United States the conservative Republicans return to power and persist in their hostility toward the Castro regime. In this eventuality, Cuba could once again turn into a source of friction, if not an apple of discord, in relations between Moscow and Washington.

Index

A

Abalkin, Leonid 179, 180
Abrams, Elliot 205, 206
Abrantes Fernandez, José 142
Adamovich, Ales 240
Addis Ababa 102
Aeroflot 187
Afanasyev, Yuri 239
Afghanistan 13, 59, 113, 129, 133, 141, 143, 149, 164, 170, 180, 205, 240
Africa 1, 19, 23, 59, 63, 86, 95, 97, 98, 100–102, 117, 128, 143, 144, 186, 200, 204, 208
    Cone of Africa 143
    Cuban troops 203, 220
    regional conflicts 143
African National Congress (ANC) 102
agreements
    bilateral 230, 237, 238
    Cuba-U.S. 238
    intergovernmental 59
    multilateral 211
    Russian-Cuban
        electronic surveillance facilities, Lourdes 268
        trade 9, 264
    Soviet-American
        withdrawal of nuclear missiles 234
    Soviet-Cuban 40, 41, 59, 234
        commercial 9, 263
        military cooperation 41
        payments 8
        trade 8, 185, 190
    superpowers 95, 96
    trade 127, 230, 240
agriculture 74, 75, 76, 246
    credits 191
    Cuba 74, 75, 188
    "socialist" 75
    Soviet 248
    tropical products 268
Aguilera, Julio Camacho 178
Aguirre, Severo 11
AIDS virus 111
Akhromeyev, Sergei 173, 181–183, 222, 224
Albania 63, 84
    Soviet submarine base 63
alcoholism, Soviet Union 114
Aldana, Carlos 161, 193, 194, 195, 225, 227
Alekseyev, Aleksandr 5, 33, 34, 36, 38, 42, 44–46
All-Russian Congress of School Teachers 15
Allende, Salvador 93, 98

alliance 17, 64, 69
    Axis 61
    de facto 17, 60
    Soviet-Chinese 61
    Soviet-Cuban 26, 31, 55, 64, 127, 193, 199, 204, 205, 215, 216, 219, 230, 234, 236, 249, 261, 270
Alliance for Progress 85
allies, ideological 193
Alma Ata 252
America. *See* United States
    anti-Americanism 19
American Overseas Private Investment Corporation 206
ammonium 242
ammunition 62, 208, 268
Anderson, Rudolf Jr. 44, 55
Andropov, Yuri 33, 60, 61, 72, 99, 224, 225
Angola 59, 95, 101, 102, 116, 123, 129, 133, 143, 144, 149, 187, 204, 205, 208, 220, 269
    Cuban expeditionary forces 102
    "internationalist army" 116
Antigua 32
Antillana iron and steel works 191
apartheid system 143
Arab nations 95
Arbatov, Georgi 87, 88, 159, 160
Arefyeva, Yelena 182, 183
Argentina 96, 127
Arias, Oscar 208
armed conflict
    Cuban-American 39, 237, 234
    Hungary 21
    Soviet-American 42
armed struggle 11, 12, 86, 87
Armenia 131, 252
arms 96, 211
    Central America 209
    imports, Sandinistas
        moratorium 146, 148, 149
    race 97, 129, 199
    sales 267
    shipments 146
    transfer to Nicaragua 210
army tanks 266
Aronson, Bernard W. 151, 157–160, 206, 208–210, 213, 214, 221, 250
arsenals, nuclear 129
Asia 1, 19, 23, 24, 59, 86, 97, 100, 128
authoritarianism 169
Azerbaijan 252

B

Bakatin, Vadim   179
Baker, James   149, 152, 207, 208, 210–212, 220, 231, 232
Baker-Shevardnadze
 "deal"   157
 joint communiqué   156
 meeting   157
Baklanov, Oleg   177, 180, 181
Baku   178
Balaguer, José Ramón   158, 163, 164, 184, 252
balance of payments   9
balance of power   25, 47
Baltic states   178, 231, 269
 naval fleet   40
Batista, Fulgencio   3, 4, 6, 10, 11, 19, 103, 105, 106, 163
 followers   236
 military coup   3
 post-Batista   5, 13
 regime   3, 4, 12, 20, 104
  overthrow   24, 262
  U.S. support   262
Bay of Pigs invasion   20, 21, 152, 200
Bekarevich, Anatoly   25, 76
Belarus (Byelorussia)   249, 252
Beliat, Mikhail   162
Berlin   199
Bessmertnykh, Aleksandr   225, 231
"Big Brother"   61
bilateral
 discussions   60, 208, 210
 exchanges on Cuba
  Soviet-American   204
 negotiations   209
Biotechnological Center   247
Bipartisan   Accord   on   Central
 America   207, 209
Biryuzov, Sergei   34
Bishop, Maurice   98, 99
Black Sea   100
blackmail   15
Blasier, Cole   230, 236
blockade of Cuba   15, 59, 73, 93, 176, 246, 252, 266, 267, 271
 "new economic"   246
Bluefields   101
Bogomolov, Pavel   168, 177
Bolivia   116
Bolshevik Party   72, 271
bombers, Soviet   55
bombing raids   45
Borge, Tomás   152
Borovik, Genrikh   159

Brady Plan   133
Brazil   2, 63, 89, 96
Brezhnev, Leonid   22, 57–60, 72, 73, 81, 86, 87, 90, 91, 94, 95, 99, 102, 164, 201, 203, 235
 Brezhnev doctrine (doctrine of limited sovereignty)   18.
 visit to Cuba   130
Britain   15
Bulgaria   74, 113, 174, 189
Burbulis, Gennady   239
Burlatsky, Fyodor   45, 46, 159
Bush, George   147, 176, 207, 209, 212, 214, 220, 231
 administration   144, 146, 149, 151, 156, 206, 207, 210, 215
  democratic changes in Cuba   217
 visit to Moscow   231
Bush-Gorbachev summit   158, 161, 213, 214

C

Cabrisas, Ricardo   191
Camarioca   240
Cambridge, Massachusetts   32, 35
Camp David   15, 214
Canada   2, 187
Capital Bank   160
capitalism   4, 19, 23, 79, 115, 164, 167, 177, 195, 242, 243, 248, 267
capitalist countries   12, 13, 24
"capitalist medicine"   122
Caribbean   1, 15, 17, 19, 42, 51, 54, 63, 73, 79, 98, 101, 135, 201, 203–205, 209, 210, 270
 crisis   57, 58
 Russian military presence   266
 Soviet military   62
 U.S. nuclear weapons   135
cars   76, 82
Carter, Jimmy   156, 202, 203, 235
Castro, Fidel
 anti-American rhetoric   4, 83, 219
 anti-Castro   9
  resolutions   221
 anti-*perestroika* stance   137
 arms   251
 assassination attempts   53
 "bourgeois origins"   9
 command center   45
 communist   10
 correspondence with Gorbechev   126
 correspondence with Khrushchev   32
 Cuban commander-in-chief   123

Castro, Fidel *continued*
  defiant attitude 215
  democrat to communist 10
  departure 206
  dictator 217
  dictatorial regime 72
  doomsday thinking 43, 236
  economic liberalization 241
  exploits in Latin America 200
  five points for peace 50, 51, 84
  foreign policy 143, 214, 222
  Gorbachev's snub 250
  guerrilla movement 7
  humanistic democracy 19
  inner circle 120
  insurgent movement 11
  interventions 241
  lecture to Gorbachev 235
  Marxist-Leninist 10, 22, 111, 123
  "Maximum Leader" 54
  message of October 27, 1962 45, 46
  New York 83, 84
  on-site inspections, consent 201
  personal integrity 271
  policy 6, 9, 19, 137, 207, 208, 240
    domestic 214, 215, 222
    economic 94, 187
    internal 179, 206
    rectification 178
  political maneuvering 90
  political skills 112
  political views 8
  popularity in Cuba 167
  prime minister 240
  propaganda 24, 170
  public humiliation 232
  "rectification of errors" 114, 115, 116,
    118, 120, 122, 132, 137
  reforms 5, 6, 10
    egalitarian 70
  regime 4, 5, 8, 9, 13, 20, 21, 25, 26, 36,
    39, 51–54, 62–64, 89, 103, 104, 106,
    117, 138, 158, 161, 162, 164, 169, 181,
    186, 200, 205, 206, 215–219, 234, 237,
    246, 251, 261, 263–267, 271
    benefits 73
    hostility to 162
    opponents 200
    resilience 265
    revolutionary 15
    Soviet assistance 160, 204, 230
    Soviet protection 16, 229
    Soviet subsidies 248
    Soviet supporters 231
  U.S. attitude toward 215
  U.S. policy 121
  revolution 4, 5, 12, 18
  revolutionary 10, 206, 270
  rumors 240
  socialism 10, 21, 22
    totalitarian 218
  'Socialism or Death!' 241
  Soviet support 13
  speech 9
    National Assembly 136
    Supreme Commander-in-Chief 42
    TV interview, October 1962 51
    views of Eastern Europe 173
    views of Soviet Union 173
    visit to Moscow 24, 38, 130, 270
Castro, Raúl 5, 9, 10, 13, 40, 41, 43, 61,
  88, 89, 92, 131, 145, 181, 182, 184, 222,
  224, 225, 239, 251
Castroite Communist Party of Cuba 12
caudillismo 69
caustic soda 190, 242
cease-fire agreement 144
Ceausescu, Nicolae 84
censorship 125
Center for American Studies in
  Havana 115, 116
Central America 99, 101, 123, 124, 130,
  133–135, 145–157, 160, 204–212, 215, 221
  agreements 151
  arms deliveries, embargo on 209
  conflict 137, 143, 145, 152, 206
    Cuban involvement 206
  liberation of Soviet policy 148
  military assistance 124
  peace process demands 208
  presidents 145, 154
  Soviet and Cuban flow of arms 209
  Soviet-American cooperation 156, 221
  tripartite consulations 147
Cerezo Arevalo, Marco Vinicio 148
Chamorro, Violeta 149, 155, 157, 158
chemicals 14, 82, 191, 240
Chernavin, Vladimir 239
Chernenko, Konstantin 72, 99
Chernobyl 170
  nuclear plant catastrophe 180
Chigir, Nikolai 58
Chile 2, 78, 93, 95, 96, 98, 150
  Chilean Communist Party (CCP) 98
  guerrilla fighters 98
  left-wing organizations 98
China 23, 60, 78, 85, 86, 90, 271
  Chinese Communist Party 86

China *continued*
  Chinese military attaché to Cuba   43
  communists   271
Chirkov, Vladislav   79, 112
chromites   14
Chumakova, Marina   169
Church, Frank   203
Churkin, Vitaly   231
CIA   53, 63, 155
Cienfuegos   62, 92, 183, 201, 202, 239
  Soviet submarine support base   223, 239
citrus fruit   14, 75, 80, 82, 125, 170, 180, 182, 190, 261, 268
civil disobedience   228
civil disturbances   167, 217
  anti-communist   19
    East Germany, 1953   19
    Hungarian Revolution, 1956   19
civil liberties   104
clandestine activities   64
CMEA. *See* Council for Mutual Economic Assistance
coal, Soviet   76
cobalt   80, 82, 268
Cold War   2, 21, 57, 64, 95, 123, 165, 176, 199, 219, 263
  post-Cold War   215
  rhetoric   15
  strategy   2
Colombia   2, 86, 87, 96, 99
colonialism   23
Columbia University, Harriman Institute for Advanced Study of the Soviet Union   160
combat   224
Comintern policy   2
Committee for the Defense of Human Rights in Cuba   239
Committees of the Defense of the Revolution (CDR)   72
"Committees of the Poor" *(kombedy)*   72
commodities   82, 185, 268, 269
  Cuban   80
  prices   190
Commonwealth of Independent States   252
communications   191
communiqués, Soviet-Cuban   14, 93, 127, 130
communism   24, 87, 88, 122, 128, 217, 262
  threat   199
Communist Party   12, 18, 72, 95, 118–121, 125, 134, 151, 163, 177, 184
  Chinese   86
  discipline   125

El Salvador   154
  Moscow's   262
  officials   143
  Russian   177
  structures   269
  Ukrainian   119
Communist Party of Cuba (CPC)   4, 71, 92, 105, 174, 178, 181, 193, 241
  Americas Department   151
  Central Committee   89, 93, 113, 118, 143, 147, 161, 184, 193
  Politburo   244
  Congress   244
  CPSU   181
  Fourth Congress   114, 185, 240, 241, 243, 244
Communist Party of the Soviet Union (CPSU)   5, 35, 49, 69, 71, 72, 85, 87, 89, 92, 105, 111, 114, 117, 134, 137, 141, 142, 170, 174, 193, 194, 207, 225, 227, 229, 241
  archives   32
  Central Committee   1, 8, 33, 34, 56, 57, 89, 95, 117–119, 125, 128, 131, 132, 138, 142, 143, 162, 165, 167, 177, 180, 183, 193, 194, 211, 224, 240
    Cuban section   177
    Ideological Department   177
    International Department   5, 9, 12, 86
    Politburo   72, 76, 117, 138, 177
    Presidium   5, 8, 21, 34, 40, 61
  "construction of communism"   87
  Cuban Communist Party   4, 10, 71, 174, 181, 193
  headquarters   142
  International Department   98
  regional committee   119
  theorists   10
  Twenty-eighth Congress   181
  Twenty-first Congress   11
communists   2, 10–12, 13, 32, 103, 105, 194, 240, 241, 266, 269
  Chinese   78, 271
  Cuban   4, 12, 13, 18, 78, 89, 244, 248
  East European   78
  ideology   142, 262
  leaders   2, 71, 78, 84
    East European   271
  monopoly   178
  morals   87
  movement   89
  participation   7
  parties   89
    Latin American   12

communists *continued*
   West European 91
   Polish 173
   Russian 263, 267
   society 88, 103
   Soviet 12, 78
      orthodox 165
   threat 11
   Vietnamese 78
   world movement 86
comrades-in-arms 193
concessions 206, 215, 233
conflict resolution 143, 160
conflicts 208, 225
   East-West 236
   military 237
   regional 123, 129, 216, 218
confrontation
   Cuban-American 220
   East-West 127, 199
   global 32, 200
      Soviet 200
      USSR 7
   Soviet-American 25, 62, 69, 123, 182
Congo 59
Congress of People's Deputies 141
Congress of the Federation of Cuban
   Women 174
conservatives, Soviet 241
construction and transport equipment 242
consumer goods 71, 76, 78
Contadora 99, 124
Continental Companies 159
Contras 123, 135, 144, 146, 147, 221
   U.S. military aid 144, 146
cooperation 41, 59, 64, 69, 86, 135
   bilateral 86, 127
   economic 128, 191, 243, 271
   Moscow-Havana
      political 96
   political 60
   Russian-Cuban
      economic 263, 267, 268
      military, 1990-1995 181
      trade and economic 263
   Soviet-American 158, 218, 231
      Central America 156
   Soviet-Cuban 17, 82, 98, 166, 179, 215,
      247, 249, 261
      culture 133
      economic 133, 138, 139, 179, 180,
      191, 192, 243, 248, 263, 264
      foreign policy matters 192
      military 9, 41, 62, 63, 127, 165, 182,

200, 208, 209, 213, 216, 223, 236, 239,
   251, 261
   political 84
   political, Angola 102
   politics 133
Cord, Vincent 98
corruption 18, 71, 115, 142, 270
Costa Rica 148
cotton 76, 188, 240, 242
Council for Mutual Economic Assistance
   (CMEA) 93, 94, 100, 129, 175, 176, 185,
   188, 189, 191, 243, 244
   Charter 94
   countries 243
   XXVI meeting 94
counterrevolutionaries 23, 49, 72, 74, 124,
   162, 175
   Cuban 159
   exiles 18
   Miami 162
coup
   August 1991 coup in Moscow 181, 183,
      193, 214, 216, 228-230, 240, 251
   d'état, Fulgencio Batista 3
   post- 230
"covert actions" 49, 53
Cox, Thomas E. 206
credits 70, 76, 82, 83, 206, 240
   energy projects 191
   non-repayable 77
   Russian 268, 269
   Soviet 70, 125
   technical assistance 265
   trade 188
crime rate 114
Crisis of October (See Cuban Missile Crisis or Missile Crisis of October 1962)
Cristiani, Alfredo 123, 150, 151, 154
Cuba
   agriculture 74, 75, 76, 268
      monocrop dependence 189
      production 188
   aid, Soviet 118, 125, 131, 206, 230
   Air Force 62, 63, 227
   air space violations 50
   airfields 62, 183
   allies 51
   ammunition 62
   Angola 101
   anti-aircraft defense forces 44
   armed forces 23, 54, 63, 183
      Soviet weapons and training 62
   arms
      deliveries 181, 210

Cuba *continued*

arms
deliveries to Nicaragua 211–213
for defense 61
Soviet 89, 92, 204, 211
army 21, 48
execution of prisoners 104
officers, Soviet 9
assistance, Soviet 76, 77
balance of payments 9
Biotechnological Center 247
bourgeois leaders 18
citrus fruit 14, 75, 80, 82, 170, 180, 182, 261, 268
civil liberties 104
"comandantes of the revolution" 144
commitments, Soviet 185
commodities 80
communication with Soviet
Leaders 225
Communist Party 4, 10, 71, 174, 181, 193
Popular Socialist Party (PSP) 11
communists 4, 5, 18, 84, 89, 105, 240, 244, 248
"communist threat" 11
leaders 5
corruption 71, 142
Council of Ministers' Executive
Committee 245
counterrevolutionaries 159
crisis 32, 35, 42, 51, 58
defense 32–35, 38, 39, 45, 48, 57, 59, 62, 237
capabilities 232
expenditure 71
deficit 9, 76, 187
deliveries
Russian 263, 271
Soviet 194
Soviet shortfalls 242, 244, 245
democratic evolution 217, 218
diaspora 162
"dogmatic copying" Soviet methods 132
domino theory 36
economic aid 38, 63, 77, 80, 90, 125, 127, 138, 204, 206, 207, 213, 215, 218, 240, 261
economic and military aid 17, 160, 179, 186, 194, 204, 206, 207, 219, 240
economic and social consequences 262
economic and technical cooperation with USSR 247, 250
economic dependence 84
on Eastern Europe 189

on USSR 13, 189, 207
United States 13
economic development 77, 94, 120, 245
projects 243
economic
hardships 186, 222
infrastructure 266
interests in USSR 252
liberalization 241
policy 86
projects 76
strategy 188
economy 10, 14, 71, 73, 74, 76, 77, 79, 117, 120, 138, 175, 179, 186, 188–190, 216, 243, 244, 246, 249, 250, 251, 261, 262, 266, 267, 271
monocultural 189
Soviet-type centrally planned 78
education 112, 125
embassy 158, 163
in Moscow 179
Soviet 180
emigration 104
enemies 185
U.S. imperialism 242
export industries 268
exports 14, 15, 188, 220, 243
biotechnological products 247
from Soviet Union 240
pharmaceuticals 247
to Soviet 190
to USSR 125
untraditional 188
financial solvency 187
FMLN forces, assistance to 220
foreign language
English 247
Russian 247
foreign policy 71, 85, 126, 143
"de-Sovietization" 236
"internationalist" 71
fraternal friendship and cooperation 128, 130
GNP (gross national product) 77, 117, 187
goods 13
government 2, 4, 35, 118, 142
grants, Soviet 70
hospitals 247
"hour of glory" 223
human rights 164, 166, 192
activists 163, 165
violations 104, 106, 165, 263
imports 14, 75, 76, 80, 188, 246
independence 12
industry 14, 76, 186

Cuba *continued*
  inspections, on-site   201
  integration   189, 243
  intelligence operations   155
    files on all important Soviets   178
  internal problems   22, 126, 217
  invasion   45, 47, 48, 53
    U.S.   33, 46, 47, 52, 224, 235
  investments
    foreign   243
    Russian   268
    Soviet   75
  Island of Freedom   75
  isolation   34
  Kalashnikovs   62
  living standards   117
  loans   77, 136
    Soviet   190
  machinery, Soviet   248
  mass exodus of Cubans   162
  militarization of society   71
  military   142, 145, 182, 223
    bases   36, 39, 52, 54, 182, 215
    delegation visit to Moscow   267
    elite   118
    equipment, Soviet   203
    establishment   164, 271
    links, Soviet   182, 231, 239
    links with Russia   264
    presence, foreign   233
    presence in Africa   144, 203
    presence, Russian   266
    presence, Soviet   53, 223, 234, 235,
      237, 251
    Soviet   9, 43, 64, 216, 238
    strategy, Soviet   183
    supplies   216, 223, 232, 247, 251
    tanks, Soviet   251
    training   8
  military assistance   222
    Nicaragua   210
    Panama   210
    Soviet   9, 17, 38, 41, 63, 77, 83, 90,
      161, 181, 209, 212–214, 222, 231, 232
  Moscow's ally   248
  nonaligned country   96
  organization of labor   120
  patronage to Nicaragua   99
  people   23, 24, 56
  pharmaceutical factories   247
  policy   86, 208, 219
    Central America   210
    defense of national interests   24
    internal   126, 217
    Russian   265

  Soviet   165, 182, 251
  U.S.   59
  political
    advantage   17
    ally   131, 215
    climate   217
    dissidents   163, 165
    persecution   263
  political, economic, and military sup-
    port, Soviet   229
  political prisoners   104, 106, 271
  pro-Iraqi position   166
  "profiteers"   115
  re-exporting   77, 81
    oil   247
  rebuilding   262
  regime   4, 15, 21, 52, 59, 103, 169, 179,
    251, 265
  Revolutionary Armed Forces   251
  revolutionary government   51, 103, 122
  Russian financial commitments   267
  Russian supplies   265
  Russia's Latin American partner   263
  schools   247
  security   33, 39, 48, 54, 59, 89, 223, 225,
    237, 238
    American threat   222
  shipping costs   190
  ships, chartered   245
  social and economic problems   222
  social experiment   261
  social development   245
  social system   236
  Soviet domain   42
  Soviet facilities   62
  Soviet ideological influences   249
  Soviet market
    buying capacity   190
    dependence on   187
  Soviet supplies   240, 250, 261, 262
  Soviet support   219
  Soviet-sponsored projects   265
  special treatment by Russia   265
  standard of living   78
  state bureaucracy   71
  strategic advantage   17
  "strategic reserves"   187
  strategic target   41
  "subversive" activities   211, 219
  sugar   170
  territorial waters   43, 50
  training center   203, 235
    withdrawal   239
  troops   15, 43, 60, 72, 116, 123, 251

Cuba *continued*
  deployment, Soviet   41, 237
  Soviet   39, 41, 49, 165, 166, 202, 203,
    213, 223, 224, 231, 232, 234–237, 239
  Cuban to Angola   102
  U.S.   49, 216
  withdrawal, Russian, from
    Cuba   263, 264
  withdrawal from Africa   220
  withdrawal from Angola   102, 144
  withdrawal, Soviet   165, 209, 216,
    232–234, 237–239, 250
  withdrawal, training center No.
    12   239
  withdrawal, U.S.   233, 238
  trucks, Soviet   248
  unequal exchange   191
  university studies in USSR   247
  value to USSR   18
  wealth of the state   122
  "wooden pesos"   124
  writers translated into Russian   249
Cuban American National Foundation 159,
  162, 221, 229, 236, 246
Cuban Armed Forces Museum   223
Cuban Center of American Studies
  North American department   49
"Cuban factor"   145
Cuban Foreign Ministry   232
Cuban Foreign Service   163
Cuban lobby   177, 178, 185
  Soviet establishment   250
Cuban Ministry of External Affairs   143,
  147, 264
Cuban Ministry of External Relations   252
Cuban Missile Crisis 24, 31, 32, 35, 41, 44,
  51-53, 55, 60, 64, 84, 87, 165, 200, 218,
  233, 234
  tripartite conference   49
Cuban nation   244
Cuban National Assembly   51, 132, 134
Cuban opposition   252
Cuban problem   200, 214, 215
Cuban Republic   56, 194
Cuban Revolution   8–12, 16, 17, 20–25, 33,
  35, 71, 90, 117, 133, 147, 154, 170, 179,
  184, 195, 205, 233, 244, 270
  true friends of   179
Cuban revolutionaries   70, 73, 187
Cuban State Council   112, 136
Cubanologists   169
cultural exchanges   8, 59, 249
  capitalist   249
  Soviet-Cuban   249
culture   127, 129

currency   82
  convertible   245
  foreign   75, 76, 81, 265
    income   77
    shops   155
  hard   8, 80, 81, 82, 124, 182, 185, 190,
    247, 264
Czechoslovakia   9, 18, 74, 90–92, 98, 113,
  132, 174
  Soviet invasion of   18, 90

D

Darusenkov, Oleg   177
debt   124, 135, 136
  cancellation   135, 136
  Cuban   76, 124, 135, 136, 269
    to Russia   266, 269
  dollar debt   77
  for Soviet arms, Cuban   63
  repayments   135
  ruble debt   269
  service   76
  "sugar debt"   81
  Third World   124
Declaration of San Isidro de Coronado 154, 155
del Pino, Rafael   63, 227
democracy   4, 103, 132, 142, 152, 154,
  169, 177, 178, 181, 216, 217, 269
  Cuba   103
  evolution in Cuba   218
  pluralism   156
  socialist   177
Democratic Party of Russia   240
democratization   99, 124, 141, 144, 218
democrats, Soviet   241
Derbentsky, Nikolai   178
destabilization   208
détente   15, 86, 92, 95, 97, 199, 200
  Soviet-American   200
dialogue   214, 215, 219, 221
  Cuban-American   221
  Soviet-American   212, 214, 216, 231
    Central American conflict   206
  Washington-Havana   211
Diaz, Helena   115
dictatorship   6, 217, 227, 243
disarmament   96, 123, 129, 205, 266
  unilateral   178
disintegration, USSR   246, 262, 265, 267
division of authority   42
Dobrynin, Anatoly   202
doctrine of limited sovereignty (Brezhnev
  doctrine)   18
dogmatism   183

dollars 190, 268
  Cuban dollar debt 77
Dominican Republic 86
Dorticós Torrado, Osvaldo 22, 45
drug(s)
  smuggling 142
  trade 155
Dubchek, Alexandr 270
Dubinin, Yuri 212
Duncan, Walter Raymond 69
duplicity 270
dyarchy 4, 5
Dzasokhov, Aleksandr 193

E

East Berlin 132
East Germany 19, 74, 98, 113, 132, 189
East-West
  class struggle 69
  competition 78
Eastern Europe 19, 72, 75, 77, 78, 91, 94,
  100, 111, 114, 158, 166, 167, 175, 176,
  178, 187, 189, 190, 218, 261, 265, 271
  Castro's views 173
  communist leaders 271
  socialism, collapse 219
  socialist states 84, 92, 112, 189
  totalitarian socialist system 261
economic
  blockade of Cuba 49, 187
    Russia 252
    United States 266, 267
  blockade of Panama
    United States 155
  concessions 206
  crisis
    Russia 265
    USSR 125
  development 87, 116
    projects 243
  integration 243
  liberalization 241
  policy 86
  sanctions 89, 205, 206, 261
    Panama 155
  systems 269
economy
  Cuba 266, 267, 271
  monocultural 189
  Russian 271
  Soviet-type 78
education 14, 70, 73, 103, 125, 127, 129
EFE, Spanish news agency 158
egalitarian society 19

Egypt 1, 15, 59, 129
Eisenhower, Dwight D. 13, 15
Ekaterinburg 119, 264
El Salvador 101, 123, 135, 145, 147, 148,
  150, 151, 153, 154, 160, 204, 208, 212,
  213, 215, 220
  army 208
  Communist Party 154
  Cuba's role 208
  elections 151
  FMLN forces 212
  government 148, 151, 152, 208
  guerrillas 101, 150, 154, 155
  insurgents 150, 151
  revolution 154
  U.S. military aid 135, 149, 208
elections 145, 147
  democratic 154, 156, 220
    Cuba 219
  El Salvador 151
  Nicaragua 149, 152–156, 221
  observers
    U.S. Congress 156, 157
    UN 156
  Polish 173
  Russia, 1991 267
  Sandinistas 154, 156
  supervised 144
electricity 186
electronic surveillance facilities, Lourdes
  62, 165, 183, 223, 239, 264, 266, 268
electronics 191
emigration 104
employment 103
Endara, Guillermo 155
energy resources 124
Engels, Friedrich 78
English 247
equipment 77, 82, 188, 190, 261
Escalante, Anibal 5, 12, 84, 89, 90
Escalona, Juan 193, 227
Esquipulas Agreement 124, 135, 145, 154,
  207, 212, 215
Estonia 252
Ethiopia 59, 129, 269
Europe 1, 20, 21, 24, 41, 54, 75, 91, 94,
  95, 97, 100, 155, 183, 247, 250
European Bank for Reconstruction and
  Development 206
"Evil Empire" 223
exchange rate 244
exiles (Cuban) 20, 21, 50, 161, 162
  community 54, 160
    Miami 161

exiles (Cuban) *continued*
  United States 160–162, 220, 246
  counterrevolutionary 18
  invasion of Cuba 21, 200
  organizations 64, 200, 217, 239
    "anti-Cuban reactionary" 158
    Miami 161, 231
    Spain 263
    United States 64, 161, 162, 217, 246, 263
expansionism, messianic 199
Export-Import Bank 206
exports 82, 188, 189, 243
  biotechnological products 247
  Cuba 14, 188, 268
  pharmaceuticals 247
  Soviet Union 14, 191, 240

F

Falin, Valentin 193, 194
farms 75, 134
  products, Soviet 176
Fascell, Dante B. 159, 229
fertilizers 14, 76, 190, 240, 242, 268
feudalism 7
fidelismo 69
Finland 13
  Soviet sugar 13
fish 242, 268
Florida 159, 160
FMLN (Farabundo Martí National Liberation Front) 101, 124, 135, 144, 148,
  150–155, 206, 208, 211, 212, 214
  Cuban assistance 135, 213, 220
foodstuffs 14, 75, 81, 188, 190, 191, 261, 263
  shortages 75, 242
foreign domination 270
foreign policy 58, 89, 95, 143
  Cuban 71, 85
  internationalist 71
  Soviet 35, 83, 184, 192, 199, 230, 241, 261
former Soviet republics 269
Fowler, Wyche 159
France 15
Franqui, Carlos 16, 17
fraternal friendship and cooperation 59,
  128, 136, 194, 252
  Soviet-Cuban 64, 139, 159
fraternal socialist countries 72, 84, 90, 91,
  112, 117, 119, 121
fraternity 113
free choice 129
free enterprise 78
free trade zone 155
freedom 4, 10, 24, 73
friendship 17, 55, 64, 118, 249

Frolov, Andrei 194
fuel 191, 245, 246
  aviation 186
  shortages 186
  Soviet 244, 245, 248

G

García Luis, Julio 113
Garthoff, Raymond L. 64
Gelman, Aleksandr 239
General Agreement on the Integral Devel-
  opment of Sugar Production 189
General National Assembly of the
  People 16. *See also* Provisional Revo-
  lutionary Government
Georgia 159
German Democratic Republic 15, 74
German Nazi regime 72
Germany 47, 85
glasnost 112, 113, 132, 160, 177, 182
global strategy 25
Gonionsky, Sergei 6, 12
González, Ernesto 63
Gorbachev, Mikhail 99, 111, 112, 114,
  119–127, 130–132, 135, 138, 147, 149,
  151, 159, 161, 166, 168, 173–176, 179,
  182, 183, 190, 193, 200, 205, 208, 209,
  212, 214–217, 219, 223, 224, 229–236,
  238, 261, 271
  and Reagan meeting, Geneva 205
  and Yeltsin decision to withdraw Soviet
    troops from Cuba 236
  confidential correspondence with
    Castro 126
  CPSU General Secretary 35
  government 207, 210, 215
  in Washington 214
  influence on Castro 126
  new political thinking 142, 160, 192,
    195, 207
  perestroika 167
  policy 111, 195
  public snub of Castro 250
  reforms 111, 112, 115, 267
  speech to National Assembly 133, 136
  speech to UN General Assembly 133
  veiled warnings to Castro 133
  visit to Cuba 126, 127, 130–132, 137,
    139, 141, 208, 209
Gorbachev-Baker press conference 236
Gorbachev-Bush summit in Malta 150,
  207, 212, 213
GOSPLAN. *See* Soviet State Planning Commission

Grachev, Pavel 267
"gradualist" approach 217
Graham, Bob 222
grain 76, 84, 186, 188
grants 70, 77
Great October Socialist Revolution 25
Great Russia 266, 271
Grechko, Andrei 92
Greece 238
Grenada 98, 99
Gribkov, Anatoly 41, 42
Gromyko, Anatoly 34, 57, 58, 99
gross national product (GNP)
    Cuba 77, 78, 117
    Latin America 78
Group of Soviet Troops (GSF) in Cuba 44
Guantánamo 16, 50, 213, 216
    U.S. forces 231–233, 237
    U.S. naval base 49, 50, 59, 84, 216, 223, 238
Guardia brothers (Gen. Patricio de la Guardia and Col. Antonio de la Guardia) 98
Guatemala 2, 18, 21, 86, 87, 145, 148
guerrillas 11, 12, 89, 96, 98, 148, 151
    Cuba 7, 102
    El Salvador 101, 150, 154, 155, 212
    Guatemala 148
    Panama 155
Guevara, Ernesto "Che" 10, 12, 14, 17, 44, 70, 73, 86, 89, 115–117, 122
    Cuban Order of 44
Guinea 1
Guinea-Bissau 95
Gulf war 192
Guzmán, Jacobo Arbenz 2

H

Haiti 135
Handal, Shafic 154
Harriman Institute for the Advanced Study of the Soviet Union, Columbia University 160
Havana
    caves 45
    Cubanacán district 131
    declarations 85
    KGB in 33
    privileged status in Moscow 131
    relations with Moscow 55
    Revolución 16
    soap factory 192
    Soviet embassy 5, 167
    Soviet-Cuban summit 168

television 4
    Tripartite Conference 39–43, 46
Hawk's Cay U.S.-Soviet Conference 32
hegemony 228, 229
Helms-Burton bill 267
herbicides 268
heretics 72
Heritage Foundation 206
Hernández, Francisco J. 162, 229
Hernández, Rafael 49
Hidalgo, Alcibiades 237, 238
Holtz, Abel 160
Honduras 135, 145, 148, 221
hospitals 247
housing 70, 73
Hoxha, Enver 84
human rights 73, 102–105, 112, 164–166, 169, 220
    activists 163
    Nicaragua 156
    socialist countries 103
    violations 103, 104, 106, 165, 263
humanism 134
humanistic democracy 19
Humphrey, Hubert 88
Hungary 21, 113, 174, 175
    Revolution, 1956 18, 19
hurricanes 75
Hussein, Saddam 61, 215
    anti-Saddam Hussein, coalition 220

I

ICBMs (intercontinental ballistic missiles) 31, 38, 61
ideology 142, 229, 247
    communist 262
    Marxist-Leninist 18, 69
    Soviet-Cuban 25
illiteracy 4
imperialism 2, 10, 11, 23, 24, 35, 38, 43, 45, 50, 56, 70, 87, 88, 90, 91, 93, 96, 97, 104, 105, 123, 133, 144, 147, 228
    anti-imperialist 5, 7, 241
        revolution 3
    archenemy 13
    armed forces 16
    Latin America 25
    oppression 24
    "Russian" 270
    threat 17
imports 76, 80–82, 188
independence 10, 16, 19
independent states 1, 269
India 1, 59, 129

individual freedoms   217, 219, 271
Indonesia   1
industrial
   development   76
   equipment deliveries to Cuba
      Russian   271
   production, Cuba   186
   products   81
industrialization   7, 122, 124
industry   191
inequality   18
information agencies   228
Institute for U.S. and Canada Studies 159, 162
Institute of Latin American Studies 71, 76, 169, 177
insurgents   4, 11, 62
   movements in Latin America   155
insurrectional movements
   El Salvador   145
   Guatemala   145
   Honduras   145
integration   189
   Cuba   243
   economic   93, 243
   Latin American   243, 244
intelligence-gathering   62, 266
intelligentsia   3
intergovernmental agreements   59
Intergovernmental Commission
   Soviet-Cuban   179, 180
International Conference of Communist Parties   92
international law   40, 178
internationalism   128, 241
"internationalist duty"   57, 77
intervention   16, 17, 20
   nonintervention   137
invasion   20, 31, 35, 36, 47, 52, 54, 56–58, 234
   Cuba   205
investments
   foreign   243
   Latin American   243
Iran   13
Iraq   1, 13, 59, 129, 166, 192, 215, 271
iron ore   14
Island of Freedom   73, 75, 103, 121, 163, 182, 262
isolation   153
Israel   82, 95
Italy   31

J

Jackson, Henry   203

Japan   187, 231, 247, 248
Jews   72
jobs   73
Johnson, Lyndon B.   88
joint communiqué   14, 93, 127, 130
   cultural cooperation   8
   Soviet-Cuban   22, 56, 58, 59, 130
   trade and economic relations   8
Joint Soviet-Cuban Statement of May 23, 1963   56, 59, 84, 85
joint ventures   247
   construction projects   191, 266
   Russian-Cuban   264, 266
journalists   212
Julien, Claude   38
junta   144, 227
Juraguá nuclear power plant   191, 240, 265, 268

K

Kachanov, Aleksandr   82, 177
Kalashnikovs   62
Kalinin, Arnold   4
Kamentsev, Vladimir   131, 136, 137
Kamorin, Andrei   80, 241
Kapto, Aleksandr   119, 177
Karyakin, Yuri   239
Katushev, Konstantin   177
Kazakhstan   184, 252
Kazimirov, Vladimir   205
Kennedy, John F.   20, 21, 42, 43, 48, 50, 52, 53, 61, 200, 204
   administration   32, 47, 53
   Alliance for Progress   85
   assurances   57
   commitment   54, 58, 64
   missile dismantling demands   45
   non-invasion assurance   201
   October 22, 1962 speech   47
Kennedy-Khrushchev understanding   49, 52–54, 55, 57, 59, 63, 64, 201, 202, 204
KGB   33, 141, 167
Khachaturov, Karen   104, 177
Kharkov   32
Khrushchev, Nikita   1, 4, 5, 7, 8, 10, 13, 15–17, 19–24, 26, 31–46, 48, 51, 57, 58, 61, 63, 70, 72–74, 80, 84–86, 103, 165, 200, 204, 218, 233, 248, 270
   brinkmanship policy, Caribbean   15
   "capitulation" to Washington   48
   concept of missiles in Cuba   32
   conversation with Kennedy   200
   Cuba visit, 1962   60
   error of judgment   61

Khrushchev, Nikita *continued*
 "good communist" 32
 koukourouznik 74
 memoirs 31
 message to JFK 48, 200
 New York 83, 84
 nuclear gamble 234
 plan 40
 pledge 57, 59
 policy 7
 politician 32
 promises to Castro 48
 "rocket fire" statement 16
 warning to U.S. 20
Khrushchev-Castro plot 61
Kiev 32
Kim Il Sung 61
Kissinger, Henry 201, 202
Klimov, Elem 240
Klyamkin, Igor 240
Kobysh, Vitaly 35
Kolesnikov, Mikhail 268
Komplektov, Viktor 100, 148, 153, 189, 210, 220
Komsomol functionaries 120
Korea 85, 91
Kornilov, Yuri 77
Kortunov, Andrei 159
Kosygin, Aleksei 88, 93, 94, 115, 202
Kovalev, Sergei 263
Kozyrev, Andrei 192, 193, 230
Kremlin 262
Kryuchkov, Vladimir 177, 227
Kudryavtsev, Sergei 84
Kuptsov, Valentin 194
Kuusinen, Otto 61
Kuwait 61, 166

L

labor productivity 71, 78, 79, 88, 187
Lage, Carlos 184, 185
landowners 6
language 247
Laos 85
latifundia 7
Latin America 1–4, 6, 8, 11, 19, 23–26, 33–36, 39, 54, 62, 63, 69, 70, 71, 73, 75, 78, 79, 83–86, 89, 92, 94–98, 100, 101, 104, 117, 127, 135, 145, 147, 149–151, 155, 157, 165, 169, 170, 186–188, 192, 200, 204, 208, 218, 220, 247, 262
 affairs 2
 armed struggle 86
 capitalists 244
 Comintern policy 2

communist parties 12, 91
 Cuba 188
 democracies 86
 diplomatic relations with USSR 2
 disarmament 129
 foreign debt 133
 governments 1, 124
 imperialism 25
 integration 243, 244
 investments 243
 landlords 244
 left-wing forces 2
 movements
  insurgent 155
  insurrectionist 96
 nuclear-free zone 96
 oil commitments 250
 revolutions 85, 88
 socialism 22
 Soviet policy 101, 127
Latin American Agribusiness Development Corporation 160
Latin American Directorate 158, 159, 180, 205, 222, 224, 234
Latvia 252
Law of Neutrality (U.S.) 53
Legvold, Robert 160
Lenin, Vladimir 6, 7, 26, 71, 78, 79, 89, 103, 115, 122, 134, 141, 243
 legacy 142
 motto 244
Leningrad (Saint Petersburg) 100, 141, 263
 CPSU Regional Committee 178
Leonov, Nikolai 5
Levchenko, Leonid 242
Liberal Union of Cuba 239
liberation 12, 24, 25
 Soviet policy in Central America 148
Libya 192, 271
Ligachev, Yegor 177
literature
 Cuban 249
 Russian and Soviet 249
Lithuania 174, 252
loan repayments 136
London 206, 209
Lourdes 62, 165, 239
 electronic surveillance facilities 62, 165, 183, 223, 239, 264, 266, 268
Luanda 102
Lukyanov, Anatoly 184, 193, 227
lumber 268
Luque, Roberto 168

M

M/S Baltika 8
machinery 14, 15, 77, 82, 84, 188, 190, 191, 248, 261, 268
Makhov, Aleksandr 162, 163
Malinovsky, Rodion 32–35, 40–42, 47, 55
Malmierca Peoli, Isidoro 143, 166, 220
Mamedov, Georgi 147, 166
Managua 99–101, 124, 146–148, 150, 154, 157, 158, 208, 262
Manuel Rodriguez Front 98
Mao Zedong 61, 86
Maputo 102
maritime communication 264
maritime navigation 127
market economy 70, 74, 111, 115, 217, 248, 266, 267, 269
market principles 115
Martinez, Oswaldo 116
Marx, Karl 78, 122
  dogma 123
Marxism 69, 244
Marxism-Leninism 7, 10, 11, 18, 22, 24, 36, 84, 103, 128, 132, 133, 169
Marxist 87
  dictum 189
  ideology 78
  regimes
    Africa 19
    Asia 19
  revolutionary experiments 200
  rulers 102
Marxist-Leninist 72, 98, 123
  Castro, Fidel 22, 111
  dogmas 26, 73
  ideology 69, 263
  indoctrination 103
  party 7
  regimes, Africa 204
  system 73
  teaching 103
  theory 7, 70, 86, 123
  utopia 270
Mas Canosa, Jorge 159, 160, 162, 229, 239
Matos, Huber 6
McNamara, Robert 53
meat 188, 240, 242
media
  censorship 125
  mass 176, 227
  Soviet 4, 6, 177, 184, 228, 241
medical care 70, 73, 103, 170
medical equipment 125, 190, 268

and medicines 268
medical facilities, Cuba 125
medical treatment 170, 180
Mediterranean 63
Melnikov, Ivan 193
Mendelevich, Lev 55
mercenaries 105
metal 14, 82, 240, 242, 268
Mexico 99, 127, 151
Miami 158–163, 167, 231, 232, 262, 271
  conference on regional problems 161
    Soviet-American 213
  Turkey Point nuclear power plant 63
Middle East 63, 88
MiG-29 fighters 213, 216, 222
Mikhailov, Sergei 23
Mikoyan, Anastas 5, 7, 8, 14, 33– 36, 38, 61, 165, 224, 234
Mikoyan, Sergo 33, 35, 57, 159, 169, 177, 234
militant group 143
militarization of society 71
military 41
  advisers 9
  aggression 17
  alliance 64
  assistance 83, 124, 209, 211
    mutual 60
    Soviet 17
  bases, Soviet 182
  buildup 144
  conflict 41, 237
  coup 167
  dictatorship 155
  establishment, Cuban 271
  foreign intervention 75
  intervention against Cuba 15
  links, Russian-Cuban 250, 264
  maneuvers, U.S. 232
  strategists, Soviet 251
  training 8
milk 188, 240, 242, 246
minerals 230
Mirabal, Rafael 163
Miret, Pedro 104
Miró Cardona, José 5, 6
Missile Crisis of October 1962 24, 31, 32, 35, 41, 43, 44, 51–53, 55, 60, 64, 84, 89, 165, 200, 217, 218, 233, 234
  first tripartite conference 49
  negotiations 49
missiles 15–17, 31–35, 37–45, 47, 48, 50, 51, 52, 55–57, 61, 66, 151, 224
  American in Turkey 48, 52
  ballistic missile production 1

bases 32, 33, 35, 36, 62, 270
  Cuba 32, 33
  defense of Castro's regime 35
  deployment 35, 40, 52, 201
    in Cuba 56, 61
    secret 52
  dismantling 50
  forces 34, 44, 48
  initiative 52
  intermediate-range ballistic missiles (IRBMs)
    United States 31
  launching pads 45
  nuclear 202
    sea-based ballistic missiles 202
  sites 42, 44, 47
  sites, Soviet 42, 44
  Soviet medium-range "R-12" 223
  surface-to-air 150, 151, 212
  thermonuclear 56
  Turkey 32, 33
  withdrawal of 35, 45, 50–52, 55, 57
    Soviet 35, 55, 166
Moa 192
Moiseyev, A. 241
Moiseyev, Mikhail 182, 222, 224
Moldova 252
Moncada barracks assault 3
Mongolia 60, 113, 269
monocrop dependence 189
monocultural structures 78
Montaner, Alberto 239
Morocco 82
Moscow
  "anti-Cuban" stand
    UN Human Rights Commission 264
  "betrayal" of Cuba 58
  Communist Party organization 262
  coup, August 1991 181, 214
  Cuban embassy 36, 141, 179
  Cuban lobby 185
  failed coup attempt 216
  "fraternal relations" 33
  Grand Kremlin Palace 22
  Institute for U.S. and Canada Studies 159
  Institute of International Relations 231
  Institute of Latin American Studies 23
  Institute of World Economy and International Relations 23
  messianic expansionism 199
  new policy toward the U.S. 165
  political capital in Washington 205
  Red Square 24
  relations with Havana 55, 189
  "selling out" Cuba 48
  strategists 21
  television 230
  trials 163
  verbal declarations 57
Moscow-Havana axis 69
Moscow-Havana connection 199
Moscow-Miami Dialogue 158, 159, 162, 213
Moskovsky Komsomolets 169
Moss, Ambler H., Jr. 159
Mozambique 59, 95, 129
multilateral talks 144
multiparty system 220
Museum of the Cuban Armed Forces 223
Muslim world 63
mutual extermination 51

N

Namibia 95, 102, 123, 143, 144, 208, 210
Nasser, Gamal Abdel 7
National Assembly 135
  Castro's speech 136
  Gorbachev's speech 136
National Front for the Total Independence of Angola (UNITA) 102, 123, 149
National Institute of Agrarian Reform 8
national liberation movement 17, 23–25, 85, 97, 143
national resources, Soviet 261
nationalism 69, 269
nationalization
  American properties 13
  business 19
  private enterprises 22
  property 13
NATO 2, 91, 97, 204
  military doctrine 41
  troops 47
naval blockade 51
Nazis 46
negotiations 145, 146, 168
New Jewel Movement (NJM) 98
New York 8, 47, 83, 84, 96, 166
newspapers 266
newsprint 76, 82, 187, 240
Nicaragua 99–101, 113, 135, 144–151, 153–158, 160, 208, 212, 213, 221, 262
  armed forces 144, 145, 157
  arms shipments, Soviet 157, 210, 211
    through Cuba 211
  cease-fire agreement 144
  Contras 123, 144, 146
    U.S. military assistance 135
  counterrevolutionaries 124

Nicaragua *continued*
  Cuban arms deliveries   210–213
  Cuban military assistance   210
  Cuban patronage   99
  economic aid, Soviet   153
  elections   147, 149, 152–156
    supervised   144
  electoral process   221
  human rights   156
  internal affairs   222
  military aid, Soviet   146, 157
  military assistance to Panama   210
  military representatives   100
  Port of Corinto   100
  Revolution   153, 154
  Sandinistas   99
    government   146, 147
    Soviet military aid   146
  socialism   152
  socialist revolution   153
  Soviet-supplied weapons   212
nickel   14, 76, 77, 80–82, 170, 180, 182, 261, 268
  concentrates   80, 137, 268
  mining industry, Cuban   81
  plant   82, 240
    equipment   268
Nikolayenko, Valery   166, 237, 239, 250
Nixon, Richard M.   201
"No. 12 Training Center"   224
non-invasion assurances   201, 216
  U.S.   51, 52, 53, 54
  Washington   231
Non-Proliferation Treaty   91, 96
nonaggression assurances   213
nonaligned movement   99, 127, 150, 186, 202, 203
noncapitalist development   1, 7
Noriega, Manuel   155, 156, 210
  "dignity battalions"   156
  illegal drug trade   155
North Korea   63, 78, 113, 192, 271
North Yemen   59
North-South relations   123
Norway   183
Novikov, Aleksandr   184
nuclear
  arms race   92, 199
  attack   39, 43, 46, 47
  blackmail   15
  catastrophe   234
  conflict   16, 38, 43, 47
  extermination   234
  fallout   62
  holocaust   50
  missiles   42, 43, 44
  power plant   240
  retaliation   47
  strike   45, 46, 47
    capabilities   1, 25, 31, 41
  tests   85
  war   42, 43, 61, 62, 129, 199
    against United States   32
  warheads   31, 33, 40
  weapons 33, 41–44, 47, 66, 95, 202, 211
    ban   129
nuclear umbrella   54, 60
nuclear-free status   135
nuclear-free zone   96, 129
Núñez Jiménez, Antonio   8

O

Ochoa Sanchez, Arnaldo   142, 193
  trial   163, 271
Odessa   32
oil   8, 13–15, 77, 80–82, 84, 89, 100, 153, 180, 186, 188, 190, 230, 240, 242–245, 263, 271
  deliveries   81, 243
  for Cuba   248, 250
  Latin American   250
  prices   182, 246
  production   246, 250
  refinery   240
    Cuban   14, 264
  refining   14, 191
  Russian   263, 264, 268, 269
  Soviet   13–15, 76, 80–82, 186, 242–245, 248, 250
    deliveries   243
    production   250
    progressive supply reduction   244
    re-export   247
    shipments   250
  subsidies   125
  Venezuelan   250
Oliver, Spencer   159
one-party
  rule   72
  socialist regimes   71
  system   25, 177, 219
  totalitarian socialist state   25
open markets   74
Operation Anadyr   34, 40, 55
opposition, Cuban   252
Organization of American States (OAS) 150
Orlov, Vladimir   74
Ortega, Daniel   101, 124, 144–149, 152, 154, 155, 157, 158

Ortega, Humberto   144, 145, 157
Orwellian "double-speak"   34

P

Paltyshev, Nikolai   193
Panama   99, 155, 156, 221
   military assistance
      Cuban   210
      Nicaraguan   210
   pro-American regime   155
   relations with Washington   156
   Soviet consular office   156
   war zone   155
Pankin, Boris   230, 232, 233, 239
Pavlov, Yuri   159, 178, 220, 222, 305, 306
peace   50, 51, 61, 84, 85, 124, 129, 134,
   135, 147, 151, 160, 173, 204, 205, 208,
   209, 210, 215, 218, 220
   Soviet "peace initiatives"   83
   Soviet, "Program of Peace"   95
   unilateral treaty   15
peace-loving forces   35
peasants   3, 11, 12, 134
   Cuban   74
   farms   134
   market   114
   Soviet   74, 75
Peking   24, 56, 83, 86, 92
Pentagon   15, 53, 62, 216, 223
peoples' liberation struggle   92
people's militia battalions   48
"people's war" doctrine   61
perestroika   111, 114, 118–122, 125, 126,
   132, 137, 138, 148, 160, 162, 167, 168,
   173, 174, 177, 179, 182, 207, 218, 247
Peru   86, 87, 93
pesos, "wooden"   124
petrochemicals   191
petroleum   245
   products   8, 14, 240
      Soviet   14, 242
Petrov, Yuri   119, 120, 121, 150, 151, 167,
   185, 251, 262, 264
Petrovsky, Vladimir   192
pharmaceuticals   190, 191, 247
   and biological industries   191
   factories   247
   industry credit   191
Philippines   238
Piñeiro, Manuel   147, 151
Pinochet, Augusto   98
pirate attacks   49, 50
planes   248
   Soviet long-range reconnaissance   183

U-2 spy planes   15
Pliyev (Pavlov), Issa   41, 42
pluralism   99, 144, 152, 156, 177
Poland   113, 149, 174, 175
policies   142, 147, 173
   USSR toward Cuba   176
Politburo   117, 128, 130, 138, 143, 146,
   157, 165, 177, 178, 183, 184, 211, 262
   CPC Central Committee   244
political
   agreement   130
   and economic reforms, Russian   269
   concessions   209
   dissidents   72, 103, 163, 165, 168
      Cuban persecution of   263, 271
   friendship   249
   pluralism   144, 152, 177
   prisoners   106
   repression, Cuba   166
Pollo, Jorge   44, 50
Polozkov, Ivan   177
Ponomarev, Boris   9
Popular Socialist Party (PSP)   3, 5–7, 11–
   13, 22, 89
Popular Unity coalition   98
ports, Cuban   83
poverty   18, 266
pragmatists   26
Prague   91, 92, 132, 270
press   129, 228, 239
   American   11, 160, 211
   commentaries, Soviet   16, 22
   communiqué, Soviet Union   13
   conference
      Gorbachev-Baker   236
      Havana   237
   Cuban   228
   Russian   32, 263
   Soviet   167, 168, 170, 182–186, 220
   Western   184
   world   232
Pretoria   102
prices   80, 82, 261
   concessionary   76
   monopoly   245, 246
   oil   246
      Russian   263
   petroleum   245
   rubbish-heap   245
   subsidies   76, 77, 80, 240
   sugar   14, 85, 246, 248
      Cuban   263
   world market   8, 85, 245, 246
Primakov, Yevgeny   179

prisons 104, 229
 Cuban 271
private enterprise 70, 78
pro-Western democratic parties, Russia 266
"profiteers" 115
"progress of mankind" 26
"progressive national-democratic regimes" 10
proletarian
 internationalism 18
 revolution 7
propaganda 12, 24, 34, 70, 72, 103, 106, 122, 135, 146, 170, 203, 270
 anti-Castro 104
 "bourgeois" 23
 campaigns 100
 imperialist 270
 war 83
property
 American property in Cuba 20
 confiscation of 20
 nationalized 13
 private 78
 redistribution 70
protocol on trade, 1961, Soviet-Cuban 14
Protocol on Trade and Payments for 1994 268, 269
 Annex II 268
protocol visits 249
protocols on trade and economic cooperation, 1991, Soviet-Cuban 263
Provisional Government of the Republic of Cuba 4
Provisional Revolutionary Government 16. See also General National Assembly of the People
 foreign policy platform 16
public health 129
public ownership 78
Puerto Rico 50, 96
Punta Gorda 82
putsch, August 1991 (See coup, August 1991)
putschism 3, 11, 227, 228

R

radio frequencies 178
Radio Martí 221
Rashidov, Sharaf 34, 40, 86
 Uzbekistan Communist party 34
rationing 75, 77, 186
 bread 186
 consumer goods 76
 starvation 262

raw materials 77, 81, 82, 97, 180, 187, 230, 263
 Soviet 82, 244, 247, 261
re-exports of Soviet oil 247
reactionary oligarchies 93
Reagan, Ronald 127, 203, 205, 209
 administration 54, 144, 209
Rebel Army 6
rebel movement 11
rebels 6
reciprocity 213
reconciliation 168, 250
recreation 170, 180, 267
"rectification of errors" 114–116, 118, 120, 122, 132, 137
Red Square 24, 141, 270
reforms 113, 167, 168
 agrarian 12
 "bourgeois-democratic" 4
 democratic 127, 216
 economic 10, 12, 98, 130, 266
 Russia 266
 Russia, free market 265
 egalitarian 8, 70
 land 6
 social 12
 USSR 118, 121, 122, 127
 economic 124
 internal 127
 political 111, 120, 124, 130
regimes
 anti-communist 2
 anti-Western 8
 bourgeois 86
 landlord 2
 left-wing 19, 143
 Guatemala 21
 radical 143
 leftist 98, 204
 Marxist-Leninist, Africa 204
 "progressive" 97, 204
 socialist, Cuba 265
 totalitarian 61, 71, 97, 230
 messianic 71
regional conflicts 142, 143, 146, 164, 205, 207, 208, 210, 213, 216, 218, 221
 negotiated settlements 208
relations 33, 86, 126, 127, 204, 215
 bilateral 127, 145, 221, 236
 Cuban-American 56, 145, 176, 204, 210, 214–216, 218–221, 266, 267
 diplomatic 2, 4, 5
 USSR and Cuba 181
 East-West 15, 91, 92, 123
 economic 191, 245

international 84, 236
normalization 204, 210, 211, 215, 216, 218–221, 225
  U.S.-Cuban 204, 210, 211, 216, 220, 221, 225, 266
North-South 123
political 127, 269
Russian-Cuban 127, 252, 262–264, 266, 267, 271
  economic 267, 269
  political 268, 269
Soviet-allies 193
Soviet-American 15, 22, 59, 62, 64, 97, 164, 179, 199, 205, 214, 215, 218, 219, 231, 232, 235
  diplomatic 200, 202
Soviet-Cuban 4, 5, 9, 25, 32, 33, 48, 55, 62, 69, 71, 86, 92, 123, 125, 126, 128, 137, 139, 158, 160, 161, 165, 175, 180, 182–185, 192, 206, 217, 225, 231, 233, 236, 238, 244, 261
  bilateral economic 85
  economic 71, 77, 79, 83, 125, 130, 136, 138, 176, 181, 182, 185, 191, 194, 214, 230, 240, 251, 252
  political 64
superpowers 123
USSR-outside world 229
USSR-South American Continent 127
Republic of South Africa 143
  apartheid system 143
retaliatory actions 21
Revolution 229
  Cuban 9–12, 16, 17, 20–25, 33, 35, 71, 117, 154, 161, 165, 170, 184, 195, 233, 244, 270
  Nicaraguan 153, 154
  Sandinista 147, 153
revolution 6, 10, 12, 18, 19, 22–25, 71, 73, 85, 175, 185, 204
  anti-imperialist 3
  bourgeois democratic 7
  Castro, Fidel 5, 6, 7
  Cuba 162, 169, 185, 234, 242
  Cuban-model 188
  El Salvador 154
  enemies of 72, 104
  Latin America 189
  national democratic 5
  post- 104
  process 175
  socialist 6, 18, 21, 23, 24, 86, 154, 188
    Cuban 23, 24
revolutionaries 21, 72

Cuban 187
Grenadian 98
Latin American 83
radical 3, 271
revolutionary
  armed struggle 86
  class struggles 12
  intellectuals 85
  movements 2, 26, 86, 245
    Central America 148
    Guatemala 148
    guerrilla 89
  process 25, 103, 184
  regime 13
  workers 85
Revolutionary Armed Forces 251
Revolutionary Cuba 24
Revolutionary Directorate 6, 12, 22
Ribbentrop-Molotov pact 61, 141
Riga, Latvia 174
rightist governments 92
Risquet, Jorge 147
Roa, Raúl 191, 192
road-construction equipment 76
Roca, Blas 5, 6, 7, 11, 12
Rodriguez, Carlos Rafael 7, 71, 79, 84, 94, 112, 136
Romania 84, 113, 166
Rome 206
Rosales del Toro, Ulises 181, 182, 222, 224, 225
Ross, Robert 160
rubles 14, 76, 80, 185, 240, 269
  Soviet 269
  "wooden" 82
Ruiz Hernández, Henry 152, 153
"Rus-Cuba" project 268
Russia 5, 9, 23, 72, 186, 192, 247, 249, 252, 262, 271
  academic community 263
  agricultural machinery 268
  army recreational facilities 267
  army tanks 266
  authors 249
  civil war of 1918-1922 72, 75, 270
  credit for Cuba 268, 269
    technical assistance credits 265
  Cuban debt 269
  Cuban literature translations 249
  Cuban military delegation visit to Moscow 267
  Cuban ruble debt 269
  deliveries to Cuba 263
    industrial and transport equipment 271

Russia *continued*
    democratic parties, pro-Western   266
    dyarchy period 1917   5
    economic crisis   265, 266
    economy   264, 271
    election, 1991   267
    financial commitments to Cuba   267
    foreign debtors   269
    foreign policy   271
        planners   266
    Great Russia   266, 271
    investments in Cuba   266, 268
    Latin American partners   263
    military links with Cuba   264
    military strategists   266
    national interests   263
    October Socialist Revolution, 1917 71, 103
        seventy-third anniversary   184
    oil   263, 264, 268, 269
    parliament   266
    policy toward Cuba   262, 265
    radio-electronic base at Lourdes   268
    recreational facility   267
    revolutionary experience   24
    Soviet-sponsored projects   265
    special treatment of Cuba   265
    State Duma   267, 269
        International Affairs Committee   267
    supplies to Cuba   265
    trade and economic cooperation with
        Cuba   263
    world affairs   266
Russian Bolsheviks   271
Russian Committee for Cooperation with
    Latin America   104
Russian Communist Party   177
    communists   267
Russian Democratic Party   240
Russian Federation   236, 252, 262, 266
    Ministry of Defense   264, 268
    Ministry of External Economic
        Relations   264
    Ministry of Foreign Affairs   264
    parliament   263
    Supreme Soviet
        Presidium   154
Russian Revolution of 1917   5
Russian Social Democratic party   239
Russian-American talks   266
Ryzhkov, Nikolai   176, 177, 190

S

SAC bombers   31
safra   74
Saint Petersburg (Leningrad)   263

Sakharov, Andrei   141
SALT II (Soviet-American Strategic Arms
    Limitation Treaty)   202, 203, 223
Sanchez Parody, Ramón   147, 214, 220, 223
sanctions   205–207
    Cuba   50, 204, 206
    economic   205
    military   17
    Panama   155
    political   205
    Soviet   137
    U.S.   75, 261
Sandinista National Liberation Front
    (FSLN)   144
Sandinistas   99, 100, 101, 144, 146, 149,
    152, 154, 155, 157, 158, 212, 221
    agreement   156
    army   99, 100
    elections   153, 154, 156
    government   146–149, 152, 153, 157,
        206, 208
        policy   100, 222
        Soviet military aid   134, 149
        U.S. undeclared war against   208
    leaders   147, 152, 153, 154
    moratorium on Soviet arms shipments
        146, 149
    regime   100, 153
    Revolution   99, 100, 147, 152, 153
    rule   99
    Soviet arms   100
        deliveries   210
Santa Clara automobile repair and mechani-
    cal plant   192
Santa Fe II document   209
Santiago de Cuba   3
Schlesinger, Jr., Arthur   42
science   127, 129
    development   188
scientists   14
secrecy   40
security   129, 134
self-determination   129, 241
Senate Foreign Relations Committee   203
Shenin, Oleg   177, 183, 194, 227
Shevardnadze, Eduard   35, 99, 100, 119,
    131, 139, 142, 143, 147–152, 164, 166,
    173, 175, 179, 192, 208, 210, 211, 219,
    220, 224
    resignation   227
    visit to Cuba   148, 173
    visit to Managua   148
Shevardnadze-Baker meetings   207
Shevchenko, Arkady   8, 42

shipping costs 190
Shliapnikov, German 100
Shmelyov, Nikolai 125, 159
shortfalls
    Soviet deliveries to Cuba 242, 244, 245
    Soviet-supplied commodities 242
Shumeiko, Vladimir 264
Sierra Maestra
    -style insurrectionist movements 86
    mountains 7
Sizov, Gennady 180
slavery 134
Slezkin, Lev 25
Smith, Lawrence J. 159, 229
Snam, Aleksandr 73
social injustice 270
social justice 18, 154
socialism 4, 8–11, 17–19, 21–25, 36, 38,
    51, 69, 70, 72–74, 79, 86, 87, 91, 94, 96,
    98, 99, 103, 104, 106, 111, 112, 115, 122,
    128, 132–134, 137, 160, 168, 169, 174,
    175, 177, 184, 189, 193, 218, 229, 241,
    243, 245–248, 270, 271
    bankruptcy of 200
    collapse 219
    Cuba 22
        "construction of" 200
    economic performance 126
    enemies 185, 227
    foundations of 227, 241
    Latin America 22
    Nicaragua 152
    "path to" 72
    perfection of 242
    preservation 217
    "sociolismo" 114
    Soviet 200, 271
    Soviet model 18
    totalitarian 17, 73, 141, 218
        Soviet 19
socialist 248
    anti-socialist forces 106, 174
    camp 38, 39, 102, 188, 189, 219, 220, 245
        origin 246
    cause 249
    community 18, 113
        Cuba 262
        defensive capacity 234
        East European 189
    countries 24, 72, 87, 96, 113, 124, 128,
        167, 187, 191, 220
        Cuba 36, 60
        East European 60, 242
    Cuba 26

cultural exchanges 249
democracy 105, 177
doctrine 22
dogma 153
economic integration 129
economies 85, 248
experiment 79
    Grenada 99
model 73, 74, 79
nation 87
option 216
political system 111
principles 249
promises 270
reality 270
reforms 19, 22, 102
regimes 70, 72, 173
revolution 2, 21, 23, 70, 86, 100, 103, 154
    China 23
    Cuban 24
    Latin America 188
    Nicaragua 153
    Russia 23
society 267
states 25, 70, 84
system 75, 78, 113, 126, 128, 138, 178,
    193, 200, 267
    Cuban 267
    totalitarian 71, 132, 227, 261
transformation 7, 20, 26, 99, 243
    East European countries 19
    world civilization 26, 61
solidarity 16
Solovyev, Yuri 178
Somalia 59, 129
Somoza, Anastasio 99
South Africa 95, 102, 123, 143
    allies 123
    apartheid system 144
        government promises 144
    forces in Angola 102
South America 135
South Korea 36, 61
    U.S. occupation 85
South Vietnam 36
    U.S. military intervention 85
South Yemen 59, 129
South-West Africa 208
South-West African Peoples Organization
    (SWAPO) 102
Southern Atlantic 135
    zone of peace and cooperation 135
sovereignty 241
    Cuban 225

"Soviet brothers" 73
Soviet experience 72
Soviet market
  Cuban buying capacity 190
Soviet Ministry of Defense 60, 166
Soviet Peace Committee 158, 159, 162
Soviet State Planning Commission
  (GOSPLAN) 76, 77, 81
Soviet Union 269. *See also* USSR
  Afghanistan's war 141
  Africa 19
  agriculture 248
    production 246
  aid 76, 77, 125
    Cuba 118, 206, 207, 230
  aircraft 102
  alcoholism 114
  allies 31, 130, 131, 148
  ambassadors 119, 121
  Angola
    logistical support 102
    military advisers 102
  armed forces 41, 47, 61, 182, 224
  arms 61, 63, 64, 92, 134, 212
    deliveries to Cuba 181, 210
    deliveries to Nicaragua 211
    deliveries to Sandinistas 210
    moratorium to Sandinistas 148, 155
    shipped through Cuba to Nicaragua 211
    to Cuba 211
  Asia 19
  assistance 76
    and support to Cuba 261
    programs 112
    to Cuba 77
  authors 249
  autonomous producers 185
  Baltic republics 174
  bombers 35, 55
  bureaucracy 83
  Castro's views 173
  China 60
  citrus fruit, Cuban 80, 82, 261
  civil conflict 242
  commitment 14
    to Castro's regime 20
    to Cuba 57, 58, 60, 185, 223
  Committee of Solidarity with the Peoples
    of Latin America 177
  Committee of State Security (KGB) 5
  conservatives 227, 241
  consular office, Panama 156
  consumer goods, per capita
    production 19

Cuban debt 124, 135, 136
Cuban lobby 250
Cubanologists 104, 169
Cuba's economic dependence 207
cultural exchanges 249
de-Cubanization 142
decolonization 1
defense industry 180
deliveries to Cuba
  MiG-29 fighters 216, 222
  shortfalls 242, 244, 245
democratic forces
  victory 249
Democratic Party of Russia 240
democrats 241
diplomacy 214
diplomatic relations
  Central America 148
diplomats 121
  in Havana 120
disintegration 246, 251, 262, 265, 267
economic aid 79, 90, 118, 120, 125,
  127, 136, 138, 207
  Cuba 77, 80, 82, 182
  foreign countries 77
  Nicaragua 149, 153
  to Cuba 38, 127, 240
economic and military aid 1, 5, 17, 19
  Afghanistan 240
  Cuba 1, 17, 18, 26, 179, 186, 194,
  240, 261
  to Cuba 204–207, 213, 214, 219
economic and military ties with
  Cuba 251
economic and political demise 261
economic and technical assistance
  programs with Cuba 250
economic and technical cooperation
  with Cuba 247
economic assistance
  from U.S. 207
  to Cuba 204, 206, 207, 215, 218
economic commitments 14
  to Cuba 124, 192
economic crisis 125, 207
economic dependence, Cuba's 189
economic dislocation 250
economic management
  decentralization 191
  system 126
economic model 187
economic projects in Cuba 240
economic resources 70
economic restructuring 120

Soviet Union *continued*
  economic system   248
  economy   85, 200, 204
  embassy   44, 46, 118
    in Havana   120
    in Washington   57
  enemies   185
  exports   14, 77, 82, 191
    Cuba   190, 240
    resources   207
  foreign ministry
    U.S.A. and Canada Department   143
  foreign policy   1, 18, 35, 83, 139, 142,
    143, 148, 184, 192, 199, 218, 230, 241,
    252, 261
  foreign trade organizations   136, 246
  fraternal friendship   128, 176
  friendship and cooperation
    Cuba   184, 193
  friendship and loyalty, Cuba's   188
  friendship with dictatorial regimes   192
  fuel   244, 245, 248
  General Staff   41
  GNP (gross national product)   204
  government   4, 8, 13, 32, 35, 37, 39,
    43, 50, 114, 117
    corruption   18
  grants   54
  ideological currents   184
  imports from Cuba   80
  inability to defend Cuba militarily   225
  industrial   and   technological
    development   247
  industrial production   124, 240
  information agencies   228
  intelligence   5, 97
  internal affairs   185
  internal changes   199
  internationalist duty   56, 57, 77
  investments   21, 75
  journalists   12
  leaders   26, 31
  "left-wing conservatives"   166
  living standards   117
  loan guarantees   190
  long-term interests   142
  machinery   14, 15, 248
  market economy   111, 217
  media   4, 6, 184, 228, 241
  merchant fleet   250
  MiG-23 fighters   62, 63, 202, 203
  MiG-29 fighters   63, 211, 213
  military   16, 18, 25, 62, 63
    Caribbean   62
    Cuba   238

  military activities
    Western Hemisphere   236
  military advisers   9, 43
    Cuba   216
  military aid
    Cuba   161, 231, 232
    Nicaragua   146, 147, 149
    Sandinistas   146, 149
  military and economic aid to Cuba   176
  military and space technology   19
  military assistance   54, 60, 90, 127
    to Cuba   9, 16, 17, 21, 38, 63, 77,
    181, 209, 212, 222
  military bases   37, 39, 52, 215
  military defense of Cuba   224
  military equipment   203
  military establishment   42, 168, 178
  military links with Cuba   182, 202, 231, 239
  military power   47
  military presence   34
    Caribbean   62
    Cuba   53, 223, 234, 235, 237, 251
  military strategists   251
  military strategy, Cuba   183
  military supplies to Cuba   216, 247
    reduction of   223
  military withdrawal from Cuba   209
  military-industrial complex   82, 181
  mineral resources   81
  missiles
    bases   270
    deployment in Cuba in 1962   201
    surface-to-air   212
  Mongolia   60
  national interests   26
  national resources   261
  Navy   62
  new political thinking   128, 195
  "order and discipline"   177
  parliament   139
  petroleum products   8, 14, 240, 242
  planes   248
    long-range reconnaissance   62, 183
  policy   211
    Cuba   165, 176, 182, 251
    internal   252
    Latin America   101
    makers   25, 62, 146
    of democratization   144
    toward Cuba   25, 215
    toward Nicaragua   211
  political ally in Cuba   215
  political, economic, and military
    support   229

Soviet Union *continued*
  political pluralism 216
  political ties with Cuba 182
  political treaty with Cuba 127–130
    mutual military assistance clause 128
  press 182–186, 220
    commentaries 16, 22
    communiqué 13
  principal provider for Cuba's needs 204
  public 162
  raw materials 82, 176, 180, 204, 230,
    244, 261
  restructuring process 181
  revolutionary changes 131
  revolutionary minded people 185
  revolutionary process 184
  rubles 185, 240
  security threat 21
  share in Cuba's trade 187
  shipping costs 190
  ships 83, 102, 186
  Social Democratic party 239
  Soviet-sponsored projects 265
  strategic interests, Cuban context 31
  strategic plans 47
    Caribbean 201
  strategic position 38
  supplies to Cuba 240, 242, 250, 261, 262
  tanks 251
  territorial problem with Japan 231
  theatrical companies
    performance in Cuba 249
  Trade Exhibition 6
  training center in Cuba 203, 224, 235
    withdrawal 239
  troops 41, 60, 62, 174, 202, 203, 236, 237
    Afghanistan 143, 205
    in Cuba 34, 165, 166, 203, 213, 224,
    231, 232, 234–237, 239
    in Cuba, deployment 237
    Lithuania 174
    withdrawal from Cuba 165, 216,
    232–234, 237–239, 250
  trucks 248
  U.S. economic and technological
    aid 176
  U.S. monitoring station 182
  unearned income 114
  unequal exchange 191
  university education 112
    Cuban students 247
  war material to Cuba 251
  weapons 150
Soviet-American
  agenda 200

    conference 158
    confidential and public exchanges 202
    consultations on Central America 221
    contacts 222, 223
      diplomatic 213
      on regional conflicts 208
    exploratory talks 216
    joint efforts 208
    talks, Wyoming, 1989 149
Soviet-American Strategic Arms Limitation
    Treaty. *See* SALT II
Soviet-Cuban
    Declaration, February 4, 1974 95, 105
    division of authority 42
    joint documents 84
    joint statement 85
    political discussions 101
    unity 95
Soviet-supplied material resources 125
Spanish Inquisition 72
Spanish translations of Soviet and Russian
    works 249
spare parts 264, 268, 271
sports 127, 129
Stalin, Joseph 1, 2, 46, 72, 74, 103, 122, 134, 163
Stalin-Mao Zedong-Kim Il Sung plot 61
standard of living 78
Stankevich, Sergei 264
Starkov, Vladislav 159
starvation 96
    rations 262
State Duma, Russian 267, 269
Statsenko, Igor 44
steel 82, 240, 242
steel mill 14
strategic arms limitations 96
strategic balance 35
strategic confrontation
    Soviet-American 62
strategic imbalance 15
strategic nuclear forces 31
strikes 114
Suarez, Luis 115
submarines 31, 62, 92, 183, 202, 223
    ballistic missile 202
    base 62, 201, 202, 239
      Albania 63
      Cienfuegos 183, 201, 202, 223, 239
    nuclear 62
    nuclear missiles 31
subsidies 70, 76, 125, 170, 188, 230, 240, 248
    oil 125, 188
    price 76
    Soviet 70, 175, 188, 230, 248, 250

Soviet sugar-petroleum 188
sugar 125, 188, 189, 246
trade 170
subversion 207, 208
Suchlicki, Jaime 78, 213
Suez Crisis, 1956 15
sugar 8, 9, 13, 14, 77–85, 94, 114, 125,
137, 170, 176, 180, 188, 189, 190, 214,
230, 243–248, 261, 263, 265, 268–271
beets 80, 81, 248, 265
borrowed 81
cane cultivation 188
Cuban 8, 9, 13–15, 74, 76, 80, 81, 85,
176, 180, 182, 188, 243, 244, 245, 248,
261, 263, 268, 269, 271
deliveries to Russia 264
exports to Russia 264, 265
demands 81
exports 188, 189, 264, 265
factories, Cuban 80
foreign 81
General Agreement on the Integral Development of Sugar Production 189
harvest, Cuban 76, 268
industry 74, 189, 191, 264
Russian 265
Soviet 80
international market 74
Iraq 13
prices 14, 80, 83, 85, 182, 190, 243, 246
production 13, 189
Cuba 74, 75, 80, 81, 265, 268
Soviet 13, 80
quota
Cuban 81, 271
U.S. 13, 271
Russian dependence on imported 265
Russian purchases 269
sales, Cuban 81
Soviet 13, 80, 81, 248
sugar cane cultivation 188
"sugar debt" 81
supplier, Cuba 189
supplies 265
U.S. 246
Suleimenov, Oldzas 184
sulfur 190, 240, 242
summits 137, 138
conference of nonaligned nations 202
Gorbechev-Bush 231
Malta 176, 212
meeting in Paris, four-power 15
Moscow 231
Soviet-American 126, 200, 221

Soviet-Cuban 127, 130, 131, 137, 138,
168, 175
Washington 161
superpowers 15, 19, 64, 173, 199, 207, 219
arms race 200
politics 130
supplies to Cuba, energy 217
Supreme Soviet. *See* USSR: Supreme Soviet
Sverdlovsk 119
Syria 1, 59

T

Tajikistan 252
Tanan, Piotr 43, 48
tanks, Soviet 251
TASS 58, 88, 91, 94, 136, 180, 192, 193, 228
taxation, indirect 70
Tbilisi, Georgia 174, 178
technical assistance 118, 127, 240
Russian 265
Soviet 14, 76, 77, 79
to Cuba 76, 77, 82
technology 1, 18, 37, 111, 127, 247
terrorism 11, 49, 104, 199, 271
thermal power plants 14, 240
Third African Department, (USSR Foreign
Ministry) 143
Third Reich 229
Third World 17, 19, 26, 57, 83, 96, 124,
131, 133, 143, 176, 186, 195, 206, 219,
236, 265, 267, 269
countries 7
debt 124
crisis 123
Soviet influence 19
thought control 219
threat 61, 175
timber 76, 82, 188, 190, 242
tin 14, 190
tires 240, 242, 268
Tito, Josip 84
Torricelli bill 267
Torrijos Herrera, Omar 156
totalitarian
control 18, 271
one-party system of government 73
totalitarianism 169, 199
tourism 129, 191
trade 7, 70, 76, 80, 82, 83, 114, 117, 126–
130, 136–138, 176, 179, 185–188, 190,
192, 217, 248, 252, 264, 267, 268, 271
alternative markets 188
barter 263, 265, 269
bilateral 14, 123, 126, 128, 136, 179,

trade *continued*
190, 250, 264, 268
　Cuban-East European　176
commodities　185
credits　76, 82, 83, 125, 187, 188
　Western countries　187
Cuba　187, 188, 252
　East European partners　176
　with USSR　246
deficit　94
　Cuban　82, 191
foreign　7, 82, 114, 124, 187
　demonopolization, USSR　124
imbalance　125
mutual obligations　123
protocol　264
Protocol on Trade and Payments for
　1994　268, 269
relations　13, 175, 176, 230
Russian-Cuban　252, 263, 267, 268
Soviet foreign trade organizations　246
Soviet-Cuban　14, 80, 130, 136, 137,
　179, 185, 188, 251, 252
terms　188, 245
unequal　175, 176
volume　185
world market prices　175, 176, 185,
　188–190, 244, 245
Trade Union Center of the Workers of Cuba 176
Transcaucasia　174
translation of literature　249
transportation　191
Travkin, Nikolai　240
treaty　53, 59, 60, 127–130, 133, 135
Treaty of Friendship and Cooperation
　(Soviet-Cuban) 128, 129, 133, 137, 263
Treaty of Tlatelolco　96, 135
Treaty on Non-Proliferation of Nuclear
　Weapons　129
Trejo, Carlos　164
Tri-Continental Conference　86
trilateral conferences (U.S.-Soviet-Cuban)
　Cuban Crisis　32, 35
trilateral Havana conference　41
trilateral negotiations　233
tripartite conference, Havana, January 1992 39
tripartite consultations (Soviet-Cuban-Nica-
　raguan)　147
trucks　76, 82, 248
Tsagolov, Kim　159
Turkey　31–33, 48, 52, 183
Turkey Point nuclear power plant　63
Turkmenistan　252
26th of July Movement　6, 8, 11, 12, 18, 22,
　262

TV Martí　161, 178, 221
　transmissions to Cuba　210

U

U.S.-Soviet Conference, Hawk's Cay,
　Florida　32
U.S.-Soviet Understanding of 1962　201–
　203, 211, 212, 216, 223
U.S.-Soviet-Cuban trilateral conference 32, 35
U.S.S. Enterprise　43
Ukraine　120, 166, 249, 252, 265, 269
　Ukrainian Communist Party
　　Central Committee　119
undercover police agents　72
underdevelopment　18
unearned income　114
unemployment　18
unilateral disarmament　178
Union Republics　251
UNITA　102, 123, 149
United Nations　2, 36, 52, 83, 96, 100, 133,
　150, 164, 192, 233
　General Assembly　133, 135, 267
　human rights　166
　Human Rights Commission　164, 192,
　　221, 229, 264
　　Geneva　106, 166, 192, 263
　　resolution condemning Cuba　174
　　Soviet representation　165
　observers　156
　Secretary General　228
　Security Council　164, 166
　　anti-Hussein coalition　220
United Revolutionary Organizations 12, 22
United States　1, 2, 7, 9, 10, 13–17, 19, 21,
　24, 31–39, 41–43, 46, 47, 49–51, 53–55,
　57, 58, 63, 64, 83, 86, 87, 95, 97, 100,
　104, 105, 127, 135, 142–146, 149–153,
　155, 167, 173, 174, 176, 178, 181, 183,
　188, 189, 195, 199, 202–206, 209–215,
　218–220, 225, 227, 250
　administrations　43, 50, 53, 127
　　policy on Nicaragua　146
　　subsequent　53, 54
　　successive　54
　aggression　34, 224, 237, 238, 261
　　nonaggression assurances　213
　Air Force　43
　allies　145, 187, 203
　　NATO　97
　　European　1, 21
　anti-Castro sentiments　216
　armed forces　1, 16
　attack　60

Soviet missile sites 47
blockade of Cuba 15, 176, 187–189, 204, 220, 236, 246, 266, 267, 271
blockade of Panama 155
Capitol Hill 216
Central Intelligence Agency (CIA) 2
Congress 206, 217, 223, 263
elections observers 156, 157
Helms-Burton bill 267
military aid to Contras 144
Torricelli bill 267
Department of State 205
diplomacy 144
dollars 190, 268, 269
economic assistance to USSR 176, 207
economic interests in Cuba 9
economic potential 15
economic sanctions 17, 75
Cuba 13
enmity to the Cuban revolutionary regime 219
Export-Import Bank 206
forces 16, 20, 42, 47, 49
government 91
"gradualist" approach, opponents 217
Guantánamo naval base 49, 50, 213, 216, 231–233, 237, 238
hostility to Castro's regime 8, 54, 204, 205, 215, 218, 272
House of Representatives 229
Foreign Affairs Committee 159, 230
ideological services 178
imperialism 16, 23, 56
intelligence 34, 40, 55, 62
-gathering facilities 183
interests in Europe 20
intervention 18, 43
invasion 31, 33, 36, 42, 48, 52, 235
Cuba 224
non-invasion assurances 45, 51, 52, 54, 216, 231
Law of Neutrality to Cuba 53
Library of Congress 230
market 271
mid-term congressional elections 33
militarists 35
military activities 62, 213, 216, 231, 232, 237
Cuba 209, 216, 231
military aid 134
El Salvador 135, 150
Nicaraguan Contras 146
military bases 178
military force 201
military intervention 21, 22, 37, 39, 51, 52, 54, 156, 173
Cuba 22, 54, 57
South Vietnam 85
military power 15, 35
Navy 43
Pentagon 216
planes 44, 45, 50, 183
policy 252
Central America 211
Cuba 50, 59, 161, 206, 214–218, 220, 221, 225
makers 54
Moscow's new 165
public opinion 217
reconnaissance aircraft flights over Cuba 216
reprisals 19
Republican conservatives 272
Republican opposition 235
security interests 213
Caribbean 54
security markets 206
State Department 156, 157, 210, 212, 213, 221, 223, 236
bilateral meeting with USSR in Geneva 205
strategic forces 47
superiority 25, 33
supremacy 270
technological power 236
Universal Declaration of the Rights of Man 102
University of Havana 115
University of Miami 78, 213
Graduate School of International Studies 159
Institute for Soviet and East European Studies 160
Urals 82, 120
Urrutia Lleó, Manuel 4, 5, 6
Uruguay 96, 127
USSR (Union of Soviet Socialist Republics) 252. *See also* Soviet Union
Academy of Sciences 71
Institute of United States and Canada 158
Committee for State Security 104
Constitution, Article six 141
Council of Ministers 1, 6, 93, 179, 202
economic links with Cuba 82
economic management
decentralization 124
fiftieth anniversary 94
Foreign Ministry 8, 100, 117, 128, 139, 142–147, 151–153, 156–167, 178, 182, 205, 210–214, 221–223, 225, 270

USSR, Foreign Ministry *continued*
 1991 directive   215
 bilateral meeting with U.S. in Geneva   205
 Human Rights Department   164
 Latin American Department   118
 Latin American Directorate   55, 113, 147, 167, 234
 United States and Canada Directorate   147
 Foreign Service   122
 Ministry of Defense   182, 222–224
 Ministry of External Economic Relations   250
 Ministry of Interior   104
 Ministry of the Maritime Fleet   83
 Provisional President   228
 State Commission on External Economic Relations, Cuban section   177
 State Committee for Economic Ties with Foreign Countries, Havana   82
 State Committee for the State of Emergency (GKCh)   228
 Supreme Soviet   22, 51, 176, 184, 193, 227, 239
 chairman of the Presidium   22
 Committee on International Affairs   193
USSR-Latin America Association of Friendship and Cultural Ties   168
Ustinov, Viacheslav   238, 250
utopian ideas   73
Uzbekistan   252

V

Valenta, Jiri   160
Valladares, Armando   106, 229
Valletta   212
Vandalic actions   87
Varadero, Cuba   125, 179
Venedictov, Dmitry   177
Venezuela 2, 86, 87, 92, 99, 127, 151, 250
Viera, José Raúl   183, 220
Vietnam   36, 59, 60, 63, 78, 87, 88, 91, 95, 113, 128, 269
violence   168, 207, 217, 271
vodka   114
Volkov Cemetery   141
Volsky, Viktor   169, 177
Voronkov, Gennady   44
Vorontsov, Yuli   201
Vorotnikov, Vitaly   154, 177
vote   167

W

wages   70
war   20, 23, 37, 39, 46, 50, 51, 53, 56, 61, 62, 85, 88, 98, 200, 208
 Afghanistan   164, 170, 180
 Angola   187
 atomic   37
 civil   175
 conditions   23
 guerrilla   155
 Gulf   192
 material   251
 nuclear   199
 of attrition   20
 of extermination   46
 thermonuclear   35, 39, 46, 51, 58
 world   85
warheads
 atomic   66
 nuclear   31
Warsaw Pact   1, 91, 92
 countries   41
Warsaw Treaty Organization   58
warships   92, 232
Washington   1, 9, 12, 15, 16, 21, 22, 32, 33, 40, 41, 49, 52–54, 58, 83, 86, 91, 92, 97, 98, 102, 123, 124, 135, 143–149, 154, 156, 161, 165–167, 175, 176, 182, 187, 189, 200–202, 204, 205, 207, 208, 213, 232. *See also* United States
weapons   8, 9, 37, 42, 55, 57, 61, 62, 70, 98, 135, 145, 146, 204, 208–213, 251
 chemical   129
 Cuba   251
 nuclear   33, 39, 41, 43, 44
 Soviet   9, 55, 212
 Soviet-supplied   150
 thermonuclear   97
 to Nicaragua via Cuba   210
Weiser, Sherwood   159
West Berlin   1, 15
Western democracies   78, 102
Western Europe   79, 155, 187, 218, 265
 U.S. military presence   97
 U.S. political presence   97
Western Hemisphere   23, 25, 36, 145, 178
 Cuba, Soviet beachhead   219
 Soviet military activities   236
Western imperialism   24, 61, 70, 72, 97
Western powers   1
Wiarda, Howard J.   10
workers' party   95
world affairs   266

world democratic community 266
world development 139
world market 8, 77, 80–83, 265, 269
  capitalist 94
world market prices 14, 85, 175, 176, 185,
  189, 190, 244–246, 248, 263
  sugar 188
  trade 245
world order 236
world progressive movement 245
world revolutionary process 25, 70, 87
world socialist revolution 26
World War I 75
World War II 2, 75, 102
World War III 56
World Youth Festivals 5
Wyoming 210
  Soviet-American talks 149

Y

Yakovlev, Aleksandr 131, 179
Yanayev, Gennady 193, 194, 227, 228
Yankee empire 174
Yankee imperialism 3, 91, 228
Yazov, Dmitry 157, 177, 182, 224
Yeltsin, Boris 78, 119, 228–232, 236, 239,
  251, 252, 262–266, 269
  and Gorbachev decision to withdraw So-
    viet troops from Cuba 236
  free market economic reforms 265
  government 263, 269
  policy toward Cuba 263
  political outcast 262
Yugoslavia 84
Yushenkov, Sergei 239

Z

Zakharov, Vasily 42
Zhirinovsky, Vladimir 266, 267
Zimbabwe 95

About the Author

Yuri I. Pavlov served as Soviet Ambassador to Costa Rica from 1982 to 1987 and ambassador to Chile from 1990 to 1991. He headed the Latin American Directorate of the USSR Foreign Ministry from 1987 to 1990. As leader of the Soviet delegation during the Soviet-American talks on Central America, he was instrumental in negotiating the peace settlement. Ambassador Pavlov also represented the USSR Foreign Ministry in bilateral talks on Central American problems in London, Madrid, Rome, and Peking from 1988 to 1990.

Ambassador Pavlov played a key role in Moscow's reassessment of the Castro regime and was the first Soviet Foreign Ministry official to establish personal contacts with leaders of the Cuban-American community in the United States. After resigning from the Soviet Foreign Service in 1991, he became a senior research associate at the North-South Center, University of Miami and is now a visiting scholar in international studies at Oregon State University in Corvallis.

As head of the Latin American Directorate, Ambassador Pavlov was directly involved in Soviet contacts with Cuba, including preparations for the Soviet-Cuban Summit in Havana, where he accompanied Mikhail Gorbachev in April 1989; the re-evaluation of relations with Cuba after the talks; and frequent bilateral talks in Havana with senior Cuban officials. In 1989 he accompanied Foreign Minister Eduard Shevardnadze when he met with Fidel Castro in Cuba, Daniel Ortega in Nicaragua, and other Latin American leaders in New York.

Yuri Pavlov was born in Viazma, in the Smolensk region of Russia, in 1931. He earned a diploma with distinction, the equivalent of a five-year master's degree, from Moscow State Institute of International Relations, with majors in international relations, history, and political economy. In addition to Russian, he speaks English, Spanish, French, German, and Ukrainian.

Among his postings as a career diplomat, Ambassador Pavlov served as first secretary at the Soviet Embassy, London; head of the Australia-New Zealand Section of the Foreign Ministry, Moscow; minister-counselor, Canberra; deputy head of the second European Division, Moscow; ambassador to Costa Rica; head of the Latin American Directorate of the Foreign Ministry, Moscow; and ambassador to Chile. He holds the diplomatic rank of Ambassador Extraordinary and Plenipotentiary.

Production Notes

This book was printed on 60 lb. Glatfelter Natural text stock with a 10 point CIS cover stock.

The text of this volume was set in Garamond, with Helvetica for the headlines and subheads, for the North-South Center Press, using Aldus PageMaker 5.0, on a Macintosh Centris 650 computer. It was designed and formatted by Stephanie True Moss.

The cover was created by Mary M. Mapes using Adobe Photoshop 2.5 for the duotone photograph and Quark XPress 3.31 for the composition and color separation, on a Macintosh IIci.

The text was edited by Kathleen A. Hamman and Jayne M. Weisblatt.

The index was compiled and created by Stephanie True Moss for this printing.

This publication was printed by Edwards Brothers, Inc., Lillington, North Carolina, U.S.A.